Confucian Democracy in East Asia

This book explores a mode of democracy that is culturally relevant and socially practicable in the contemporary pluralistic context of historically Confucian East Asian societies, by critically engaging with the two most dominant theories of Confucian democracy – Confucian communitarianism and meritocratic elitism. The book constructs a mode of public reason (and reasoning) that is morally palatable to East Asians who are still saturated in Confucian customs by reappropriating Confucian familialism, and using this perspective to theorize on Confucian democratic welfarism and political meritocracy. It then applies the theory of Confucian democracy to South Korea, arguably the most Confucianized society in East Asia, and examines the theory's practicality in Korea's increasingly individualized, pluralized, and multicultural society by looking at cases of freedom of expression, freedom of association, insult law, and immigration policy.

Sungmoon Kim is an associate professor of political theory at City University of Hong Kong. He received his Ph.D. in political science from the University of Maryland at College Park and previously taught at the University of Richmond. His research interests include comparative political theory, democratic theory, and history of East Asian political thought.

Confucian Democracy in East Asia

Theory and Practice

SUNGMOON KIM
City University of Hong Kong

CAMBRIDGE
UNIVERSITY PRESS

CAMBRIDGE
UNIVERSITY PRESS

32 Avenue of the Americas, New York NY 10013-2473, USA

Cambridge University Press is part of the University of Cambridge.

It furthers the University's mission by disseminating knowledge in the pursuit of education, learning, and research at the highest international levels of excellence.

www.cambridge.org
Information on this title: www.cambridge.org/9781107641211

First published 2014

Printed in the United States of America

A catalog record for this publication is available from the British Library.

Library of Congress Cataloging in Publication data
Kim, Sungmoon.
Confucian democracy in East Asia : theory and practice / Sungmoon Kim.
pages cm
Includes bibliographical references and index.
ISBN 978-1-107-04903-1 (hardback) – ISBN 978-1-107-64121-1 (paperback)
1. Democracy – East Asia. 2. East Asia – Politics and government. I. Title.
JQ1499.A91.K54 2014
321.8095–dc23 2013039644

ISBN 978-1-107-04903-1 Hardback
ISBN 978-1-107-64121-1 Paperback

to my parents

Contents

Acknowledgments

Nowadays, political theorists are under immense pressure to choose a certain, highly technical, type of political theory or clarify the genre of their work, most often between analytical political philosophy, history of political thought, or critical theory. In this milieu, increasingly, to write a book that does not fit neatly in one particular genre of political theory often proves to be a liability: methodological impurity, the fit problem with leading journals, and, ultimately, the identity problem – a political philosopher, a political theorist, an intellectual historian, or a social critic? But, traditionally, political theory has always been in part normative-analytical, in part evaluative-descriptive, and in part historical-textual, and as a discipline it has long resisted being identified with one particular genre precisely because of what it deals with, that is, the entirety of political life, which requires skills and insights from all subgenres of political theory to make holistic sense of our political life. This is what my teachers at Yonsei and Maryland taught me, and although as a student I was sometimes frustrated by their methodological eclecticism and strong emphasis on the supreme task of political theory (particularly democratic theory) – to articulate and help improve what the citizens of a theorist's concern are already doing – I now realize and appreciate the deepest intellectual debt I owe to them.

At Yonsei, Hahm Chaibong, my faculty mentor, first introduced me to the world of Western and East Asian political thought and comparative political theory, then a nascent field, and always encouraged me to conceive of Confucian political theory in terms of the *identity* question that East Asians – Koreans in particular – are struggling with between their Confucian tradition and the imported modernity of liberal democracy. I am deeply grateful for his instruction and mentorship. Thanks are also due to Jang Dong-jin, who taught me contemporary political theory, especially John Rawls's political philosophy and the liberal-communitarian debate, and who found in me, then a junior, a promising young theorist and urged me, though with his usual anxiety about his student's job security, to further my study in political theory. While I received a seminal course of training in Western political theory at Yonsei, I owe my education in Confucian philosophy and Korean political thought to the work of a group of scholars at the Academy of Korean Studies where I did my M.A., especially Kim Hyong-hyo, Han Hyong-jo, Choi Jin-deok, Park Byoung-ryun, Lee Wan-bum, and the late Chung Young-guk, who introduced me to the world of classical Chinese and the Korean-Confucian philosophical tradition.

I first engaged in comparative political theory at Maryland when I began to write a Ph.D. dissertation titled "A Post-Confucian Civil Society: Liberal Collectivism and Participatory Politics in South Korea," and though this book is not based on my dissertation (except Chapter 8), I owe all the knowledge and training required to write this book to my teachers at Maryland, especially Jim Glass, Charles Butterworth, Stephen Elkin, and, above all, Fred Alford, my dissertation supervisor and academic mentor, whose insight into human psychology and great skill to make political theory relevant to everyday life deeply inspired me to engage in a kind of political theory that weaves political theory and political reality. Special thanks go to Benjamin Barber, who not only introduced me to the field of democratic political theory but also supported both my project and the way I do political theory with unflagging enthusiasm and support. Especially, collaboration with him on democratic theory and global interdependence, which began after graduation and has extended to the present, has helped me develop myself into a more competent political theorist. I am grateful for his continued support, collaboration, and mentorship.

I presented portions of this book at various institutions and academic events, and I am grateful for the helpful comments from the people at those venues. By naming them, I acknowledge once again my gratitude for their generous support: Han Do-hyun for inviting me to the Institute for Modern Korea at the Academy of Korean Studies; Han Hyongjo and Choi Jin-deok for inviting me to the Department of Philosophy at the Academy of Korean Studies; Kim Sung Ho, Seo Jungmin, and Lee Byoungha for inviting me to the Department of Political Science at Yonsei University; Kim Bumsoo, Kim Youngmin, Richard Kim, Fred Dallmayr, Brooke Ackerly, and Eirik Harris (who is now my colleague) for their valuable comments at the Korean Political Theory Workshop at Seoul National University; Sor-hoon Tan, Russell Fox, and Doh Chull Shin for their helpful comments at the 2011 American Political Science Association meeting; and Leigh Jenco, Justin Tiwald, Baogang He, Joseph Chan, and the late Robert Bellah for their comments and encouragements at two comparative political theory conferences held at City University of Hong Kong in 2010 and 2011.

Benjamin Barber, Stephen Angle, Fred Dallmayr, Justin Tiwald, Hwa Yol Jung, Owen Flanagan, and Susan Lee read the entire or substantive portions of the manuscript, and I am grateful for their helpful comments and criticisms. My colleague Ruiping Fan provided written comments on Chapter 6, where I critically engage with his Confucian familism, and I owe thanks to him. My deepest gratitude in writing this book goes to P. J. Ivanhoe, my colleague, mentor, and friend, who read the whole manuscript at least three times, provided extensive written comments on each chapter, and corrected all kinds of grammatical mistakes and expressive infelicities in the various stages of the manuscript writing. Without his enthusiastic support and appreciation of the value of my work, I could not even have begun to write this book. I am deeply grateful for his friendship and support.

I am also grateful to Robert Dreesen, my editor at Cambridge University Press, for recognizing the value of the manuscript and giving it a shot with the external review process. I owe many thanks to other editorial staff including Elizabeth Janetschek for facilitating the publication process.

A New Staff Start-up Grant from City University of Hong Kong enabled me to initiate the seminal research for Chapters 4 and 11, and a multiyear grant from the Academy of Korean Studies enabled me to start and finish this book project. I hereby acknowledge that this research was supported by an Academy of Korean Studies Grant funded by the Korean Government (MEST) (AKS-2011-AAA-2102).

Finally, I want to thank my family: first and foremost my parents, Kim Jungseop and Woo Kyungja, for their great sacrifices for the education and well-being of their two children. To them I dedicate this book. My wife Sejin and my son Seoyoon are the greatest sources of joy and happiness in my life, and their support and understanding have enabled me to come this far as a scholar.

Article-length versions (though all revised here) of six of the chapters have been published previously, and I am grateful for permission to draw on them.

Chapter 1 is based on "The Anatomy of Confucian Communitarianism: The Confucian Social Self and Its Discontent," *Philosophical Forum* 42 (2011): 111–30; with permission from John Wiley & Sons.

Chapter 2 is based on "The Virtue of Incivility: Confucian Communitarianism beyond Docility," *Philosophy and Social Criticism* 37 (2011): 25–48; with permission from SAGE Publications.

Chapter 3 is based on "To Become a Confucian Democratic Citizen: Against Meritocratic Elitism," *British Journal of Political Science* 43 (2013): 579–99; with permission from Cambridge University Press.

Chapter 4 is based on "A Pluralist Reconstruction of Confucian Democracy," *Dao* 11 (2012): 315–36; with permission from Springer Science+Business Media B.V.

Chapter 8 is based on "The Politics of *Jeong* and Ethical Civil Society in South Korea," *Korea Journal* 46 (2006): 212–41 and "Transcendental Collectivism and Participatory Politics in Democratized Korea," *Critical*

Review of International Social and Political Philosophy 11 (2008): 57–77; with permission from Taylor & Francis.

Chapter 11 is based on “The Logic of Multiculturalism and Korean Democracy,” *Citizenship Studies* 17 (2013): 353–68; with permission from Taylor & Francis.

Introduction

Toward Confucian Democratic Theory

The Plasticity of "Democracy" in the East Asian Political Discourse

One puzzling phenomenon in modern political science and political theory is that as democracy has become ubiquitous in many parts of the world and democratic values have become increasingly accepted as universal human values, the term "democracy" has become almost a cliché, losing its definitional political meaning. This is especially so among East Asians who have yet to establish (full) democracy, despite their strong desire for it, and those who have attained it only recently through bloody fights against authoritarian forces. On one extreme, democracy means everything good: political stability, economic development, quality of life, full protection of individual human rights, maximal respect of diversity, and so on. On the other extreme, democracy is associated with the detriments that Western liberal democracies are currently struggling with, such as unbridled egoism, consumerism, erosion of the common good, and social anomie – all of which might ultimately contribute to high divorce rates, dysfunctional families, juvenile violence, and so on.

For those who are in the first extreme, democratic struggle aims primarily to "remedy evils experienced in consequence of [existing or] prior political institutions."[1] Thus understood, democracy not only is compatible with but also can provide optimal political and societal conditions for a market economy, rights-based individualism, value pluralism (or cultural pluralism), a vibrant civil society, and social justice. In a democracy, the argument goes, we can have all these goods simultaneously and without any internal contradictions, if we, the citizens, so will it; if any of these goods are missing or if there is any tension between these goods in our putatively democratic system, quite simply our democracy has not reached its pinnacle, or in political scientific language, our

[1] John Dewey, *The Public and Its Problems* (Athens: Swallow Press, 1954), 84.

democracy has not yet been consolidated. Originally conceived negatively as the absence of evils, therefore, democracy in this understanding turns out to be "democratic faith," an optimistic belief in the omnipotence of democracy.[2]

For those on the other extreme, however, democracy is the source of "Western evils" and the global resurgence of democracy as the only legitimate political regime is more than alarming. Here, democracy is nothing more than mob rule, namely, rule by the ignorant and self-interested many, where tyranny of majority is the defining characteristic.[3] Of interest, however, the focus here is not on the Tocquevillian or Millian apprehension that the tyrannical majority suffocates individual souls and makes liberal self-experiment and democratic self-government impossible. Quite the contrary, the key argument is that in a democracy, tyranny of majority is inevitable precisely because of democracy's preoccupation with individualism, whatever that may mean practically (individual self-interest, individual self-identity, or individual self-government); democratic accommodation of individual self-interest erodes the common good, democratic respect for individual self-identity destroys social harmony, and democratic commitment to individual self-government threatens political order. Committed to political equality (thus ignoring the importance of excellence and merit) and upholding self-interested and rights-based individualism (thus jeopardizing public interest and common good), democracy turns out to be an anathema.

However, democracy is neither omnipotent nor impotent, and neither understanding of democracy captures the core tenets of democracy as a political system and as a social practice.

Contra the first view, democracy is not the comprehensive package of all good things we cherish qua human being. Democracy includes both the political system in which power resides not in kings or aristocrats but in ordinary citizens who are free and equal, and its underlying public culture that makes popular sovereignty not merely a political slogan but a palpable social reality. Therefore, collective self-determination and protection of citizens' basic rights are central to democracy, and together they can undergird political equality and thus realize popular sovereignty.[4] Deeply concerned with what the citizens

[2] Patrick J. Deneen, *Democratic Faith* (Princeton: Princeton University Press, 2005).

[3] Most notably, the Chinese Confucian scholar Jiang Qing asserts that "[t]he major flaw of democracy is the uniqueness of the legitimacy of the popular will. The exaggerated importance given to the will of the people leads to extreme secularization, contractualism, utilitarianism, selfishness, commercialism, capitalization, vulgarization, hedonism, mediocritization, this-worldliness, lack of ecology, lack of history, and lack of morality." Jiang Qing, *A Confucian Constitutional Order: How China's Ancient Past Can Shape Its Political Future*, ed. Daniel A. Bell and Ruiping Fan, trans. Edmund Ryden (Princeton: Princeton University Press, 2012), 33.

[4] See Benjamin R. Barber, *Strong Democracy: Participatory Politics for a New Age*, 20th anniversary ed. (Berkeley: University of California Press, 2003); Ian Shapiro, *Democratic Justice* (New Haven: Yale University Press, 1999). By "the citizenry's basic rights" I mean the rights that people are entitled to qua citizens in a democratic polity, not natural rights that they putatively possess in the natural state qua human beings. Following Corey Brettschneider, we can call rights of the

commonly share – legally, politically, and public culturally – and trusting the citizenry's capacity to resolve common problems through public deliberation and contestation (i.e., through *civic* virtue), democracy is often in tension with value pluralism that stresses diversity more than public commonality, rights-based individualism that puts the individual right before the common good, and social justice, the attainment of which is sometimes sought by circumscribing democratic deliberation and contestation both in the legislature and, more important, in civil society. In short, democratic politics is premised on the realistic observation that good democratic citizenship is not always congruent with good membership or with one's unique individuality.[5] The virtue of democratic politics, instead, lies precisely in the way it resolves such tensions, however temporarily – not by appealing to abstract moral principles but by all affected citizens participating in public deliberation.[6]

From the perspective of democracy understood in terms of collective self-determination and protection of citizen rights, the second view is equally, if not more, problematic. Although the view is mistaken, in a sense it is natural that democracy is idealized by its proponents, most of whom are not educated in democratic theory and principles, particularly those under authoritarian regimes. What is needed for them is John Dewey's reminder that "political forms do not originate in a once for all way [and] the greatest change, once it is accomplished, is simply the outcome of a vast series of adaptation and responsive accommodations, each to its own particular situation."[7] In contrast, the problem of the second view lies in the stark "East versus West" dichotomy, but its complete rejection of democracy is based on the massive confusion that identifies democracy with everything one finds abhorrent in existing Western liberal democracies, be it market consumerism, rights-based individualism, or the morally irresponsible political system of one person, one vote, which only justifies and ineluctably results in mob rule.

The fact that democracy is premised on the assumption of citizens' political equality and the conviction that democracy proffers us a societal and political

former kind "democratic rights." Corey Brettschneider, *Democratic Rights: The Substance of Self-Government* (Princeton: Princeton University Press, 2007). On the "co-originality" of collective self-determination and democratic rights, see Jürgen Habermas, *Between Facts and Norms: Contributions to a Discourse Theory of Law and Democracy*, trans. William Rehg (Cambridge, MA: MIT Press, 1996) and Joshua Cohen, "Democracy and Liberty," in *Deliberative Democracy*, ed. Jon Elster (Cambridge: Cambridge University Press, 1998).

5 On this so-called incongruence thesis between democratic citizenship and associational membership (and/or individual plurality), see Nancy L. Rosenblum, *Membership and Morals: The Personal Uses of Pluralism in America* (Princeton: Princeton University Press, 1998).

6 Amy Gutmann and Dennis Thompson, *Democracy and Disagreement: Why Moral Conflict Cannot Be Avoided in Politics, and What Should Be Done about It* (Cambridge, MA: Belknap, 1996); James Bohman, *Public Deliberation: Pluralism, Complexity, and Democracy* (Cambridge, MA: MIT Press, 2000); John S. Dryzek, *Deliberative Democracy and Beyond: Liberals, Critics, and Contestations* (Oxford: Oxford University Press, 2000); Barber, *Strong Democracy*.

7 Dewey, *Public and Its Problems*, 84.

condition that can best accommodate individual self-identity and self-interest should not mislead us to conclude that it is grounded in and also engenders atomistic individualism and/or neoliberal consumerism, only to erode the communal bond and impair the common good.[8] Likewise, democracy's ability to accommodate value pluralism should not be misunderstood as democracy's acquiescence to the "perils of pluralism." While respecting value plurality and associational freedom, democracy offers political institutions and a civil society that can mitigate (if not eliminate) social ills resulting from the vicissitudes of pluralism. We cannot oppose democracy by identifying it in terms of the things that democracy actively opposes or aims to mitigate. This is more than a categorical mistake. Its political cost is simply huge.

East Asian Particularism Revisited

This book is motivated by the conviction that democracy, properly understood, is desperately needed in East Asia, where political regimes remain authoritarian or only partially democratic. In this regard, this book shares the first view's faith in democracy enabling a viable and flourishing social and political life for its citizens, with the additional aim of articulating the societal conditions of democracy, originally of Western provenance, under which democracy would work best in East Asian – historically Confucian – societies, accommodating other social goods and values that are not necessarily democratic. The central thesis of this book is that in East Asian societies democracy would be most politically effective and culturally relevant if it were rooted in and operates on the "Confucian habits and mores" with which East Asians are still deeply saturated, sometimes without their awareness – in other words, if democracy were a *Confucian democracy*.[9]

[8] According to some strong democrats, quite the contrary is the case. See Benjamin R. Barber, *Consumed: How Markets Corrupt Children, Infantilize Adults, and Swallow Citizens Whole* (New York: Norton, 2007); Sheldon S. Wolin, *Democracy Incorporated: Managed Democracy and the Specter of Inverted Totalitarianism* (Princeton: Princeton University Press, 2008).

[9] Whether citizens in East Asian, historically Confucian, countries are still deeply soaked in Confucian habits and mores is an important empirical question, and this book, which aims at a normative political theory of Confucian democracy, does not attempt an empirical test for my foundational sociological observation. Instead, for such empirical evidence, I draw attention to recent social scientific studies relying on public opinion surveys and their statistical analysis. See Doh Chull Shin, *Confucianism and Democratization in East Asia* (New York: Cambridge University Press, 2012); Chong-Min Park and Doh Chull Shin, "Do Asian Values Deter Popular Support for Democracy in South Korea?," *Asian Survey* 46 (2006), 341–61; Yu-Tzung Chang and Yun-han Chu, "Traditionalism, Political Learning and Conceptions of Democracy in East Asia" (Asian Barometer Working Paper Series No. 39, National Taiwan University, Taipei, 2007); Yu-Tzung Chang, Yun-han Chu, and Frank Tsai, "Confucianism and Democratic Values in Three Chinese Societies," *Issues & Studies* 41 (2005), 1–33. Readers may object that survey data alone are short of providing compelling evidence for the claim that East Asians still possess the Confucian habit of the heart by pointing to some methodological limits inherent in the survey-based research on values, and, to be sure, the scientific validity of such

Even though Confucian democracy sounds foreign or even anachronistic to many East Asians, many of whom attribute their sufferings following the "Western impact" in the late nineteenth and early twentieth centuries to Confucianism, particularly its failure to modernize the state and society, Confucian democracy is hardly a novel idea among East Asian political scientists and political theorists and Western academics active in East Asia. In fact, in the course of refuting Samuel Huntington's provocative claim that "Confucian democracy" is a contradiction in terms and Francis Fukuyama's end of history thesis that liberal democracy is the only morally and politically legitimate universal value in the post–Cold War era, scholars of East Asia have actively searched for Confucian democracy as the viable political alternative to Western liberal democracy.[10] Although the debate remains ongoing as to whether Confucian democracy is possible both in theory and in practice, and if possible what it should look like, in the past two decades, three dominant theses have emerged in the discourse of Confucian democracy, namely, the particularism thesis, the communitarianism thesis, and the meritocracy thesis.[11]

(1) The particularism thesis declares that Confucian democracy is a valid East Asian response to cultural imperialism, political hegemony, and ethical monism implicated in the globalization of liberal democracy. Confucian democracy offers political institutions and a civil society that are most suitable to East Asia's particular cultural context.

research hangs critically on the reliable definitions of the key concepts (say, "Confucianism") and the proper measurements of the variables (e.g., family-oriented worldview, filial piety, ritual propriety, deference, respect of elders, social harmony, etc.). That said, it is worth noting that a good number of interpretive – sociological, philosophical-anthropological, social psychological, and legal – studies on Confucian values and practices among East Asians (particularly South Koreans), which occasionally draw on survey data, content analysis, and/or in-depth interviews, generally suggest the same conclusion. For such studies, see Byung-ik Koh, "Confucianism in Contemporary Korea," in *Confucian Traditions in East Asian Modernity: Moral Education and Economic Culture in Japan and Four Mini-Dragons*, ed. Tu Weiming (Cambridge, MA: Harvard University Press, 1996); Geir Helgesen, *Democracy and Authority in Korea: The Cultural Dimension in Korean Politics* (Surrey: Curzon, 1998); C. Fred Alford, *Think No Evil: Korean Values in the Age of Globalization* (Ithaca: Cornell University Press, 1999); Su-young Ryu, "Han'gukinui yugyojeok gachicheukjeongmunhang gaebal yeon'gu" [Item Development for Korean Confucian Values], *Korean Journal of Management* 15 (2007), 171–205; Chaihark Hahm, "Disputing Civil Society in a Confucian Context," *Korea Observer* 35 (2004), 433–62.

10 Samuel P. Huntington, *The Third Wave: Democratization in the Late Twentieth Century* (Norman: University of Oklahoma Press, 1991), 307; Francis Fukuyama, *The End of History and the Last Man* (New York: Free Press, 1992).

11 While the first two theses are almost unanimously affirmed by the advocates of Confucian democracy, the third thesis is controversial. For instance, Sor-hoon Tan, a strong advocate of Confucian communitarian democracy, is critical of political meritocracy (actually, meritocratic elitism) of the kind advanced by other Confucian communitarians such as Daniel Bell. For Bell's argument for political meritocracy in China, see Daniel A. Bell, "Taking Elitism Seriously," in *Beyond Liberal Democracy: Political Thinking for an East Asian Context* (Princeton: Princeton University Press, 2006). Tan's criticism of Bell is found in her "Beyond Elitism: A Community Ideal for a Modern East Asia," *Philosophy East and West* 59 (2009), 537–53.

(2) The communitarianism thesis asserts that as Western liberal democracy is predicated on the assumption of rights-based individualism, and since rights-based individualism is incompatible with Confucian role-ethics and a communitarian culture and philosophy, the most appropriate mode of democracy in East Asian societies is a Confucian communitarian democracy.

(3) The meritocracy thesis proclaims that Confucian democracy offers a political alternative to liberal representative democracy, which is structurally inhibited from producing responsible and sound long-term public policies due to staggering electoral pressures on representatives from ordinary citizens who are largely self-interested, shortsighted, and of mediocre intelligence. By contrast, Confucianism upholds a political meritocracy understood as rule by the "best and brightest."

Although the mode of political practice that I am proposing in this book embraces some elements from all three theses either explicitly or implicitly, my proposal is significantly different from the existing suggestions.

Let me begin with the particularism thesis. Indeed, there is a danger of value monism in the presumption that the transition from an authoritarian regime to democracy in East Asian societies is completed with the establishment and consolidation of a Western-style liberal democracy, an assumption that is most salient in the political scientific studies of democracy.[12] And given its nature as a sociopolitical practice involving constant social, political, and cultural adaptations and reformulations, democracy cannot be reduced to a set of moral and political principles, and must be context-sensitive and culturally grounded. There is no disagreement here with the conviction that Confucian democracy can offer an important pluralist corrective to global value monism and cultural universalism from the perspective of East Asian particularism (if not parochialism).

However, I disagree with the core claim of the particularism thesis – that Confucian democracy and liberal democracy are diametrically opposed to each other and that in East Asia the former must replace the latter in both political institutions and civil society.[13] Confucian critics of liberal democracy tend to identify liberal democracy solely in terms of rights-based individualism as if liberal democracy is founded on, and thus is not possible without, it. Since

[12] Juan L. Linz and Alfred Stepan, *Problems of Democratic Transition and Consolidation: Southern Europe, South America, and Post-Communist Europe* (Baltimore: Johns Hopkins University Press, 1996); Larry Diamond, *Developing Democracy: Toward Consolidation* (Baltimore: Johns Hopkins University Press, 1999); Doh Chull Shin, "On the Third Wave of Democratization: A Synthesis and Evaluation of Recent Theory and Research," *World Politics* 47 (1994), 135–70; Shin, *Confucianism and Democratization*.

[13] This claim is most salient among Chinese scholars such as Jiang Qing, Kang Xiaoguang, and Chen Ming. See *Zhengzhi Rujia: Dangdai Rujia de zhuanxiang, tezhi yu fazhan* [Political Confucianism: Contemporary Confucianism's Challenge, Special Quality, and Development] (Beijing: San lian shu dian, 2003); *Renzheng: Zhongguo zhengzhi fazhan de disantiao daolu*

rights-based individualism is culturally and philosophically incompatible with Confucianism, which is at its core a communitarian ethics, and since rights-based individualism and communitarian ethics are diametrically opposed, the critics' reasoning goes, Confucian democracy is both philosophically and practically inconceivable without going *beyond* liberal democracy.[14] The problem with this incompatibility claim is that it reduces politics (and political theory and practice) to a self-contained philosophical or ethical thesis. At the heart of this claim lies the assumption that philosophical incompatibility directly leads to political incompatibility and that mutually incompatible ethical systems cannot coexist (or cohabit) or dialectically interact with each other.[15] It is, however, beyond this book's scope to examine whether or not Confucianism as a philosophical system is incommensurable with rights-based individualism.[16] So let us put this purely philosophical question aside and instead focus on two methodological problems in the theorization(s) of Confucian democracy thus far.

First, I find it problematic to think of Confucian democracy as a purely philosophical construct. The strategy has been, first, to reconstruct Confucian ethics or Confucian political philosophy with reference to ancient Confucian classics in the communitarian perspective and, second, to present it as an alternative political vision and practice to liberal democracy. But this produces mainly a philosophical reconstruction of Confucianism in light of contemporary

[Humane Government: A Third Road for the Development of Chinese Politics] (Singapore: Global Publishing, 2005); "Modernity and Confucian Political Philosophy in a Globalized World," in *Contemporary Chinese Political Thought: Debates and Perspectives*, ed. Fred Dallmayr and Zhao Tingyang (Lexington: University Press of Kentucky, 2012), 110–30 for each scholar's view. Kang's core argument is available in English in "Confucianism: A Future in the Tradition," *Social Research* 73 (2006), 77–120. One important exception is Sor-hoon Tan, who argues that "[t]he challenge for those supporting Confucian democracy is to articulate an alternative that would be sensitive to cultural requirements while taking seriously the liberal concern about governmental and social tyranny." See her *Confucian Democracy: A Deweyan Reconstruction* (Albany: State University of New York Press, 2003), 12.

14 The strongest advocate of this position is Henry Rosemont. See his "Why Take Rights Seriously? A Confucian Critique," in *Human Rights and the World's Religions*, ed. Leroy Rouner (Notre Dame, IN: University of Notre Dame Press, 1988), 167–82; "Rights-Bearing Individuals and Role-Bearing Persons," in *Rules, Rituals, and Responsibility*, ed. Mary I. Bockover (Chicago: Open Court, 1991), 71–101; "Human Rights: A Bill of Worries," in *Confucianism and Human Rights*, ed. Wm. Theodore de Bary and Tu Weiming (New York: Columbia University Press, 1998), 54–66.

15 For a recent criticism of this view, see Stephen C. Angle, *Contemporary Confucian Political Philosophy: Toward Progressive Confucianism* (Cambridge: Polity, 2012).

16 For some pioneering studies on this subject, see Joseph Chan, "Confucian Perspective on Human Rights for Contemporary China," in *The East Asian Challenge for Human Rights*, ed. Joanne R. Bauer and Daniel A. Bell (Cambridge: Cambridge University Press, 1999), 212–37; Seung-Hwan Lee, "Was There a Concept of Rights in Confucian Virtue Based Morality?," *Journal of Chinese Philosophy* 19 (1992), 241–61. Also see essays included in de Bary and Tu, *Confucianism and Human Rights* and Justin Tiwald, "Confucianism and Human Rights," in *Handbook of Human Rights*, ed. Thomas Cushman (London: Routledge, 2012), 244–54.

communitarianism without construction of a *Confucian democracy* that is politically relevant in existing East Asian societies both as a political system and as a social practice. The intention is to contrast Confucian democracy to liberal democracy, but in the end communitarian Confucianism and liberal rights-based individualism are contrasted.[17] The democracy part remains untouched.

Therefore, scholars remain unclear regarding whether or not Confucian democracy thus understood can be a robust democratic political practice in any realistic sense without having liberal constitutionalism (consisting of checks and balances, an independent judiciary, judicial review, etc.) as an institutional backdrop. In this sense, it is quite ironic that when some of the Confucian critics of liberal democracy articulate their Confucian democratic institutional vision more directly, quite often they do not merely go beyond liberal democracy but leave out democracy in toto.[18]

Second and related, it is just as problematic to understand liberal democracy as a purely (deontological) philosophical system. It is true that while many liberal philosophers (especially in the Kantian-Rawlsian strand) construct their normative political theory of liberal democracy on the assumption of rights-based individualism, there is a valid normative and methodological ground for disagreement with such attempts. In fact, the communitarian critiques of liberalism in the West during the 1980s and the 1990s revolved around just this problem. More specifically, when communitarians criticized John Rawls's *A Theory of Justice*, their major focus was on his philosophical apparatus of the original position and the Kantian deontological reconstruction of the liberal self as a socially unencumbered self.[19] Put differently, the debate was between social, civic, or communitarian liberals and deontological liberals, not between antiliberals and liberals.[20] None of the communitarian critics of (deontological) liberalism took issue with liberalism as a political system (i.e.,

[17] See David L. Hall and Roger T. Ames, *The Democracy of the Dead: Dewey, Confucius, and the Hope for Democracy in China* (Chicago: Open Court, 1999); Sor-hoon Tan, "Confucian Democracy as Pragmatic Experience: Uniting Love of Learning and Love of Antiquity," *Asian Philosophy* 17 (2007), 141–66; Tan, *Confucian Democracy.*

[18] This is clearly true of Daniel Bell and Tongdong Bai (See Chapter 3 for my critical examination of their institutional proposals) and less so of Hall and Ames, who take issue with the Western rule of law but do not advance alternative Confucian political institutions except Confucian ritualism. Tan's view is similar to those of Hall and Ames, but her critique of liberal democracy is more moderate and sensitive. It is still unclear though whether Tan endorses liberal constitutionalism as an integral element of her Deweyan Confucian democracy. For a pointed criticism of Bell's institutional proposal, see Fred Dallmayr, "Exiting Liberal Democracy: Bell and Confucian Thought," *Philosophy East and West* 59 (2009), 524–30.

[19] Most representative are Michael J. Sandel, *Liberalism and the Limits of Justice* (Cambridge: Cambridge University Press, 1982) and Michael Walzer, *Spheres of Justice: A Defense of Pluralism and Equality* (New York: Basic Books, 1983).

[20] Although I appreciate Stephen Holmes's presentation of liberalism as political theory and practice, I think his charge of communitarians as antiliberals is too strong, even misleading. See his *The Anatomy of Antiliberalism* (Cambridge, MA: Harvard University Press, 1996).

liberal constitutionalism) or as a political practice (i.e., public freedom and citizen rights). It is one thing for Confucian communitarian democrats, who are deeply inspired by Western communitarians, to engage critically with a certain brand of liberal political philosophy; it is another to reduce liberal politics to deontological liberalism.

This is not to argue that Confucian democrats must embrace liberal politics, specifically liberal constitutional politics. My point is that if there is no inherent and foundational connection between deontological liberalism, the main focus of the Confucian criticism of liberalism, and liberal-democratic and constitutional politics, there is no strong reason to present Confucian democracy and liberal democracy as polar opposites. Again, democracy can mean or include many different things, but at its core, it is a political system and a sociopolitical practice, not a philosophical idea or an ethical precept.

East Asians no longer live in a traditional Confucian society, where Confucian political doctrines and moral precepts enjoyed cultural and ideational monopoly in both central government and local communities, and virtually all East Asian societies have been more or less liberalized, pluralized, and democratized, compared to their old Confucian counterparts. Although some Confucian philosophers continue to raise skepticism about the relevance of human rights in the East Asian context, reiterating the philosophical incompatibility claim, rights discourse and rule of law have become integral parts of East Asian life. Only very few East Asians self-consciously identify themselves as "Confucians," and a very small number of them wish to return to an old-style Confucian regime, however "noble" it would appear from a contemporary philosophical and atheistic viewpoint.[21]

Confucian democracy as a political vision and practice must be socially relevant in contemporary East Asian societies and must be able to appeal to ordinary East Asian citizens who now belong to various moral, philosophical, cultural, and religious communities. However, the *idea* of Confucian democracy that is philosophically constructed in reference to ancient Confucian classics without much consideration of its social relevance in modern and pluralistic East Asian societies can hardly achieve this crucial political goal.[22] Therefore,

[21] Certainly, Jiang Qing is one example of such (religious) "Confucians" who differentiate themselves from (secular) "Confucianists." For Jiang's distinction between Confucians and Confucianists, see his *Confucian Constitutional Order*, 47. To be fair, while envisioning Confucian constitutionalism by returning the sovereign authority back to heaven (or its representatives, viz., Confucian scholars), Jiang clearly says that he is not a reactionary but a reformer who embraces China's republican historical context.

[22] It should be clarified that my problem with the philosophical construction of Confucian democracy lies not so much in its attempt to reconstruct Confucian political philosophy with reference to Confucian classics as such (there is nothing wrong with this endeavor) but in its failure to address the central feature of democracy as collective self-determination, particularly in the modern societal context. In this regard, it is surprising that recent "Deweyan" Confucian democrats do not pay enough attention to Dewey's analysis of social and practical *conditions* under which politically significant problems arise and "publics" (in Dewey's distinct sense) emerge.

I suggest a more political version of Confucian democracy: instead of trying to surpass liberal democracy, East Asians should attempt to *Confucianize* partially liberal and democratic regimes that currently exist.

This suggestion is based on my observation that the real problem East Asians are struggling with is not so much the putative philosophical incompatibility between Confucianism and liberalism but the frustrating reality that the (more or less) democratic institutions that they (or their leaders) have imported from the West do not work as the theories of liberal democracy claim. Of course, no political regime can operate precisely as political theory stipulates. But East Asians are currently experiencing more than the usual discrepancy between theory and practice. The gist of the East Asian problem lies in the systematic discord between the more or less liberal-democratic institutional-political hardware and the social-cultural software that should operate it. Put differently, liberal discourse and liberal-democratic institutions are not socially relevant in East Asian societies, where citizens are soaked in Confucian habits and mores, often without self-awareness.[23] The result is the widespread complaint that there is no genuine democracy in East Asia, followed by the common suggestion for the transformation of East Asian societies and its civic culture through "attitudinal, cognitive, and behavioral" changes among the East Asian citizenry.[24]

From the perspective of cultural pluralism, however, this attempt to attain a perfect congruence between democratic institutions and their underlying civic culture is overbearing.[25] The Confucian democracy that I am proposing in this book is predicated on the Confucian habits and mores that citizens, while subscribing to different comprehensive moral doctrines, broadly share as the core components of their public culture and as the affective sources for their public reasoning. In this suggested Confucian democracy, the formal political structure is largely undergirded on liberal-democratic political institutions as they offer sophisticated institutional mechanisms to check the arbitrary power of the power-holders, thereby protecting the citizenry's public freedom and each individual citizen's constitutional rights.[26] Rendering

For more on this point, Sungmoon Kim, "John Dewey and Confucian Democracy: Toward Common Citizenship," *Constellations* (forthcoming).

[23] See Koh, "Confucianism in Contemporary Korea"; Alford, *Think No Evil*.

[24] See, for example, Doh Chull Shin and Chong-Min Park, "The Mass Public and Democratic Politics in South Korea: Exploring the Subjective World of Democratization in Flux," in *How East Asians View Democracy*, ed. Yun-han Chu, Larry Diamond, Andrew J. Nathan, and Doh Chull Shin (New York: Columbia University Press, 2008).

[25] For instance, Doh Chull Shin asserts, "To operate the institutional hardware, a democratic political system requires 'software' that is congruent with the various hardware components" (Shin, *Confucianism and Democratization*, 7).

[26] Of course, this formal liberal-democratic political structure is open to Confucian revisions. But it is not prudent to refuse to adopt liberal-democratic political institutions simply because they are not East Asian or Confucian in origin when they better protect public freedom and political rights than old or reformed Confucian institutions. In this regard, I strongly agree with Stephen

this apparently liberal-democratic regime *Confucian*, thus making it socially relevant and culturally grounded, are the ceaseless translations of political, putatively liberal, rights in Confucian terms or their reappropriation in reference to Confucian public reason. In Chapters 9 and 10, I show what such mutual adaptations between Confucian public culture and liberal rights look like in a Confucian democracy.

Beyond Thick Confucian Communitarianism and Meritocratic Elitism

1. Thick Confucian Communitarianism

While virtually all Confucian political theorists and philosophers uphold the communitarianism thesis and an equally good number of scholars agree that political meritocracy is an integral element of Confucian democracy, there is a meaningful difference between what I call thick Confucian communitarians and advocates of meritocratic elitism. The most notable difference is that the meritocracy thesis as stipulated earlier is supported only by the latter. Although the Confucian democracy that I propose embraces both communitarian and meritocratic components, it accepts the communitarian thesis only partially and completely rejects the meritocracy thesis.

The communitarian thesis supports thick Confucian communitarianism.[27] The following statement by David Hall and Roger Ames most succinctly illustrates the core tenets of thick Confucian communitarianism: "[The Confucian] stress upon a tacit, affective consensus celebrated through ritualized roles and practices that do not require raising difference to the level of consciousness, promotes authentic social harmony.... Consensus is primarily unspoken. The essentially aesthetic dimension of ritual practice promotes communication at a level of precluding the necessity of debate."[28] The communitarianism thesis consists of four main claims: (1) the Confucian self is fundamentally a social self (the social self claim); (2) contra the liberal morally autonomous and

Angle when he says that objective liberal-democratic political structures consisting of a constitution, laws, and rights are not merely compatible with Confucianism, but rather are "required" by Confucianism (Angle, *Contemporary Confucian Political Philosophy*, 29).

27 Its advocates include David Hall, Roger Ames, Henry Rosemont, Sor-hoon Tan, Russell Fox, and Craig Ihara. Besides the works of Hall and Ames, Tan, and Rosemont, see Russell A. Fox, "Confucian and Communitarian Responses to Liberal Democracy," *Review of Politics* 59 (1997): 561–92; Craig K. Ihara, "Are Individual Rights Necessary? A Confucian Perspective" in *Confucian Ethics: A Comparative Study of Self, Autonomy, and Community*, ed. Kwong-loi Shun and David B. Wong (Cambridge: Cambridge University Press, 2004). Theodore de Bary also calls his social vision "Confucian communitarian," but unlike thick Confucian communitarians, he finds that moral individualism and human rights are integral to Confucian communitarianism. See Wm. Theodore de Bary, *Asian Values and Human Rights: A Confucian Communitarian Perspective* (Cambridge, MA: Harvard University Press, 1998). Also see David B. Wong, "Rights and Community in Confucianism," in Shun and Wong, *Confucian Ethics* for a similar view.

28 Hall and Ames, *Democracy of the Dead*, 182.

self-choosing self that is starkly opposed to community, the Confucian social self is symbiotic with community because it performs ritualized roles, or more radically, it *is* its various social roles (the role ethics claim); (3) premised on the assumption of the social self, Confucian role ethics not only works through but normatively cherishes ritual aestheticism (the ritual aestheticism claim); and finally (4) Confucian ritual aestheticism upholds social harmony as the quintessential sociopolitical value in a Confucian communitarian democracy and as an aesthetic state of affairs it is qualitatively different from, perhaps even opposed to, a political consensus that is attained through a dialogical communicative process that involves negotiation, bargaining, deliberation, and contestation (the social harmony claim).

In Chapters 1 and 2, I critically examine these four claims in detail from both Confucian and democratic perspectives. Here let me briefly address two problems, methodological and political. First, the communitarianism thesis is exposed to two methodological problems.

The first methodological problem is related to the question of whether Confucianism originally presented by the tradition's founding masters (Confucius, Mencius, and Xunzi) indeed upholds role ethics, which is the core assumption in the communitarianism thesis. What is involved here is a purely academic philosophical question of how to *interpret* Confucian classics, and it is beyond the scope of this book to address the ongoing debate between those who interpret (ancient) Confucian ethics as role ethics (such as Roger Ames and Henry Rosemont)[29] and those who interpret it as a kind of virtue ethics (such as Philip Ivanhoe and Bryan Van Norden).[30] Without subscribing myself to Confucian virtue ethics (as its proponents are primarily interested in apolitical moral virtues that any human being must cultivate to live a flourishing human life), let me raise skepticism to the role ethics claim: however social or relational, the Confucian social self cannot merely play various social roles, and there is ample textual evidence that Confucian philosophers took an individual's moral and political agency quite seriously.[31]

The second methodological problem is already noted in my refutation of the particularism thesis. That is, the communitarianism thesis wrongly identifies Confucianism, philosophically reconstructed in the communitarian (and putatively democratic) spirit, with Confucian democracy – a democratic political system and practice that is characteristically Confucian – which must be

[29] Roger T. Ames, *Confucian Role Ethics: A Vocabulary* (Honolulu: University of Hawaii Press, 2011).

[30] For the virtue ethical interpretation of (ancient) Confucianism, see Philip J. Ivanhoe, *Ethics in the Confucian Tradition: The Thought of Mengzi and Wang Yangming* (Indianapolis: Hackett, 2002); Ivanhoe, *Confucian Moral Self Cultivation* (Indianapolis: Hackett, 2000); Bryan W. Van Norden, *Virtue Ethics and Consequentialism in Early Chinese Philosophy* (Cambridge: Cambridge University Press, 2007).

[31] See Joseph Chan, "Moral Autonomy, Civil Liberties, and Confucianism," *Philosophy East and West* 52 (2002), 281–310.

concerned with the political question of how to improve the citizenry's collective life in the contemporary Confucian society, a life that is stricken with a variety of social, economic, and political injustice. Philosophical Confucian democracy highlights the normative appeal of Confucian democracy as a communitarian social vision, and there is indeed much to appreciate in it, especially when democracies all over the world are invasively threatened by consumerism and market totalitarianism. However, philosophical Confucian democracy is critically limited in presenting itself to citizens in East Asia as a politically attractive social practice, as long as it remains primarily a philosophical argument for ritual aestheticism as an alternative (not just complement) to rights-based individualism and rule of law. Its political efficacy is significantly reduced unless it is socially grounded and politically effective in societies where the stringent East-West dichotomy is no longer feasible. Echoing Western communitarians, Confucian communitarians criticize the (deontological) liberal notion of the rights-bearing individual as socially implausible because it is presented as socially unencumbered. This is a reasonable and important criticism. However, ironically, while their political proposal is almost completely based on ancient Confucian classics, there are hardly any references (or relevance) to existing East Asian societies, and the specific problems that they are wrestling with.

In a sense, the political problems of the communitarianism thesis are the natural corollary of the methodological problems just sketched, but their ramifications are far more serious as they are directly related to politics. Here, too, let me point out two specific problems.

First, by deeming all four claims in the communitarianism thesis as inexplicably intertwined, Confucian communitarians fail to note that interpreting Confucian ethics as role ethics is distinct from normatively advocating ritual aestheticism and social harmony. Suppose Confucian ethics does support role ethics. Does Confucian role ethics leave any room for the citizen to play a political role in a Confucian yet democratic society? Can democratic citizenship fit nicely into the five cardinal human relationships (*wulun* 五倫), around which Confucian ethics was traditionally centered?[32] Confucian communitarians often present equal participation in the communal semiotics of Confucian rituals (*li* 禮) as analogous to equal political participation, and relying on this equation they say that ritual aestheticism is at the core of Confucian democracy, replacing dialogical public deliberation and harmony-destroying political contestation. The problem is that moral equality assumed in Confucian ritual practice (that *anyone* can participate in the *li*, thereby becoming morally good) does not necessarily establish political equality, where everyone is a free and equal citizen regardless of his or her ritualized roles in the society.[33]

[32] The five cardinal human relationships refer to ruler-minister, father-son, husband-wife, old-young, and friend-friend relationships. See *Mencius* 3A4.

[33] See Edward Shils, "Reflections on Civil Society and Civility in the Chinese Intellectual Tradition," in Tu, *Confucian Traditions in East Asian Modernity*. It is for this reason that Fred Dallmayr suggests adding civic relations to the traditional Confucian five cardinal relationships to make

By failing to distinguish political equality from moral equality, Confucian communitarians reduce Confucian democratic *politics* to Confucian role *ethics*, reiterating the traditional Confucian faith in the seamless continuum between ethics and politics. The result, however, is not the ideal Confucian gemeinschaft as Confucian communitarians wish to have but the absence of a robust democratic citizenship.[34] Members in the Confucian ritual-constituted moral community may live a vibrant and fiduciary social life, and fiduciary communal life certainly makes democracy (if it exists) work better. But communal membership is not directly analogous to democratic citizenship. In reality, we can have abundant social capital in local communities in a nondemocratic, even authoritarian, regime, as powerfully demonstrated by Sheri Berman's study of the collapse of the Weimar Republic, which enjoyed a plethora of social capital in local communities.[35] In the absence of a robust democratic citizenship, strong emphasis of civility is likely to promote docility, democracy's worst enemy according to Alexis de Tocqueville. What we need is a democratic civil society that is rooted on Confucian habits and mores but qualitatively different from a Confucian ritual-constituted gemeinschaft that aims at an organic whole.

The second political problem of the communitarianism thesis derives directly from the first one. Simply put, aiming at an aesthetic organic whole, Confucian communitarianism is critically limited in coming to terms with the fact of value pluralism that increasingly characterizes East Asian societies. Even though Confucian communitarians acknowledge the ethical importance and the reality of value pluralism in principle (which is evident in Hall and Ames's and Tan's works), their strong opposition to dialogical communication and democratic conflict resolution through public deliberation and contestation should make pluralistic East Asian citizens wonder how a genuine respect for value pluralism is possible in a Confucian communitarian democracy. By substituting aestheticism for politics, Confucian communitarians valorize tacit consensus and organic social harmony. In so doing, however, they completely dismiss how *power* surreptitiously works in achieving such consensus and harmony. Put differently, they do not pay attention to the quintessentially political question, *harmony according to whose judgment?*

Harmony as conceived by ancient Confucians is attained only when the Way (*dao* 道) prevails and the Way prevails only when the sage-king, the Confucian equivalent of the Platonic philosopher-king, reigns. Only then will everyone play their *proper* social roles, without any moral and political transgressions,

Confucianism safe in a modern democratic society. See Fred R. Dallmayr, "Confucianism and the Public Sphere: Five Relationships Plus One?" in *The Politics of Affective Relations: East Asia and Beyond*, ed. Chaihark Hahm and Daniel A. Bell (Lanham, MD: Lexington Books, 2004).

34 Shaun O'Dwyer, "Democracy and Confucian Values," *Philosophy East and West* 53 (2003), 39–63; Kim, "John Dewey and Confucian Democracy."

35 Sheri Berman, "Civil Society and the Collapse of the Weimar Republic," *World Politics* 49 (1997), 401–29.

although they would not fully understand why and in what sense what they do is proper. It is the sage-king (or Heaven's delegate) alone who possesses the inscrutable measure of what is proper and the holistic understanding of the ethical and cosmological meaning of such roles in the moral universe.[36] Of interest, when they uphold the organic whole, ritual aestheticism, and tacit social harmony in reference to ancient Confucian texts, Confucian communitarians never allude to the underlying institutional model that can allegedly achieve all of them.[37] In modern East Asian societies where the sage-king paradigm and moral/value monism affiliated with it have become nearly obsolete and individuals are adopting different value systems, it may not be so politically prudential or even morally undesirable to attempt to establish a democratic regime undergirded on thick or organic Confucian communitarianism.[38]

2. *Meritocratic Elitism*

Compared to the particularism and communitarianism theses, the meritocracy thesis of Confucian democracy is a recent academic phenomenon mainly among Chinese or pan-China-based scholars.[39] Many of its advocates largely agree with Confucian communitarians that Confucian democracy is a kind of communitarian project and it can be a genuine alternative to liberal democracy.[40] Advocates of Confucian meritocracy and thick Confucian communitarians part company, however, when it comes to democracy: while the latter is strongly committed to democracy and political equality in principle, despite some problems in their theorization(s) of Confucian democracy, the former expresses deep dissatisfaction with democracy itself. Even though none of the supporters of meritocracy present themselves as antidemocrats by embracing at least "some" democratic elements in their suggestion of Confucian political

[36] Among the three ancient Confucian masters, Xunzi most clearly illustrates the origin of proper roles and social positions under sage kingship. See *Xunzi* 9:3; 19:1a-b. Also see *Mencius* 3A4.

[37] The reason seems to have to do with the fact that these scholars reinterpret ancient Confucian texts in light of Deweyan pragmatism, thereby dismantling Confucian cosmology and political metaphysics implicated in the Confucian rule by ritual (*lizhi* 禮治) and presenting Confucian ritualism in nonreligious aesthetic terms.

[38] On the "sage-king paradigm" in Chinese (especially Confucian) intellectualism and political philosophy, see Julia Ching, *Mysticism and Kingship in China: The Heart of Chinese Wisdom* (Cambridge: Cambridge University Press, 1997). Also see Jiang, *Confucian Constitutional Order*, 49–52.

[39] In addition to Jiang Qing, Kang Xiaoguang, and Daniel Bell, these scholars include Ruiping Fan, Tongdong Bai, Chenyang Li, and Joseph Chan. See Ruiping Fan, *Reconstructionist Confucianism: Rethinking Morality after the West* (Dordrecht: Springer, 2010); Tongdong Bai, "A Mencian Version of Limited Democracy," *Res Publica* 14 (2008), 19–34; Chenyang Li, "Equality and Inequality in Confucianism," *Dao* 11 (2012), 295–313; Joseph Chan, "Democracy and Meritocracy: Toward a Confucian Perspective," *Journal of Chinese Philosophy* 34 (2007), 179–93.

[40] Daniel A. Bell, *East Meets West: Human Rights and Democracy in East Asia* (Princeton: Princeton University Press, 2000).

institutions, I consider them opponents of democracy.[41] Since I examine their position(s) in detail in Chapters 3 and 7, here, as I did with the communitarianism thesis, I will just point out one crucial problem of the meritocracy thesis, which is both methodological and political.

The problem is rooted in the way meritocratic elitism is justified. Most tellingly, Daniel Bell, one of the most active and influential advocates of the meritocracy thesis, explains why meritocratic elitism can be a realistic political option in East Asian societies: "A Western democrat might favor letting 'the people' decide. The idea here is that ordinary citizens can be trusted to make sensible choices as to capable rulers.... The problem with this view, however, is that politicians often get elected by pandering to the short-term interests of the populace.... Perhaps the situation is different in East Asia. Ordinary people seem to have imbibed the Confucian ethic of respect and deference toward educated and public-spirited politicians."[42] The problem of this statement, which is widely shared by advocates of Confucian meritocratic elitism, lies in the unfair comparison between potential problems of representative democracy and putative virtues of Confucian meritocracy. Is it fair to compare good Confucian ethics, which is reconstructed solely with reference to ancient Confucian classics, to bad liberal practices that betray liberal ethics and ideals?[43] Furthermore, is the "respect and deference toward educated and public-spirited politicians" a distinctively Confucian ethic?[44]

Since James Madison, no conscientious liberal constitutionalist has understood modern representative democracy merely as a system that lets the people decide whatever they want. Quite the contrary, meritocracy understood as good leadership/statesmanship has been an integral part of liberal representative democracy, and liberal democrats have always tried to constrain unrestrained democratic populism by means of various constitutional-institutional

[41] Joseph Chan's attitude toward democracy, however, is quite complex. On the one hand, he appears to be much more liberal-democratic than other scholars advocating Confucian meritocracy, but on the other hand, he acknowledges the moral and political value of democracy merely for instrumental reasons. Though it is unfair to call Chan an opponent of democracy, it is certain that he is not wholly committed to democracy, and Chan justifies his position in terms of "Confucian perfectionism." See his *Confucian Perfectionism: A Political Philosophy for Modern Times* (Princeton: Princeton University Press, 2013).

[42] Bell, *Beyond Liberal Democracy*, 162–3.

[43] Bell illustrates the Confucian tradition of respect toward the "best and brightest" merely by referring to a couple of sporadic passages in the *Analects* of Confucius (Ibid., 153–4).

[44] According to Doh Chull Shin's recent survey research, only 33 percent of Chinese citizens are attached to meritocratic moral leadership, and, even more striking, those who are firmly attached to this putatively "Confucian" value amount to only 1.9 percent. All the more strikingly, popular attachment to the nondemocratic model of meritocratic government turns to be more pervasive throughout the non-Confucian region than the Confucian region of Asia. See Shin, *Confucianism and Democratization*, 120, 138. For a classical study on this subject, see Lucian W. Pye, *Asian Power and Politics: The Cultural Dimensions of Authority* (Cambridge, MA: Belknap, 1985).

apparatuses including checks and balances and judicial review.[45] Equally important, in liberal representative democracy good leaders are not deemed to be elitist rulers, but are those who are capable of getting their hands dirty in making tough political decisions for the sake of the public good and who can take full political responsibility for their decisions, including impeachment and even imprisonment, should they have violated the law or democratic procedures. In other words, the defining characteristics of political meritocracy in a liberal democracy are political responsibility and democratic accountability.[46] Political representatives and public officials assume leadership, but they are in no way elitist rulers.

As I noted earlier, it is both possible and politically desirable to Confucianize democratic institutions so that they can be socially relevant and politically effective in East Asian societies, into which they (at least some skeletons of the institutions) have been imported thus far. However, it is simply wrong to present Confucian meritocratic elitism as a political alternative to liberal democracy because there is no inherent contradiction between political meritocracy and liberal representative democracy. In the absence of better institutional mechanisms for democratic accountability, representative democracy is neither an object to be overcome nor a Western ideal to be blindly emulated. Rather, it is something to be culturally accommodated.

In sum, political meritocracy should be pursued not outside democratic political institutions but within them (especially in the accountability mechanism), within institutions that are at once supported and constrained by Confucian democratic civil society. Only then can we realize Confucian meritocracy that is both nonelitist and democratically accountable.

Toward Confucian Democratic Civil Society

Thus understood, the institutional backbone of the Confucian democracy that I propose in this book does not necessarily lie in formal political institutions, the key players of which consist mainly of professional politicians and public officials. What makes Confucian democracy culturally distinctive (as Confucian) and politically vibrant (as democratic) is the existence and invigoration of what I have been calling "Confucian democratic civil society," where Confucian habits and mores are retained, reproduced, and reappropriated.[47] It

[45] Alexander Hamilton, James Madison, and John Jay, *The Federalist Papers*, ed. Garry Wills (New York: Bantam Books, 1982).

[46] See William A. Galston, "Toughness as Political Virtue," *Social Theory and Practice* 17 (1991), 175–97; Dennis F. Thompson, *Political Ethics and Public Office* (Cambridge, MA: Harvard University Press, 1987), especially chap. 1, titled "Democratic Dirty Hands."

[47] Though I generally embrace the established formal-judicial understanding of civil society in the social science literature as "a realm of organizations, groups, and associations that are formally established, legally protected, autonomously run, and voluntarily joined by ordinary citizens" (see Marc M. Howard, *The Weakness of Civil Society in Post-Communist Europe* [Cambridge:

is in the Confucian civil society that citizens are inculcated in Confucian public reason (which is familial sentimental rather than purely rational) and can cultivate the virtue of Confucian civility. Furthermore, it offers an open public space where all affected citizens can freely deliberate about and even contest the social norms implicated in Confucian civility, thus enriching and reformulating Confucian public reason in a more inclusive way. Formal political institutions can be Confucianized, and political leaders and public officials can be democratically accountable and civically virtuous, only if there exists a vibrant Confucian and democratic civil society. Therefore, though the overall purpose of this book is to construct a new model of Confucian democracy, its primary focus centers on Confucian civil society – more specifically, how to empower it as a formidable bulwark for public freedom and democratic citizenship, and how it can meet the challenges of value pluralism.

Aims and Outlines of the Book

This is a book about democracy, a democracy that is culturally relevant and politically practicable in Confucian East Asia, which is increasingly becoming pluralized and multiculturalized. It is not primarily about Confucianism, nor is it aimed at a philosophical reconstruction of the *idea* of Confucian democracy. My aim in this book is not to accommodate the East Asian social and political reality to philosophical Confucianism, which many Confucian political philosophers do on the assumption that the current East Asian reality is deviant from, hence morally and politically rectified by, the pure Confucianism conceived by the ancient masters, unencumbered by the historical Confucianism of premodern East Asia. I do not believe philosophical Confucianism – a Confucianism systematically reconstructed with reference to ancient Confucian classics – can save morally decadent East Asian societies that are increasingly Westernized, rights-based, and interests-oriented.

The Confucianism that I am focused on in this book is what still *characterizes* East Asian societies as distinctively Confucian (in the sense that any outsider would observe and characterize as such),[48] despite their increasing liberalization,

Cambridge University Press, 2003], 34–5), I am especially interested in the normative dimension of civil society, that is, as a public sphere that interconnects individual agency to citizenship, with an understanding that the practical connotations of the terms "individual" and "citizenship" and their cultural mode of connection, namely "civility," can vary across culture. For my theorizations of Confucian civil society, see Sungmoon Kim, "Self-Transformation and Civil Society: Lockean vs. Confucian," *Dao* 8 (2009), 383–401 and "Beyond Liberal Civil Society: Confucian Familism and Relational Strangership," *Philosophy East and West* 60 (2010): 476–98.

48 I suspect that some scholars who are methodologically savvy or those who are interested to know what kind of a philosophical Confucianism is alive in East Asia may find my loose and largely sociological understanding of "Confucianism" utterly unsatisfactory. Self-consciously Confucian scholars such as Jiang Qing might have some answers for them, but honestly I do not know whether the Confucianism that is still practiced in East Asia (as statistically attested

pluralization, and individualization. I am referring to the Confucian habits and mores with which East Asian citizens are still deeply saturated, and the Confucian public culture and public reason that they, who as individuals subscribe to different moral, philosophical, and religious doctrines, commonly share as public citizens. This does not mean that I do not revisit classical Confucian texts at all. As a matter of fact, I do frequently (especially in Chapters 2, 5, and 6). But when I do, my interest is not so much in the philosophical reconstruction of Confucianism as such but in a Confucianism (politically and civically reconstructed), which can help us to make better sense of what citizens in East Asia are already doing and expand our understanding of what counts as democratic in the Confucian societal, cultural, and ethical context.[49] In Chapter 2 I call such a reconstructed Confucianism "civil Confucianism" and distinguish it from thick Confucian communitarianism and meritocratic elitism.

In short, while Confucian democracy is undergirded in practice by Confucian habits and mores, as a political theory it is predicated on civil Confucianism that philosophically *articulate*s, rather than frames, the nature of Confucian habits and mores that are always in play in East Asia, and *illuminates* the Confucian civilities that they produce. Though Part II, in which I construct a political theory of Confucian democracy and civil society with reference to Confucian classics (especially the *Mencius*), precedes Part III, in which I examine the Korean practice of Confucian democracy, it is indeed chapters in Part III that inspired those in Part II. For this reason, the chapters in Part III should not be misunderstood as a case study prepared to test the (normative) theory constructed in Part II scientifically.[50]

My goal in this book, therefore, is philosophically modest and politically pragmatic, which is to make democracy, originally of Western provenance, work well in the societies whose public culture is characteristically Confucian. Contra the particularism thesis examined earlier, my central argument is that for the citizenry's public life to be politically free and socioculturally vibrant,

as well as generally observed) can be clearly defined in the way that can satisfy methodologists or philosophers. The same complaint can be leveled at, say, Robert Bellah and his colleagues' modern classic *Habits of the Heart: Individualism and Commitment in American Life* (Berkeley: University of California Press, 1985) where Bellah and company investigate the American habits of the heart as well as (and even) to Alexis de Tocqueville, who first noted uniquely American social habits and mores, without defining what exactly they consist of, in his monumental work *Democracy in America*, ed. and trans. Harvey C. Mansfield and Delba Winthrop (Chicago: University of Chicago Press, 2000), but I wonder whether this type of a complaint can make any practical contribution to the enhancement of democracy in East Asia (or America), which is this book's central aim. In this regard, Robert Bellah's following statement is worth serious attention: "Why something so obvious should have escaped serious analytical attention is itself an interesting problem" (Robert N. Bellah, "Civil Religion in America," in *The Robert Bellah Reader*, ed. Robert N. Bellah and Steven M. Tipton [Durham, NC: Duke University Press, 2006], 225).

49 I share this spirit with Benjamin Barber. See *Strong Democracy*, xxvi.

50 So, one way to read this book – especially for those who wonder what I mean by Confucian habits and mores and how they actually operate in East Asia – is to read Part III before Part II.

democracy and Confucianism must be mutually adapting to each other, thereby creating favorable societal conditions for a Confucian democracy.

Furthermore, in the Confucian democracy that I propose, Confucianism is no longer a universalist and all-encompassing philosophical doctrine and/or political metaphysics that is ethically monistic and culturally monolithic. Instead, having been accommodated to democratic conditions (political equality, collective self-determination, and value pluralism), Confucianism is civically recast as civil Confucianism. Here, democracy, thus modified, does not operate on liberal civility but on Confucian civility, and it serves the telos of good government as stipulated in the traditional Confucian virtue politics (*dezhi* 德治), namely, the moral and material well-being of the people.

This book consists of three parts. In Part I, I critically examine the communitarianism and meritocracy theses. In Chapter 1, I revisit two claims of the Confucian communitarianism thesis (the social self claim and the role ethics claim). Here I first examine whether it is justifiable to dismiss liberal ethics of moral individualism and liberal political theory of social contract based on the implausibility of modern ontology. I then challenge the Confucian communitarians by asking how their claim that the Confucian self is a social self can justify their ethical claim that the Confucian social self is also a civil self. After identifying Confucian moral agency in three terms – contextual self-reflexivity, moral judgment, and social criticism – I argue that the communitarianism thesis renders Confucian communitarianism less democratically robust and is predisposed to political conservatism.

Then in Chapter 2, I turn to the third and fourth claims of the communitarianism thesis – the social harmony claim and the ritual aestheticism claim. I argue that to make Confucian communitarianism a viable political practice, namely *civil Confucianism*, its one-sided emphasis on civility must be balanced with what I call "Confucian incivility," a set of Confucian social practices that may temporarily upset the existing social relations and yet ultimately help those relations become more enduring and viable. My central argument is that "Confucian civility" encompasses both social-harmonizing civilities that buttress the moral foundation of the Confucian social order and some incivilities that upset that foundation, albeit temporarily, to revise and thereby revitalize it.

In Chapter 3, which is the last chapter of Part I, I critique the meritocracy thesis of Confucian democracy from the standpoint of Confucian democratic civil society. Here I argue not only that there is no strong textual ground for the Confucian justification of meritocratic elitism but also that the meritocracy thesis severely suffers democratic deficit resulting from its strong emphasis on the governability of the people as opposed to their political transformability. I then introduce my own vision of Confucian democracy by claiming that (1) Confucian virtue politics (*dezhi* 德治) can be creatively reappropriated in democratic civil society in terms of cultivating civility in ordinary people who belong to different moral communities; (2) in the modern East Asian social context, the Confucian ideal of benevolent government can be better attained through democratic contestation by victims of socioeconomic injustice in the public space of civil society than by thin/minimal democracy controlled by meritocratic elitism.

In Part II, I articulate my own vision of Confucian democracy, namely, *Confucian pluralist democracy*, far more systematically and in greater detail, which extends from the mere sketch in the final part of Chapter 3.

In Chapter 4, I articulate how Confucian democracy should come to terms with the moral well-being of citizens in a pluralist societal context by reconstructing Confucian democracy into a robust democratic political theory and practice. To do so, I first investigate the core tenets of value pluralism with reference to William Galston's political theory, and then construct a political theory of Confucian pluralist democracy by critically engaging with the communitarian and meritocracy theses in the existing suggestions of Confucian democracy. In this chapter I advance a threefold argument: (1) the unity in Confucian democracy should be interpreted not as moral unity but as constitutional unity; (2) Confucian virtues should be differentiated (or pluralized) between moral virtues and civic virtues; and (3) in Confucian democracy minorities have the constitutional right to contest public norms in civil society.

In Chapters 5 and 6 I further articulate the nature of public reason in a Confucian pluralist democracy and my vision of Confucian democratic welfarism. In Chapter 5, I argue that Confucian public reasons are not so much rationalist constraints or deontic principles but consist of moral sentiments or civil passions that dispose citizens who share common (yet publicly contestable) legal, social, and political institutions to have common concerns about their public life. Drawing on the core Mencian-Confucian assumption that Confucian *ren* 仁 is rooted in filial love and fraternal affection, I reconstruct Confucian public reason as affective concerns and argue that the defining characteristic of Confucian public reason is familial moral sentimentalism, especially what I call *critical affection*, which makes public reason(ing) reflective, self-regulative, and inclusive. Finally, I argue that Confucian public reason thus understood is open to democratic revision and contestation because of the norm of inclusiveness implicated in familial affection.

Chapter 6 relates the core argument that I developed in Chapter 5 to a defense of democratic welfarism by developing a political vision of Confucian social justice that is robustly democratic and justifiable in light of Confucian public reason(s). I argue that Confucian family-oriented welfarism, or simply Confucian familism, according to which it is wrong for one to love strangers (including one's fellow citizens) as one's core family members, seriously violates the Confucian principle of the familial as the political in which the state is envisioned as an extended family. After revealing the libertarian and strong economic meritocratic implications in the suggestion of family care, I argue that Confucian familism must be revamped into Confucian familialism that puts vulnerability before merit. By focusing on vulnerability and interdependency, I defend Confucian democratic welfarism not in terms of economic egalitarianism but on the basis of political equality and democratic citizenship.

In Chapter 7, I advance my own idea of political meritocracy in the context of Confucian pluralist democracy that I have reconstructed in previous chapters. As a critical rejoinder to advocates of meritocratic elitism, I make a threefold argument: (1) political meritocracy is highly compatible with, even integral to, representative democracy, if the selection model of political representation is preferred to the sanction model (the selection thesis); political meritocracy can be Confucian democratic if (2) political representatives and public officials see themselves as public servants as opposed to elitist rulers (the public servant thesis) and (3) representatives exempt themselves from protection from public insult, thus exposing themselves to open and free public criticism when they have breached public faith (the no insult thesis).

Part III extends the theory of Confucian pluralist democracy constructed thus far to a particular East Asian country – South Korea. My choice of South Korea as a case that practically reflects as well as normatively inspires Confucian pluralist democracy is twofold[51]: first, among East Asian countries, South Korea has experienced the most radical and thorough Confucian societal transformation since the foundation of the Chosŏn dynasty (1392–1910); second, South Korea, despite its heavy Confucian moorings, has been successfully democratized and maintains a robustly democratic regime and a highly vibrant civil society, which are rarely found in new democracies established in and after the third wave of democratization.

In Chapter 8, I relate the Confucian familial moral sentimentalism that I have discussed in Chapter 5 to an exposition as well as exploration of the Korean-Confucian public reason by articulating the civil nature of critical affection and the civic virtue that it gives rise to. Special focus will be on the Korean experience of *chŏng*, familial affectionate sentiments and the uniquely

[51] Methodologically speaking, my approach in this part is close to what Stephen Salkever calls "explanatory evaluation," an Aristotelian methodology that aims to integrate theory into practice and facts into values (or vice versa). Salkever's following statement best captures this part's (and this book's) pronounced spirit of linking a social science of democracy (empiricality) to a political theory of democracy (normativity): "The separation between political philosophy and political science, or between normativity and empirical political theory, carries with it or implies a number of important assertions about the character of things known and the way they are knowable. Chief among these is the distinction between facts and values or goods, and the claim that facts are known empirically while values are either not objectively knowable or knowable in some a priori way.... I have in mind primarily the way in which the distinction between political philosophy and political science (as well as the more general distinction between moral philosophy and social science) works to separate the processes of evaluation and explanation, of critique and understanding, against the intentions of many within the discipline to practice a political science that is both evaluative and explanatory" (Stephen G. Salkever, *Finding the Mean: Theory and Practice in Aristotelian Political Philosophy* [Princeton: Princeton University Press, 1990], 14).

Korean-Confucian civic virtue called "*uri*-responsibility" (we-responsibility), a collective moral responsibility that *chŏng* induces.[52] After critically examining the familial-relational characteristic of the Korean idea/practice of *uri* and two – positively affective and critically affective – dimensions of *chŏng* (*miun chŏng* and *goun chŏng*), I then discuss the civic/political implications of *uri* in democratic civil society by likening it to the Rousseauian general will and highlight the Confucian cultural character of *uri*-responsibility by comparing it with two Kantian-liberal accounts of responsibility. I present Korea's *chŏng*-based civil society as one particular mode of Confucian democratic civil society that I have developed in Part II.

After reconstructing the Korean-Confucian public reason and civic virtue with reference to *chŏng* in Chapter 8, in Chapter 9, I then turn to an exploration of a mode of liberalism that is culturally relevant and socially practicable in South Korea's given cultural (Confucian) and political (democratic) context from the perspective of ordinary Korean citizens. After discussing the cultural unfamiliarity of ordinary Koreans with the basic assumptions of liberalism and their practical implications on daily life, I show how ordinary Koreans can, nevertheless, create a uniquely Korean-style liberalism by appealing to their Confucianism-based social mores and public reasons. This chapter concludes by stressing that liberal democracy is practically possible in Korea's Confucian societal context and Confucian democracy is not an antithesis of liberal democracy but rather the outcome of the manifold cultural translations of liberalism and democracy.

In Chapter 10, I illuminate the mutual adaptations between traditional Confucian culture and the new liberal-democratic way of life in democratized Korea. More specifically, I discuss how social norms implicated in Article 311 of the Korean criminal law (namely, *moyokjoe*, which literally translates as insult law), which I argue reflects a uniquely Korean Confucian communitarian mode of civility, balances well with expressive liberty, one of core democratic rights that, according to liberals, holds *intrinsic* moral value. I argue that (1) norms of Confucian civility in Korea, often considered at odds with ethical pluralism, underpin a democratic civil society that is internally pluralistic, thereby making Korean democratic civil society characteristically Confucian; and (2) democratic socialization in turn has increasingly sensitized ordinary Korean citizens to the possibility that too much emphasis on civility by the government is likely to degenerate it into docility, which works only to impair the regime's democratic vitality and political freedom.

Chapter 11, the final chapter, turns to the increasing multiculturalization of South Korean society. Here I attempt to construct a normative framework of

52 Throughout this book, for Romanization of Korean characters, I employ the Korean Ministry of Education system promulgated in 2000, except in the cases of Chosŏn and *chŏng*, for which I rely on the traditional McCune-Reischauer system, for the sake of consistency with the Romanization practices in my published works.

Korean multiculturalism in the Confucian public-societal context of Korean democracy by focusing on the political implications of the claim to cultural rights (the so-called logic of multiculturalism) and cultural pluralism that it is likely to entail for Korean democracy. After examining the logic of multiculturalism that often puts multiculturalism in tension with liberal democracy, I critically examine Will Kymlicka's liberal resolution of the potential tension between multiculturalism and liberal democracy. I then construct a normative framework of Korean multiculturalism with reference to Confucian public reason that I have illuminated in Chapter 5.

PART I

BEYOND THICK CONFUCIAN COMMUNITARIANISM AND MERITOCRATIC ELITISM

1

Beyond Thick Confucian Communitarianism I: The Confucian Social Self and Its Discontent

The recent resurgence of Confucianism in social and political theory is largely (if not exclusively) affiliated with the communitarian discontent and critique of liberalism in the West (particularly in North America) over the past two decades.[1] Echoing Western communitarians who find fault with rights-based individualism as psychologically hollow (because of its assumption of the self-choosing, socially unencumbered self), ethically unpalatable (because of its priority of the right over the good), and politically undesirable (because of its tendency to erode communal bonds and civic virtue),[2] recent Confucian political theorists criticize liberalism as too self-centered in its valorization of individual autonomy, will, choice, and (negative) freedom at the expense of communal solidarity and common good.[3] Despite the still theoretically

[1] Michael B. Sandel, *Liberalism and the Limits of Justice* (Cambridge: Cambridge University Press, 1982). Also, see Michael Walzer, *Spheres of Justice: A Defense of Pluralism and Equality* (New York: Basic Books, 1983); Charles Taylor, *Sources of the Self: The Making of the Modern Identity* (Cambridge, MA: Harvard University Press, 1989); Alasdair MacIntyre, *After Virtue: A Study in Moral Theory* (Notre Dame, IN: Notre Dame University Press, 1984).

[2] Among recent Confucian scholars, Joseph Chan parts company with communitarian Confucianists and Deweyan Confucian democrats by trying to reveal noncommunitarian, more individualistic values in the Confucian tradition. See his "Moral Autonomy, Civil Liberties, and Confucianism," *Philosophy East and West* 52 (2002), 281–310 and "A Confucian Perspective on Human Rights for Contemporary China," in *The East Asian Challenge for Human Rights*, ed. Joanne R. Bauer and Daniel A. Bell (Cambridge: Cambridge University Press, 1999), 212–37. Notwithstanding his being a great champion of Confucian fiduciary society (a version of communitarian society), Tu Weiming, too, cherishes the value of moral individualism in Confucianism (particularly in Neo-Confucianism). See his "Confucianism and Liberalism," *Dao* 2 (2002), 1–20.

[3] Russell A. Fox, "Confucian and Communitarian Responses to Liberal Democracy," *Review of Politics* 59 (1997): 561–92; Daniel A. Bell, *East Meets West: Human Rights and Democracy in East Asia* (Princeton: Princeton University Press, 2000); Bell, *Beyond Liberal Democracy: Political Thinking for an East Asian Context* (Princeton: Princeton University Press, 2006); Wm. Theodore de Bary, *Asian Values and Human Rights: A Confucian Communitarian Perspective*

ambiguous connection between the democratic political regime and the communitarian society,[4] many advocates of "Confucian democracy" recognize the communitarian elements in Confucianism as essential in the making of a viable Confucian democracy that is distinct from liberal individualistic democracy.[5]

However, "Confucian communitarianism" as a political vision and practice is not without problems, the problems communitarianism is generally exposed to. Most important, it is still unclear whether communitarianism is theoretically superior to liberalism, or at least whether communitarianism can withstand the liberal critique of it. For instance, as far as I know, communitarians (including Confucian communitarians) have not yet successfully met the challenges that Stephen Holmes raised two decades ago.[6] Holmes claims that while critiquing the liberal valorization of the unencumbered self, communitarians go to the other extreme by valorizing the "social self." But why is the social self a better self than the autonomous self?[7] Is "social" not a descriptive, rather than evaluative, term?[8] Also, can sociality and individuality not be dialectically intertwined rather than starkly opposed by mediation of liberal political institutions and social practices?[9] Then, are communitarians not confusing a particular version of liberal *theory* predicated on a speculative Cartesian

(Cambridge, MA: Harvard University Press, 1998). However, it must be noted that these scholars do not necessarily agree on what kinds of communitarian values in Confucianism are to be reinvigorated and further cultivated.

4 For example, Benjamin R. Barber argues that for a viable democracy, what is needed is not so much a communitarian civil society as what he calls "a strong civil society," which is a participatory civil society. See his *A Place for Us: How to Make Society Civil and Democracy Strong* (New York: Hill and Wang, 1998).

5 This tendency is easily found in a group of "Deweyan Confucian democrats." See David L. Hall and Roger T. Ames, *The Democracy of the Dead: Dewey, Confucius, and the Hope for Democracy in China* (Chicago: Open Court, 1999); Sor-hoon Tan, *Confucian Democracy: A Deweyan Reconstruction* (Albany: State University of New York Press, 2003).

6 Stephen Holmes, "The Permanent Structure of Antiliberal Thought," in *Liberalism and Moral Life*, ed. Nancy L. Rosenblum (Cambridge, MA: Harvard University Press, 1989), 227–53. This essay later evolved into a monograph, *The Anatomy of Antiliberalism* (Cambridge, MA: Harvard University Press, 1996).

7 Some Confucian communitarians are quite adamant in submitting this claim. Their reasoning is that the Confucian self is fundamentally a relational self, and rather than performing the social roles, it *is* the roles, lacking any core self. Since in Confucianism, they continue, virtue is disclosed (not exercised) in the faithful performance of the given social roles, only the Confucian social/relational self can be virtuous even without forming a virtuous *self*. See Henry Rosemont, "Rights-Bearing Individuals and Role-Bearing Persons," in *Rules, Rituals, and Responsibility*, ed. Mary I. Bockover (Chicago: Open Court, 1991), 71–101; Hall and Ames, *Democracy of the Dead*, 101–17, 197–203.

8 Holmes writes, "The relation between master and slave is no less 'social' (though it is less desirable) than the relation between intimate friends" ("Permanent Structure of Antiliberal Thought," 231).

9 According to Adam B. Seligman, the essence of modern Western "civility" lies in the individualized and internalized mode of sociality. See his *The Idea of Civil Society* (Princeton: Princeton University Press, 1992).

epistemology of atomistic individualism[10] with liberal social and political *practice*, which relies on a liberal education aimed at inculcating liberal virtues and characters?[11] Are communitarians not mistaken when they think liberalism is essentially antisocial while the gist of liberalism lies in its *reformulation* (not abnegation) of the relationship between the self and society? Any attempt to justify Confucian communitarianism not merely as an antiliberal ideology but, more important, as a viable political vision and practicable theory, should be able to address (and overcome) these important challenges.

In this chapter, I carefully examine two core claims of the communitarianism thesis in the recent formulations of Confucian democracy – namely, the social self claim and the role ethics claim.[12] I start with the social self claim, Confucian communitarianism's central assumption and its quintessential argumentative weapon against liberalism, which stipulates that the Confucian self is a social self, not a self-choosing autonomous individual, and that it is in great harmony with society, rather than starkly opposed to it as liberalism contends. To do so, I first investigate whether it is justifiable to dismiss liberal ethics undergirded on moral individualism, and liberal political theory pivoted around the assumption of social contract on the ground of the implausibility of modern ontology from a practical standpoint.

More specifically, I raise the suspicion that Confucian communitarians are guilty of categorically confounding ontological questions with ethical and political ones in their critique of liberal individualism. I then challenge Confucian communitarians by asking the following question: If, as they claim, the Confucian self is a social self and, in the most authentic sense, "I" as the social self am not merely the performer of the social roles but *am* these very social roles, how can we identify the moral agency of the Confucian social self? In what sense is the Confucian social self an ethical as well as civil self? Furthermore, if the Confucian self is a social self, how can one make sense of the moral pitfalls of the existing community? How is social criticism possible

[10] One example is John Rawls's idea of "original position." However, Rawls explicitly says that this is merely a conceptual apparatus necessary to derive fair principles of justice that are unadulterated by natural and social contingencies, factors that are irrelevant from a moral perspective. In making the actual liberal society viable, Rawls admits, cultivating good liberal characters in various civic associations is critical. Many (Confucian) communitarian critics of Rawls often fail to distinguish Rawls's speculative claims from his practical claims. For an illuminating essay on this issue, see Erin M. Cline, "Rawls, Rosemont, and the Debate over Rights and Roles," in *Polishing the Chinese Mirror*, ed. Marthe Chandler and Ronnie Littlejohn (New York: Global, 2008), 77–89.

[11] That liberalism as social and political practice is buttressed in reality by liberal virtues and liberal characters has been forcefully submitted by "civic liberals." See, among others, Stephen Macedo, *Liberal Virtues: Citizenship, Virtue, and Community in Liberal Constitutionalism* (Oxford: Clarendon, 1990) and Amy Gutmann, *Democratic Education* (Princeton: Princeton University Press, 1988).

[12] The third and forth claims – the ritual aestheticism claim and the social harmony claim – will be discussed extensively in Chapter 2.

in Confucian communitarianism? After identifying Confucian moral agency in three terms – contextual self-reflexivity, moral judgment, and social criticism – I conclude that the Confucian communitarian characterization of the Confucian self as social roles is likely to predispose Confucian communitarianism to political conservatism.

What *Kind* of Social Self?

Virtually all (including Confucian) communitarians start their critique of liberalism by taking issue with the post-Enlightenment notion of the rights-bearing, autonomous individual. Apparently, their biggest problem with the liberal conception of the self is that it, being radically deracinated from any relevant social moorings, is not only ahistorical and thus fundamentally unreal, but also does serious disservice to common social life because of its obsessive preoccupation with the individual right over the common good. In fact, as both Cartesian epistemology and Hobbesian social contract theory suggest, liberalism's rights-based individualism is predicated on the assumption of the autarchic core self – be it mind or ego – existing prior to society and common bond. Its political implication is that liberal man, originally perfectly free in the presocial state, stands in stark contrast to society. For this liberal self, the only meaningful freedom is a negative freedom, freedom from external interference.

What is radically missing in this liberal portrayal of the self and its (anti) relation to society, however, is the defining characteristic of the real human being, namely, man's sociality and its background social environments and relationships. Therefore, Sor-hoon Tan, a key Deweyan Confucian communitarian, upholds Dewey's notion of the social self that in her view is remarkably similar to Confucius's understanding of the self. She says, "The difference between Dewey's conception of self and the prevalent liberal conception is that, for Dewey, the 'inner depths' [that make the liberal self presocially perfect] do not exist prior to an individual entering into relations with the rest of the world; they are acquired in association with others, through experience involving interaction with our environment both social and natural."[13] Similar to Dewey, Tan concedes that "there is no getting away from the fact that individuals are selves." But she raises an important question: "What kind of self? Social but unique or unencumbered but autonomous?" Tan then, agreeing with Dewey, rightly argues that a self (ought to) develop into a "person," by which she means "the uniqueness of individuality," in marked contrast to rights-bearing individualism's abstract individuality.[14] Thus, at issue is not so much individuality as social individuality.[15] And, in Tan's interpretation, Confucius's supreme concern was with (re-)creating social individuality, when

[13] Tan, *Confucian Democracy*, 23.
[14] Ibid., 24.
[15] Ibid., 35.

he famously said in *Analects* 12:1 that "through self-discipline (*keji* 克己) and observing ritual propriety (*fuli* 復禮) one becomes authoritative (*ren* 仁) in one's conduct."[16] Put differently, a morally cultivated man, by practicing ritual propriety in the complex web of human relationships, is the most authentic and authoritative person in Confucianism.[17] Ultimately, the liberal opposition of the self against society is mistaken. As Dewey and Confucius show, the self is fundamentally a social self in which self and society are harmoniously reconciled and where their relationship turns out to be mutually constitutive.[18] In the most profound sense, individuality is an organic sociality,[19] from which social harmony entails.

Admittedly, this brief summary of Tan's key argument does not exhaust her complex philosophical comparison between Dewey and Confucius and her normative vision of Confucian communitarian democracy, which I largely share.[20] Nor does it represent any comprehensive political theory of *the* Confucian form of communitarianism.[21] Nevertheless, it definitely helps us understand what I call the communitarianism thesis, the core argument of the philosophical discussions of Confucian communitarianism advanced so far. First, the Confucian self is a social self particularly in and through the practice of ritual propriety (*li* 禮). Second, in this idea of the social self not only does the tension between self and society dissolve, but through the practice of ritual propriety, they are "aesthetically" intertwined. Third, being radically situated, the Confucian social self *discloses* its agency by actively performing its social roles in a ritualistically ordered society.[22] Therefore, the radical reflexivity, so central to the post-Enlightenment Western problematic of the self, is not an issue in early Confucianism and in Confucian communitarianism that is inspired by it.[23] Finally, the ideal society composed of "individuals-in-their-relations"

16 Ibid., 35–9. The reader should be reminded that this translation of *Analects* 12:1 that Tan adopts is from Roger T. Ames and Henry Rosemont Jr., *The Analects of Confucius: A Philosophical Translation* (New York: Ballantine Books, 1998), 152. However, this translation is far from conventional, especially when it comes to the translation of *ren*, which casually translates to benevolence, humanity, or human heartedness, as "authoritative."

17 Also, see Hall and Ames, *Democracy of the Dead*, 204–14.

18 Tan, *Confucian Democracy*, 30–32.

19 Ibid., 53–62.

20 In this regard, it is unfortunate that less attention has been paid to the last chapter of Tan's *Confucian Democracy*, where she discusses, albeit briefly, how her vision of Confucian democracy supports political activism (such as the farmer's movement) and political institutional reform in China.

21 For instance, while many Confucian communitarians such as Tan, Hall, Ames, Rosemont, and Fox are particularly interested in the social harmonizing roles of the Confucian rituals, Bell is much more concerned with the general communitarian themes including community, common good, and civic virtue.

22 Fox calls this type of agency "an immanent sociality" (Fox, "Confucian and Communitarian Responses to Liberal Democracy," 574). Also, see Herbert Fingarette, *Confucius: The Secular as Sacred* (New York: Harper, 1972).

23 Tan, *Confucian Democracy*, 30.

is essentially a *li*-based consensus-enhancing harmonious community that is distinct from (even opposed to) the gesellschaft of social contract.[24] The fundamental premise of the aforementioned Confucian communitarian assumptions is that the Confucian self is a *li*-mediated social self.[25]

At first glance, the Confucian social self seems quite an improvement compared with the liberal autonomous self, and arguably, this is the very tactic that Confucian communitarians employ by tacitly associating the archaic self (*ji* 己) that is to be disciplined by the *li* in the formula of *ke ji fu li* with the liberal rights-bearing self, which Confucian communitarians generally deem as self-assertive. Here, the liberal rights-bearing and morally autonomous person is tacitly rendered as a presocial (or antisocial), perhaps even a selfish, man. This tactic, however, is heavily problematic because of two related confusions. The first confusion resides in the monolithic understanding of the social self, which stems from the infelicitous ethical blurring between the liberal moral self and the Hobbesian amoral self. The second and more problematic confusion originates from the misunderstanding of the political theory of social contract from the viewpoint of the Cartesian ontology of atomistic individualism. Let us begin with the first confusion.

Undoubtedly, the social self is a better self than the antisocial self that disrupts social order and civil peace – the self consumed by such boisterous passions as rage, envy, jealousy, hatred, and resentment. Therefore, if the essential premise of Confucian communitarianism is the ontological understanding of the Confucian self as a social self,[26] and if its goal is to defend the Confucian social self as ethically superior to the liberal self, then it must be demonstrated how effective the Confucian self actually is, compared to the liberal self, in dealing with those antisocial passions that are prone to relegate a civil society into an uncivil state, which Hobbes identified in terms of the state of nature.[27]

The major problem with this first confusion is that there is no justification to equate the morally autonomous self with the antisocial self. Quite the contrary, the autonomous self that liberals such as Kant and Rawls champion is a moral

[24] Ibid., 63–112; Hall and Ames, *Democracy of the Dead*, 193–6. Also, see Chenyang Li, "The Confucian Ideal of Harmony," *Philosophy East and West* 56 (2006), 583–603 for a philosophical discussion of the concept of Confucian harmony (*he* 和) and Albert H. Chen, "Mediation, Litigation, and Justice: Confucian Reflections in a Modern Liberal Society," in *Confucianism for the Modern World*, ed. Daniel A. Bell and Chaibong Hahm (Cambridge: Cambridge University Press, 2003), 257–87, for the practical implications of the Confucian ideal of *he* in the modern society.

[25] Sor-hoon Tan, "From Cannibalism to Empowerment: An Analects-Inspired Attempt to Balance Community and Liberty," *Philosophy East and West* 54 (2004), 52–70; Tan, *Confucian Democracy*, 79–88.

[26] An irony, then, is that this ontological claim is a universal claim – that is, it specifically speaks not of the *Confucian* self per se, but of *all* kinds of self, which is exactly what Dewey did.

[27] See Sungmoon Kim, "Self-Transformation and Civil Society: Lockean vs. Confucian," *Dao* 8 (2009), 383–401 for how the Confucian *li* can resolve antisocial passions in a nonrationalist way.

and civil self that is qualitatively different from, in fact even starkly opposed to, the Hobbesian antisocial, hence amoral and uncivil, self. Confucian communitarians often (mistakenly) regard all modern Western conceptions of the self that rely on psychological constructs such as "mind," "ego," or "self" as some sort of atomistic self.[28] More problematically, they further understand the liberal claim to right, autonomy, freedom, or equality – the quintessential *moral* concepts in the liberal political tradition – as an expression of the atomic self's inorganic and anomic state of mind.[29] However, it is important to note that Kant's autonomy, for example, is qualitatively different from Hobbes's freedom: While Kantian autonomy is accompanied by moral as well as civil and legal responsibilities for the *social* consequences of the freely chosen action,[30] Hobbesian freedom means the arbitrary wielding of untrammeled passion, without control by reason and thus without any relevant moral idea or ethic of responsibility. Because it is merely *compelled* by the unbridled and uncontrollable passion (especially the passion for the mastery of others) rather than freely and responsibly chosen by the rational thinking agent, Hobbesian freedom is nothing but pathological hubris. Confucian communitarians do not pay heed to this critical point, failing to distinguish liberal moral individualism, to which sociality is central, from amoral atomistic individualism that liberals attempt to overcome.[31]

Therefore, the Confucian communitarian claim that the social self is better than the liberal morally autonomous self begs a much more sophisticated philosophical investigation. As it stands, the claim is at best controversial. For by "the morally autonomous self" virtually all major modern liberal thinkers meant the "social self" who can responsibly participate in the social contract, a uniquely modern moral and political arrangement of the common life. In my view, a fairer claim – though this is still a problematic claim because of the second confusion that Confucian communitarians frequently suffer, which will be discussed shortly – would be that there can be two distinct kinds of social self: the Confucian social self whose individual moral autonomy is compatible with (even empowered by) certain kinds of heteronomy[32] and the liberal

[28] Hall and Ames, *Democracy of the Dead*, 209.

[29] Ibid., 68–77; Tan, *Confucian Democracy*, 17–22; Rosemont, "Rights-Bearing Individuals and Role-Bearing Persons," 84–9. Modern thinkers such as Locke, Smith, Kant, Hegel, and Weber painstakingly invented these moral concepts with the view of the characteristically modern and politically liberal civil society by transforming the Hobbesian antisocial self into a moral self. See Seligman, *The Idea of Civil Society*, 25–52, 70–99.

[30] Immanuel Kant, *The Metaphysics of Morals*, trans. Mary J. Gregor (Cambridge: Cambridge University Press, 1996).

[31] This problem is generally found in Chinese Confucians such as Jiang Qing, Kang Xiaoguang, and Chen Ming. See note 13 in Chapter 1.

[32] Some Confucian ethicists argue that from the Confucian viewpoint, a person's important moral decisions (such as medical decision) can reasonably be affected by other members of society, especially by his or her family members, and this does not necessarily interfere with his or her personal moral agency. On the Confucian family-oriented moral heteronomy, see Ruiping Fan,

social self for which moral autonomy means a person's independent power to make a moral decision solely based on his or her own conception of the good. Both types of social self are morally superior to the Hobbesian antisocial self. However, whether the Confucian social self is morally superior to the liberal social self is open to debate. Again, this evaluation should depend, at least in part, on which social self is more effective in resolving the antisocial passions. Confucian communitarians, however, rarely come close to this point because of their habitual confusion between the liberal moral self and the Hobbesian amoral self.

A more serious problem, insomuch as Confucian communitarianism is a *political* vision, is the second confusion, the problematic tendency to reduce the political theory of social contract to the Cartesian epistemology of atomistic individualism. For example, David Hall and Roger Ames, prominent Deweyan Confucian democrats, contend,

> The rule of law functions to protect the individual citizen against the state, and against the tyranny of the majority. In Confucian China, law develops to articulate administrative duties and to overcome the deficiencies of ritual in maintaining social stability. "The evolution of law in China may be described as a *devolution* of ritual (*li*) into law (*fa*) and of law into punishment (*xing*)." A principle implication of Western legal mechanisms into contemporary China may occasion significant disruption in the sense of social obligations that bind the community. In particular, the Western contractual understanding of law – interpreted by appeal to the model of social contract or of commercial contract – has traditionally made little sense to the Chinese.[33]

To begin with, it is simply a mistake to understand Western constitutional law that "protects the individual citizen against the state and against the tyranny of the majority" solely in terms of the scheme of either punitive law or commercial law. Constitutional law that is concerned with democratic citizenship and/or protection of democratic rights and is based on mutual consent by *all* members of political society is qualitatively different from criminal law and commercial law, both of which come under constitutional boundaries. The more serious problem, however, lies in the entrenched perception of social contract as merely an artificial and mechanical tie between self-seeking atomistic individuals, a sort of "Western evil" disrupting the sense of social obligations that bind the community. Put differently, it is a view that opposes social contract to community or "social organism" that is deeply problematic, even untenable.

"Self-Determination vs. Family-Determination: Two Incommensurable Principle of Autonomy," *Bioethics* 11 (1997), 309–22; Julia Tao and Andrew Brennan, "Confucian and Liberal Ethics for Public Policy: Holistic or Atomistic?," *Journal of Social Philosophy* 34 (2003), 572–89.

33 Hall and Ames, *Democracy of the Dead*, 216. The quote inside is from Julia Ching, "Human Rights: A Valid Chinese Concept?," in de Bary and Tu, *Confucianism and Human Rights*, 24. For a similar negative view on social contract, see Tan, *Confucian Democracy*, 188.

Ironically, however, it was exactly for holding this sort of conception (in fact misconception) of democracy – democracy as the rule of mass and as a mere numerical aggregate of atomistic individuals devoid of any organic reality or vision, or merely a mechanical social contract – that Dewey criticizes Henry Maine in an essay titled "The Ethics of Democracy." In this essay, Dewey argues that democracy is not a simple conglomeration of atomic units based on a very thin contractual tie. Quite the contrary, democracy is a form of ethical society *generating* a thick and organic citizenship, and of interest, Dewey emphasizes, it is social contract that imparts an organic life to democracy.

> The essence of the "Social Contract" theory is not the idea of the formulation of a contract; it is the idea that men are mere individuals, without any social relations *until* they form a contract. The method by which they get out of their individualistic condition is not the important matter.... The notion, in short, which lay in the minds of those who proposed this theory was that men in their natural state are non-social units, are a mere multitude; and that some artifice must be devised to constitute them into political society. And this artifice they found in a contract which they entered into with one another.[34]

According to Dewey, "social organism" does not mean a community of unmediated affection. Its authentic meaning is that "men are not isolated non-social atoms, but are men only when in intrinsic relations to men."[35] That is, "in an organism man is essentially a social being."[36] This is not a mere tautology because Dewey's key point is not so much sociality as the social self's *given* quality but sociality as a resolving quality (hence "civility") the self has *attained* through a confrontation with the problematic situation.[37] Classical liberals identified the most problematical human situation in terms of the state of nature, which is nothing other than a presocial, prepolitical situation of hubristic private autarchy.

Given my discussion thus far, it can now be agreed that none can deny the sociological *fact* that human beings are social beings, and that no sensible liberal democrat would endorse Cartesian individualism, which is limited to atomistic subjectivism as the foundation of both ethical and political visions (if so, he or she would be a narcissistic solipsist rather than a liberal). More important, it is liberalism's quintessential normative claim that a man *ought to*

[34] John Dewey, "The Ethics of Democracy," in *John Dewey: The Early Works*, vol. 1, ed. George E. Axetell and Jo Ann Boydston (Carbondale: Southern Illinois University Press, 1969), 231.

[35] Ibid.

[36] Ibid., 232.

[37] According to Corey Brettschneider, who is inspired by Rousseau and Rawls, social contract can be recast democratically, as a democratic theory that morally justifies both democratic citizenship, which Dewey captures in terms of social organism, and the citizenry's democratic rights. Brettschneider calls a democratic theory of social contract "democratic contractualism." See his *Democratic Rights: The Substance of Self-Government* (Princeton: Princeton University Press, 2007), 54–70. Also see Benjamin R. Barber, *Fear's Empire: War, Terrorism, and Democracy* (New York: Norton, 2003), 88–91.

be social, though there is an ongoing dispute among the liberals on the issue of how social a man should be.

Hence whether man is social or autarchic cannot be at the heart of the liberal and (Confucian) communitarian debate. Rather, the real question is whether man, essentially a social being, acts civilly or uncivilly, and, accordingly, how to make an otherwise uncivil man civil.[38] The trouble is that any communitarian valorization of the social self over the autarchic self that it often mistakenly identifies as the liberal self does not necessarily imply the ethical claim that the social self is a civil self rather than an uncivil self, which is in other words a pathologically social self. Given that the social self can always turn into an uncivil one (people become uncivil precisely because they are social beings), the statement that the Confucian self is a social self is by no means ethically substantive. It is a descriptive statement that concerns ontology, not an evaluative claim concerned with ethics and politics, a domain of man's active moral agency. Here a brief revisit to modern contractarian tradition can be helpful.

When early liberals such as Hobbes and Locke described the state of nature as the uncivil state where men are entangled in the life-and-death struggle with one another, they were actually wrestling with a quintessential political problem – how to bring uncivil social men preoccupied with their passions and desires under constitutional order, thereby rescuing the civil society (the commonwealth) from the uncivil state, or the state of nature where there is presumably (if not literally) no law, no justice, and no society.[39] Though contemporary liberals at times seem single-mindedly focused on the contrast between civil *society* and the state (or the government) in the political theory of social contract (hence paying far more attention to "contract'" than "social"), it should not be forgotten that for early liberals, the more important political problem was the contrast between *civil* society and the state of nature.[40] In other words, what mattered most to them was the civil and organically integrated order of the political society that, despite its fundamental modern transformation, could still be reminiscent of the essential ethical characteristics of the ancient regime.[41]

[38] Unlike Confucian communitarians, Stephen C. Angle attempts to reconstruct ritual propriety into Confucian civility that stands between (personal) ethics and (impersonal) law. See his *Contemporary Confucian Political Philosophy: Toward Progressive Confucianism* (Cambridge: Polity, 2012), chap. 6.

[39] Richard Boyd, *Uncivil Society: The Perils of Pluralism and the Making of Modern Liberalism* (Lanham, MD: Lexington Books, 2004). On the liberal constitutional political implications of Hobbes's political theory, see Richard E. Flathman, *Thomas Hobbes: Skepticism, Individuality, and Chastened Politics* (Lanham, MD: Rowman & Littlefield, 2002).

[40] See John Dunn, "The Contemporary Political Significance of John Locke's Conception of Civil Society," in *Civil Society: History and Possibilities*, ed. Sudipta Kaviraj and Sunil Khilnani (Cambridge: Cambridge University Press, 2001).

[41] On the ancient theme integrated in Hobbes's political philosophy, see Leo Strauss, *The Political Philosophy of Hobbes: Its Basis and Its Genesis* (Chicago: University of Chicago Press, 1952).

My point is threefold: first, for classical and contemporary civic liberals, social contract theory was and is intended to be the political theory composed of a uniquely modern organic social and political order, not a Cartesian individualist theory that justifies a gesellschaft of purely mechanical human relations; second, the main concern of social contract theory is not so much the ontological question of whether or not man is social but the ethical and political question of how to transform uncivil man into civil man and further into a public-spirited citizen; third, consequently, the successful defense of Confucian communitarianism against the Cartesian epistemology of modern liberalism is still short of, or even irrelevant to, critiquing the morality of liberal politics and the ethics of rights-based individualism.

I do not deny that the current version of rights-based individualism, dominant in the United States, is problematic – for one, because of its absolutist claim that excludes self-restraint and sacrifices common solidarity.[42] I also concede that the global dissemination of this particular version of liberalism is a serious problem. However, we should not mistake the currently dominant extreme version of rights-based individualism for the kind of individualism that its early modern originators actually had in mind (i.e., moral and social individualism), especially since they founded the political theory of liberal constitutionalism on it.

Thus understood, it is even more problematic to oppose communitarianism to liberal moral/social individualism and to the liberal politics of social contract, however opposed it may be to Cartesian individualism. In this regard, it is revealing that three key advocates of communitarianism (Walzer, Sandel, and Taylor) have reservations about being labeled communitarians. None of them deny wholesale the ethical and political value of moral individualism; nor do they understand communal bonds and moral/social individualism as mutually exclusive. Quite the contrary, their shard conviction is that moral individualism and viable communitarianism reinforce each other and, in a profound sense, are mutually constitutive. Here the rights discourse is not in itself the problem; it is rather an important component of (liberal) social life that must be reasonably moderated and balanced with the view of the common good. None of them problematize liberalism on the basis of ontology;[43] rather, they uphold a liberalism that is civic/public-minded – whatever the name is, civic liberalism, liberal republicanism, or communitarianism – while resisting Cartesian ontology and criticizing its transgression into the realm of politics and ethics.

[42] For this reason, Mary Ann Glendon, renowned legal philosopher and one of the most vehement critics of the recent "rights talk" in the United States, ascertains that what is needed is a reasonably moderate version of rights-bearing individualism, not its complete disavowal. See her *Rights Talk: The Impoverishment of Political Discourse* (New York: Free Press, 1991). In this view, to mock the Bill of Rights as "A Bill of Worries" is to throw out the baby with the bath water. See Rosemont, "Human Rights," 54–66.

[43] This point is most clearly made by Charles Taylor in his classical essay, "Cross-Purposes: The Liberal-Communitarian Debate," in Rosenblum, *Liberalism and the Moral Life*, 159–82.

In the end, then, the question is not an ontological, but an ethical one: What *kind* of social self is the Confucian self? More specifically, to make Confucian Communitarianism morally attractive and politically compelling, we must explicate why liberal civility (and liberal social and political theory) is unpalatable to Confucian civility (if there is such a thing)[44] and what it consists of. Put differently, we must clarify what makes Confucian communitarianism a uniquely *Confucian* ethical and political vision and practice. In this regard, it is important that a good number of Confucian communitarians explicitly subscribe to Henry Rosemont's claim that Confucian ethics is a form of "role-ethics"[45] and develop their Confucian communitarian arguments based on it. In the next section I examine whether the theories of Confucian communitarianism relying on Confucianism's supposed role-ethics are tenable by critically investigating first Rosemont's argument and then its Confucian communitarian appropriation.

The Moral Agency of the Social Self

In his essay "Rights-Bearing Individuals and Role-Bearing Persons," Rosemont famously describes Confucianism in terms of its role-ethics[46]:

44 Confucian communitarians generally believe that Confucian rituals (*li*) are the core elements of Confucian civility, or, at minimum, they are what make the Confucian self civil. However, although largely sanguine about the possibility of Confucian civil society, Edward Shils, renowned sociologist, laments that Confucius omitted the specifically civil category of civil society because he never made a place for "the citizen in relation to other citizens." Edward Shils, "Reflections on Civil Society and Civility in the Chinese Intellectual Tradition," in Tu, *Confucian Traditions in East Asian Modernity*, 38–71, esp. 66. Also, see Fred R. Dallmayr, "Confucianism and the Public Sphere: Five Relationships Plus One?," in Hahm and Bell, *Politics of Affective Relations*, 41–59.

45 These scholars include Hall, Ames, Tan, Fox, and A. T. Nuyen. For Nuyen's position, see his "Moral Obligation and Moral Motivation in Confucian Role-Based Ethics," *Dao* 8 (2009), 1–11.

46 In this section, my discussion will be mainly focused on Rosemont, one of the strongest defenders of Confucian role ethics. Rosemont's view of the Confucian self is widely shared by Confucian communitarians such as Hall, Ames, and Tan. For example, Hall and Ames state that "Confucian selves are 'individuated' as a complex of constitutive roles and functions associated with their obligations to the various groupings to which they belong.… The identification of the person with roles is not in any sense a collectivist understanding.… Rather, the roles are constitutive of what one in fact is. In the absence of the performance of these roles, nothing constituting a coherent personality remains: no soul, no mind, no ego, not even an 'I-know-not-what'" (David L. Hall and Roger T. Ames, "A Pragmatic Understanding of Confucian Democracy," in Bell and Hahm, *Confucianism for the Modern World*, 135–6). Ames reaffirms this position when he says that "for Confucius, there is no individual – no 'self' or 'soul' – that remains once layer after layer of social relations are peeled away. One is one's roles and relationships." Roger T. Ames, "Confucianism: Confucius (Kongzi, K'ung Tzu)," in *Encyclopedia of Chinese Philosophy*, ed. Antonio S. Cua (New York: Routledge, 2003), 61. For the most comprehensive account of Confucian role-ethics, see Roger T. Ames, *Confucian Role Ethics: A Vocabulary* (Honolulu: University of Hawaii Press, 2011).

[F]or the early Confucians there can be no me in isolation, to be considered abstractly: I am the totality of roles I live in relation to specific others. By using the term "roles" here I do not wish to imply that the early Confucians were the forerunners of the discipline of sociology. They emphasize the interrelatedness of what I am calling "roles," that is to say, they are cognizant of the fact that the relations in which I stand to some people affect directly the relations in which I stand with others, to the extent that it would be misleading to say that I "play" or "perform" these roles; on the contrary, for Confucius I am my roles. Taken collectively, they weave, for each of us, a unique pattern of personal identity, such that if some of my roles change, others will of necessity change also, literally making me a different person.[47]

Here Rosemont presents two claims: first, from a Confucian standpoint, a human being is fundamentally a social being and, second, the Confucian relational self is not so much a moral agent performing its social roles but essentially *is* such roles. These two claims, however, are not logically related to each other as it may appear at first glance. First, the claim that the self is by nature social is not exclusively Confucian but universally applied to many versions of the *actual* self, not philosophically abstracted, deeply embedded in actual social contexts, whatever they may be.[48] As I have argued, what differentiates *this* particular (e.g., Confucian) social self from *that* particular (e.g., liberal) social self is the kind and the quality of sociality. That is to say, one can claim that the Confucian social self is a relatively thicker social self than its liberal counterpart, because while Confucian social action is crucially mediated or sometimes motivated by the *li*, liberal social action, in its most authentic sense, is driven from within by means of what Locke called "inward civility." At any rate, to say that the Confucian self is a social self conveys no substantial meaning. Moreover, it is farfetched to say that a social self *is* the Confucian self. These statements are hardly significant from an ethical or political standpoint.

What is significant is Rosemont's second claim that the Confucian self is not merely a social self but *is* essentially its social roles. Here Rosemont's Confucianism (and Confucian communitarianism relying on it) parts company with any version of liberal ethics and social/political theory. As Rosemont rightly argues, liberal rights-based individualism is premised on the assumption of the autonomous self. What he fails to note is that the liberal autonomous self is itself a particular mode of the social self whose moral autonomy is exercised in concrete social contexts and in relation to particular human

[47] Rosemont, "Rights-Bearing Individuals and Role-Bearing Persons," 90.

[48] The claim that the self is interdependent/relational rather than independent/autarchic is one of the core claims of the care ethicists. According to them, it is a universal claim applied to *any* self. See Virginia Held, *The Ethics of Care: Personal, Political, Global* (New York: Oxford University Press, 2006). Of note, but not surprising, almost all of such ethicists are feminists, who are careful to insist on the importance of respect for individuals. Women in particular have often been largely absorbed into the lives of men, and this is morally reprehensible. I am not sure how role ethicists can meet the feminist challenge. Michael Slote makes this point extremely well. See his, *The Ethics of Care and Empathy* (London: Routledge, 2002).

beings. An example may be helpful. Suppose an impoverished boy, born and raised by a helpless single mom living in a slum, threatened a stranger with a dagger, took his wallet, ran away, and was eventually caught. A typical liberal response to this case may be that even though the cause of this poor boy's desperate action might be understandably traceable and attributable to his dismal social conditions and dysfunctional personal relationships, all of which were arguably beyond his control, he must be held personally responsible for his criminal action. He should be held responsible not only because of the action's logical betrayal of its original freedom (or the right to free action), but, more important, because of the negative social consequences that his action brought about. Furthermore, the boy's action is also politically problematic because it involves a serious violation of social trust and mutuality embodied in the social contract that now punishes him. From the liberal perspective, not punishing him is to treat him as if he was completely under the sway of the necessity of natural causes, hence allowing him no moral and political agency as a thinking and actionable person. What all of this amounts to is that in liberalism only a morally autonomous person is thought to be a responsible, thus a civil, social member and a legitimate partaker of the liberal (and democratic) political community.

By radically identifying the Confucian self in terms of its social roles, however, Rosemont leaves no room for autonomous moral agency in Confucian social action. Furthermore, by rejecting the idea that a Confucian social self plays or performs its social roles, Rosemont (or his version of Confucianism) forecloses the very possibility of *any* form of moral agency. In other words, according to Rosemont's Confucianism, social roles are not external to the self, not something to be assumed then performed by the self's internal core. Rather, they are the essential constituents of the core of the self, thereby dissolving the core itself. As Philip J. Ivanhoe argues, at the very least, Rosemont's position suggests that the core of the self evaporates up and condenses into the matrix of one's social roles and at the extreme, his view is that there never was or shall be a core to the self.[49] Yet, from an ethical and political standpoint, the greater problem in Rosemont's depiction of the Confucian self, greater than the absence of the core self or the appropriator and performer of the roles, is his complete dismissal of moral agency that demonstrates the ethical quality of the self in the performance of the roles.

By the Confucian social self's moral agency and its ethical quality I mean two potentially conflicting things. First, although Confucianism does not embrace purely individualistic conceptions of liberty and equality cherished in liberal social and political ethics but rather accepts a family-oriented, reasonably hierarchical, social order, the Confucian self can still exercise its sociality (i.e., civility) by voluntarily performing its social roles and thereby positively

[49] Philip J. Ivanhoe, "The Shade of Confucius: Social Roles, Ethical Theory, and the Self," in Chandler and Littlejohn, *Polishing the Chinese Mirror*, 41.

demonstrating its ethical quality in terms of excellence. In this regard, I agree with Ivanhoe when he says,

> [W]hat matters is not so much the role that one plays but *how* one plays it. What makes one a good ruler, minister, father, mother, or child is not the role *per se* but the virtues one expresses through these various roles. Rulers, ministers, fathers, mothers, sons and others all are to be benevolent, trustworthy, courageous and the like. The way in which benevolence, courage, or some other particular virtue is manifested will often differ depending upon the role that a good person fulfills, but the various roles described by early Confucians all afford one the opportunity to develop and express a range of common virtues.[50]

From this Confucian *virtue ethics perspective* in which the fact of human (especially familial) relationality is presupposed,[51] the boy in my hypothetical case is guilty not because of his self-contradicting betrayal of his moral right and freedom, nor because of his violation of liberal citizenship in terms of mutuality and trust embodied in the idea of social contract. His culpability is the result of the serious transgressions of multiple moral boundaries by his actions. According to Confucian virtue ethics, only by reflexively and respectfully observing such boundaries can he become a morally responsible person, that is, as a filial son in the family, as a trustworthy neighbor in the village, and as a loyal subject (or as a faithful citizen in today's more or less democratic political circumstances) in the state. In other words, this boy must not commit violent robbery, because it goes against his filial piety (*xiao* 孝) to his mother, his fraternal responsibility (*ti* 悌) to his siblings, his trustworthiness (*xin* 信) to his neighbor, and his loyalty (*zhong* 忠) to the state. From this standpoint, the Confucian social self's moral agency is exercised in terms of responsibility to multiple moral boundaries, and its ethical quality is revealed in the (excellent) fulfillment of such moral responsibilities.

Here arises a problem, however., hence my second point. In the ideal world, moral responsibilities such as *xiao*, *ti*, *xin*, and *zhong* can be in great harmony: a filial son can simultaneously be a fraternal brother, trustworthy neighbor, and loyal subject (or faithful citizen). In the nonideal world, however, not only are

[50] Ibid., 39. Still, Rosemont explicitly argues that roles are not something *performed* or *played* but are ontologically constitutive of the self. Of course, as Ivanhoe does, we can, in the name of philosophical charity, take Rosemont's claim not quite literally, but it should nevertheless be noted that Rosemont's "role ethics" risks reducing Confucian ethics to Confucian ontology. Among Confucian communitarians, Tan is least susceptible to this problem given her far more complex account of the Confucian social self than Rosemont's (and Hall and Ames's). Most telling, in no place does Tan claim that the Confucian self *is* social roles, despite her strong emphasis of the importance of ritual in her proposed Confucian democracy.

[51] The Confucian moral virtue par excellence that best represent the spirit of *ren* is filial piety (*xiao* 孝) and by extension filiality (*xiaoti* 孝悌). This Confucian emphasis of filiality as the pillar moral virtue makes Confucian virtue ethics qualitatively different from Western (most famously Aristotelian) virtue ethics. See Chenyang Li, "Shifting Perspectives: Filial Morality Revisited," *Philosophy East and West* 47 (1997), 211–32.

the moral boundaries frequently overlapping (or even blurred), but sometimes, and perhaps more important, moral obligations can be in great tension. For example, if the ruler demanded it, should a Confucian-scholar in the middle of his or her three-year mourning quit this important Confucian moral duty and join the government to fulfill his or her moral obligation to the state? Which moral obligation should be given priority in this problematic situation – *xiao* or *zhong*? In this case, the ethical quality of the Confucian social self cannot simply be found in the excellence with which he is performing his ritualistically given social roles. What is at stake is moral judgment to critically adjudicate the gravity of *zhong* vis-à-vis *xiao* (or vice versa) in the given situation.[52]

To summarize the argument thus far, first, even for the Confucian social self an inner moral perplexity at some point is inevitable, though I concede that such moral perplexity can at most times be mitigated effectively by the faithful yet reflective practice of ritual propriety.[53] Second, without conceding the inner capacity of moral judgment to the Confucian social self in the event of moral perplexity, it would be very hard to justify the claim that the Confucian self is an ethical self. These observations help clarify my key point that we cannot afford to dismiss the *relative* autonomy of the Confucian self's moral agency from the social roles to which it is ritualistically attached.

Rosemont-inspired Confucian communitarians may counter by saying that they never downplay the Confucian self's moral agency, and indeed their claim is not without justification. First, despite generally embracing Rosemont's emphasis of social roles as constitutive of the Confucian self, Confucian communitarians largely acknowledge the Confucian self-reflexivity of the social self in the ritualistic practice of its social roles. Second, some Confucian communitarians have paid attention to the possibility of conflict between moral obligations of the Confucian self, though without further exploring the theoretical implications of this recognition on their assumed understanding of the Confucian social self.[54] Otherwise stated, despite their problematic understanding of the Confucian social self, Confucian communitarians have a relatively fair understanding of the Confucian social self's reflective moral agency *within* the social context. What these scholars overly downplay is my third point about the Confucian social self: Without embracing a certain epistemic and ethical *distance* between the self and the world and thereby some necessary

[52] For a revealing case that actually took place during the Chosŏn dynasty (1392–1910) in Korea, see Sungmoon Kim, "Trouble with Korean Confucianism: Scholar-Official between Ideal and Reality," *Dao* 8 (2009), 29–48, 43–4.

[53] On the moral reflexivity involved in the authentic and authoritative practice of ritual propriety, see Karyn Lai, "*Li* in the *Analects*: Training in Moral Competence and the Question of Flexibility," *Philosophy East and West* 56 (2006), 69–83.

[54] See Sor-hoon Tan, "Between Family and State: Relational Tensions in Confucian Ethics," in *Mencius: Contexts and Interpretations*, ed. Alan K. L. Chan (Honolulu: University of Hawaii Press, 2002), 169–88.

estrangement of the self from the social roles it plays, it is logically impossible for the Confucian social self to cast a critical eye on the world (the very source of the "social," which presumably constitutes the Confucian social self's self-identity), thereby reforming the world. In short, what is missing in current versions of Confucian communitarianism is the Confucian self's critical moral agency *toward* the existing social context.[55]

Confucian communitarians (particularly Hall and Ames and Rosemont) may wonder how it is possible that a Confucian self that is fundamentally fused with society (hence the "social self" as they call) can maintain an epistemic and ethical distance from the social world. They may suspect that by assuming an epistemic and ethical distance between the self and the world, I inadvertently render the Confucian self as standing in opposition to the social world. They may object, isn't the radical opposition between the self and the world a typical mode of "Socratic citizenship" in which a philosophic man transcends, critiques, and reforms the cave-like self-rationalizing, self-perpetuating social convention by shedding new epistemic and ethical light on it?[56] How is such an epistemic and ethical transcendence possible in Confucianism, which, they argue, conceives of no epistemic dualism of philosophy and politics or of individual man and social convention?

Here we should be reminded that classical Confucians (especially Confucius and Mencius) never were complacent, however gracious, performers of their roles as father, teacher, or minister in any static sense. In actuality, they took pains to reform the world by re-creating – not merely reproducing – the past, wandering around the world (thus partially alienating themselves from family obligations) to draw then-existing rulers to the Kingly Way (*wangdao* 王道).[57] In other words, they were not merely part of the existing social rituals, customs, and conventions, but, more often, were vehement critics of them. For example, despite Confucius's modest self-identification as a mere transmitter of past traditions,[58] he was the social critic who, similar to a wooden bell clapper, awoke the morally depraved world by a pragmatic use of the past. "A border official at Yi asked for an interview with the Master [Confucius], saying: 'I have always been accorded an interview with those distinguished persons who have made their way here.' Confucius's followers presented him. On taking his leave, he said: 'Why worry over the loss of office, my friends? All under

[55] Once again, Sor-hoon Tan is less susceptible to this criticism. In fact, Tan's recent essays clearly show that her vision of Confucian democracy is more critically democratic and socially progressive than other Confucian communitarian democrats'. For instance, see her "Our Country Right or Wrong: A Pragmatic Response to Anti-democratic Cultural Nationalism in China," *Contemporary Pragmatism* 7 (2010), 45–69.

[56] On "Socratic citizenship," see Dana Villa, *Socratic Citizenship* (Princeton: Princeton University Press, 2001).

[57] *Analects* 2:11.

[58] *Analects* 7:1.

Heaven (*tian* 天) have long since lost their Way (*dao* 道), and Heaven is going to use your Master as a wooden bell-clapper.'"[59] True, the Confucian social critic is not a solitary individual citizen similar to Socrates, who retreated to his private station to philosophically contemplate on ephemeral social conventions from the standpoint of pure reason; nor does he or she withdraw to his or her psychological citadel to engage in self-dialogue with his or her own demons in philosophic contemplation.[60] Without assuming the existence of the inscrutable inner core self (i.e., psyche) and without self-isolating philosophic contemplation in his or her private station, however, the Confucian critic is still able to *transcend* the world (and his or her moral obligations to it as ritually stipulated) and critically recast it. Shmuel Eisenstadt and Benjamin Schwartz famously called this nonphilosophic Confucian ethical transcendence "this-worldly transcendentalism," a moral transcendence *toward* this world.[61] In the Confucian ethico-political tradition, it refers to the self's ethico-political empowerment to critically reevaluate the existing social and political state from the enlarged moral perspective of Heaven (*tian* 天).[62]

It is by no means my intention to suggest that Confucian communitarianism as a contemporary political vision is doomed to fail without reinvigorating the philosophy of Heaven. Nor is it important, insomuch as Confucian communitarianism is a *political* vision, to rekindle the long debate on the nature of Confucian transcendentalism.[63] In fact, my consistent claim throughout this

[59] *Analects* 3:24.

[60] On this point, see Marion Hourdequin, "Engagement, Withdrawal, and Social Reform: Confucian and Contemporary Perspective," *Philosophy East and West* 60 (2010), 369–90; Sungmoon Kim, "Confucian Citizenship? Against Two Greek Models," *Journal of Chinese Philosophy* 37 (2010), 438–56.

[61] Shmuel N. Eisenstadt, "This Worldly Transcendentalism and the Structuring of the World: Max Weber's 'Religion of China' and the Format of Chinese History and Civilization," *Journal of Developing Societies* 1 (1985), 168–86; Benjamin I. Schwartz, "The Age of Transcendence," in *China and Other Matters* (Cambridge, MA: Harvard University Press, 1996), 64–8.

[62] Cf. *Analects* 7:23; 9:5; 14:35. It is beyond the scope of this book to thoroughly investigate the Confucian philosophy of Heaven and its ethico-political implications, for which see Philip J. Ivanhoe, "Heaven as a Source for Ethical Warrant in Early Confucianism," *Dao* 6 (2007), 211–20 and also Rodney L. Taylor, "The Religious Character of Confucian Tradition," *Philosophy East and West* 48 (1998), 80–107. What is worth noting here is that while acknowledging the this-worldly transcendental dimension of Heaven, Deweyan Confucian communitarians generally disagree with the (this-worldly) transcendental interpretation of (ancient) Confucianism, at the heart of which lies Heaven's religious quality. For instance, Roger Ames asserts, "[For Confucius] 'Heaven' itself is a faceless amalgam of ancestors rather than some transcendent creator deity" (Ames, "Confucianism," 61; also see Tan, *Confucian Democracy*, 138–9). Though Heaven is certainly not a transcendent creator, it is heavily problematic to understand Heaven as totally devoid of any transcendental meaning, value, or intention.

[63] The Deweyan-Confucian communitarians' understanding of Confucian transcendentalism is critically indebted to Fingarette's illuminating study on the sacred dimension in the apparently secular practice of ritual propriety. However, nearly three decades ago, Benjamin I. Schwartz criticized Fingarette's interpretation of Confucianism that in his view unjustly subjugates *ren*, which has a profound religious quality, to *li*, its socially expressed mechanisms. See his *The World of Thought in Ancient China* (Cambridge, MA: Harvard University Press, 1985), 78–85.

book is that Confucian democracy should be a robustly democratic political theory and practice and is not premised on traditional Confucian political metaphysics and moral cosmology. My point is that the Confucian communitarian notion of the Confucian social self as a bundle of social roles cannot account properly for the Confucian self's critical moral agency toward the social context in which it is situated.

The Confucian social self may not possess the inscrutable inner core self in terms of soul (psyche), mind, or ego, but it does have its deep inner world that early Confucians conceptualized in terms of *xin* 心 (heart-and-mind) that enables an ordinary person to become a courageous moral and political critic.[64] The Confucian social self may not be squarely opposed to the world since it is never, ontologically or ethically, severed from it; yet, it occasionally becomes discontent with the way it is. As Tu Weiming famously noted, an authoritative Confucian person (*junzi* 君子) is in the world, but not of the world, and it is for this reason that Confucian intellectuals were able to step back from and confront the world of realpolitik and transform it from within.[65]

Conclusion

The Confucian self is not only ethical but also civil by respectfully and reflectively observing ritual propriety that helps subdue one's private/selfish desires and passions, by sometimes struggling with conflicting moral obligations, and by occasionally being critical of the status quo. However, by defining the Confucian social self as social roles and Confucian sociality as mere role enactment, not only have Confucian communitarians (inadvertently) confounded ontology and ethics, but, more important, they have created a theoretical difficulty for making sense of the Confucian self's moral agency by associating any claim to the inner world with the distinctively modern Western discourse of individualism. Even when they acknowledge Confucian moral agency, contra their key assumption of the Confucian social self, their primary focus is on self-reflectivity within the given social context and to a lesser degree on the Confucian self's moral judgment in the face of conflicting moral obligations. They, however, rarely pay attention to Confucian critical moral agency toward the existing social and political world.

The result is that Confucian communitarianism has become predominantly concerned with self-growth and social harmony in the given societal context while losing a grip with Confucianism's equally important vision of the ethico-political transformation of the world. Even if most (if not all) Confucian communitarians are simultaneously claiming themselves to be the

[64] For an excellent account on the transcendental/critical capacity of *xin*, see Chung-ying Cheng, "A Theory of Confucian Selfhood: Self-Cultivation and Free Will in Confucian Philosophy," in Shun and Wong, *Confucian Ethics*, 124–47.

[65] Tu Weiming, *Way, Learning, and Politics: Essays on the Confucian Intellectual* (Albany: State University of New York Press, 1993), 10.

advocates of Confucian democracy (especially in the Deweyan strain), their communitarianism, because of its particular assumption of the Confucian self, is critically limited in grappling with how to cultivate in East Asian people such key democratic political civilities as social criticism of and political dissent toward the existing sociopolitical arrangement. Rather, recent theories of Confucian communitarianism, preoccupied with the issues of social harmony and stability, are more or less politically conservative. As a theory, Confucian communitarianism is highly compatible with, even better realizable in, a benevolent authoritarian political regime, and yet very few Confucian communitarians (such as Daniel Bell) openly concede that Confucian communitarianism can be more easily affiliated with meritocracy and elitism than with full-fledged democracy.[66]

This is not to suggest that political conservatism is inherently problematic, nor is it to argue that Confucianism is by nature a radical political vision. My point is that the widely received understanding of the Confucian self as social roles is likely to *predispose* Confucian communitarianism toward a form of political conservatism. However, if the moral agency of the Confucian self is taken more seriously and if it is acknowledged that Confucian moral agency includes social criticism toward the existing social context as well as moral reflexivity within the given social context, Confucian communitarianism can develop into a more politically dynamic and more democratic vision and practice for modern East Asian societies, into what can be called "civil Confucianism." I turn to civil Confucianism in the next chapter.

[66] In an excellent essay, Shaun O'Dwyer takes issue with the elitism and meritocracy in Hall and Ames's ideal of Confucian democracy precisely from a Deweyan participatory democratic political perspective. See his "Democracy and Confucian Values," *Philosophy East and West* 53 (2003), 39–63. Unlike most other Confucian communitarians, though, Tan supports political equality and participatory democracy (*Confucian Democracy*, 100–122).

2

Beyond Thick Confucian Communitarianism II: Toward Civil Confucianism

As we have seen in the previous chapter, the Confucian communitarian critics of liberalism (and liberal democracy) argue that as an ethical theory liberalism is much too individual-centered and its staggering emphasis on individual right is fundamentally at odds with the obvious human condition that man or woman is radically situated in the particular social context in which the social roles that one plays are prior to one's individual right and moral autonomy. They also argue that as a political theory liberalism is flawed because of the legalistic assumptions embedded in it: by envisioning the social and political world purely in terms of right, (negative) freedom, and law, liberal political theory dismisses what makes man or woman an ethical being and what makes society a fiduciary community in which men and women are expected to act *properly* toward one another, thereby enriching their communal bonds and mutual trust. At the heart of the Confucian communitarian critique of liberalism is that unlike liberalism placing a supreme moral value on legality, Confucianism as an ethical and political discourse centers on the idea of civility (particularly *li*-based civility),[1] in and through which social relations, otherwise purely legal and lacking in common identity, can be refurbished into thick civic bonds of mutual trust.

[1] No doubt, civility is a modern Western social ideal, and in the strict liberal sense it is inconceivable without the political backdrop of modern constitutionalism in which individuals *qua* strangers meet one another as citizens. And it is for this reason that Edward Shills, being positive about the Confucian notion of civil society, thought that Confucianism lacks civility that governs citizen relation. See Edward Shils, "Reflections on Civil Society and Civility in the Chinese Intellectual Tradition," in Tu, *Confucian Traditions in East Asian Modernity*, 66–7; also see Fred Dallmayr, "Confucianism and the Public Sphere: Five Relationships Plus One?," in Hahm and Bell, *Politics of Affective Relations*. Despite this original liberal definition of civility, however, throughout this book I use the term "civility" very broadly and in a generic sense, meaning it to be a quality that makes man sociable and society (or social relation) fiduciary.

Although the Confucian communitarian claim that liberalism glosses over the social value of civility in its valorization of individual right and legality is oversimplified,[2] it is widely observed that recent liberalism is increasingly subscribing to the "absolutist" claim to right (such as the right to privacy) and thus in practice (if not in theory) to atomistic individualism that Alexis de Tocqueville pointed out as the self-undermining feature of modern liberal democracy. In this respect, the Confucian communitarian critique of liberalism (and liberal democracy) is not completely misplaced or particularly novel. What usually goes unnoticed (thus untackled), however, is that Confucian communitarianism, too, is exposed to the liberal rejoinder of (originally Western) communitarianism, especially liberalism's *political* critique of communitarianism[3] – that is, how to prevent civility from deteriorating into docility. For instance, while acknowledging in principle the social value of civility (such as togetherness, discipline, and mutuality) in any viable liberal society, George Kateb, a prominent liberal individualist, nevertheless argues,

> When mutuality passes beyond relief of the needy to a greater effort to persuade or entice people to care actively for one another's well-being, individualists bridle.... Even worse, the tendency of such guided or administered or engineered mutuality is to work with the same effect of docility as those things individualism fears precisely because they are immediate sources of docility: greater togetherness, greater discipline, and greater group identity. Some of this tendency is already present in the work of such social liberals as T. H. Green and John Dewey, both of whom urge so much mutuality that they betray the very idea of rights. They make rights merely instrumental to a society-wide abstract mutuality. Liberal individualism can have no difficulty with measures to alleviate suffering: it does not aspire to repeal basic morality, which mandates such alleviation. Beyond the relief of misery, however, social projects often appear to promise more docility, whatever else they may achieve.[4]

[2] One of the problems with the Confucian communitarian critique of Western liberalism is that it does not do justice to liberalism by failing to differentiate classical liberal political theory into which the idea of civility was integrated and recent liberalism, which has lost that ideal. See for instance, Immanuel Kant, *The Metaphysics of Morals*, trans. Mary J. Gregor (Cambridge: Cambridge University Press, 1996) and James Schmidt, "Civility, Enlightenment, and Society: Conceptual Confusions and Kantian Remedies," *American Political Science Review* 92 (1998), 419–27 for classical liberalism and see Mary A. Glendon, *Rights Talk: The Impoverishment of Political Discourse* (New York: Free Press, 1990) for the state of recent liberalism. For an illuminating discussion of the virtue of civility in modern liberal theory and practice, see Adam B. Seligman, *The Idea of Civil Society* (Princeton: Princeton University Press, 1992).

[3] As I discussed in Chapter 1, no thoughtful liberal denies the validity of communitarianism's key onto-epistemological claim that communal values and common identity are constitutive of individual identity. That is, liberals do not intend to deny that man is a social being and the quintessential value of civility in making liberalism a viable sociopolitical practice. What liberals find problematic in communitarianism is what it advocates, not necessarily what it is premised on.

[4] George Kateb, *The Inner Ocean: Individualism and Democratic Culture* (Ithaca: Cornell University Press, 1992), 226.

According to Kateb, liberal individualism is qualitatively different from atomistic individualism, which does not involve the idea of civility at all. On the contrary, liberalism is deeply concerned with, even undergirded by, such civil qualities as togetherness, mutuality, self-discipline, and common identity, and it is an ethical theory in its own right that is committed to the *negative* principle such as the elimination of injustice or the alleviation of suffering.[5] Therefore, what distinguishes liberalism from communitarianism is not so much whether or not there are notions of social self and civility (as is often assumed by Confucian communitarians), but whether the ethical concern is positive or negative. Otherwise stated, the issue is how social an individual can be reasonably expected to be and how thick civility (and citizenship) should be. Kateb's central contention is that thick civility (and strong democratic citizenship) is self-undermining because, instead of contributing to voluntary social cooperation among self-governing individuals, it will more likely promote social conformism in the name of self-discipline and social cooperation.[6]

Kateb's point seems to pose a more formidable challenge to Confucian communitarians, compared to their Western counterparts, because of their profound emphasis on ritual (*li* 禮) as the key mechanism of social harmony (*he* 和) and its theoretical reliance for social harmony on the ideal of *zhengming* 正名 (literally, the rectification of names), which stipulates that one ought to fulfill faithfully one's given social roles and that not transgressing one's social boundaries constitutes the core of morality, as is famously expressed by Confucius: "[Let] the ruler be a ruler, the minister a minister, the father a father, and the son a son."[7] While occasionally alluding to customs, mores, and traditions in terms of "the habits of the heart" that undergird the backdrop of a liberal civil society, however, Western communitarians rarely (almost never) endorse the kind of *li*-mediated social hierarchy and so-called role-ethics according to which moral agency consists primarily in one's commitment to the *li* and fulfillment of the social roles.

Then the question we should raise is this: if as Confucian communitarians assume, (1) the Confucian self is a role-playing social self, (2) the five cardinal human relations in Confucianism (*wulun* 五倫) presuppose a *more or less* fixed social hierarchy and the particular roles that are to be faithfully played in it,[8] and

[5] Also see Judith N. Shklar, *The Faces of Injustice* (New Haven: Yale University Press, 1990); Iris M. Young, *Inclusion and Democracy* (Oxford: Oxford University Press, 2000); Philip Pettit, *Republicanism: A Theory of Freedom and Government* (Oxford: Oxford University Press, 1997).

[6] Also see Dana Villa, *Public Freedom* (Princeton: Princeton University Press, 2008), chap. 3.

[7] *Analects* 12:11. All English translations of the *Analects* of Confucius (*Lunyu* 論語) in this chapter are adopted from Roger T. Ames and Henry Rosemont Jr., *The Analects of Confucius: A Philosophical Translation* (New York: Ballantine Books, 1998).

[8] Virtually no Confucian communitarian who cherishes the value of the *li* asserts that *li*-mediated social hierarchy is a rigorously fixed, socially petrified residue from the past. On the contrary, it is agreed that *li* allows an individual room for moral reflection and the occasion for incremental reform.

finally (3) the ritualistic performance of such roles is considered as generating Confucian civilities such as deference (*rang* 讓), respectfulness (*jing* 敬), humility (*gong* 恭), and sense of shame (*chi* 恥), thereby contributing to social harmony,[9] then how can Confucian communitarianism avoid the problem of docility, a complacency to the existing social order?

In this chapter, I critically examine the remaining two core claims of the communitarianism thesis that I left unresolved in the previous chapter – namely, the ritual aestheticism claim and the social harmony claim. I argue that to make Confucian communitarianism a viable *political* vision, its emphasis on *li*-based civility and social harmony, however important in creating a characteristically "Confucian" civil society, must be balanced with what I call "Confucian incivility," a set of Confucian social practices that temporarily "upset" the existing social relations and yet which, ironically, help those relations become more enduring and viable.[10] My central argument is that the Confucian social self can exercise its critical moral agency by upsetting and yet without completely transgressing the conventional ritual boundaries set by the *wulun*, and that in a profound sense "Confucian civility" encompasses both social-harmonizing civilities that buttress the moral foundation of the Confucian social order and some incivilities that aim to revise and thereby revitalize that foundation. The defining characteristics of Confucian incivilities are summed up as deferentially remonstrative and respectfully corrective (usually in the familial relations), but they are sometimes uncompromising and even involving contestation (especially in the political relations). I conclude by examining the implications of the virtue of Confucian incivility for constructing a less conservative and more sociopolitically vibrant version of Confucian democracy than the prevailing suggestions of Confucian communitarian democracy.

The Virtue of Civility and Its Limits

The revival of civility in recent social and political theory is closely associated with the excessive rights-bearing individualism in contemporary liberalism, the corresponding erosion of community in liberal-democratic life, and the disappearance of common good in liberal political discourse.[11] Simultaneously, contemporary liberal-democratic society is increasingly characterized by what John Rawls famously called "the fact of pluralism" in which groups and communities

[9] Sor-hoon Tan, "Can There Be a Confucian Civil Society?," in *The Moral Circle and the Self: Chinese and Western Approaches*, ed. Kim-chong Chong, Sor-hoon Tan, and C. L. Ten (Chicago: Open Court, 2003), 210–11.

[10] By "incivility," however, I do not mean "unsociability," which makes society *uncivil*, driving it to a war-like state as depicted by Hobbes and Xunzi.

[11] Robert D. Putnam, *Bowling Alone: The Collapse and Revival of American Community* (New York: Touchstone, 2000); Michael J. Sandel, *Democracy's Discontent: America in Search of a Public Philosophy* (Cambridge, MA: Belknap, 1996); Glendon, *Rights Talk*.

of differing comprehensive doctrines pursue moral (and sometimes political) autonomy from the national moral community.[12] In the face of excessive self-assertion in terms of individual right on one side and growing interest in collective/group rights on the other – both being claimed vis-à-vis common identity and common good – civility has emerged as a quintessential political virtue in Western liberal political discourse. Edward Shils offers one of the most authoritative definitions of civility from a liberal political perspective:

> Civility is a belief which affirms the possibility of the common good; it is a belief in the community of contending parties within a morally valid unity of society. It is a belief in the validity of legitimacy of the governmental institutions which lay down rules and resolve conflicts. Civility is a virtue expressed in action on behalf of the whole society, on behalf of the good of all the members of the society to which public liberties and representative institutions are integral. Civility is an attitude in individuals which recommends that consensus about the maintenance of the order of society should exist alongside the conflicts of interests and ideals.... Civility is a virtue because it permits a variety of substantive interests and ideals or virtues to be cultivated and because it attempts to keep a balance among the parties to the conflicts by an example and an insistence on self-restraint. It is a restraint on the passion with which interests and ideals are pursued.[13]

Central to civility is its unifying function by which a society sustains order and preserves both common good and shared (political) identity. It is by virtue of civility that conflicts of interests and moral values endemic in the liberal-democratic politics can be peacefully resolved. In other words, civility is of great political significance not necessarily because it can avoid conflicts of both material and ideal interests, which are quite natural in the modern pluralistic society, but because of its noncoercive way of resolving conflicts through the exercise of example and self-restraint. Even though civility is a belief in the possibility of the common good, it "has less specific substantive content and it is concerned with compromises among a plurality of values and with compromises of the demands of parochial parts of the society with the interest of the society as a whole."[14] Put differently, civility is what makes democratic peace with our fellow citizens (mostly strangers) possible. As Stephen Carter argues, it is a precondition of democratic dialogue: "Democracy demands dialogue, and dialogue flows from disagreement. But we can, and maybe must, be relentlessly partisan without being actively uncivil. Indeed the more passionate our certainty that we are right, the more urgent our need to practice the

[12] John Rawls, *Political Liberalism* (New York: Columbia University Press, 1993). Also see William A. Galston, *Liberal Pluralism: The Implications of Value Pluralism for Political Theory and Practice* (Cambridge: Cambridge University Press, 2002) and *The Practice of Liberal Pluralism* (Cambridge: Cambridge University Press, 2005).

[13] Edward Shils, *The Virtue of Civility: Selected Essays on Liberalism, Tradition, and Civil Society*, ed. Steve Grosby (Indianapolis: Liberty Fund, 1997), 4.

[14] Ibid., 70.

art of civility – otherwise, we make dialogue impossible, and the possibility of dialogue is the reason democracy values disagreement in the first place."[15]

What is particularly important is that civility is an ethical quality that is cultivated by virtue of self-restraint. From the standpoint of civil politics, what is problematic about the recent rights-based individualism is not so much the discourse of right or individualism itself. The actual problem lies in its being too absolutist to the extent that individual right can no longer be balanced with the common good. Thus, civil politics, while being discontented with the recent tendency in liberal discourse to place the right over the good, does not attempt to replace the right with the good. Rather it aims to moderate the absolutist claim to right and unbridled self-interest so that right and interest can be compatible with those of others by helping redefine them in light of the common good. Hence Carter says, "The Constitution protects a variety of rights, but our moral norms provide the discipline in their exercise. Sometimes what the moral norm of civility demands is that we restrain our self-expression for the sake of our community."[16]

In sum, civil politics stipulates that only where there is the "civil collective self-consciousness" can we commit ourselves to the common good;[17] only among the self-restrained individuals is a civil dialogue possible; only where there is a civil dialogue can the peaceful and morally justifiable resolution of conflicts of interests and moral values be achieved; and finally only where there is a public consensus and the common good can one's (civil) right as a member of civil society be fully respected and one's (social) individuality be empowered.

At this point, it seems necessary to note that recent liberalism, after the years-long debate with communitarianism, has improved its social and political theory by actively embracing the key tenets of civil politics mentioned earlier, thus consciously distancing it from deontological liberalism premised on the assumption of an unencumbered, morally autonomous, rights-bearing self. To distinguish this new version of liberalism from deontological liberalism, we may call it "civic liberalism."[18] And, not surprisingly, civic liberalism shares many of the concerns and emphases of the communitarian critics of deontological liberalism: its insistence on the importance of responsible citizenship, the

[15] Stephen L. Carter, *Civility: Manners, Morals, and the Etiquette of Democracy* (New York: Basic Books, 1998), 24.

[16] Ibid., 69.

[17] Shils, *Virtue of Civility*, 71.

[18] Thomas A. Spragens, *Civic Liberalism: Reflections on Our Democratic Ideals* (Lanham, MD: Rowman & Littlefield, 1999); Richard Dagger, *Civic Virtues: Rights, Citizenship, and Republican Liberalism* (Oxford: Oxford University Press, 1997); William A. Galston, *Liberal Purposes: Goods, Virtues, and Diversity in the Liberal State* (Cambridge: Cambridge University Press, 1991); Stephen Macedo, *Liberal Virtues: Citizenship, Virtue, and Community in Liberal Constitutionalism* (Oxford: Clarendon, 1990); James T. Kloppenberg, *The Virtues of Liberalism* (Oxford: Oxford University Press, 1998).

norms of civic virtue (or civility), and its discontent with the public discourse and the political order focused almost exclusively on individual rights.[19] Even though liberal individualists do not stress too strongly the vital significance of civility because of their supreme concerns with individual right (vis-à-vis the government and to a lesser degree fellow citizens), they, nevertheless, and as we have already seen in Kateb, admit its quintessential political value.

What distinguishes communitarians from both liberal individualists and civic liberals is not so much their interest in civility (vis-à-vis the right) as their enthusiasm to put the core argument of deontological liberalism in reverse,[20] that is, to place the common good and civility prior to the right,[21] or further to reintroduce classical (most often Aristotelian) virtue ethics in place of modern individualism and its attendant rights discourse.[22] Put differently, rather than trying to dialectically balance the right with the good and civility, communitarians are supremely interested in replacing the political discourse concentrated on the right with that of the common good and civility, regarding them as generally incompatible. Whereas civility presupposed in civic liberalism is in a mutually constitutive relation with the right,[23] civility conceived by communitarians is operating on the strategies of integration and identification. In communitarianism, community is closer to a gemeinschaft of natural affection than to a society of civil collective self-consciousness, and the kernel of civil politics is understood as consisting in achieving common identity and social harmony.

The problem is that communitarian civility is likely to inculcate docility within the heart of the "social self" – a mode of the self that communitarians valorize and which they argue is in contradistinction to the autonomous self that liberalism is alleged to cherish. Communitarians assert against deontological liberals that ethics has nothing to do with one's ability to abide by formal rules that are given a priori and independently of the social and cultural context; on the contrary, it is concerned with how well someone fulfills his or her social roles by internalizing moral goods defined by the community in which

19 Spragens, *Civic Liberalism*, xvi.

20 By communitarians, I am particularly referring to those who strongly oppose the kind of rights-based individualism that Confucian communitarians are most willing to ally themselves with, such as Alasdair MacIntyre and Ronald Beiner. Other communitarians like Michael Sandel and Charles Taylor, rather than attempting a foundational critique of liberalism, are trying to accommodate the originally republican ideas of common good, citizenship, and moral character into the existing Western liberal-democratic settings. Michael J. Sandel, *Liberalism and the Limits of Justice* (Cambridge: Cambridge University Press, 1982) and Charles Taylor, *Sources of the Self: The Making of the Modern Identity* (Cambridge, MA: Harvard University Press, 1989). But even these more liberal-minded communitarians scarcely talk about the virtue of incivility.

21 Ronald Beiner, *What's the Matter with Liberalism?* (Berkeley: University of California Press, 1992).

22 Alasdair MacIntyre, *After Virtue: A Study in Moral Theory* (Notre Dame, IN: University of Notre Dame Press, 1984).

23 That is, respect of right is considered one of the essential liberal civilities. See Macedo, *Liberal Virtues*; Dagger, *Civic Virtues*.

he or she is radically situated, that is, by cultivating a good character, which is a uniquely human quality that is identifiable and appraisable only within a particular social and cultural context. But it is this radical contextualism that facilitates docility that makes people want to be led by, and thus to be more deferential toward, either personal or impersonal authorities. It is, however, distinct from submission that is more overtly political. According to Kateb, in the secular community docility is working through the *aesthetic mentality*.

Some communitarian critics long for a society whose customs, manners, visible surfaces, and daily transactions (public and private) all seem designed or composed and therefore seem to have strong and unmistakable meanings and to fit together to create one great composition, one great meaning.... In effect, the communitarians ask us to give up the will to have moments of transcendence in which one tries to see one's society as from a distance or a height, or in which one tries to see it as an alien or an enemy does or could. Instead, one should treat society as prior, that is, as always prepared to receive everyone, as all-enclosing and wiser than oneself. Every society provides the script, and in good societies all play their parts and say their lines unselfconsciously.[24]

In other words, communitarianism, albeit unwittingly, obviates what is political (i.e., self-government, political liberty, civil dialogue, conflict resolution and the common good) in its aesthetic mentality, the mentality to envision the society in an organic sense and in terms of a seamless whole. Here a good character is not something to be cultivated by means of reason-giving civil dialogue among the self-reliant, loosely connected, individuals (more accurately, strangers) of different moral values and diverse material interests.[25] Rather, a good character is understood primarily in terms of one's excellent fulfillment of one's parts and roles in society. Therefore, some communitarians, such as MacIntyre, liken moral practice to a sort of "game" (in the Wittgensteinian sense) in the context of which criteria of good and bad performances inhere and participants have roles and obligations in light of such criteria.

To be sure, a communitarian community is qualitatively different from a totalitarian community that is individuality-suffocating, in that it is predicated on and further nourishes what Charles Taylor calls "strong evaluational agency," a moral agency that is cultivated within the community context.[26] In this conceptualization of moral agency, "the individual is an ineluctably moral being for whom fundamental moral questions *inescapably pre-exist* and she is compelled to seek answers to these inescapable questions and by doing so she is moved to embrace certain fundamental values and ideals that we

[24] Kateb, *Inner Ocean*, 228.

[25] Among Confucian political philosophers, Stephen C. Angle draws attention to the value of (civil) dialogue in the contexts of Confucian ethical cultivation and politics. See his *Sagehood: The Contemporary Significance of Neo-Confucian Philosophy* (Oxford: Oxford University Press, 2009), 172–6.

[26] See Charles Taylor, "What Is Human Agency?," in *Philosophical Papers*, vol. 1 (Cambridge: Cambridge University Press, 1985).

deem incomparably more important than others but that provide the standpoint from which these must be weighed, judged, decided about."[27] In other words, the moral agent postulated in communitarianism entertains "contextual individuality." However, communitarians rarely go further than this. Their supreme interest in the preservation of the ever-eroding traditional moral communities puts a critical obstacle to understanding how to revise, revitalize, and ultimately transform such communities so that they can be commensurate with changing social conditions and moral perspectives. And yet, from the civic liberal standpoint, the essence of moral autonomy resides exactly in these capacities to revise, revitalize, and transform the existing community (hence better preserving it), which requires a person to keep a creative tension between the moral context in which he or she is socially embedded and his or her critical moral self.[28]

By identifying autonomy in terms of unencumbered selfhood devoid of *any* moral concern for community, however, communitarians emphasize less the more practical (in contrast to deontological) understanding of autonomy in terms of revisability and transformability. Because of their understanding of individuality as contextual individuality (i.e., reflexivity), communitarians approach civility predominantly in terms of context-adaptability (i.e., social order and harmony), but rarely in terms of context-revisability/transformability. Its political consequences are, first, a one-sided, largely conservative understanding of civility and, second, a certain anxiety toward the moral capacity to disrupt, albeit temporarily, the existing social (particularly political) relationships, even though it is ultimately for its moral betterment. In short, communitarians rarely acknowledge and are quite reluctant to embrace incivility emanating from one's critical context-destabilizing moral agency as the integral part of civility that preserves the backbone of civil society.

The problem is that this critical absence of interest in the political virtue of incivility in Western communitarianism is now being reproduced in the accounts of Confucian communitarianism. In the remainder of this chapter, therefore, I revisit the core arguments of Confucian communitarianism and attempt to reconstruct a more civil account of it.

Li, Civility, and Confucian Communitarianism

By identifying "liberalism" singularly with deontological liberalism and thus failing to appreciate civic liberalism, Confucian communitarians who are critical of rights-based individualism seem to do injustice to modern liberalism as

[27] Ranjoo S. Herr, "Cultural Claims and the Limits of Liberal Democracy," *Social Theory and Practice* 34 (2008), 25–48, 42 (with paraphrasing).

[28] For some illuminating accounts on this creative moral tension, see Galston, *Liberal Purposes*, 22–41 and Michael Walzer, *Thick and Thin: Moral Argument at Home and Abroad* (Notre Dame, IN: University of Notre Dame Press, 1994), 85–104.

a social and political tradition. However, a more serious problem than their casual misunderstanding of liberalism is the political implications of their habitual affiliation of civility with communitarianism – that is, their assumption that civil politics relies on social conventions (whether tradition, custom, habit, or ritual) for its practical force, and therefore is in contrast to social destabilization generated by disagreement, contestation, or conflicts. Certainly, the purpose of civil politics is essentially conservative in that it is committed to arriving at the common good by peacefully and consensually resolving social (both material and ethical) conflicts that would be intractable where there is no civility (i.e., in the state of nature).[29] What Confucian communitarians have been relatively dismissive of is the fact that in civil politics the *process* by which to arrive at a consensus or the common good is just as important as the consensus itself, and that such a process does not preclude reasonable yet temporarily destabilizing contention or conflict among citizens.

This is not to say that Confucian communitarians completely ignore the issue of process. As a matter of fact, Confucian communitarians have great interest in the way in which Confucianism *dissolves* – rather than resolves through a civil dialogue – social conflicts and reproduces social harmony through the appropriate (*yi* 義) practice of Confucian rituals (*li*). Sor-hoon Tan argues,

> It is the interaction between ritual practice and appropriateness that results in a growth in meaning that is widely shared and transmitted across generations, a growth in the organizing, articulating, and practicing continuity linking physically separate individuals constituting community. This intertwining of the personal and the communal in the ritual practices-appropriateness conjunction is central to achieving a social harmony that would preclude the oppression of individuals and the stagnation of societies.[30]

I do not believe that Tan's neo-Deweyan attempt to revivify the *li* from a pragmatic perspective by unearthing the values of reflexivity and a sense of appropriateness in their social practice is in itself problematic. In fact, although Western thinkers have rightly warned of the tyrannical elements in ritual practice because of its proclivity toward blind adherence to existing social conventions,[31] Confucius indeed opposed such ritualism when he advocated the *li*. For Confucius, *li* was not what Weber termed the routinized or petrified form of charisma that exerts a mere traditional authority of the past. It was rather a vibrant ensemble of social practices grounded in and guided by its original spirit, namely, *ren* 仁, which holds a present meaning in its performance.

[29] Michael Oakeshott, a well-known conservative scholar and one of the champions of civility (and civil association), defines politics in terms of "the activity of attending to the general arrangements of a set of people whom chance or choice have brought together" (*Rationalism in Politics and Other Essays* [Indianapolis: Liberty Fund, 1991], 44).

[30] Sor-hoon Tan, *Confucian Democracy: A Deweyan Reconstruction* (Albany: State University of New York Press, 2003), 84.

[31] For instance, see Ernest Gellner, *Conditions of Liberty: Civil Society and Its Rivals* (New York: Penguin, 1996).

Confucius therefore wondered, "What has a person who is not benevolent (*ren*) got to do with observing ritual propriety (*li*)?"[32] In other words, *li* is the color and *ren* is the unadorned textile – although color and textile are inseparable in the concrete form of gamut, each is meaningless without the other.[33] A certain mode of reflexivity is essential in the practice of *li*: "What could I see in a person ... who in observing ritual propriety (*li*) is not respectful (*jing* 敬)?"[34] In this respect, a blind adherence to rituals of the past actually deserts the purposes of the *li* and thus ruins the spirit of *ren* (humanity). Again, what is required is a sense of appropriateness (*yi*) to figure out what type of action is proper and necessary in the given social context.

> The use of a hemp cap is prescribed in the observance of ritual propriety (*li*). Nowadays, that a silk cap is used instead is a matter of frugality. I would follow accepted practice on this. A subject kowtowing on entering the hall is prescribed in the observance of ritual propriety (*li*). Nowadays that one kowtows only after ascending the hall is a matter of hubris. Although it goes contrary to accepted practice, I still kowtow on entering the hall.[35]

In other words, a Confucian moral agent can exercise his or her moral agency in terms of reflexivity and can entertain his or her contextual individuality. Russell Fox takes a further step by asserting that one's reflexive practice of the *li* involves action and such a ritualistic action is a public *act*. By voluntarily and reflectively participating in the ritualistic order, Fox continues, not only can one, together with others, disclose authority, but more important, one can oneself become an authoritative person – the author of one's own life.[36]

The problem, however, is that the community conceived by Confucian communitarians is more or less organic as it is assumed to be preexisting and thus social continuity is taken for granted. Here a person's freedom is exercised not so much in terms of context-revising/transforming talk and action but in terms of context-adapting/clarifying reflexivity, that is, the social self's personal appropriation of the constitutive logic and operational meaning of the *preexisting* and considerably *stable* social context into which one was born and in which one constantly finds oneself.[37]

This does not imply that the *li*-following Confucian social self, as described by communitarian Confucians, does not undergo what John Dewey called "problematic situations," which enable a context-revising critical moral agency.

[32] *Analects* 3:3.

[33] *Analects* 3:8.

[34] *Analects* 3:26. Also see *Analects* 15:18, where Confucius stresses the importance of a sense of appropriateness in the practice of the *li*.

[35] *Analects* 9:3.

[36] Russell A. Fox, "Confucian and Communitarian Responses to Liberal Democracy," *Review of Politics* 59 (1997), 577n44.

[37] As I noted in Chapter 1, Tan's endorsement of the political activism like the farmers' movement in China critically remedies this weakness of Confucian communitarianism as a political theory and practice.

However, the degree and scope of the problem with which one is confronted in one's everyday practice of the *li* should not be exaggerated. The problem to be solved in one's practice of the *li* is whether or not to follow the *li*, or whether or not to perform one's particular roles that are socially given – a daughter, a father, a teacher, or a citizen.[38] Herbert Fingarette's following statement describes well the nature of the problem that a role-performing Confucian social self must deal with:

In both passages [*Analects* 12:10, 12:21], the meaning is not that of a mind in doubt as to which course to choose but of a person being inconsistent in his desires or acts. Paraphrasing the theme of these texts: one wants someone – perhaps a relative – to live and prosper, but out of anger, one wishes that he perish or one actually endangers him out of a blind rage. In such conflict, the task is not posed as one of *choosing* or *deciding* but of *distinguishing* or *discriminating* (*pien*) the inconsistent inclinations.... In short, the task is posed in terms of knowledge rather than choice. *Huo*, the key term in the passages, means here "deluded or led astray by an un-*li* inclination or tendency." It is not doubt as to which to choose to do.[39]

To submit voluntarily and unswervingly to the order of the *li* and thereby attain the context-clarifying moral capacity (also social knowledge and self-authority), what is required, according to Confucius, is the virtue of self-restraint, as he famously said, "[b]y overcoming one's [private or selfish] self (*ke ji* 克己) and returning to the *li* (*fu li* 復禮)."[40] What is more intriguing and important from the political standpoint is the tactic many Confucian communitarians deliberately employ to counter the narcissistic individualism saturated in contemporary liberal culture. That is, the reverse logic in the formula of *ke ji fu li*, which stipulates that through the voluntary and unswerving submission to the order of the *li* (*fu li*), one can effectively constrain one's otherwise unregulated self (*ke ji*) and only by virtue of *li*-guided self-restraint can one become a responsible and trustworthy, or "civil," partaker of moral community (*wei ren* 爲仁). Characteristic of the Confucian *li*-abiding civil self are such self-constraining virtues as deference, respectfulness, humility, and sense of shame,[41] which together can be called "Confucian civilities." Confucian communitarians argue, only in the *li*-ordered moral community can one effectively empower one's authoritative individuality, and only by mediation of *li*-induced Confucian civilities (particularly sense of shame) can self and society be mutually constitutive, transforming society into a fiduciary community.[42]

[38] David L. Hall and Roger T. Ames, *The Democracy of the Dead: Dewey, Confucius, and the Hope for Democracy in China* (Chicago: Open Court, 1999), 209.

[39] Herbert Fingarette, *Confucius: The Secular as Sacred* (New York: Harper & Row, 1972), 22–3.

[40] *Analects* 12:1.

[41] *Analects* 15:18; 6:27; 14:27.

[42] Tan, *Confucian Democracy*; Hall and Ames, *Democracy of the Dead*. Also see Sor-hoon Tan, "From Cannibalism to Empowerment: An Analects-Inspired Attempt to Balance Community and Liberty," *Philosophy East and West* 54 (2004), 52–70.

I strongly agree that *li* can be reinvented as the generic foundation of Confucian civilities and that self-restraining Confucian civilities can provide a great bulwark for a viable democracy (only if under a relevant constitutional order) by forestalling atomistic individualism that simply bears no sense of civility.[43] What is problematic about recent formulations of Confucian communitarianism is not so much its generic theory as its strong aestheticism that prefers a prepolitical, nondialogic, ritualistically orchestrated "tacit" consensus in the name of "authentic social harmony," as David Hall and Roger Ames claim: "Stress upon a tacit, affective consensus celebrated through ritualized roles and practices that do not require raising difference to the level of consciousness, promotes authentic social harmony.... Consensus is primarily unspoken. The essentially *aesthetic* dimension of ritual practice promotes communication as at a level precluding the necessity of debate."[44] I suspect that "a tacit consensus precluding the necessity of debate" is not only impossible, even in an ideal community of perfect ritualism (not to mention in a highly urbanized industrial East Asia), but also undesirable because of what it likely entails – docility. Perhaps we can try to achieve this type of *li*-guided nonadversary and noncontentious compromise, if not necessarily tacit, in local communities, workplaces, families, and various forms of private associations.[45] However, it must be remembered that a nonadversary and well-ordered ritual society is not only possible but also can flourish under a benevolent authoritarian regime, as was historically the case with Chosŏn Korea (1392–1910), which allegedly entertained a full-blown Confucian ritual society from the sixteenth century,[46] but was notoriously intolerant of ethical pluralism, attacking those who held different ethical (and ethico-political) standards and convictions by labeling them "the Despoilers of the Way."[47]

Clearly, Confucian incivilities may not able to make a Confucian civil society democratic; but it seems they can prevent a Confucian civil society from deteriorating into a rigidly hierarchical, nonpluralistic authoritarian society. Then, the challenge is to retrieve the habits of incivility endorsed but not fully articulated in the Confucian social and political tradition and cultivate them to

[43] See Chapters 3 and 4.

[44] Hall and Ames, *Democracy of the Dead*, 182.

[45] See Albert H. Chen, "Mediation, Litigation, and Justice: Confucian Reflections in a Modern Liberal Society," in Bell and Hahm, *Confucianism for the Modern World*. According to Jane Mansbridge's classic work, unitary democracy is indeed more suitable for such small, intimate groups and associations than adversary democracy. See her *Beyond Adversary Democracy* (Chicago: University of Chicago Press, 1980).

[46] Martina Deuchler, *The Confucian Transformation of Korea: A Study of Society and Ideology* (Cambridge, MA: Council on East Asian Studies, Harvard University, 1992).

[47] Martina Deuchler, "Despoilers of the Way – Insulters of the Sages: Controversies over the Classics in Seventeenth-Century Korea," in *Culture and the State in Late Chosŏn Korea*, ed. JaHyun K. Haboush and Martina Deuchler (Cambridge, MA: Council on East Asian Studies, Harvard University, 1999).

make Confucian communitarianism more socially and politically vibrant. But before exploring Confucian incivility, let us first examine the philosophical justification for Confucian incivility by revisiting Confucius, Mencius, and Xunzi, three masters of classical Confucianism.

The Social Meaning of *He Er Bu Tong* 和而不同

Even though the view that Confucianism is inherently associated with authoritarianism is now nearly obsolete, the equally troublesome assumption that an ideal Confucian person (*junzi* 君子) is complacent or docile, rather than self-assertive and socially critical, is still persistent. In a sense, such a view is not totally invalid because Confucius describes the *junzi* in such self-restraining terms – for example, as "having a sense of appropriate conduct (*yi*) as one's basic disposition (*zhi* 質), developing it in observing ritual propriety (*li*), expressing it with modesty (or self-restraint), and consummating it in making good on one's word (*xin* 信)."[48] Likewise, when Confucius and his disciples were talking about *li*, emphasis was on their self-restraining and social harmonizing functions.[49] At one point, Confucius even lamented the reality in which the faithful practice of the *li* (particularly in serving the ruler) was often misunderstood as "acting unctuously."[50]

Of interest, though, classical Confucians were keenly aware of the potential social evils arising from the faithful yet uncritical practice of the *li* and thus made every effort to clarify what the *li* entail socially and politically by distinguishing two related sets of frequently equated concepts – harmonization (*he* 和) and identification (*tong* 同) on one hand and exemplary person (*junzi*) and village-worthy (*xiangyuan* 鄉愿) on the other.

In *Analects* 13:23, Confucius explicitly differentiates the exemplary persons (*junzi*) from the petty men (*xiao ren* 小人) in terms of *he* and *tong*: "Exemplary persons seek *he* not *tong*; petty persons are the opposite." What, then, is meant by *he* as a social virtue squarely opposed to *tong* in Confucianism? To use the analogy of music (to which the concept of *he* is etymologically related), harmony is what results when sounds respond to one another appropriately. Furthermore, as Chenyang Li rightly argues, the most authentic meaning of *he* (as harmony) comes from "the rhythmic interplay of various sounds, either in nature or between human beings, that is musical to the human ear."[51] Here the key word is "various" because harmony presupposes the existence of different things, different perspectives, or different views on various issues.[52] In stark

[48] *Analects* 15:18.
[49] *Analects* 12:1; 16:5.
[50] *Analects* 3:18.
[51] Chenyang Li, "The Confucian Ideal of Harmony," *Philosophy East and West* 56 (2006), 583–603, 584.
[52] Ibid., 586.

contrast, there is no such presupposition of diversity in the concept of *tong*. *Tong* leads a person and society only to a single, dead, monotonous end.

Most Confucian communitarians seem to agree with this well-received understanding of *he* (vis-à-vis *tong*) and indeed their idealized Confucian fiduciary community is a harmonizing society, not a stagnant society of *tong*.[53] What I find problematic in Li's (and Confucian communitarian) description of harmony is the claim that harmony *implies* a certain favorable relationship among different things/views/ideas.[54] According to Li, harmony is something to be *disclosed* out of diversity. Otherwise stated, harmony is essentially an aesthetic phenomenon. Certainly, this understanding of harmony makes perfect sense in the appreciation of art and music where the "magical" process of harmonization does not render itself to rational scrutiny.[55]

What distinguishes social and political life, however, is that there is no magic in attaining social and political harmony (and common good) except by means of respectful, reasonable, and disciplined dialogic interactions among individuals who hold not only diverse but also conflicting views. In most social and political affairs (especially in the modern world), there is no implied harmonious order of various things, the beauty of which can somehow be revealed to a morally elevated person, say, *junzi*. A more realistic observation is that the beauty of social and political life lies in the consensus arriving (or common good-arriving) human activities, which is dialogical in nature. We should not forget that Confucius, abhorrent of the eloquence of spoken language,[56] never advocated a complete ritualism unguided by an intelligent and disciplined use of verbal communication.[57]

Thus understood, *he* is (and should be) a characteristically human social and political process of harmonization in which different and even conflicting views, ideas, or perspectives held by different individuals are resolved not only by aesthetic ritualism but equally important by social and political communication, which sometimes involves tension and even, I argue, contestation especially in the democratic societal context. On the contrary, *tong* refers to the pathological proclivity to secure consensus (and collective identity) to the exclusion of the harmonizing social and political process.

53 See Russell A. Fox, "Activity and Communal Authority: Localist Lessons from Puritan and Confucian Communities," *Philosophy East and West* 58 (2008), 36–59.

54 Li, "The Confucian Ideal of Harmony," 584.

55 On the harmony-achieving "magic" of the *li*, see Fingarette's aforementioned book (note 39), by which many Confucian communitarians are inspired.

56 *Analects* 1:3; 15:27; 17:7; 17:17. For an insightful essay exploring the political implications of Confucius's largely negative attitude toward language, see J. G. A. Pocock, "Ritual, Language, Power: An Essay on the Apparent Political Meanings of Ancient Chinese Philosophy," in *Politics, Language and Time: Essays on Political Thought and History* (New York: Atheneum, 1971), 42–79.

57 *Analects* 11:21; 12:3; 14:20.

This reinterpretation of *he* and *tong* from the social and political perspective leads to a renewed understanding of *junzi* and *xiangyuan*. Simply put, *junzi* is a person willing to commit himself to such a harmonizing, consensus-arriving social and political process, whereas *xiangyuan* is a person who is single-mindedly concerned with sustaining the preexisting, conventional social norms, and does not consider consensual process to achieve such norms or the plurality of human life. *Junzi*, therefore, is the kind of person who likes to associate himself with those who have deep appreciation of human plurality and of the moral value of commonality in the face of human plurality, thus differentiating himself from a *xiangyuan* who has no such appreciation.

In marked contrast, as the complacent observer of the social convention (including rituals), a *xiangyuan*'s single greatest concern is to be loved by all, which is good only in appearance, but not good at all in reality. Thus Confucius said, "The *xiangyuan* is excellent (*de* 德) under false pretense."[58] Mencius gives a detailed description of a *xiangyuan*:

> [*Xiangyuan* is the man who says,] "What is the point of having such great ambition? Their [those who are wild and unconventional, rushing for the Way] words and deeds take no notice of each other, and yet they keep on saying, 'The ancients! The ancients!' Why must they walk alone in such solitary fashion? Being in the world, one must behave in a manner pleasing to this world. So long as one is good, it is all right." He tries in this way cringingly to please the world. It is the kind of person, "you cannot find anything, if you want to censure him; you cannot find anything either, if you want to find fault with him. He shares with others the practices of the day and is in harmony with the sordid world. He pursues such a policy and appears to be conscientious and faithful, and to show integrity in his conduct. He is liked by the multitude and is self-righteous."[59]

Mencius's point is that *xiangyuan* possesses no critical mind toward the existing social world and thus social relationships. It is not because he is unharmonious with the world that he is not authentically virtuous; rather, it is his remarkable ability to be harmonious with *any* world (community or social relationship) that is so appalling from the Confucian ethical perspective. The so-called virtue the *xiangyuan* has embodied in himself, which Confucius disparaged as "virtue under false pretense," is nothing but docility. The commitment to pursue harmony in a civil manner is a dramatic expression of care and respect; it is difficult and requires compromising one's own desires and ideals. This is something wholly lacking in the *xiangyuan*.

Therefore, what matters is not so much the harmony between the self and the world, which is the key problematic of Confucian communitarianism. The real issue is whether or not the harmony between the self and the world is under one's ceaseless critical moral scrutiny and therefore whether or not the harmony between the self and the world is open to revision and further

[58] *Analects* 17:23.

[59] *Mencius* 7B37. All English translations of the *Mengzi* 孟子 in this chapter are adopted from *Mencius*, trans. D. C. Lau (New York: Penguin, 1970).

reformulation. While the *xiangyuan* takes for granted the existing social world (in this regard, he is merely a conventionalist) and strives for slavish adaptation to it, the *junzi* asks relentlessly whether the existing social order and convention deserve continued moral allegiance and explores a better alternative. As such, as Tu Weiming aptly puts it, a *junzi* is in the world but, unlike *xiangyuan*, he is not of the world.[60] In the *xiangyuan*, civility deteriorates into docility because of the lack both of reflexivity in the practice of the *li* and of critical mind toward the existing social world. In *junzi*, on the contrary, civility stays alive because of its continual revision and reinvention. I understand such moral power to keep civility vibrantly alive (thereby keeping docility at bay) as the virtue of incivility.

Retrieving and Cultivating the Virtue of Confucian Incivility

Incivility (as distinct from uncivility) is part of civility. But it is a particular kind of civility in that it is what makes civility as the generic social underpinning a living moral and social-political virtue. It is true that classical Confucians never offered a systematic account of Confucian incivility as the invigorating force of the moral system of Confucian *li*-mediated civility. But this does not invalidate the virtue of incivility in Confucian social and political ethics.[61] In fact, for classical Confucians the virtue of incivility was deemed the other side of the same coin (hence not self-consciously asserted) of the virtue of civility, a moral value that they took pains to revivify in the morally deteriorating, increasingly uncivil world. What is interesting is that as advocates of ethics of differential love and treatment, classical Confucians conceived of the intensity of incivility differently, depending on whether the given social relation is familial or nonfamilial (particularly political). This distinction is particularly important when it comes to political relations because while envisioning the political ruler in the image of the father, Confucians still maintained the distinction between familial and political relations – the former based on the principle of familiarity (*qin-qin* 親親) and the latter on that of righteousness (*Jun chen yi he* 君臣義合).[62]

[60] Tu Weiming, *Way, Learning, and Politics: Essays on the Confucian Intellectual* (Albany: State University of New York Press, 1993), 11.

[61] Some recent scholars exploring the contemporary relevance of Confucianism, though, appreciate the virtue of incivility, such as social criticism, without referring to it as such. See Brooke A. Ackerly, "Is Liberalism the Only Way toward Democracy? Confucianism and Democracy," *Political Theory* 33 (2005), 547–76; Stephen C. Angle, *Contemporary Confucian Political Philosophy: Toward Progressive Confucianism* (Cambridge: Polity, 2012), chap. 7.

[62] Conventionally, *qin-qin* is juxtaposed with *zun-zun* 尊尊, which means to revere who is politically authoritative. Confucius, however, never presented the ruler-subject (minister) relation in terms of *zun-zun*, which is quite compatible with *Jun wei chen gang* 君爲臣綱 ("The ruler is the subject's supreme lord"), the moral-political principle created during the Han dynasty (206 B.C.E.–220 C.E.) in which Confucianism was thoroughly fused with Legalism. Rather than viewing the ruler-subject relationship in terms of dominance and subservience, Confucius understood it

In Familial Relations

In Confucian social ethics the principle of familiarity as the ethical guidance governing the members of the family (the parents in particular) is exercised by means of filial and fraternal responsibility (*xiaoti* 孝悌). And in Confucian classics such as *Lunyu* and *Mengzi*, filiality is often presented as the supreme practical moral virtue embodying the spirit of *ren*, the generic moral virtue in Confucian ethics. Given the prominent status of filiality in the Confucian ethical system, scholars such as Qingping Liu call Confucian ethics somewhat pejoratively "consanguinitism," which suppresses both individuality and sociality.[63] In this view, both filiality and the principle of familiarity inculcate in the person a submissive attitude, namely, docility.

As many of Liu's critics have argued,[64] characterizing Confucian ethics as consanguinitism does not do justice to the profound ethical meaning implicated with filiality and the principle of *qin-qin* (vis-à-vis *zun-zun* 尊尊). But it cannot be easily dismissed that Confucian family-oriented ethics (or simply "Confucian familism") is likely to promote docility. For example, while stressing the core ethical value of filiality, Youzi, one of Confucius's disciples, said, "It is a rare thing for someone who has a sense of filial and fraternal responsibility (*xiaodi* 孝弟) to have a taste for defying authority. And it is unheard of for those who have no taste for defying authority to be keen on initiating rebellion. Exemplary persons (*junzi*) concentrate their efforts on the root, for the root having taken hold, the way (*dao* 道) will grow therefrom. As for filial and fraternal responsibility, it is, I suspect, the root of authoritative conduct."[65] Confucius, too, when asked about filial conduct (xiao 孝), replied by saying, "Do not act against [the will of the parents],"[66] and also by saying, "In serving your father and mother, remonstrate with them gently. On seeing that they do not heed your suggestions, remain respectful and do not go against [their will]. Although concerned, voice no resentment."[67]

What is often glossed over is that Confucius (and Confucians) embraced as part of filial and fraternal responsibility (i.e., as civility) actions that upset, albeit temporarily, the given, admittedly hierarchical, moral boundaries and relations such as (gentle) remonstration and admonition. For example, in the

as based on the moral principle of righteousness (*yi*), hence his assertion that one can rightfully withdraw from the world (and the government), when there is no Way. Even though Confucius did not spell out *qin-qin* as well in the *Analects* (*Lunyu* 論語), it corresponds well with his general view of family relation.

63 Qingping Liu, "Filiality versus Sociality and Individuality: On Confucianism as 'Consanguinitism,'" *Philosophy East and West* 53 (2003), 234–50.

64 See the articles in the March and June 2008 issues of the journal *Dao*, which were contributions to the symposium titled "Filial Piety: Root of Morality or Source of Corruption." Most articles there offer critical rejoinders from various fronts to Liu's provocative interpretation of Confucian ethics as consanguinitism.

65 *Analects* 1:2.

66 *Analects* 2:5.

67 *Analects* 4:18.

passage just quoted from the *Analects* (4:18), even though Confucius's eminent concern seems to be with children's moral power (i.e., filiality) to constrain themselves within the moral boundary set between themselves and their parents, and to remain responsible to it, he does accept remonstration as the way to exercise its filiality as long as it does not go against the very spirit of filiality, although it would upset the existing moral relationship. *Xiaojing* 孝經 (*The Book of Filial Reverence*), which became canonized during the Han dynasty in which Confucianism was tethered with Legalism and *xiao* 孝 (filial piety) with *zhong* 忠 (loyalty), records the conversation between Confucius (C) and Zengzi (Z), Confucius's disciple who is most famous for his great filial piety.[68]

Z: I would presume to ask whether children can be deemed filial simply by obeying every command of their father.

C: What on earth are you saying? What on earth are you saying? Of old, an Emperor has seven ministers who would remonstrate with him, so even if he had no vision of the proper way, he still did not lose the empire. The high nobles had five ministers who would remonstrate with them, so even if they had no vision of the proper way, they still did not lose their states. The high officials had three ministers who would remonstrate with them, so even if they had no vision of the proper way, they still did not lose their clans. If the lower officials had just one friend who would remonstrate with them, they were still able to preserve their good names; if a father has a son who will remonstrate with him, he will not behave reprehensively. Thus, if confronted by reprehensible behavior on his father's part, a son has no choice but to remonstrate with his father, and if confronted by reprehensible behavior on his ruler's part, a minister has no choice but to remonstrate with his ruler. Hence, remonstrance is the only response to immorality. How could simply obeying the commands of one's father be deemed filial?[69]

Likewise, while acknowledging the general principle that father and son had better not demand goodness from each other (by means of admonition and remonstration),[70] Mencius was not ashamed of his friendship with Kuang Zhang, whom people found unfilial but who in reality came to be at odds with his father because of his relentless remonstration with him over a moral issue.[71] Here we should not mistakenly assume that Mencius, who was in favor of a father's authority over his son, prohibited a son's remonstration with his father.

[68] Even though the authenticity of this conversation is questionable, it does not hurt my key argument that Confucianism embraces a son's moral remonstration with his father as part of filial responsibility. Quite the contrary, *Xiaojing*'s notoriety that the book itself was fabricated precisely to give predominance to authority figures (like king and father) reinforces my argument – that is, even *Xiaojing*, as conservative as it is, admits what I call Confucian incivility as integral to Confucian civility.

[69] *Xiaojing* 15. The English translation is adopted from Henry Rosemont Jr. and Roger T. Ames, *The Chinese Classic of Family Reverence: A Philosophical Translation of the Xiaojing* (Honolulu: University of Hawaii Press, 2009), 114.

[70] *Mencius* 4A18.

[71] *Mencius* 4B30.

Rather, what Mencius was concerned about was the mutual estrangement between father and son, namely, a complete disruption of their moral relationship. For Mencius, what was troublesome was extreme remonstration that would lead to estrangement; like Confucius, he embraced gentle remonstration as part of filial responsibility.

Even Xunzi, otherwise known as Mencius's archrival, offered strong defense of the occasion in which a son can be reasonably disobedient to the father and is even required to show moral remonstration, and called it "great filiality."

> Of filial sons who do not follow the course of action mandated by their fathers, there are three types. If following the mandated course would bring peril to his family whereas not following it would bring security, then the filial son who does not follow his commission still acts with true loyalty. If following his mandated course would bring disgrace on his family whereas not following it would bring honor, then in not following the mandated course he still acts morally. If following the mandated course would cause him to act like a savage whereas not following it would cultivate and improve him, then in not following it he still acts with proper reverence. Hence, if it were possible to have followed the course, not to have done so would constitute not being a proper son. If it were impossible to follow the course, to have done so would be disloyalty. If a son understands the principles of when to follow and when not to follow and is able to be utterly respectful and reverent, loyal and honest, straightforward and diligent, so that he carefully attends his conduct, then he may properly be called "greatly filial."[72]

From the shared emphasis on the necessity of filial remonstrance of these three canonical Confucians, three points can be gleaned. First, in Confucianism family is not posited as possessing unalloyed moral identity and monolithic moral value (most likely the father's moral value) that must be uniformly imposed on every member of the family. What is striking in the passages from the Confucian classics is that moral pluralism within the family is treated not as an anomaly (hence as something to be eliminated) but as integral to any ordinary family life (and by extension social life). Second, Confucianism takes harmony within the family not as primordially granted in terms of consanguinity but as a state that has to be socially achieved through the harmonizing process that involves incivilities such as (gentle) remonstration and admonition – the Confucian equivalents to civil dialogue. In other words, the moral and social system of Confucian civility, to which filiality is central, embraces incivility as its indispensable part. Finally, and more generally speaking, the virtue of incivility lies in its unique moral power by which to revise the existing (often morally problematic) social relationship and thereby reinvigorate social viability.

It is important to note that in Confucianism what is civil is not merely what is rational as is in liberalism.[73] Rather, Confucian civility encompasses both

[72] *Xunzi* 29:2. The English translation of the *Xunzi* 荀子 is adopted from John Knoblock, *Xunzi: A Translation and Study of Complete Works*, 3 vols. (Stanford: Stanford University Press, 1988, 1990, 1994).

[73] Recently, though, political theorists have shown that even deontological liberalism, characteristic of John Rawls's and Jürgen Habermas's rationalist political theories, does not completely

rational and sentimental elements as the ethical system of the *li* is rooted in the complex psychosocial mixture of what we now analytically differentiate as reason and emotion. This means that Confucian civil talk does include some affective sentiments. Or rather, in a profound sense, Confucian civility (including incivility) is grounded in affective emotions. Hence, Mencius defended the plaintive note (*yuan* 怨) in the chapter titled "Xiao Pan (小弁)" in the *Shijing* 詩經 against the charge that it was the poem of a petty man (*xiao ren* 小人) by saying, "The plaintive note is due to the poet's feeling of intimate concern for his parent (*qin-qin* 親親). To feel this is benevolence (*qin qin ren ye* 親親仁也).... Not to complain about a major wrong committed by one's parent is to feel insufficient concern; on the other hand, to complain about a minor wrong is to react too violently. Insufficient concern and too violent a reaction are both actions of a bad son."[74]

To distinguish *yuan* (whose common English translation is resentment) in the sense that Mencius is employing here from the Western concept of resentment, which denotes antisocial or uncivil passion, let us call it "affective resentment." Then, we can conclude that Confucian incivility (particularly in the context of familial relations) is animated by affective resentment; ironically, it is by virtue of affective resentment that what Xunzi calls "great filiality" (*da xiao* 大孝) can be achieved. By implication, civility, for its viability, must be buttressed by the appropriate use of incivility.[75] In the end, a Confucian family is not a static haven of enlarged affection but a dynamic ethical arena in which each member experiences personal moral growth through dialogic interactions.

In Political Relations

Even though in Confucianism the political relation between ruler and subject is commonly rationalized in familial terms, classical Confucians (particularly Confucius and Mencius) believed the relation was essentially a moral one mediated by the principle of *yi* (righteousness). Of course, the righteous relationship between ruler and subject (*Jun chen yi he*) is qualitatively different from social contract theory, particularly of the Hobbesian kind, because its semifamilial moral relation makes both parties (yet more so for the subject) difficult to dissociate from the other.

On the other hand, the ruler-subject relation is also distinct from the principle of *Jun wei chen gang* ("The ruler is the subject's supreme lord") established

dismiss sentimental components. See Patchen Markell, "Making Affect Safe for Democracy? On 'Constitutional Patriotism,'" *Political Theory* 28 (2000), 38–63 and Sharon R. Krause, *Civil Passions: Moral Sentiment and Democratic Deliberation* (Princeton: Princeton University Press, 2008). I come back to this issue in Chapter 5, where I articulate what Confucian public reason consists of.

74 *Mencius* 6B3.

75 The political implication of the idea of "affective resentment" will be further illuminated in Chapters 5 and 8. Here suffice it to say that in a viable Confucian democratic society, dissent is expressed as a form of care; dissent is always a call to improve the society.

during the Han dynasty, in that it is more concerned with the moral quality of the relationship, not with the inseparable and rigidly hierarchical relationship as reformulated under imperialism. It was by having in mind the righteous relationship between ruler and subject that Confucius was able to urge his students not to take public office if the Way does not prevail (*Bang wu dao ze bu shi* 邦無道則不仕).[76]

In traditional Confucian politics, when the ruler went astray (hence signaling no Way in his court), one of the most powerful weapons that a subject could avail himself of in demanding the ruler to maintain righteousness in their moral-political relationship was to withdraw to his hometown as a form of remonstration. But the most common way, and the very method classical Confucians recommended, was verbal remonstration. For instance, Confucius, who recommended gentle remonstration in the case of the father-son relationship, opted for a more intense form of remonstrance when it came to the subject's remonstration with the ruler: "Let there be no duplicity and take a stand against him (*Wu si ye er fan zhi* 勿斯也而犯之)."[77] This statement may seem to be contrary to Youzi's statement that we have already seen earlier – that a person who has a sense of filial and fraternal responsibility (*xiaoti*) would rarely have a taste for "defying authority" (*fan shang*).[78] However, it is not far-fetched to assume that by *shang* 上 Youzi meant primarily (if not exclusively) an authority figure (say, father) in familial relations, not necessarily a political authority. Besides, "rarely" (*xian* 鮮) is not tantamount to "never."

What is certain, though, is that Confucius thought a minister is the one who serves his lord with the Way (*dao* 道) and resigns when he cannot.[79] And it is for this reason that he blamed his former student Ranyou who was then working for the Ji clan (the usurper of Lu, Confucius's home country) for failing to save his lords from grave impropriety such as the use of the imperial eight rows of eight dancers in the courtyard of their estate.[80] Furthermore, when Ranyou, in gathering revenues for the Ji clan, added even more to their coffers, Confucius urged his students to "sound the charge and attack" him.[81] What was lacking in Ranyou was the virtue of incivility, the moral power to correct (*zheng* 正) and remonstrate with those who wielded the political power.

On the other hand, Confucius exhorted rulers to express civility and heed subjects' loyal and faithful incivility, namely, their moral-political remonstrations. When Duke Ding inquired whether there was any one saying that could ruin a state, Confucius replied, "A saying itself cannot have such effect, but there is the saying, 'I find little pleasure in ruling, save that no one will take

[76] *Analects* 8:13; 14:1; 15:6.
[77] *Analects* 14:22.
[78] *Analects* 1:2.
[79] *Analects* 11:24.
[80] *Analects* 3:6.
[81] *Analects* 11:17.

exception to what I say.' If what one has to say is [morally] good (*shan* 善) and no one takes exception, fine indeed. But if what one has to say is not good and no one takes exception, is this not close to a saying ruining a state?"[82] Here Confucius explicates clearly that the ruler and the subject, to achieve benevolent (*ren*) government, must engage in civil dialogue: the subject must take exceptional measures (e.g., remonstration) if what the ruler is saying is not efficacious (*shan*); the ruler, on the other hand, must be open to such exceptional measures (namely, incivilities) for the sake of the common good, which is the proper aim of the state. In the same vein, Mencius rationalized the subject's intensive remonstration with the ruler by saying somewhat paradoxically that "[t]o curb the lord is to love him."[83]

Mencius, however, went further than Confucius in his justification (or espousal, rather) of the subject's remonstration with the ruler to the extent to which the subject's moral-political obligation of remonstration was recast into a moral privilege (even a kind of political *right*) bestowed by Heaven on the Way-following scholar-officials.[84] "The great man (*da ren* 大人)[85] alone can rectify the evils in the prince's heart (*ge jun xin zhi fei* 格君心之非). When the prince is benevolent, everyone else is benevolent; when the prince is dutiful, everyone else is dutiful; when the prince is correct, everyone else is correct. Simply by rectifying the prince (*yi zheng jun* 一正君) one can put the state on a firm basis."[86] Once elevated to be a moral privilege, in Mencius, the righteous duty to rectify the ruler (*ge jun* 格君 or *zheng jun* 正君) is then diametrically opposed to docility. "The great man," argued Mencius, "does not consider obedience or docility (*shun* 順) the norm (*zheng* 正), which is nothing but the way of a wife or concubine."[87] If the ruler demands from his subjects (unconditional) obedience or docility, and further harasses and punishes those who have offered him a righteous remonstration, it is as though he treats them as an "enemy."

If a prince treats his subjects as his hands and feet, they will treat him as their belly and heart. If he treats them as his horses and hounds, they will treat him as a stranger. If treats them as mud and weeds, they will treat him as an enemy (*kouchou* 寇讎).... Today when a subject whose advice has been rejected to the detriment of the people

[82] *Analects* 13:15 (translation modified).

[83] *Mencius* 1B4. Also see *Xunzi* 32:2–3.

[84] This, however, is not to argue that Mencius did not cherish the virtue of self-restraining civilities such as *gong*, *jian*, *xiao*, and *di* 弟 (see *Mencius* 4A16; 6B2).

[85] In *Mencius* 3B3, Mencius defines the great (*da ren* or *da zhang fu* 大丈夫) as a man who "lives in the spacious dwelling, occupies the proper position, and goes along the highway of the Empire [and who,] when has achieved his ambition, shares these with the people; when has failed to do so, practices the Way (*dao*) alone."

[86] *Mencius* 4A20.

[87] *Mencius* 3B2. I admit that here Mencius's view is arguably masculine and it is far from my intention to argue that docility is a woman's virtue. My point is simply that Mencius did not consider docility a virtue.

has occasion to leave, the prince puts him in chains, makes things difficult for him in the state he is going to and takes his land the day he leaves. This is what is meant by "enemy" (*kouchou*). What mourning is there for an enemy?[88]

Mencius's reasoning is strikingly radical: if the ruler treats his subjects as an "enemy" by imposing docility on his subjects (and further by punishing them unrightfully), the righteous relationship (*yihe* 義合) between them becomes null and void. Not only that, upon the catastrophic dissolution of the relationship, the subject is morally entitled to regard his ruler as a stranger (that is, as "nobody" with whom he has no meaningful relational ties) and can even treat him as an enemy. Since there is no moral relationship, there is no moral obligation left for the subject to pay due ritual propriety (such as mourning) to the ruler. In extreme circumstances, subjects (particularly ministers of royal blood) can rightfully replace the ruler.[89]

Civil Confucianism toward Confucian Democracy

I do not think Confucian communitarianism is a misguided political project toward Confucian democracy. Quite the contrary: considering numerous social and political problems explicitly and/or implicitly associated with increasingly individualistic liberal democracy, and given that this particular mode of democracy has become the "only game in town" (as political scientists call it) in today's globalized and still globalizing world, the pursuit of Confucian communitarianism is culturally meaningful and politically important. Therefore, my purpose here should not be misunderstood as denouncing Confucian communitarianism because of its potential problems, especially its tendency to cultivate docility. My aim is rather to explore how Confucian communitarianism can be saved from such potential problems by reinventing communitarian Confucianism into *civil Confucianism* by reconceiving Confucianism in the light of the virtue of incivility, an ethical resource indispensable to maintaining a self-revising, thus more viable, civil society.

Finally, I want to close by discussing a methodological merit of theorizing civil Confucianism in the political theoretical construct of Confucian democracy as a political vision and social practice.

Despite growing interest in Confucian democracy both in empirical political scientists and in normative political theorists/philosophers over the past two decades, there has been a noticeable gap between these two groups of scholars in understanding Confucian democracy. The first group, consisting of empirical political scientists, attributes East Asian countries' dramatic and remarkably

88 *Mencius* 4B3.

89 *Mencius* 5B9. In this sense, we may call Mencius the first political theorist of political liberty in the Confucian tradition. See Sungmoon Kim, "The Origin of Political Liberty in Confucianism: A Nietzschean Interpretation," *History of Political Thought* 29 (2008), 393–415.

successful democratization in the 1980s and afterward to their contentious civil societies (e.g., Taiwan and South Korea).[90] Some of these scholars suspect and attempt to prove that the contentious and deeply ethical character of these civil societies in East Asia has a profound connection with their traditional Confucian culture.[91]

What is problematic about Confucian communitarianism is that its characteristic emphasis of social harmony and personal moral growth does not adequately come to terms with the real political experiences of the East Asian societies. More specifically, Confucian communitarianism, as currently formulated, does not do a good job in explicating politically important questions such as why East Asians grew discontented with the incumbent authoritarian regimes, on what cultural and ethical ground they were able to justify their contentious civil actions against existing political regimes, and how they are still struggling with their new democracies. In short, while possessing an excellent virtue when it comes to consolidating an institutionally stable democratic regime, Confucian communitarianism is critically limited in understanding and also rendering political support to democratizing and newly democratized East Asian countries.

By making incivility indispensable and integral to Confucian communitarianism, civil Confucianism paves, both theoretically and practically, a much smoother path toward Confucian democracy. Not only does it admit the virtue of civility that is necessary at the stage of democratic consolidation, but it also embraces incivility by which to express moral and political discontent toward the existing social and political order. Although civil Confucianism is not directly tantamount to Confucian democracy, it is no doubt a great vehicle toward Confucian democracy in both transitioning and consolidating periods.

[90] Muthiah Alaqappa (ed.), *Civil Society and Political Change in Asia: Expanding and Contracting Democratic Space* (Stanford: Stanford University Press, 2004); David C. Schak and Wayne Hudson (eds.), *Civil Society in Asia* (Burlington, VT: Ashgate, 2003); Sunhyuk Kim, *The Politics of Democratization in Korea: The Role of Civil Society* (Pittsburgh: University of Pittsburgh Press, 2000).

[91] Hein Cho, "The Historical Origin of Civil Society in Korea," *Korea Journal* 37 (1997), 24–41; Sangjun Kim, "The Genealogy of Confucian *Moralpolitik* and Its Implications for Modern Civil Society," in *Korean Society: Civil Society, Democracy, and the State*, e. Charles K. Armstrong (London: Routledge, 2002), 57–91.

3

Against Meritocratic Elitism

Though some still remain skeptical of the possibility of Confucian democracy as an integrated value system,[1] a great number of scholars who study East Asia are increasingly persuaded that Confucian democracy can offer a viable political alternative to liberal democracy. As we have seen in the preceding chapters, the most dominant mode of Confucian democracy suggested thus far is a Confucian communitarian democracy, and its advocates have been mainly concentrated on the communitarian critique of liberal rights-based individualism by drawing attention to the "democratic" values implicated in Confucian ritual practices.

As Daniel Bell argues, however, recent studies of Confucian democracy lack detailed institutional prescriptions. In Bell's view, by understanding democracy as a set of values, a way of life, or a set of social conditions, the existing literature of Confucian democracy dismisses the dimension of democracy as a political system, thus offering no practical contribution to the constitutional design of Confucian democracy in the nonideal situation.[2] Bell's key argument is that Western-style liberal democracy is not plausible in Confucian societies, where there remains a strong tradition of respect for meritocratically chosen political elites, and therefore the most culturally relevant form of democracy in such societies is a meritocratic democracy.[3] Thus Bell says that in Confucian societies "it is tempting to conceive of the possibility of reconciling the Confucian

[1] For such skepticism, see Chenyang Li, "Confucian Value and Democratic Value," *Journal of Value Inquiry* 31 (1997), 183–93; Ruiping Fan, *Reconstructionist Confucianism: Rethinking Morality after the West* (Dordrecht: Springer, 2010).

[2] Daniel A. Bell, *Beyond Liberal Democracy: Political Thinking for an East Asian Context* (Princeton: Princeton University Press, 2006), esp. chap. 6 ("Taking Elitism Seriously: Democracy with Confucian Characteristics").

[3] As I noted in the Introduction (note 44) by drawing on Doh Chull Shin's recent survey data, however, this claim is not empirically supported.

emphasis on rule by wise and virtuous elites with the democratic values of popular participation, accountability, and transparency."[4] In the same vein, Joseph Chan concludes his essay on the possibility of Confucian democracy by saying, "How to combine democracy and meritocracy is one of the most interesting and challenging issues for Confucianism today."[5] Echoing Bell and Chan, Tongdong Bai asserts that Confucian democracy should be a limited or thin democracy in which popular sovereignty or the citizens' political equality is properly limited by Confucianism's meritocratic/elitist consideration.[6]

As an institutional mechanism to reconcile meritocracy and democracy, Bell and Bai propose the exam model and leveled model, respectively. Bell's exam model, which is inspired by the imperial civil service examination system employed in premodern China, proposes a bicameral legislature with a democratically elected lower house and an upper house – which Bell names Xianshiyuan (賢士院) or House of Virtue and Talent – composed of deputies selected on the basis of competitive examination. What is distinctively "Confucian" about this proposal, according to Bell, is its resolution of the possible gridlock between the two houses by means of "a constitutional formula providing supermajorities in the upper house with the right to override majorities in the lower house."[7]

While Bell's model, focused on the legislature, supports a limited representative democracy, Bai's leveled model is less agreeable with competitive election because of its entanglement with special interests, and thus is more geared toward meritocracy. According to Bai's model, common people are allowed to participate in local affairs, with which they are familiar, but not in higher level (i.e., national or central governmental) affairs that are beyond their grasp. Only local officials can participate in decision-making processes in the national/central government because they are "free from specialized jobs and exposed to policy-making on a local level that is itself often connected with policies on a higher level."[8] That is, Bai's model embraces electoral democracy on a local level but rejects any democratic procedures on the national level.[9]

Certainly, the meritocratic approach of Confucian democracy has a few theoretical and practical advantages. First, it transcends the conventional

4 Bell, *Beyond Liberal Democracy*, 152.

5 Joseph Chan, "Democracy and Meritocracy: Toward a Confucian Perspective," *Journal of Chinese Philosophy* 34 (2007), 191.

6 Tongdong Bai, "A Mencian Version of Limited Democracy," *Res Publica* 14 (2008), 19–34.

7 Bell, *Beyond Liberal Democracy*, 171.

8 Bai, "Limited Democracy," 28.

9 In Bai's essay, the distinction between exam model and leveled model is not always clear. In fact, Bai admits that the two models are "complementary and can be further combined." Ibid., 29. For example, public officials can be recruited through the competitive civil examinations. What is unclear in Bai's proposal, however, is whether or not it embraces the liberal constitutional separation of the three branches of the government and how they operate relative to one another. If the existence of the three branches of the government is assumed in his model, it is still unclear how legislators, for instance, are selected.

opposition between Western liberal democracy and Confucian authoritarianism, the problematic dichotomy to which many social and political scientists including Samuel Huntington subscribe. While doing justice to Confucianism's meritocratic characteristics, Confucian democracy of this kind tries to accommodate – yet only minimally – the democratic value of popular participation (if not the democratic ideal of popular sovereignty). Second, without resorting to the liberal constitutional mechanism of checks and balances among the three branches of government, it can still safeguard itself from the evil of democratic tyranny or the tyranny of majority that an electoral democracy (especially in newly democratized countries) is susceptible to.

That being said, however, both the proposal and the models of Confucian meritocratic democracy are problematic. First, proponents of Confucian meritocratic democracy present Confucianism as naturally upholding political elitism, but this presentation is premised on the mistaken assumption that political elitism is the natural corollary of Confucian virtue politics (*dezhi* 德治). While the latter (*dezhi*) was upheld by all classical Confucians who were genuinely committed to the Confucian ideal of benevolent government (*ren zheng* 仁政), a form of government that best serves the moral and material welfare of the people, the former (political elitism), which emerged only after the *politicization* of Confucianism during the imperial period, was essentially of a Legalist origin, concerned more with the security and stability of the state than with the welfare (particularly the moral well-being) of the people.[10] The realization that Confucian virtue politics as a form of moral statesmanship is qualitatively different from meritocratic elitism, and that it is committed to the moral and material well-being of the people, should encourage any contemporary Confucian, particularly a *Confucian democrat*, to find a way to realize this Confucian moral commitment in drastically altered socioeconomic, cultural, and political environments in modern East Asian societies. I seriously doubt that meritocratic elitism can serve the *differentiated* welfare of the people in modern East Asia who are increasingly pluralistic (ethically, politically, and culturally) and simultaneously plagued by massive socioeconomic inequalities.

Second, the proposed models of Confucian meritocratic democracy fail to reflect the recent political experiences in democratized (or still democratizing) East Asian societies in, for instance, South Korea and Taiwan. Democratization there was vitalized by active civil societies, and it is widely agreed that the presence of active and viable civil society is indispensable to their continued democratization or democratic consolidation.[11] Moreover, the models' top-down

[10] On the formation and development of the exam-based bureaucratic system during imperial China, see Etienne Balazs, *Chinese Civilization and Bureaucracy*, trans. H. M. Wright, ed. Arthur F. Wright (New Haven: Yale University Press, 1964).

[11] See Sunhyuk Kim, "South Korea: Confrontational Legacy and Democratic Contributions" and Yun Fan, "Taiwan: No Civil Society, No Democracy," both in Alaqappa, *Civil Society and Political Change in Asia*.

approach to governance and their singular focus on the *governability* of the people dismiss wholesale the moral and political transformative power of democratic civil society – the power of reinventing private individuals absorbed in their private interests into public-spirited citizens. By regarding the people only as myopic consumers in both the economic and political marketplace, the meritocratic institutionalization of Confucian democracy is likely to promote passive consumerism rather than democratic citizenship, without giving full credit to their moral capacity to become citizens, namely, their moral and political *transformability*: one of the most characteristic and persistent features of the Confucian tradition.

In this chapter, I attempt to critique the meritocratic justification of Confucian democracy from the standpoint of democratic civil society by shifting the focus from *governability* of the people to their *transformability*. My central claims are, first, that Confucian virtue politics can be creatively reappropriated in a democratic civil society in terms of cultivating public civility in the ordinary people who belong to different moral communities;[12] second, in modern East Asian societies the ideal of Confucian benevolent government can be better attained by means of democratic contestation especially by the victims of socioeconomic injustice in the public space of civil society than by thin/minimal democracy controlled by meritocratic elitism. That is, the *differentiated* welfare of the people can be served more effectively and legitimately in a Confucian democratic regime only if there is a viable "Confucian civil society," *a democratic civil society operating on Confucian public civility and serving the differentiated moral and material well-being of the citizens.*

Confucianism, Meritocracy, and Democracy: A Critical Investigation

Admittedly, Confucian politics is a virtue politics as premodern Confucians understood it in terms of *dezhi* 德治. Central to Confucian virtue politics is the assumption that the ruler's moral virtue is the single greatest locomotive of good government, which critics of Confucianism such as Hanfeizi, the famous Legalist, found utterly naïve.[13] The gist of Confucian virtue politics can be recapitulated as follows: only a ruler who is morally virtuous by correcting himself or by cultivating his moral goodness can govern the people properly, that is, make them equally morally good.[14]

This does not mean that Confucians persist in any mythical causality between the ruler's moral virtue and good government. To attain good

[12] This normative claim is supported by actual political experience in East Asian societies. For an interesting study on Taiwan, see David C. Schak, "The Development of Civility in Taiwan," *Public Affairs* 82 (2009), 447–65.

[13] Eric L. Hutton, "Han Feizi's Criticism of Confucianism and its Implications for Virtue Ethics," *Journal of Moral Philosophy* 5 (2008), 423–53.

[14] See *Analects* 2:3.

government, namely "benevolent government" (*ren zheng* 仁政), the ruler's moral virtue must be socially mediated by benevolent public policies.[15] But Confucians never doubt that it is the ruler's moral virtue that propels him to implement benevolent public policies and thereby realize benevolent government. The question is whether Confucian virtue politics implies meritocratic elitism.

Originally, Confucian virtue politics presupposed only *one* ruler, namely the king, and its goal lies in making the incumbent king, who has assumed the throne according to his hereditary right, morally virtuous so that he can commit himself to the material and, more important, moral welfare of the people. The problem is that Confucian virtue politics can hardly be effective in the nonideal world where the king is not necessarily virtuous. Even if he is morally virtuous, the king alone cannot handle all public affairs properly to ensure his government is benevolent. Therefore, a king needs those who can aid his government and, more important, those who can enlighten him about the Dao by teaching Confucian classics or by remonstrating with him (according to Confucian rituals) if he goes astray. Those who take part in government should be "good and wise" to assume the role of the king's aide or teacher, or ideally both. This is the ideal of the Confucian "scholar-official" that, I believe, has inspired many proponents of Confucian meritocracy (especially Bell).[16] If Confucian meritocracy means rule by the good and wise, then, it can be admitted that meritocratic elitism is implied in Confucian virtue politics.

The meritocratic elitism that contemporary Confucian proponents propose, however, is a normative belief that "only those who acquire knowledge and virtue ought to participate in government, and the common people are not presumed to possess the capacities necessary for substantial political participation."[17] Such a view obscures the original Confucian concern with whether those who actually take part in government *really* aid the king properly with benevolent public policies or make him virtuous. What is more salient is the question of who is *entitled* to take part in government. Thus it is understandable why contemporary proponents of Confucian meritocracy distinguish citizens into two classes – intellectual elites on one hand and the common people on the other. For instance, Daniel Bell draws attention to two phrases in the *Analects* to support this distinction of the citizens.[18]

[15] See Sungmoon Kim, "The Secret of Confucian *Wuwei* Statecraft: Mencius's Political Theory of Responsibility," *Asian Philosophy* 20 (2010), 27–42.

[16] Bell, *Beyond Liberal Democracy*, 164–5. Also see Jiang Qing, *A Confucian Constitutional Order: How China's Ancient Past Can Shape Its Political Future*, ed. Daniel A. Bell and Ruiping Fan, trans. Edmund Ryden (Princeton: Princeton University Press, 2012), 48–55, which inspired Bell's Confucian bicameralism.

[17] Bell, *Beyond Liberal Democracy*, 154.

[18] Ibid., 153n8. In fact, Bell cities one more (*Analects* 12:19), but I do not see its relevance to the so-called Confucian tradition of respect for a ruling elite.

The Master said, "The common people can be induced to travel along the way, but they cannot be induced to realize it."[19]

Confucius said, "Knowledge acquired through a natural propensity for it is its highest level; knowledge acquired through study is the next highest; something learned in response to difficulties encountered is again the next highest. But those among the common people who do not learn even when vexed with difficulties – they are at the bottom of the heap."[20]

Unfortunately, Bell does not explain why he thinks these phrases vindicate Confucius's endorsement of meritocratic elitism as a *political rule*. All I see in the phrases (particularly in the second), though, is the philosophical rationale for why common people should be educated – an idea that was quite revolutionary in Confucius's own time[21] – and Confucius's lamentation concerning *some* hopeless cases.[22] The first quote has nothing to do with the cognitive limitation of the common people. According to Ames and Rosemont, the point here is that everyone can find a place on the Way (*dao* 道), even when they do not participate in constructing it, which is the task of the cultural heroes of every generation.[23] If Ames and Rosemont are correct, what is at issue is not so much the contrast between political elites and ordinary people but the contrast between the makers of the Way (sage-kings such as Yao, Shun, Yu, Tang, Wen, and Wu) and its ardent followers.[24] This interpretation is also consistent with Mencius's statement that "people [under a sage-king] move daily towards goodness without realizing who it is that brings this about."[25] At any rate, the passages are not about who is entitled to participate in government but on the need of moral education or the "educability" of the people, nor do the passages imply or justify a political rule of a few elites over the many.[26]

Tongdong Bai offers a more textually grounded justification for Confucian meritocratic democracy and the text he focuses on is the *Mengzi*. Bai begins by quoting Mencius's famous answer for the question of whether a ruler should

[19] *Analects* 8:9. Unless noted otherwise, all English translations of the *Lunyu* 論語 in this chapter are adopted from Roger T. Ames and Henry Rosemont Jr., *The Analects of Confucius: A Philosophical Translation* (New York: Ballantine Books, 1998).

[20] *Analects* 16:9.

[21] See H. G. Creel, *Confucius and the Chinese Way* (New York: Harper & Row, 1960), 75–99.

[22] Such "helpless cases" (i.e., those who refused to be educated) include Zai Wo, Confucius's own student (*Analects* 17:21).

[23] Ames and Rosemont, *Analects of Confucius*, 243n125.

[24] If we understand the ancient sage-kings as the founders of the constitution based on Confucian ritual (*li* 禮), Confucius's key concern in *Analects* 8:9 seems to be with civic virtue (a willingness to follow the Kingly Way), not with elitist rule.

[25] *Mencius* 7A13 (modified). Unless noted otherwise, all English translations of the *Mengzi* 孟子 in this chapter are adopted from *Mencius*, trans. D. C. Lau (New York: Penguin, 1970).

[26] On the "educability" of the people and its Confucian democratic implications, see Fred Dallmayr, "Exiting Liberal Democracy: Bell and Confucian Thought," *Philosophy East and West* 59 (2009), 524–30.

work in the field like his subjects. "There are affairs of great men, and there are affairs of small men.... There are those who use their minds and there are those who use their muscles. The former rule; the latter are ruled. Those who rule are supported by those who are ruled. This is a principle accepted by the whole world."[27] If we dismiss the context of this passage,[28] it seems to endorse meritocratic elitism, a rule by great men (*da ren* 大人), who use their minds, over the small men (*xiao ren* 小人), who use their muscles such as artisans and farmers. Bai understands the gist of the passages as follows:

> [T]he priority for the "great men" or rulers of focusing on how to promote the material and moral well-being of the "small men" or the common people makes it impossible for them to do any menial tasks. Similarly, it is implied that those whose time and energy is consumed by daily labour, thus rendering them unable to pay any serious attention to political matters, cannot undertake the task of ruling the state. The labourers Mencius talks about are farmers and artisans, but it is reasonable to include in this group a lot of today's "white-collar" professionals, such as scientists, engineers, doctors, financiers, teachers, and so on ... because many of them are consumed by their daily work, and many have limited knowledge about public affairs or anything outside of their narrow specializations.[29]

Bai, however, overlooks the fact that sage-king Shun and Yi Yin, sage-king Tang's sagacious minister, were formerly farmers who never had formal training or experience in public affairs. Shun and Yi Yin, who must have been "consumed by daily labor," were handpicked by sage-kings Yao and Tang solely on the basis of their excellent moral virtue.[30] Contrary to Bai's expectation, Mencius acclaims the appointment of these former farmers to the highest public post because for Mencius the most important (if not the only) qualification for public service is moral goodness, which does not necessarily have to be accompanied by knowledge, foresight, or even a settled character. When the state Lu wished to entrust the government to Yuezengzi, Mencius's student, an inquiry was raised about the key qualification to become a good official and whether or not Yuezengzi possessed them. "'Has Yuezengzi great strength of character?' 'No.' 'Is he a man of thought and foresight?' 'No.' 'Is he widely informed?' 'No.' 'Then why were you so happy that you could not sleep [upon hearing Yuezengzi's possible appointment]?' 'He is a man who is drawn to the good.' 'Is that enough?' 'To be drawn to the good is more than enough to

[27] *Mencius* 3A4 (quoted from Bai, "Limited Democracy," 26).

[28] The context is that Mencius was challenging Zhen Xiang (ultimately, his teacher Xu Xing, the Agriculturalist, who was persuaded that the wise ruler shares the work of tilling the land with his people). Mencius's main point here is not so much about the division of labor between two distinct social classes of people but about the seriousness of the work the ruler (the king in this case) does, which is rarely recognized by ordinary people because it does not appear to "produce things."

[29] Bai, "Limited Democracy," 26.

[30] *Mencius* 5A1 for Shun and 5A7 for Yi Yin.

cope with the whole world, let alone the state of Lu.'"[31] Therefore, Bai's claim that those involved in menial work cannot become great men and thus are not qualified to take part in government does not find strong support in Mencius's political thought.[32] Moreover, it is problematic to identify great men and small men purely in *political* terms (as rulers and commoners) because for Mencius what distinguishes one from the other is not so much sociopolitical status but moral character. "He who is guided by the interests of the parts of his person that are of greater importance is a great man; he who is guided by the interests of the parts of his person that are of smaller importance is a small men," says Mencius.[33]

This is not to argue, however, that Mencius was a (proto-)democratic thinker, as is often claimed.[34] Living in the ancient feudal world, Mencius never challenged the existing social distinction between the aristocratic class and the laypeople. In fact, he (and all other premodern Confucians including Confucius) never questioned the moral legitimacy of the monarchical system even if he believed the ideal way to transmit the throne was by abdication (*shanrang* 禪讓).[35]

Bai, however, attempts to take full advantage of the social distinction of the people that is presupposed in the text of the *Mengzi* when he says "the 'people' in *Mencius* should be translated literally as 'the men in the capital (*guo ren* 國人),' who were originally taken to be superior to the people in the 'wild' (*ye ren* 野人).... Therefore, it is reasonable to take 'the men in the capital' as the common people in general."[36] Bai's point is that not all commoners are allowed to take part in government; only a qualified few are. Bai's interpretation, however, is mistaken in that it takes Mencius's acquiescence to feudal aristocracy for his active espousal of it by equating feudal aristocracy with Confucian moral meritocracy.

[31] *Mencius* 6B13. Here Mencius reminds us that Confucian meritocracy, where the only meaningful "merit" is one's moral virtue, is far from an epistocracy of the brightest as the contemporary advocates of meritocratic elitism often claim.

[32] Bai presents Mencius as holding a pejorative view of menial works because they are "animals' activities." But nowhere in the *Mengzi* does Mencius present menial works as animals' activities. In my view, the Mencius in Bai's interpretation is more Aristotelian than Mencian. On the Aristotelian contempt of menial works in terms of animal activities, see Hannah Arendt, *The Human Condition* (Chicago: University of Chicago Press, 1958).

[33] *Mencius* 6A15.

[34] For an important corrective to this widely held view, see Justin Tiwald, "A Right of Rebellion in the *Mengzi*?," *Dao* 7 (2008), 269–82.

[35] *Mencius* 5A5. That being said, it is highly controversial whether Mencius actively advocated abdication. For an argument countering this view, see Yuri Pines, *Envisioning Eternal Empire: Chinese Political Thought of the Warring States Era* (Honolulu: University of Hawaii Press, 2009), 71–6; Sungmoon Kim, "Confucian Constitutionalism: Mencius and Xunzi on Virtue, Ritual, and Royal Transmission," *Review of Politics* 73 (2011), 371–99.

[36] Bai, "Limited Democracy," 27.

Certainly, Mencius maintains that morally cultivated persons (great men) *should* rule those who are not (small men). In this regard, it can be rightly claimed that Mencius supports "meritocracy," in which merit (i.e., moral virtue) *ought* to be the most important qualification for political leaders and public officials. However, there is no compelling reason to believe that Confucian moral meritocracy thus envisioned ought to be nested in rigid sociopolitical distinctions among people. The fundamental confusion in recent proposals for Confucian meritocracy is that they see meritocracy as one of the particular systems of political government on par with monarchy, aristocracy, or democracy.

However, meritocracy (as Confucians understood it) refers only to the *character* of any such political system, not the institutional distribution of power itself. It should be recalled that premodern Confucians were strongly convinced that Confucian moral meritocracy could be perfectly realizable under monarchical rule or alongside the aristocracy of the Confucian literati. For instance, for ancient Confucians, on whom most contemporary Confucian advocates of political meritocracy draw, meritocracy meant a political regime that operates on the ruler's moral virtue, not the political system as such. For them monarchy was the only way to organize the political regime, in which the ruler was presented as the "son of Heaven" (*tianzi* 天子), as the man who possesses the Heaven-given mandate (*tianming* 天命) to rule. Political power (i.e., the mandate to rule) was either exclusively held by the king or shared by the king and those who (i.e., Confucian scholar-officials) he appointed in his court. In the Confucian political tradition, therefore, the gist of political meritocracy consisted in how to make the ruler (and by extension his ministers) who in reality acquired his mandate to rule by hereditary right (or by the ability to pass the imperial examination) morally responsible to Heaven and by implication to people who vicariously represent the will of Heaven.

Thus understood, the political proposal to replace democracy by political meritocracy (more accurately meritocratic elitism) is not very convincing either theoretically or practically as it confounds the source and distribution of political power with the moral character of a political regime. In the complete absence of political equality, even to attempt to limit democracy by meritocratic elitism makes no sense because the democratic ideal of popular sovereignty is never acknowledged, let alone respected.

If the question is how to constrain democracy because unchecked democracy is inevitably self-undermining, there are various ways to achieve this goal – through, for instance, the constitutional mechanism of checks and balances among the three branches of government, federalism, or constitutional review.[37] None of these measures, however, aim to make democracy thin; rather

[37] These Western liberal constitutional mechanisms can be properly "Confucianized." See, for instance, Tom Ginsburg, "Confucian Constitutionalism? The Emergence of Constitutional Review in Korea and Taiwan," *Law & Social Inquiry* 27 (2002), 763–99.

they aim to make democracy work without violating its ideal. Still, Confucian democrats should demand that democratically elected political leaders and public officials who are constrained by democratic constitutional rules and procedures be morally excellent and exemplary. But this demand would be effective only where there is the Confucian "habits of the heart" among citizens. Only such citizens can appreciate the value of Confucian morals and civilities; only such citizens can demand political leaders and public officials to be committed not only to democratic rules and procedures but *also* to moral excellence. Only at the citizens' demand would political leaders and public officials then aspire to possess *good character*.[38]

Confucian meritocratic democrats may wonder how Confucian public virtues can come about in the absence of moral leadership that would make the people *virtuous* in the first place. But a robustly democratic Confucian polity "leaves it primarily up to families, local governments, schools, religious and workplace associations, and a host of other voluntary groups" to teach and transmit Confucian civic virtues from one generation to the next.[39] That is, in a Confucian democracy, civic virtue is inculcated spontaneously in the heart of every citizen through their participation in various social institutions in civil society rather than deliberately infused by elitist leaders by means of paternalistic moral education.

It is often claimed that the civil examination system can help institutionalize Confucian moral meritocracy. However, apart from the fact that no classical Confucian advocated civil examination as the method for recruiting governmental officials,[40] many premodern Confucians (particularly Neo-Confucians) historically regarded civil examination as the single greatest obstacle to their study (and repossession) of the Dao, and thus a source of self-alienation.[41] More important,

[38] Advocates of meritocratic elitism often claim that political meritocracy should be taken seriously as an alternative to representative democracy predicated on the principle of "one person, one vote." This claim is heavily problematic because representative democracy, mostly operating on the selection or trustee model of political representation, is a kind of political meritocracy. See Nannerl O. Keohane, *Thinking about Leadership* (Princeton: Princeton University Press, 2010). I see no compelling reason why Confucian democracy should not be supported by a representative democratic system that I think best institutionalizes the accountability mechanisms. See Chapter 7 for more detailed discussion on this point.

[39] Here I am referring to Mary A. Glendon's "Forgotten Questions," in *Seedbeds of Virtue: Sources of Competence, Character, and Citizenship in American Society*, ed. Mary A. Glendon and David Blankenhorn (Lanham, MD: Madison Books, 1995), 2.

[40] The preferred method was either invitation by the ruler or recommendation by Confucian masters.

[41] For instance, from the late sixteenth century to the end of the Chosŏn dynasty (1392–1910), many orthodox Cheng-Zhu Neo-Confucians in Korea refused to take the civil examination to preserve the purity of what they called the "study of Dao" (*daoxue* 道學). See Insoo Woo, *Joseonhugi sanlimseryeok yeon'gu* [A Study on the Backwoods Literati Forces in Late Chosŏn Korea] (Seoul: Iljogak, 1999). Also see Sungmoon Kim, "Confucian Charisma and the True Way of the Moral Politician: Interpreting the Tension between Toegye and Nammyeong in Late Sixteenth-Century Joseon," *Review of Korean Studies* 7 (2004), 201–30.

there is no guarantee that legislators or public officials selected through the universal and competitive examination will actually prove to be morally good, just as there is no assurance that any democratically elected politician will indeed commit to democratic principles, rules, and procedures. Only a civil society operating on Confucian social mores and civilities can ensure a meritocratic Confucian democracy. Without the presence of a viable Confucian civil society both civil examination and democratic election are likely to create a new aristocratic class, as was the case with premodern Confucian China and Korea.[42]

Democracy as Collective Self-Determination and Equal Citizenship

Joseph Chan complains that recent literature on Confucian democracy often conflates the endorsement of democratic values with the endorsement of democratic institutions by ignoring that in the most proper sense democracy is "a mode of decision making about collectively binding rules and policies over which the people exercise control."[43] After defining democracy in such institutional terms, Chan then draws attention to the distinction between the *constituents* of democracy and the *conditions* that make it work satisfactorily.

> [H]owever important these conditions [such as a culture of tolerance, civility and civic duties, a vibrant civil society, a participatory culture, public reason and deliberation, etc.] are, they are merely conditions of a democracy, not its defining constituents.... This point is important ... for according to some interpretations, Confucianism does endorse consultation, tolerance, civility, or even a participatory community. But these interpretations, even if true, are still far from being able to show that Confucianism endorses democracy as a political system.[44]

Chan's point is highly relevant to more community-oriented Confucian democrats who present Confucian democracy as a kind of communitarian cultural-political vision and practice.[45] Indeed, preoccupied with the social and cultural conditions that make democracy work, Confucian communitarians do not pay due attention to the possibility that communities can still be vibrant under nondemocratic political systems (for instance, under a benevolent monarchy). As political scientist Sheri Berman has shown in her article on the collapse of the Weimar Republic, rich social capital in civil society can easily be exploited by authoritarian forces unless democratic political institutions (particularly a democratic party system) are firmly established.[46]

[42] See Benjamin A. Elman, *A Cultural History of Civil Examinations in Late Imperial China* (Berkeley: University of California Press, 2000) for China and James B. Palais, "Confucianism and the Aristocratic/Bureaucratic Balance in Korea," *Harvard Journal of Asiatic Studies* 44 (1984), 427–68 for Korea.

[43] Chan, "Democracy and Meritocracy," 181.

[44] Ibid., 182.

[45] See Chapters 1 and 2 for the core tenets of Confucian communitarianism.

[46] See Sheri Berman, "Civil Society and the Collapse of the Weimar Republic," *World Politics* 49 (1997), 401–29.

The problem is that in actual social and political reality it is difficult to distinguish democracy as a particular institutional arrangement of power vividly from democracy as a way of life. By definition, democracy is a regime in which people are at once the rulers and the ruled. In democracy key political decisions with regard to who will be rulers (and the ruled) and under what terms they will be rulers (and the ruled) are decided by the people. In other words, what is central to democracy is the *collective self-determination* of the people, and this is what constitutes democracy as a political rule.[47] And yet, collective self-determination is predicated on a characteristically democratic mode of living, on the life of active citizenship. Benjamin Barber thus says, "The most important fact about citizens is that they are defined by membership in a political community and enact their civic identities only to the extent that they interact with other citizens in a mutualistic and common manner. Political judgment is thus 'we-judgment' or public judgment or common-willing (in Rousseau's phrase, general willing). *I* cannot judge politically, only *we* can judge politically; in assuming the mantle of citizenship, the I becomes a We."[48] Democratic institutions and procedures that Chan understands as the constituents of democracy are in fact the institutionalized expressions of the citizenry's collective self-determination, and they are meaningful only if they are responsive and accountable to the collective will of the people.[49]

This clarification is of crucial significance in the context of East Asian politics. Admittedly, predemocratic authoritarian regimes in South Korea and Taiwan were formally democratic governments founded on liberal-democratic constitutions. But it is generally agreed that both South Korean and Taiwanese societies have been democratized only recently precisely because the "democratic" institutions in the predemocratic periods did not represent the people and were not accountable to the people's collective will. For the citizens of South Korea and Taiwan, therefore, democratization was the process of reclaiming their collective self-determination, their fundamental political freedom hijacked by a handful of political elites. For them, democratic consolidation means the institutionalization of the democratic political system that is genuinely committed to the enhancement of equal citizenship and individual citizen empowerment. Thus understood, seeing the components of democratic

[47] See Ian Shapiro, *Democratic Justice* (New Haven: Yale University Press, 1999); Benjamin R. Barber, *Strong Democracy: Participatory Politics for a New Age*, 20th anniversary ed. (Berkeley: University of California Press, 2003).

[48] Benjamin R. Barber, *The Conquest of Politics: Liberal Philosophy in Democratic Times* (Princeton: Princeton University Press, 1988), 200–201.

[49] By "active citizenship" I do not mean an old-style republican citizenship that puts active political participation above everything else. Even Barber's "active citizenship," which I endorse, is much more moderate than this and quite practicable in a modern pluralist society: "Citizens are governors: self-governors, communal governors, masters of their own fates. They need not participate all of the time in all public affairs, but they should participate at least some of the time in at least some public affairs." (Barber, *Strong Democracy*, xxix).

citizenship such as civic virtue, participatory culture, and strong civil society merely as the conditions of democracy is problematic. Democratic citizenship is the core of democracy; not only does it make democracy work, but, more fundamentally, it is what makes a certain arrangement of power democratic.

Apart from their conflation of feudal aristocracy with Confucian moral meritocracy, what is striking about recent Confucian meritocratic democrats, insomuch as they claim themselves to be *democrats*,[50] is their lack of interest in democratic citizenship.[51] According to them, democratic citizens are no more than consumers in the political marketplace. For instance, Bell says, "Elite politics does not rule out democratic participation by ordinary citizens, but democracy will take 'minimal' forms, not much more demanding than visiting the voting booth every few years."[52] For Bai, democracy is tantamount to "one person, one vote," and this is what he means by a "full and equal participation" of the common people on a local level.[53] In this minimal understanding of democracy, there is no way to form a thick democratic citizenship, nor is it possible to empower citizens beyond the vote. Instead, meritocratic elitism promotes the opposite of citizen empowerment, namely docility, which is rationalized as a form of respect for the elite.

The reason that Confucian meritocratic democrats want democracy to be minimal is premised on the assumption that in a democracy ordinary citizens are largely absorbed in the pursuit of their own short-term self-interests. But then, as Barber argues,

> [thin democracy] yields neither the pleasures of participation nor the fellowship of civic association, neither the autonomy and self-government of continuous political activity nor the enlarging mutuality of shared public goods – of mutual deliberation, decision,

[50] Fred Dallmayr comments on Daniel Bell's book in this way: "As indicated, the book's title is *Beyond Liberal Democracy*, but one frequently gets the impression that the move is not just beyond 'liberal democracy' but beyond democracy *tout court*, leaving as a remnant only what Bell calls 'minimal democracy.'" Dallmayr, "Exiting Liberal Democracy," 526.

[51] In his earlier work *East Meets West: Human Rights and Democracy in East Asia* (Princeton: Princeton University Press, 2000), Bell supported an empowered civil society and the right to vote without fear of retaliation in Singapore (chap. 4). But in *Beyond Liberal Democracy*, whose subtitle reads *Political Thinking for an East Asian Context*, Bell makes a generalized claim that meritocratic elitism with thin/minimal democracy is suitable in East Asian Confucian societies.

[52] Bell, *Beyond Liberal Democracy*, 151. In making this argument, Bell offers a "Confucian" justification for why active citizenship is unsuitable in East Asian societies: "In East Asian societies with a Confucian heritage, where the good of the family has been regarded as the key to the good life for more than two millennia, there republican tradition is so far removed from people's self-understanding that it is a complete nonstarter. Most people have devoted their time and energy to family and other 'local' obligations, with political decision making left to an educated, public-spirited elite." Though I agree that Confucian democratic citizenship does not necessarily have to be modeled after the republican active citizenship, I do not see any compelling reason why active citizenship must be precluded from the possible Confucian democratic modes of political engagement "at least some of the time in at least some public affairs."

[53] Bai, "Limited Democracy," 26.

and work. Oblivious to that essential human interdependence that underlies all political life, thin democratic politics is at best a politics of static interest, never a politics of transformation; a politics of bargaining and exchange, never a politics of invention and creation; and a politics that conceives of women and men at their worst (in order to protect them from themselves), never at their potential best (to help them become better than they are).[54]

As we have seen, Confucian meritocratic democrats occasionally enlist the authority of classical Confucians such as Confucius and Mencius. But their view of ordinary human beings is more Legalistic (or Hobbesian) than Confucian: by finding ordinary people hopelessly fixed to their preformed preferences and interests and allowing them no moral power to transform themselves into public-spirited citizens, Confucian meritocratic democrats seek only how to best govern them. Therefore, *governability* is the only civic virtue acknowledged by the Confucian advocates of political meritocracy, but it is dubious how qualitatively different it is from docility. What is fundamentally lacking in the proposal for meritocratic elitism is the typical Confucian moral optimism as illustrated in the following passage of the *Mengzi*. "Heaven has not sent down men whose endowment differs so greatly. The difference is due to what ensnares their hearts. Take the barley for example.... If there is any unevenness, it is because the soil varies in richness and there is no uniformity in the fall of rain and dew and the amount of human effort devoted to tending it. Now things of the same kind are all alike. Why should we have doubts when it comes to men? The sage and I are of the same kind."[55]

Again, it is not my intention to argue that Confucianism is inherently democratic or that it naturally supports democracy as a political rule. My point is to raise the question of why modern Confucian democrats cannot *reappropriate* the Confucian moral optimism where everyone can be morally transformed and is even capable of becoming a sage,[56] and lends support to the democratic self-transformability of the common people. If it is agreed that moral or ethico-religious self-transformation (i.e., to become a sage) is more daunting than democratic self-transformation (i.e., to become a citizen), why should "Confucian democrats," who would embrace the classical Confucian optimism for human perfectibility, opt for a characteristically Legalistic and only minimally democratic mode of governance?[57]

[54] Barber, *Strong Democracy*, 24–5.

[55] *Mencius* 6A7. Also see *Mencius* 3A1.

[56] This Confucian moral (or spiritual) optimism does not have to be taken literally. It can be understood to mean (1) everyone can improve and the opportunity to pursue such improvement is a fundamental human good and (2) since no one knows who will succeed, we should ensure everyone has an equal opportunity to try.

[57] Bai, however, opposes democratic education and by implication democratic citizenship. See Tongdong Bai, "Against Democratic Education," *Journal of Curriculum Studies* 43 (2011), 615–22. Compare Bai's argument to that of Amy Gutmann, *Democratic Education* (Princeton: Princeton University Press, 1988).

Thus far, I have critiqued the recent proposal(s) for Confucian meritocratic democracy from both Confucian and democratic viewpoints. In the remainder of this chapter, I attempt to reconstruct a Confucian democracy that is more faithful to Confucian moral optimism, more consistent with the Confucian ideal of virtue politics, and fully democratic.

Constructing a Confucian Democratic Civil Society

In conceiving of a Confucian civil society, there can be two different approaches – cultural/evaluative and ethico-political/normative. The former, often employed by historians and social scientists, understands Confucianism as a cultural system still alive in East Asian societies and investigates the way it actually plays out in the modern social and political context. In this view, the driving force of "Confucian civil society" as a cultural practice is the self-consciousness of the key political agents in it – as the moral elite or the political vanguard of the society. According to Thomas Metzger, this elite-centered Confucian civil society has a long history, which is traced back to late imperial China.

> During the imperial period, therefore, the dominant moral rhetoric was not that of ordinary people seeking freedom by calling for limits on the power of the centralized state but that of moral virtuosi, super-citizens claiming to embody the conscience of society, looking down equally on the degeneration of state institutions and the private pursuit of economic profits, and continuing to search for some way to restore the ancient saintly *Gemeinschaft*. In other words, the utopian, top-down view of progress as based on the moral dynamism of super-citizens able to influence a corrigible state was never replaced by an un-utopian, bottom-up view of progress as based on the efforts of ordinary free citizens fallibly pursuing their economic interests and organized in a practical way to monitor an incorrigible state. When Chinese intellectuals from the late nineteenth century on started to embrace the idea of "democracy" and, later, that of "civil society," this utopian, top-down approach remained integral to their thought.[58]

If Confucianism supports meritocracy, I believe it is this kind of moral-political leadership voluntarily assumed by moral virtuosi or super-citizens in the civil society, especially at the moment of an ethico-cultural and political crisis. Meritocracy in this sense has nothing to do with *political rule* by the sociopolitical elite for the common people. The "merit" at issue here is not something that can be tested in an examination. It is the moral virtue (*de* 德) that one has cultivated in oneself by repossessing the Dao, the profound source of the moral (even spiritual) meaning of one's life, one's connection with society, and one's role in it. Therefore, this nonpolitical, essentially moral, meritocracy is more properly called an "aristocracy of the Dao."

[58] Thomas A. Metzger, "The Western Concept of Civil Society in the Context of Chinese History," in *Civil Society: History and Possibilities*, ed. Sudipta Kaviraj and Sunil Khilnani (Cambridge: Cambridge University Press, 2001), 224.

However, there are two problems with Confucian civil society understood in this way. First, "super-citizenship" implicated in the moral aristocracy of the Dao, though not aiming to institutionalize moral meritocracy in the form of political elitism, is undemocratic in the sense that the assumed moral hierarchy between super-citizens and citizens, or the top-down social perspective affiliated with the moral elitism of the super-citizens, impedes the democratic ideal of citizenship, the ideal of collective self-determination.

On a second and related point, Confucian civil society predicated on super-citizenship is short of producing democratic civility or civic virtue. The civic virtues that super-citizens exercise in the civil society are not so much those that they have cultivated in the capacity of (democratic) citizen but rather those that *extended* from moral virtues they possess as morally cultivated persons, especially (though not always) in moments of cultural and political crises. In other words, in an aristocracy of the Dao civic virtue has no independent moral ground, nor do citizenship and civil society. Here civic virtue is required only on special occasions and civil society, when created, is an ephemeral phenomenon, not a sustainable sociopolitical institution.

These two problems associated with the cultural/evaluative understanding of Confucian civil society should impel Confucian democrats to reconstruct a version of Confucian civil society that is institutionally formidable and democracy-enhancing. What is central to our task in this normative reconstruction of Confucian civil society is to reinvent an aristocracy of the Dao into an aristocracy of all, namely, into democratic citizenship.[59] The question is how to make a democratic civil society serve the moral and material well-being of the people, which is the goal of traditional Confucian virtue politics.

1. Enhancing the Moral Welfare of the Citizens

As we have seen, the supreme goal of Confucian virtue politics lies in making the people morally good. However, under the monarchical system it was the king's (ideally the sage-king's) Heaven-given mission to lead and by personal example inspire the people to goodness. Hence it was imperative for the king himself to be morally good in the first place. A political ruler as well as a moral teacher, the Confucian king therefore was called the "teacher-king" (*jun shi* 君師). Mencius illustrates the teacher aspect in the ideal of the Confucian monarch by alluding to sage-king Yao.

> This is the way of the common people: once they have a full belly and warm clothes on their back they degenerate to the level of animals if they are allowed to lead idle lives, without education and discipline. This gave the sage King (Yao) further cause for concern, and so he appointed Xie as the Minister of Education whose duty was to teach the people human relationships: love between father and son, duty between ruler and

[59] Cf. Benjamin R. Barber, *An Aristocracy of Everyone: The Politics of Education and the Future of America* (Oxford: Oxford University Press, 1992).

subject, distinction between husband and wife, precedence of the old over the young, and faith between friends. Fang Xun (Yao) said, "Encourage them in their toil, put them on the right path, aid them and help them, make them happy in their station, and by bountiful acts further relieve them of hardship." The Sage worried to this extent about the affairs of the people.[60]

In modern Confucian East Asian societies where the traditional Confucian monarchical system is completely obsolete, the ideal of the teacher-king, implicated in what Julia Ching calls the "Sage-King Paradigm," is no longer feasible.[61] Confucian meritocratic democrats still want the state (or those who compose it) to claim the role of the moral teacher attached originally to kingship (and later to the scholar-officials after the rise of Neo-Confucianism), but this is neither morally desirable nor politically efficacious in East Asia's increasingly pluralist societies.

Rather, in the modern context of pluralism and multiculturalism, the moral well-being of the people can be better achieved in various types of self-governing moral communities – whether neighborhoods, villages, (private/civic/religious) organizations/associations, or extended families. By belonging to and actively participating in these communities, individuals can not only overcome public ills commonly associated with atomistic individualism but also realize their moral ideals and cultivate moral goods that they cherish in association with others.

What makes this pluralist civil society consisting of many self-governing moral communities a "Confucian" civil society, however, is not a monolithic conception of the common good that may be authoritatively given by some elites.[62] Instead, it is through the uniquely Confucian conception and practice of public civility, which the members of civil society commonly share, that a pluralistic civil society becomes a Confucian civil society. Put differently, in Confucian democracy Confucian civility can play a critical *constitutional* role.

At the heart of Confucian public civility, which interlocks Confucian civil pluralism and Confucian constitutional democracy, are Confucian rituals (*li* 禮). I fully agree with Robert Neville, when he says, "[W]hat is a Confucian ritual except a complicated social dance form in which all can participate (democracy) and yet can play roles that recognize their vast differences from one another (pluralism)? ... The key is rituals that require affirming ritual participation without necessarily agreeing to affirm the character and values of

[60] See *Mencius* 3A4.

[61] Julia Ching, *Mysticism and Kingship in China: The Heart of Chinese Wisdom* (Cambridge: Cambridge University Press, 1997).

[62] It is not surprising that Bell supports both Confucian communitarianism and meritocratic elitism. I suspect that in Bell's ideal regime, common good is essentially what leaders call as such. In Bell's view, deliberation is not so much the citizenry's business but intellectual elites'. See Daniel A. Bell, "Democratic Deliberation: The Problem of Implementation," in *Deliberative Politics: Essays on Democracy and Disagreement*, ed. Stephen Macedo (Oxford: Oxford University Press, 1999).

those importantly different from oneself."[63] In the same spirit, I submit that in pluralist East Asia, the *li* can help moral communities upholding different moral ideals recognize others as equal members of the common public world and maintain the bond of trust necessary to sustain a discussion about issues that they face together. That is, the *li* may not (and *should not*) transform the modern pluralist civil society into a community of commonality, as Confucian communitarians wish,[64] but can nevertheless offer a constitutional forum for democratic deliberation and contestation that aims to achieve the commonality of the public world. Let me elaborate on this.

In the Confucian tradition, *li*, which refers generally to norms and standards of proper behaviors in social, ethical, and religious contexts, is understood as an externalization of *ren* 仁 (commonly translated as benevolence or human-heartedness), the Confucian moral virtue par excellence.[65] Most famously, in *Analects* 12:1, Confucius says that (only) by returning to the observance of the *li* (*fuli* 復禮) and thereby overcoming the self (*keji* 克己) can one become morally good (*ren*). Here both *li* and *ren* are presented as moral virtues in the universalist sense, concerned with a person's moral goodness qua human being, and Confucius called a morally elevated person who has successfully undergone this process a *junzi* 君子. What is important here is that by defining the *junzi* primarily as a moral person in the universalist sense and simultaneously presenting him as the model citizen, Confucius was never troubled by the possible incongruence between a moral man and a responsible citizen.[66] Most tellingly, when asked why he was not employed in governing, Confucius replied by referring to the *Book of Documents* (*Shujing* 書經), that "[i]t is all in filial conduct (*xiao* 孝)! Just being filial to your parents and befriending your brothers is carrying out the work of government."[67]

In the Confucian universalist ethics that fuses politics/civics and ethics/morals and defies the stark distinction between private and public, the independent moral importance of public virtue, a capacity to sustain the political institutions, was never consciously acknowledged.[68] Rather, such a capacity was thought

63 Robert C. Neville, *Boston Confucianism: Portable Tradition in the Late-Modern World* (Albany: State University of New York Press, 2000), 80.

64 Sor-hoon Tan, "From Cannibalism to Empowerment: An *Analects*-Inspired Attempt to Balance Community and Liberty," *Philosophy East and West* 54 (2004), 58.

65 Tu Weiming, *Humanity and Self-Cultivation* (Berkeley, CA: Asian Humanities Press, 1979), 8–10.

66 In no place in the *Analects* does Confucius define the *junzi* purely in civic terms. Instead, Confucius always presents the *junzi* as a moral person primarily (almost solely) concerned with his or her moral self-cultivation (see *Analects* 12:4; 14:24; 15:18; 15:21; 15:32; 16:10). In other words, for Confucius, civics had no moral value independent of morals. On Confucius's (and the Confucian) idea of moral self-cultivation, see Philip J. Ivanhoe, *Confucian Moral Self Cultivation* (Indianapolis: Hackett, 2000).

67 *Analects* 2:21.

68 Of classical Confucians, Xunzi seems to have grasped (without articulation) a *certain* distinction between human/moral virtue and civic/political virtue. See Sungmoon Kim, "Before and After Ritual: Two Accounts of *Li* as Virtue in Early Confucianism," *Sophia* 51 (2012), 195–210.

to be a natural extension from one's personal morality, namely one's relationship with the Dao. Thus, Mencius was able to confirm this happy continuum between morals and civics when he said, "All under heaven (*tianxia* 天下) has its basis in the state, the state in the family, and the family in one's own self."[69]

Interpreted most generously, Confucian meritocratic democrats seem to aspire to reproduce this happy congruence between personal morality and public civility in East Asian societies. However, this is an unrealizable and politically undesirable aspiration in the modern societal context of ethical/value pluralism. To be sure, as Confucian meritocratic democrats rightly claim, East Asian societies remain Confucian, and thus it is both culturally and politically futile to attempt to transplant a Western-style liberal democracy on them. However, it is certainly wrong to understand (or present) East Asian societies as *the* Confucian society in a culturally monolithic and ethically monistic sense.

What renders East Asian societies that are internally diverse *Confucian* is the distinctively Confucian character of their public culture – that is, while subscribing to different moral, philosophical, and religious doctrines, citizens in East Asia still largely share a Confucian public culture predicated on the social semiotics of Confucian rituals. In other words, they might be Christian/Muslim/Buddhist as private individuals, but they are, often unconsciously, Confucian (broadly understood) as public citizens.[70] More specifically, in East Asian societies, core Confucian values such as filiality (*xiaoti* 孝悌), trustworthiness (*xin* 信), social harmony (*he* 和), respect of the elderly (*jinglao* 敬老), and respectful deference (*cirang* 辭讓) are widely cherished as public virtues independent of an individual citizen's self-chosen religious/cultural value system, and it is through the continued practice of the *li* that these public virtues are socially available in those increasingly pluralist societies.[71]

Thus understood, in modern pluralist society, Confucian rituals should no longer be a *bonding* social capital that consolidates monocultural cohesion and ethical homogeneity, but a *bridging* social capital that helps to bond individual citizens horizontally, thereby bringing them to one common public world where they encounter one another as free and equal citizens.[72] As Sor-hoon

[69] *Mencius* 4A5 (slightly modified).

[70] For empirical evidence for this claim, see note 9 in the Introduction

[71] In this regard, I agree with Stephen Angle's idea of "ritual minimalism." Angle says, "The point of minimalism about ritual is not to minimize the significance of style, but rather to mark a distinction between the role ritual plays in all our lives, as the general social expectation of civility, and the endless opportunities we have for further perfecting our individual performances of propriety. For the purposes of civility, our motivation for following ritual is relatively unimportant; it matters little where we fall on the continuum from rigid self-control to fluid spontaneity. The latter end of the spectrum is ethically superior, but the former is sufficient for achieving the goals of civility with which we are here concerned" (Stephen C. Angle, *Contemporary Confucian Political Philosophy: Toward Progressive Confucianism* [Cambridge: Polity, 2012], 106).

[72] For an illuminating discussion of the difference between bonding social capital and bridging social capital, see Robert D. Putnam, *Bowling Alone: The Collapse and Revival of American Community* (New York: Touchstone, 2000), 18–24.

Tan rightly notes, the essence of this civically reconstructed Confucian ritual consists in the quality of communication.[73]

The communication thus enabled, however, is not so much an intracultural communication whose ultimate goal is to "overcome" differences but a democratic deliberation across differences. In this regard, my proposed Confucian democratic deliberation is differentiated from Tan's communicative model of Confucian ritualism, but it is also distinguished from liberal-democratic deliberation. First, while Tan's communicative Confucian *li*-based democracy attempts to make *li* itself the mode of communication and thus dismisses the importance of verbal, especially dialogical, communication, my proposed Confucian democratic deliberation is conducted in an active verbal dialogue among free and equal citizens. The significance of Confucian rituals in my model lies not so much in replacing words, which I find completely unrealistic, but in ritual's remarkable ability to bring diverse individuals to the common public forum by first making them exercise self-restraint (*keji* 克己). Restrained by the *li* and reminded of the Confucian public purposes that they broadly share, citizens are then capable of what Gutmann and Thompson call "mutual reciprocity," the capacity to seek fair terms of cooperation for its own sake.[74] Both the advocates of meritocratic elitism and strong Confucian communitarians (like Tan), despite their meaningful differences, prefer an aesthetic harmonization of differences, but my model aims at the political consensus among different groups and individuals and embraces a democratic contestation in civil society.

Second, there is a crucial difference between my proposed Confucian democratic deliberation and liberal-democratic deliberation. Many liberal deliberative democrats find troubling John Rawls's suggestion that deliberative procedures need accommodate only the fact of "reasonable pluralism."[75] Jack Knight and James Johnson explicate the nature of this challenge as follows: "[Rawls's claim] prejudges in an unjustifiable way the question of which sorts of argument or value are legitimately admissible to the process of political deliberation and debate."[76] Likewise Gerald Gauss argues, "Because notions of political reasonableness will be affected by our epistemic, religious, and other commitments, there is little prospect of a consensus emerging on what is politically reasonable in a society that disagrees on what is religiously, morally and epistemologically reasonable."[77] Precisely because it is not a *liberal* political practice, Confucian democratic deliberation, while embracing ethical/value

[73] Tan, "From Cannibalism to Empowerment," 58.

[74] Amy Gutmann and Dennis Thompson, *Democracy and Disagreement: Why Moral Conflict Cannot Be Avoided in Politics, and What Should Be Done about It* (Cambridge, MA: Belknap, 1996).

[75] John Rawls, *Political Liberalism* (New York: Columbia University Press, 1993).

[76] Jack Knight and James Johnson, "What Sort of Equality Does Deliberative Democracy Require?," in Bohman and Rehg, *Deliberative Democracy*, 285.

[77] Gerald F. Gauss, "Reason, Justification, and Consensus," in Bohman and Regn, *Deliberative Democracy*, 222.

pluralism, does not have to be implicated with this philosophical conundrum regarding what makes pluralism reasonable. In my model, pluralism is reasonable to the extent that it is respectful of (but not necessarily blindly deferential to) Confucian public purposes and if it is moderated by public reason nested in the moral sentiment of *ren*.[78]

My model might not be able to uphold ethical/value pluralism maximally as some liberals wish, but, again, it should not matter because my Confucian deliberative model is not a liberal-democratic political practice, nor does it intend to be antiliberal. Neither the maximal promotion of ethical/value pluralism nor finding a philosophical justification for reasonableness is my concern here. My concern is rather with a *more* earnest attention to the moral well-being of the citizens in a Confucian society who belong to different moral, religious, cultural communities, and how to accommodate human plurality *as much as possible* in the given Confucian societal context. Meritocratic elitism is far from meeting the differentiated moral needs of modern East Asians. In fact, its monistic vision of the Confucian society is likely to oppress pluralism.[79]

2. *Enhancing the Material Welfare of the Citizens*

Historically, no Confucian believed that ordinary citizens' moral well-being could be attained without first resolving the question of their material well-being.[80] Therefore, it is understandable that proponents of Confucian meritocratic democracy such as Bell claim that the most important "right" acknowledged in the Confucian ethical tradition is the "right to be fed."[81] Bell, in particular, calls a modern Confucianism that obliges the state to provide for the material well-being of the people, "left Confucianism."[82]

What is unclear to me is why Bell believes that left Confucianism is more suitable in the meritocratic setting. Can't it be equally (or even better) practicable in the democratic welfare state? In fact, noting that the Confucian state's (or a benevolent, father-like, Confucian ruler's) main obligation is to help those who are worst off,[83] Bell agrees that "Confucius (if he were around today) may

78 On public reason in a Confucian pluralist democracy, see Chapter 5.

79 Joseph Chan, who differentiates his moderate Confucian perfectionism from extreme Confucian perfectionism (of the kind advocated by Jiang Qing), is less susceptible to this criticism. See his "On Legitimacy of Confucian Constitutionalism," in Jiang Qing, *Confucian Constitutional Order*, 99–112.

80 *Mencius* 1A7.

81 Bell, *Beyond Liberal Democracy*, 44–7.

82 Daniel A. Bell, *China's New Confucianism: Politics and Everyday Life in a Changing Society* (Princeton: Princeton University Press, 2008), xv.

83 Most famously, Mencius says, "Old men without wives (*guan* 鰥), old women without husbands (*gua* 寡), old people without children (*du* 獨), young children without fathers (*gu* 孤) – these four types of people are the most destitute and have no one to turn to for help. Whenever King Wen put benevolent measures into effect, he always gave them first consideration" (*Mencius* 1B5). Also see *Xunzi* 11:12.

well have endorsed something like Rawls's difference principle."[84] Bell, however, understands the Confucian obligation to help the worst off as a matter of the state's (or the ruler's) paternalistic beneficence, but not as a matter of justice. Contra what a "left" ideology normally signifies, Bell's left Confucianism turns out to be quite conservative as it is mainly concerned with economic development and sociopolitical stability, rather than distributive justice and democratic contestation.[85]

Certainly, Confucius as a champion of sage-kingship and moral aristocracy did not support democratic contestation, nor did he advance his own political theory of justice. Nevertheless, he did believe that for a government to be benevolent, it must be committed to distributive justice. "I have heard that the ruler of a state or the head of a household does not worry that his people are poor, but that wealth is inequitably distributed; does not worry that his people are too few in number, but that they are disharmonious."[86] If the essence of Confucian benevolent government lies not so much in the people's mere material subsistence but in the just or equitable distribution of material goods, it is clear that modern Confucian democrats (particularly left Confucians) must devote themselves to achieving socioeconomic justice in the rapidly industrializing East Asian countries. In my view, it is more reasonable for the Confucian democrats to support a welfare state that is democratically controlled.[87]

By democratic control, however, I do not merely mean electoral control or representative democracy. True democratic control of the government can be achieved only if the voices of the victims of socioeconomic injustice are heard in the government.[88] Although not a democrat himself, Mencius insisted that

84 Daniel A. Bell, "Constraints on Property Rights," in Bell and Hahm, *Confucianism for the Modern World*, 223.

85 Bell, *Beyond Liberal Democracy*, 55–62. Michael Walzer criticizes Bell's left Confucianism precisely because it fails to be a left doctrine. See Michael Walzer, "Michael Walzer Responds," *Dissent* 57 (2010), 100–101, which critically responds to Bell's "Reconciling Socialism and Confucianism? Reviving Tradition in China," *Dissent* 57 (2010), 91–9. It might be unfair to say that Bell is not concerned with distributive justice at all. For instance, in chap. 3 ("Hierarchical Rituals for Egalitarian Societies") of *China's New Confucianism*, Bell makes an interesting argument that hierarchical rituals not only "provide bonds not based solely on kinship that allow people to partake of the benefits of cooperative social existence" (39–40), but also "can limit the powerful and protect the interests of the disadvantaged in the various spheres of social life where power is exercised" (46). I see partial relevance of this claim to small villages in rural China where "the powerful members of the rituals are more likely to develop a concern for the disadvantaged" (47), but I am not persuaded that hierarchical rituals can adequately come to terms with, let alone cope with, the massive socioeconomic inequalities that are bedeviling contemporary Chinese society. Even in "Constraints on Property Rights," where Bell does find some meaningful resonance between Confucian ethics and Rawls's difference principle, his concern is predominantly with how to justify individual family ownership (as opposed to individual private property ownership), and not so much with distributive justice as such.

86 *Analects* 16:1.

87 See Chapter 6 for my Confucian defense of Confucian democratic welfarism.

88 Cf. Judith N. Shklar, *The Faces of Injustice* (New Haven: Yale University Press, 1990); Iris M. Young, *Inclusion and Democracy* (Oxford: Oxford University Press, 2000).

justice (especially, distributive justice) will be attained only if the victims' perspectives (if not voices) are taken by the government seriously:

Now when food meant for human beings is so plentiful as to be thrown to dogs and pigs, you fail to realize that it is time for garnering, and when men drop dead from starvation by the wayside, you fail to realize that it is time for distribution. When people die, you simply say, "It is none of my doing. It is the fault of the harvest." In what way is that different from killing a man by running him through, while saying all the time, "It is none of my doing. It is the fault of the weapon." Stop putting the blame on the harvest and the people of the whole Empire will come to you.[89]

In this passage, Mencius makes a provocative claim, turning our conventional understanding of meritocracy upside down. His preeminent concern is not with who should rule. Of greater importance is *to what extent* the government (or the ruler) should be responsible for the people's misfortune. Mencius's point is that if people are destitute, the responsibility to provide for them falls on the public authority and the responsibility is almost limitless, irrespective of what the proximate cause of the problem is. Thus understood, the true Confucian meaning of meritocracy is the ruler's (or the government's) *expanded responsibility* for the basic needs of the people, not an epistocracy of the elite.

Mencius, however, goes even further than most contemporary welfare democrats. His most provocative argument is that the ruler's responsibility ends only when he or his government is cable of supplying "sufficient" food (and other material goods) to the people, not merely goods that barely meet their basic needs.

To punish them after they have fallen foul of the law is to set a trap for the people. How can a benevolent man in authority allow himself to set a trap for the people? Hence when determining what means of support the people should have, a clear-sighted ruler ensures that these are sufficient (*zu* 足), on the one hand, for the care of parents, and, on the other, for the support of wife and children, so that the people always have sufficient food in good years and escape starvation in bad; only when does he drive them towards, goodness; in this way the people find it easy to follow him.[90]

Drawing on this passage, particularly, I suspect, on the Chinese word *zu*, which translates in English into "sufficient," Joseph Chan calls the Confucian principle of economic justice the "principle of sufficiency."[91] I do not think that this interpretation is completely baseless as merit and contribution as criteria for economic distribution are there in Mencius's and especially Xunzi's texts. But I cannot help thinking that the emphasis is misplaced when Chan likens the Confucian principle of sufficiency to the doctrine or principle as understood by

[89] *Mencius* 1A3.

[90] *Mencius* 1A7.

[91] Joseph Chan, "Is There a Confucian Perspective on Social Justice?," in *Western Political Thought in Dialogue with Asia*, ed. Takashi Shogimen and Cary J. Nederman (Lanham, MD: Lexington Books, 2008).

contemporary "sufficientarians" such as Harry Frankfurt and Roger Crisp.[92] In my view, Chan largely bypasses Mencius's core argument, when he says, "[O]nce past the level of material sufficiency, Mencius and Xunzi do not object to economic inequalities that arise from personal factors such as merit and contribution, which are largely based on the possession of abilities (moral character and intelligence)."[93]

Certainly, as Chan rightly claims, Mencius never objected to the accumulation of money (and other material goods) on the basis of one's desert, be it natural talent or effort, nor did he support equality of outcome as contemporary egalitarians define it. That being said, acknowledging the general importance of desert is one thing and upholding the doctrine of sufficiency is another. Central to sufficientarianism is the claim that "[a] concern for economic equality, construed as desirable in itself, tends to divert a person's attention away from endeavoring to discover – within his experience of himself and of his life – what he himself really cares about and what will actually satisfy him."[94] As Frankfurt stresses, from the sufficientarian standpoint, what is problematic with egalitarianism is self-alienation, the fact that as the criterion of equality is defined by an external entity (mostly the government), an *individual person* cannot define what is materially sufficient for him or her according to his or her own value, life plan, religious faith, or taste.

Nowhere in Mencius's (or Xunzi's) text do we find this typical liberal emphasis of individual self-identity and its facilitating (sufficient) economic condition. As we have seen in the passage, Mencius's core argument is simply that there should be "sufficient" (*zu* 足) material provisions for each family. Moreover, it seems quite arbitrary to claim that Confucianism upholds the doctrine of sufficiency because Mencius happened to employ the Chinese word *zu* in his criticism of the then ruler's inhumane government without much articulation of his idea of economic justice.[95]

92 Ibid., 276n23. For Frankfurt's and Crisp's defense of the doctrine of sufficiency, see Harry Frankfurt, "Equality as a Moral Ideal," *Ethics* 98 (1987), 21–43 and Roger Crisp, "Equality, Priority, and Compassion," *Ethics* 113 (2003), 745–63.

93 Chan, "Is There a Confucian Perspective on Social Justice?," 275.

94 Frankfurt, "Equality as a Moral Ideal," 23.

95 To be fair, Chan has a more extensive argument for his "doctrine of sufficiency" than just the use of the word *zu*, but nevertheless his sufficientarian interpretation of and justification for Confucian justice has a number of both interpretive and normative problems. At some point, Chan seems to say that the Confucian perspective of social justice can be best captured in terms of sufficientarianism because sufficientarianism represents the distributive principle most preferred by perfectionism, an ethical theory in terms of which he understands the essence of Confucian ethics and politics. Indeed, scholars such as Chris Mills show how liberal perfectionism can generate distinctive distributive principles by relying on the doctrine of sufficiency (see Chris Mills, "Can Liberal Perfectionism Generate Distinctive Distributive Principles?," *Philosophy and Public Issues* 2 [2012], 123–52). However, Chan never advances a coherent theory of the Confucian doctrine of sufficiency *from* his idea of "Confucian perfectionism," nor does he clearly distinguish Confucian perfectionism (and Confucian sufficientarianism) from liberal perfectionism

My point is that there seems to be no strong reason to draw the sufficientarian implications from the Confucian principle of sufficiency, to argue that Confucianism has no problem with economic inequalities that ensue after meeting a certain threshold if only they are the result of personal deserts.[96] As Paula Casal rightly notes, "[W]hat makes a view sufficientarian is not simply the great importance it attaches to eliminating deprivation but the lack of importance it attaches to certain additional distributive requirement."[97] Highly compatible with Rawls's difference principle, the Confucian principle of sufficiency seems to be far more egalitarian than Chan understands it to be.[98]

Not surprisingly, few Confucian meritocratic democrats seem to struggle with *how* to help poor citizens have sufficient materials goods to live a decent social, economic, and moral life; nor do they seem to be interested in following up Mencius's suggestion – expand governmental responsibility (to the extent that it does not seriously compromise individual responsibility). Most important, proponents of Confucian meritocracy have rarely shown genuine interest in the victims of socioeconomic injustice, let alone enabling them to contest government policies.

Democratic civil society provides a public arena where socioeconomic victims can organize their voices, make them heard by public officials and political leaders, and demand heavy moral and political responsibility of the government for socioeconomic injustice. There are many indications that representative democracy, which according to Bernard Manin is closer to electoral aristocracy than to real democracy,[99] has failed to truly represent the interests of socioeconomic victims. Then it would be utterly unrealistic to believe that unelected political elites will always heed, let alone represent, the interests of the victims of injustice. After all, proponents of meritocratic elitism prefer elitism to democracy precisely because common people (including socioeconomic

(and liberal perfectionism). This is a serious problem that Chan must be able to address because his goal as a political philosopher is to generate a modern *Confucian political philosophy* as distinct from liberal political philosophy. For my critical engagement with Chan's sufficientarian interpretation of and justification for the Confucian sense of distributive justice, see Sungmoon Kim, "Confucianism and Acceptable Inequalities," *Philosophy & Social Criticism* (December 2013 , published online on October 15, 2013 as doi:10.1177/0191453713507015.).

96 It is worth noting that according to Steven Wall, the statement, which underlies Chan's perfectionist endorsement of Confucian sufficientarianism, that "[t]he flourishing of everyone matters; but resources and opportunities ought to be distributed so as to promote excellence, even if this results in inegalitarian distributions" does not necessarily follow from the core stipulations of perfectionism. See his *Liberalism, Perfectionism and Restraint* (Cambridge: Cambridge University Press, 1998), 16–17. I believe the same is true of Confucian perfectionism as well, unless it is clearly shown that Confucianism generates a mode of perfectionism qualitatively different from liberal perfectionism.

97 Paula Casal, "Why Sufficiency Is Not Enough," *Ethics* 117 (2007), 296–326.

98 See note 83 in this chapter.

99 Bernard Manin, *The Principles of Representative Government* (Cambridge: Cambridge University Press, 1997).

victims) are preoccupied with their narrow self-interests. However, they never attempt to distinguish the socioeconomic underdogs' legitimate demand for justice from their narrow self-interests. Nor do they acknowledge that legitimate demand for justice requires democratic contestation in the public space of civil society. Even though Confucianism is often believed to prefer a harmonious, nondisputative way of conflict resolution,[100] modern Confucian democrats cannot afford to dismiss democratic contestation when it comes to serving the differentiated welfare of the people, especially of socioeconomic victims.

Concluding Remarks

In increasingly multiculturalized and industrialized East Asia, civil society is not merely an institutional accessory to the democratic system, nor is it a social condition that makes democracy work *better*. Rather, it is an essential component of democracy because it provides a public space (not just a public sphere in the abstraction) in which (1) private individuals transform themselves into public citizens, (2) citizens belonging to different moral communities interact civically to resolve problems that face them together, and (3) citizens who have suffered injustice can organize their voices and make them heard by the government. Moreover, civil society is an indispensable element of Confucian democracy because it is where Confucian virtue politics and the Confucian ideal of benevolent government can be creatively reappropriated. In this chapter, I call a democratic civil society that operates on Confucian *li*-mediated civility and serves the differentiated moral and material well-being of the citizens "Confucian civil society."

Recent proposals for Confucian meritocratic elitism fail to meet Confucian democracy's democratic aspiration of the aristocracy of everyone and Confucian commitment to the moral and material well-being of the people. By focusing on the governability of the people and thus paying no attention to the transformability of the people, Confucian meritocratic democrats simply downplay the ethical and political power of democratic civil society in the Confucian context. They overlook the fact that without the presence of a strong Confucian civil society, a decent Confucian democratic governance can hardly be attained.

[100] Albert H. Chen, "Mediation, Litigation, and Justice: Confucian Reflections in a Modern Liberal Society," in Bell and Hahm, *Confucianism for the Modern World*, 257–87.

PART II

CONFUCIAN DEMOCRACY IN THEORY – A PLURALIST RECONSTRUCTION

4

Value Pluralism and Confucian Democratic Civil Society

Larry Diamond, a renowned political scientist, points to pluralism as one of the defining features of democratic civil society. He says, "To the extent that an organization, such as a religious fundamentalist, ethnic chauvinist, revolutionary or millenarian movement, seeks to monopolize a functional or political space in society, crowding out all competitors while claiming that it represents the only legitimate path, it contradicts the pluralistic and market-oriented nature of civil society."[1] In this brief statement, we find three important points about the nature of democracy and democratic civil society: (1) liberal pluralism is integral to democratic civil society, (2) the center of pluralism is the market, and (3) at the center of pluralism is the *plurality of material interests*. In fact, many political scientists now widely agree that the democratic movements in Central and Eastern Europe, even if galvanized by the mass public's anticommunist and procapitalistic spirit in civil society, occasionally faced difficulty transforming the national, ethically charged, civil society into various kinds of interest-based liberal pluralistic civil societies. For instance, Juan Linz and Alfred Stepan understand the most profound challenge to Polish democratic consolidation precisely in terms of the difficulty of liberal pluralism. "Ethical civil society represents 'truth,' but political society in a consolidated democracy normally represents 'interest.' In political society the actor is only seldom the 'nation,' the more routinely 'groups.' 'Internal differences' and 'conflict' are no longer to be collectively suppressed, but organizationally represented in political society. Compromise and institutionalization are no longer negative but positive values."[2] Undoubtedly, pluralism is at the core of modern

[1] Larry Diamond, *Developing Democracy: Toward Consolidation* (Baltimore: Johns Hopkins University Press, 1999), 223.

[2] Juan J. Linz and Alfred Stepan, *Problems of Democratic Transition and Consolidation: Southern Europe, South America, and Post-Communist Europe* (Baltimore: Johns Hopkins University Press, 1996), 272.

civil society, but the empirical political scientists' understanding of pluralism as plurality of material interest is significantly limited for the following two reasons. First, liberal pluralism in political science completely dismisses Hannah Arendt's insight that what is really meaningful is the plurality of the *selves* (or human *beings*).[3] In this regard, empirical political scientists make a critical mistake by understanding the core of the individual self solely in terms of material interest. Such a view is what (Nozickean) libertarianism champions, but libertarianism hardly represents the entire liberal tradition, and it certainly does not offer the best case of liberal pluralism. Second, empirical political scientists fail to appreciate Max Weber's insight that there are two categorically different kinds of "interest" – material interest and so-called ideal interest. Weber introduces this controversial concept in his famous "switchmen" metaphor: "Not ideas, but material and ideal interests, directly govern men's conduct. Yet very frequently the 'world images' that have been created by 'ideas' have, like switchmen, determined the tracks along which action has been pushed by the dynamic of interest."[4] Put differently, human action is often propelled by the moral, religious, or philosophical values, that is, the ideal interests one holds, and they are occasionally (if not always) independent of consideration for material interests. Human beings are interested not only in material goods but also in ideational values, most eminently religious and cultural values.

While from the standpoint of material interest, liberal pluralism boils down to traditional *interest politics*, which Sheldon Wolin argues was first endorsed by Machiavelli,[5] from the standpoint of ideal interest, liberal pluralism is predicated on value pluralism and freedoms of expression and association, which, according to William Galston, originated with the Reformation.[6] The paramount concern of liberal pluralism in this vein is the question of how a liberal-democratic polity should come to terms with the expressive liberty of the individual self and, by extension, of the associations formed by individuals (qua members) holding shared values. In other words, value-oriented liberal pluralism is concerned with *identity politics*.[7]

In the past decade, Confucian democrats, the majority of whom identify themselves as communitarian, have vehemently criticized liberal pluralism as interest politics on the basis that mainstream political scientists' interest-oriented liberal political prescription will only erode the social fabric of East Asian Confucian societies rather than enhance their civic-democratic capacities.[8]

[3] Hannah Arendt, *The Human Condition* (Chicago: University of Chicago Press, 1958).

[4] Max Weber, *From Max Weber: Essays in Sociology*, trans. and ed. Hans H. Gerth and C. W. Mills (New York: Oxford University Press, 1958), 280.

[5] Sheldon S. Wolin, *Politics and Vision* (Boston: Little, Brown, 1960).

[6] William A. Galston, "Two Concepts of Liberalism," *Ethics* 105 (1995), 516–34.

[7] Amy Gutmann, *Identity in Democracy* (Princeton: Princeton University Press, 2003).

[8] Among others, see Daniel A. Bell, *East Meets West: Human Rights and Democracy in East Asia* (Princeton: Princeton University Press, 2000); David L. Hall and Roger T. Ames, *The*

While resisting the mainstream political scientists' apparently libertarian prescriptions, Confucian democrats have simultaneously criticized contemporary liberalism's preoccupation with unencumbered individualism and its emphasis of the right over the good.[9] But they have rarely taken seriously, much less met, the practical challenges posed by value pluralism.[10] What should a Confucian democracy look like in a pluralist society? Can we revamp Confucian communitarian democracy, which is originally presented as a cultural alternative to Western liberal democracy, into a robust democratic political theory and practice that is plausible in the societal context of pluralism?

In this chapter, I explore a Confucian democracy that is neither thick communitarian nor liberal individualistic, but one that is most plausible as a democratic theory and practice under the context of what John Rawls calls the "fact of pluralism."[11] To do so, I first investigate the core tenets of value pluralism with reference to William Galston's political theory. There are two reasons why I focus on Galston's political theory. First, in my view, it attempts the most sophisticated political theoretical engagement with value pluralism by giving full attention to the *intrinsic* value of diversity and human plurality particularly in the modern democratic context, even though Galston's political pluralism is characteristically liberal. Second, Galston's liberal pluralism offers us a comparative philosophical standpoint in appreciating and evaluating the core tenets of Confucian pluralist democracy. After examining Galston's liberal pluralism, I then construct a political theory of Confucian pluralist democracy by critically engaging with two dominant versions of Confucian democracy – Confucian communitarian democracy and Confucian meritocratic democracy. In short, this chapter aims to further articulate how

Democracy of the Dead: Dewey, Confucius, and the Hope for Democracy in China (Chicago: Open Court, 1999); Sor-hoon Tan, *Confucian Democracy: A Deweyan Reconstruction* (Albany: State University of New York Press, 2003); Russell A. Fox, "Confucian and Communitarian Responses to Liberal Democracy," *Review of Politics* 59 (1997): 591–2. In Chapters 1 and 2, I have critically examined these and related works on Confucian communitarianism.

9 However, whether or not the Confucian democrats' double criticism of liberalism as interest-centered *and* rights-based is internally coherent is a philosophically intriguing question, because under the rubric of "liberalism," Confucian democrats often mean two different, mutually competing, schools of thought – libertarianism on the one hand and what Thomas Spragens identifies as "deontological liberalism," which is a liberalism conceived in the Original Position. See Thomas A. Spragens, *Civic Liberalism: Reflections on Our Democratic Ideals* (Lanham, MD: Rowman & Littlefield, 1999).

10 Robert C. Neville argues that the Confucian ritual is "a complicated social dance form in which all can participate (democracy) and yet can play roles that recognize their vast differences from one another (pluralism)" (*Boston Confucianism: Portable Tradition in the Late-Modern World* [Albany: State University of New York Press, 2000], 80). This is an interesting statement, but Neville does not probe into the practical question of exactly how pluralism can be realized in Confucian ritual-based democracy.

11 John Rawls, *Political Liberalism* (New York: Columbia University Press, 1993).

Confucian democracy should come to terms with the moral well-being of the citizens in a pluralist societal context.

The Challenge of Value Pluralism and Liberal Pluralism

Confucian democrats often take deontological liberalism, pivoted on the assumption of unencumbered individualism, preoccupied with individual autonomy and prioritizing the right over the good, as *the* liberalism that is culturally incompatible with Confucian ethics and mores. John Rawls is frequently criticized as the key representative of this particular version of liberalism because of his notion of the "original position," in which individuals who strive to arrive at principles of justice that would make the political society a system of mutual cooperation are divested of relevant information regarding their natural talents and social status behind the "veil of ignorance."[12]

In the preceding chapters, I have argued that the Confucian communitarian critique of rights-based liberalism (the kind early Rawls represents) is often mistaken because of its failure to distinguish between Cartesian onto-epistemology and liberal political practice. In the same vein, I think the Confucian communitarian critique of Rawls's political theory is largely mistaken because of its failure to distinguish the original position, a philosophical device, and the actual position, where *politically free and equal* citizens are *socially encumbered* as persons by various chosen and unchosen (i.e., ascriptive) social relations. That being said, considering that in *A Theory of Justice* Rawls understands the democratic citizens' freedom and equality in comprehensive liberal-moral (i.e., Kantian-Millian) terms, the Confucian critique is not completely off the mark; for the idea of "free and equal citizenship" is itself deeply implicated in the liberal moral ideal of autonomous personhood.

However, Confucian democrats have generally failed to appreciate, let alone analyze, the troubling fact that there is another version of liberalism that allegedly emerged after the Reformation, a liberalism predicated on the assumption of a radically situated selfhood. Since, as shall be shown shortly, this version of liberalism called "liberal pluralism" is neither an ephemeral phenomenon nor merely supplementary to the Enlightenment liberalism that centers on individual autonomy, it would (and should) change the way Confucian democrats think about liberalism and challenge them to reconstruct Confucian democracy as a more plausible alternative sociopolitical practice to both versions of liberalisms (Enlightenment liberalism and Reformation liberalism).[13] In

[12] John Rawls, *A Theory of Justice* (Cambridge, MA: Belknap, [1971] 1999).

[13] In the present chapter, however, I do not embark on a comparison between liberal pluralism and Confucian pluralist democracy, which is my primary concern in Chapter 11. Investigation of the core tenets of liberal pluralism, though, will help us see the unique feature of Confucian pluralist democracy.

this section, I investigate the core tenets of liberal pluralism in reference to Galston's political theory.

According to liberal pluralism (otherwise called diversity liberalism or Reformation liberalism), which is focused on liberal social and political practice rather than on the Enlightenment epistemology of the socially deracinated self, individuals are primarily the members of a particular religious or cultural community (one of the most telling examples is the Amish people) and their status as citizens is only of secondary significance. Contrary to the casual Confucian-democratic understanding of the liberal person as a self-choosing individual,[14] many individuals in actual liberal societies are radically encumbered by their mostly unchosen religious beliefs and/or cultural values that govern (even dictate) their way of life. Finding liberalism's rights discourse incompatible with Confucian rites discourse and attendant role-ethics, and assuming that the liberal rights discourse is philosophically premised on the Cartesian pure mind or Kantian unencumbered self, Confucian democrats tend to misconstrue the right to freedom of religion and/or conscience as a matter of pure individual choice, as if it grants that one can change one's religious faith (and the way of life it dictates) as freely in accordance with one's pure will.[15] However, the precise opposite is often the case: freedom of religion and/or conscience is in practice grounded in the radical unavailability of freedom of choice for a person who is radically situated in a particular religious and/or cultural community as a member – since he or she (say, a Mormon) *cannot* choose other religious/cultural values at will or freely, he or she rather takes his or her freedom as the ability to express his or her religious or cultural values that he or she did not freely choose but has deeply embodied in his or her selfhood as maximally as possible without external constraint.[16] William Galston insightfully captures this freedom/choice versus unfreedom/nonchoice dialectic implicated in the freedom of religion/conscience. "[F]rom time to time, individuals and groups have chosen to create and live in these nonchoice societies. In so doing, they enjoy what I have called 'expressive liberty' – a sense

[14] As we have seen in Chapter 1, most Confucian communitarians roundly oppose the rights discourse as such (not any particular liberal rights) as the Western presumption incompatible with the Confucian discourse of rites/rituals.

[15] See Hall and Ames, *Democracy of the Dead*, 68–75. This, however, is a problematic assumption because historically the awareness of the importance of individual rights grew with the individuals' ongoing religious-political struggles against the state and with the members of other sects and/or factions. Even for J. S. Mill, individual rights were important for a practical (not philosophical) reason – that they offered a quintessential social-political bulwark against the tyranny of the majority. See Mary A. Glendon, *Rights Talk: The Impoverishment of Political Discourse* (New York: Free Press, 1990), 52–4.

[16] It needs to be clarified that the freedom that is radically unavailable for the members of cultural/religious associations is not directly a political freedom (after all, it is not the case that government forces citizens to be religious in a certain way) but a societal freedom. It becomes a critical political question, though, when the government interferes with the internal affairs of the associations.

of identification with the organizing principles of a group or social order. In a wide range of circumstances, it would be wrong to intervene in such societies to compel them to recognize the authority of negative liberty over their own constitutive values."[17]

Here Galston argues that freedom of religion and/or conscience is not a matter of an unencumbered self's free choice but is deeply concerned with the freedom of an encumbered self in a certain religious and/or cultural group called "expressive liberty." Galston explains the critical importance of expressive liberty in liberalism in the following way: "Liberalism requires a robust though rebuttable presumption in favor of individuals and groups leading their lives as they see fit, within a broad range of legitimate variation, in accordance with their own understanding of what gives life meaning and value. I call this presumption the principle of *expressive liberty*. This principle implies a corresponding presumption (also rebuttable) against external interference with individual and group endeavors."[18]

What is interesting about expressive liberty is that it straddles positive liberty and negative liberty in an unusual manner – two kinds of liberty that Isaiah Berlin thought are incommensurable.[19] On one hand, it is a positive liberty, liberty to self-fulfillment and happiness in the identification with principles that govern the internal life of a group to which one belongs. On the other hand, the positive dimension of expressive liberty is sustained by an individual's and, in mediation of freedom of association, a group's negative liberty from external constraint. By "negative liberty," however, Galston does not mean a mere absence of external intervention or constraint. Nor does he mean by "external intervention or constraint" an obstacle standing in the way of free will or power as Thomas Hobbes understands it. In the pluralist societal context in which diverse individuals and groups exercise various forms of expressive liberty that are often in conflict with one another, negative liberty implies that "coercion [to restrict it] always stands exposed to a potential demand for justification." That is, negative liberty rests on "the insufficiency of the reasons typically invoked in favor of restricting it."[20] In this view, expressive liberty as a sort of positive liberty ought to be accommodated to the maximum extent possible, and it can be restricted only if there is a "compelling" (constitutional justificatory) reason on the part of the public authority.

In *Political Liberalism*, John Rawls, too, acknowledges the fundamental and irrevocable social change that the Reformation ushered into the modern world and identifies the defining feature of the altered social reality in terms of

[17] William A. Galston, *Liberal Pluralism: The Implications of Value Pluralism for Political Theory and Practice* (Cambridge: Cambridge University Press, 2002), 54.

[18] Ibid., 3.

[19] Isaiah Berlin, "Two Concepts of Liberty," in *Four Essays on Liberty* (Oxford: Oxford University Press, 1969).

[20] Galston, *Liberal Pluralism*, 58.

"the fact of pluralism." According to Rawls, however, diversity is not always a value, and it needs to be kept in its proper place. Not any pluralism but only *reasonable* pluralism, Rawls believes, is eligible for liberal constitutional protection and respect. In fact, when Rawls tries to "deal with" the fact of (reasonable) pluralism by means of overlapping consensus and encourages democratic citizens to appeal to public reason in public deliberation, he presents himself as a committed civic liberal for whom social cooperation, not mere toleration, is the ultimate value. Just like early modern political liberals (particularly John Locke), Rawls is deeply concerned with the "perils of pluralism" that the untrammeled claim to expressive liberty is likely to result in.

In the same liberal civic vein and strongly influenced by Rawls, Stephen Macedo says, "The point of public reasonableness is, after all, to accept the fact of reasonable pluralism, which means trying to discern principles that can be assessed and accepted by individuals who are committed to a wide range of different ways of life. In this way, citizens honor a duty of civility to one another."[21] Contra Galston championing diversity, Macedo asserts that "liberal constitutional institutions have a more deeply constitutive role than the rule of law ideal signifies: they must shape or constitute all forms of diversity over the course of time, so that people are satisfied leading lives of bounded individual freedom."[22] Upholding liberalism's positive constitutional and civic ambition, Macedo boldly declares that "liberalism is not about indiscriminate toleration."[23]

Galston opposes civic liberalism on two grounds. First, civic liberals fail to do justice to the essential characteristics of a modern world, a world "in which fundamental values are plural, conflicting, incommensurable in theory, and uncombinable in practice – a world in which there is no single, univocal summum bonum that can be defined philosophically, let alone imposed politically."[24] In other words, civic liberals do not fully appreciate a multiplicity of genuine goods or the heterogeneity of values, namely, *value pluralism*.[25] Second, in Galston's view, this failure to appreciate value pluralism as the ineluctable human condition of modernity has led some prominent liberals – to name a few, John Dewey, Jürgen Habermas, Robert Dahl, Amy Gutmann, Ian Shapiro, Stephen Macedo, as well as (albeit controversially) John Rawls – to be tempted by what he calls "civic totalism."[26] Civic totalism, the classic

[21] Stephen Macedo, *Diversity and Distrust: Civic Education in a Multicultural Democracy* (Cambridge, MA: Harvard University Press, 2000), 172.

[22] Ibid., 15.

[23] Ibid., 196.

[24] Galston, *Liberal Pluralism*, 30.

[25] Galston stresses that value pluralism is not relativism: "The distinction between good and bad, and between good and evil, is objective and rationally defensible.... [However, o]bjective goods cannot be fully rank-ordered, [which] means that there are no comprehensive lexical orderings among types of goods" (ibid., 5).

[26] William A. Galston, *The Practice of Liberal Pluralism* (Cambridge: Cambridge University Press, 2005), 3–40. Galston does appreciate Rawls's attention to value pluralism but still believes his

examples of which Galston finds in political philosophies of Aristotle, Hobbes, and Rousseau, stipulates that "politics enjoys general authority over subordinate activities and institutions because it aims at the highest and most comprehensive good for human beings" and that "civic health and morality cannot be achieved without citizens' wholehearted devotion to the common good."[27] The problem is that in the world of value pluralism the political purpose for "the highest and most comprehensive good for human beings" is simply implausible and any political attempt at it is dangerous.

This does not mean that liberal pluralism dismisses the value of public purposes or the importance of the common good altogether; quite the opposite. Galston begins his earlier work *Liberal Purposes* by saying that "the modern liberal state is best understood as energized by a distinctive ensemble of public purposes that guide liberal public policy, shape liberal justice, require the practice of liberal virtues, and rest on a liberal public culture. Liberal purposes, so conceived, define what the members of a liberal community must have in common."[28] And he clearly says that "the liberal state cannot be understood as an arena for the unfettered expression of difference" and that "in the very act of sustaining diversity, liberal unity circumscribes diversity."[29] What differentiates Galston from more civic-minded liberals is his pluralist conviction that for public purposes, the value of public institutions, and of the public activities they shape, must be understood as instrumental rather than intrinsic.[30] Galston says, "Pluralism does not abolish civic unity. Rather, it leads to a distinctive understanding of the relation between the requirements of unity and the claims of diversity in liberal politics.... Politics may be instrumentally rather than intrinsically good, and partial rather than plenipotentiary, but it is nonetheless essential."[31] Hence, from a liberal pluralist point of view, diversity is an intrinsic value, while politics is not, and neither is common citizenship. Since liberalism understands public institutions as limited rather than plenipotentiary, it endorses only the minimum conditions of public order in which a constitution represents only a "partial ordering" of value.[32]

In the end, liberal pluralism as political theory has two practical consequences that are relevant to democracy and democratic civil society. The first is

political liberalism relying on overlapping consensus to be civic totalism because it embraces only reasonable pluralism – reasonable only in light of liberal-democratic constitutional politics in the name of civic cooperation. From Galston's perspective, Rawlsian pluralist politics is too thickly perfectionist, while his is only minimally perfectionist. Of course, whether or not Galston's critique of Rawls is convincing is open to debate.

[27] Ibid., 24.

[28] William A. Galston, *Liberal Purposes: Goods, Virtues, and Diversity in the Liberal State* (Cambridge: Cambridge University Press, 1991), 3.

[29] Ibid., 3–4.

[30] Galston, *Liberal Pluralism*, 4.

[31] Ibid., 10.

[32] Ibid., 67.

"multiple sovereignties," which postulates that "our social life comprises multiple sources of authority and sovereignty – individuals, parents, associations, churches, and state institutions, among others – no one of which is dominant for all purposes and on all occasions."[33] Even "democracy," says Galston, "is not trumps for all purposes."[34] The second practical consequence of liberal pluralism is derived from the first, which is the incongruence between regime-level principles and the association of civil society. Galston says, "[P]ublic institutions must be cautious and restrained in their dealings with voluntary associations, and there is no presumption that a state may intervene in such associations just because they conduct their internal affairs in ways that diverge from general public principles."[35]

Earlier, I said that liberal pluralism poses a formidable challenge to Confucian democrats. The reason was that while they present Confucian democracy mainly as a communitarian corrective to Western liberal democracy that in their view is predicated on the assumption of unencumbered selfhood and autonomous individualism, liberal pluralism is supremely concerned with the extent of freedom of radically encumbered "social" individuals and of the associations that they voluntarily form. Now, Galston's political theory further complicates this challenge. It helps us to see that what is at stake is not so much the choice between unencumbered self and social self – the question with which Confucian communitarian democrats are preoccupied – but a much more complex choice that any real social individual is confronted with in a pluralist society – the choice between civic autonomy and cultural diversity (or value pluralism) or that between democratic citizenship (of whatever kind – be it liberal or Confucian) and associational membership. Then, a Confucian democrat is faced with a series of challenging theoretical and practical questions: Is Confucian democracy predicated on an ethical monism? Is Confucian democracy another version of civic totalism? Or is it aiming at pluralist politics undergirded by a thin notion of democratic citizenship? In a Confucian democracy may a state intervene in associations whose internal affairs do not conform to principles of the general public?

In the following section, I address these and related questions by exploring a mode of Confucian democracy that is plausible in a pluralist society. This exploration is important for the simple reason that East Asian societies are becoming increasingly pluralistic, no longer "the Confucian society" in any monolithic and monistic sense. But there is another reason that makes this exploration important. In the early 1990s, Confucian democracy was vigorously explored as a critical pluralist corrective to the hegemonic universalism (i.e., ethical, cultural, and political monism) of Western liberal democracy most

33 Ibid., 36.
34 Ibid., 9.
35 Ibid.

vividly manifested in Francis Fukuyama's end of history thesis.[36] However, because of their preoccupation with the communitarian critique of liberal democracy, Confucian democrats occasionally made and still make the similar mistake of ethical and cultural monism by assuming a given traditionally Confucian society (be it Chinese, Korean, or Taiwanese) as *the* Confucian society in which Confucian values entertain a monistic authority across the society. In consideration of logical coherence, therefore, Confucian democrats who once pressed Western liberal democrats with the charge of monism should meet the same pluralist challenge now arising from the inside. Given that East Asian Confucian societies are only partially Confucian in reality, what does it mean to search for a Confucian democracy, as distinct from liberal democracy, in such societies?

Reconstructing Confucian Democracy: From Communitarian to Pluralist

Originally sought as an alternative and corrective to the West's individualistic liberal democracy, Confucian democracy is casually presented (even assumed) as a communitarian political theory. For instance, inspired by Herbert Fingarette's insightful work on the Confucian ritual (*li* 禮), Russell Fox claims that Confucian rituals can contribute to the creation of a uniquely Confucian-style communitarian democracy.[37] By participating in rituals, Fox argues, not only can one cultivate "an immanent sociality," as opposed to sovereign individuality, but one can also become personally and socially "authoritative."[38] Fox explicates the meaning of "authority" that he believes is critical to the social vitality of Confucian communitarian democracy in reference to Roger Ames and Antonio Cua:

> Authority is "disclosed" through creativity, contextual and personal acts of *li* and thus is constantly in flux. Roger Ames writes that in a "ritual-ordered community, particular persons stand in relationships defined by creativity rather than power. This distinction between power and creativity is essential" to classical Confucianism.[39] With authority perceived as more tied to human artistry than power, there is a "transformation of all social relationships into personal relationships."[40] This elevation of personal creativity makes the exercise of authority, and the performance of *li*, an extremely intimate affair.[41]

[36] Francis Fukuyama, *The End of History and the Last Man* (New York: Free Press, 1992).

[37] Herbert Fingarette, *Confucius: The Secular as Sacred* (New York: Harper, 1972).

[38] Fox, "Confucian and Communitarian Responses to Liberal Democracy," 574.

[39] Quoted from Roger T. Ames, "Rites and Rights: The Confucian Alternative," in *Human Rights and the World's Religion*, ed. Leroy S. Rouner (Notre Dame: University of Notre Dame Press, 1988), 201.

[40] Quoted from Antonio S. Cua, "Confucian Vision and Human Community," *Journal of Chinese Philosophy* 11 (1984), 227–38, 227.

[41] Fox, "Confucian and Communitarian Responses to Liberal Democracy," 577–8.

At the heart of Fox's communitarianism is the aesthetic transformation of power into artistry and social and political relationships into intimate familial bonds through the performance of rituals. Ritual aestheticism is not peculiar to Fox's Confucian communitarian democracy, however. As we have seen in Chapter 2, some key advocates of Confucian communitarian democracy such as David Hall and Roger Ames, whose collaborative works Fox heavily draws on, and Sor-hoon Tan understand ritual aestheticism as the essence of Confucian social practice and therefore present it as the operating mechanism of their proposed Confucian democracy. Despite some variations in their theorizations, these scholars generally agree that Confucian democracy is a nonadversarial social practice, or in their preferred term, "a way of life" that is profoundly concerned with social harmony. Social harmony (*he* 和), it is accented, does not mean a static state of same-mindedness (*tong* 同) that fertilizes only pathological social conformism but a dynamic state or, in Tan's words, "ordered change," which embraces "not only diversity and contrast but also tension and resistance."[42] All in all, Confucian communitarian democrats concur that the gist of harmony, the Confucian communitarian social ideal par excellence, lies in "a unity in variety."

Thus formulated, Confucian communitarian democracy does not dismiss the value of diversity. In a pluralist point of view, however, the Confucian communitarian understanding and treatment of diversity is problematic for two mutually entwined reasons. First, it is important to note that there is a qualitative difference between "acknowledging the value of diversity" and "fully (of course within the constitutional limit) respecting diversity." Pluralists would contest that Confucian communitarians do not fully appreciate the intrinsic value of diversity and that they are predominantly focused on the state of moral unity that is (or *must* be) ultimately arrived at or "disclosed" as Fox puts it. The aesthetic synthesis of differences sounds fascinating, but it is the very impossibility of harmonization of different values that politics matters especially in a pluralist society.[43] What if individuals and associations resist accepting the political principles and social norms that govern the polity? (Recall Tibet.)[44] How can political tensions involving vehement resistance and its brutal crackdown

[42] Tan, *Confucian Democracy*, 76–7.

[43] Chantal Mouffe, *The Return of the Political* (London: Verso, 1993).

[44] With regard to the Tibet issue in China, Baogang He offers a Confucian prescription by saying that "[w]ithin a Confucian culture, with its emphasis on family, minorities are seen as younger brothers, sometimes as occasionally disobedient ones. Confucian obedience involves minority groups conforming to Confucian norms, maintaining unity and correct relations" ("Confucianism versus Liberalism over Minority Rights: A Critical Response to Will Kymlicka," *Journal of Chinese Philosophy* 31 [2004], 103–23, 115). I agree with He's reliance on Confucian familism in dealing with the multicultural problems in China, but it is questionable why minorities should be viewed as "younger" brothers, rather than just brothers or sisters. As will be clear in later chapters, the Confucian democracy that I propose in this book is more democratic egalitarian and pluralist than what He proposes.

be aesthetically harmonized? Liberal pluralists do not charge communitarians and/or civic republicans with neglecting human diversity and the multiplicity of value in toto. No sensible communitarian/civic republicans do. The point of their criticism lies precisely in the communitarian/civic-republican emphasis of (moral) unity over diversity. Confucian communitarians seem to be equally vulnerable to this charge.

Second and more important, Confucian communitarians' apparent negligence of the intrinsic value of diversity (hence their strong optimism about the possibility of aesthetic harmonization of diversity) is closely affiliated with the fact that most of them subscribe to Confucian role-ethics. For them, difference is not so much value pluralism but different roles that constitute the very core of the self, defining who one really *is*.[45] Craig Ihara says,

> Consider a company or a family where a cooperative whole is constituted through the fulfillment of role responsibilities. When a group is a kind of community working toward a common goal, talk of rights is neither necessary nor appropriate. In fact, it can be deleterious. Respect, equality, and dignity are all understood in terms of being a contributing member of a community. There will still be rules and boundaries, not because individuals in the community have rights, but because *roles have to be defined for the community to work effectively and to progress*.[46]

Whether or not Confucian democracy can or should accommodate the ethic of rights is an important question.[47] In our context, however, what is more important is to note Ihara's (and the Confucian communitarian) presumptions that individuals (in a Confucian society?) belong to one common, preexisting, community and that in such a community there exists a single moral authority that defines and allocates their proper social roles. It is simply assumed that in this idealized Confucian community individuals are governed by one authoritative moral/value system consisting of the moral discourse of *ren* 仁 (benevolence), *yi* 義 (righteousness), *li* 禮 (ritual propriety), *zhi* 智 (wisdom) and thought to be comprehensively committed to the ethics of the *wulun* 五倫, five "cardinal" human ethical bonds between ruler and ruled, between father and son, between husband and wife, between old and young, and between friends. What is completely dismissed here is the realistic attention to the possible challenge to, even rejection of, the very Confucian moral discourse and ethics by individuals subscribing to different value systems or "comprehensive moral doctrines" in Rawls's famous language. In

[45] David L. Hall and Roger T. Ames, "A Pragmatic Understanding of Confucian Democracy," in Bell and Hahm, *Confucianism for the Modern World*, 136.

[46] Craig K. Ihara, "Are Individual Rights Necessary? A Confucian Perspective" in Shun and Wong, *Confucian Ethics*, 27, emphasis added.

[47] For illuminating discussion on this issue, see David B. Wong, "Rights and Community in Confucianism," in Shun and Wong, *Confucian Ethics*; Fred Dallmayr "'Asian Values' and Global Human Rights," *Philosophy East and West* 52 (2002), 173–89; Joseph Chan, "Moral Autonomy, Civil Liberties, and Confucianism," *Philosophy East and West* 52 (2002), 281–310.

other words, Confucian communitarian democracy is tacitly predicated on the assumption of ethical monism.

Confucian communitarian democrats rarely pay attention to the fact that individuals are differently situated in society, each depending on which ethical/cultural/religious community they are a member of. Thus understood, Fox's dualism of "immanent sociality" versus "sovereign individuality" echoed by most Confucian communitarians is too simplistic to capture reality. It only diverts our attention from a more socially and politically meaningful and important tension, that is, the tension between Confucian-democratic citizenship and cultural membership. Fox (and Confucian communitarians) often glosses over the obvious fact that there are many forms of immanence, hence multiple modes of sociality, of which citizenship is only a part.

My pluralist critique of Confucian communitarian democracy thus far, however, is not to suggest the outright rejection of Confucian communitarianism as if it is disqualified to be a democratic political theory and social practice. As possessive individualism continues to go on a rampage on the global scale, the socioeconomic and political significance of communitarianism (including Confucian communitarianism) will (and should) not decrease.[48] My point is that while retaining its power to curb untrammeled private individualism, Confucian communitarianism, contrived as the cultural alternative to the West's rights-based individualism, must be significantly reconstructed into a robust *democratic political theory* that takes the fact of (reasonable) pluralism seriously. Put differently, Confucian communitarian democracy must be able to meet social and political problems arising in the modern pluralist societies that East Asian societies have become and are increasingly becoming.

Then how can we reinvent Confucian democracy from an ethically monistic or thick communitarianism into a pluralist political practice that is nevertheless devoted to the common good? I suggest three propositions: (1) the unity in Confucian democracy means not so much moral unity but constitutional unity, (2) Confucian virtues are differentiated (or pluralized) into moral virtues and civic virtues, and (3) in Confucian democracy minorities have the constitutional right to contest public norms in civil society.

1. Unity: Constitutional, Not Moral

As noted, Confucian communitarian democrats are not against pluralism. However, they hardly take the intrinsic value of diversity (value pluralism) seriously, partly because they understand human plurality in terms of different

[48] In most ethical and political theoretical literature, (Confucian) communitarianism is presented as an alternative to rights-based individualism, but it is debatable, to say the least, whether the two are indeed incommensurable as is often assumed (see Chapter 2 on this). What is certain, though, is that possessive individualism poses the biggest threat to communitarian ethos and democratic way of life. See Benjamin R. Barber, *Consumed: How Markets Corrupt Children, Infantilize Adults, and Swallow Citizens Whole* (New York: Norton, 2007).

social roles. Confucian communitarians cherish "diversity" insomuch as it can be aesthetically transformed into social harmony. For them, what holds an intrinsic value is the common (national?) community, the morals and ethics of which govern *all* individuals comprehensively.

The Confucian pluralist democrat does not lament the reality that no East Asian societies are "Confucian" in a comprehensive moral sense, nor does she strive ambitiously (or anachronistically) to make her society a communitarian whole. Appreciating the insights of communitarianism, she is wary of possessive individualism because it erodes the civic foundations of the polity, and as a democrat she attempts to moderate autonomous individualism because it tends to give too much emphasis to individual right over democratic citizenship. And as a democratic pluralist she does not hail diversity as such, but only reasonable diversity, and is deeply concerned with the unity of the polity. But she is more a constitutional democrat than a thick communitarian who, fully appreciating the intrinsic value of diversity and human plurality, finds problematic *any* (including aesthetic) attempt at a transformation of different identities into a single common whole, or multiple moral goods into a single common good. The unity she cherishes is not so much the moral unity (if at all possible), as the regime's political unity that is constitutionally secured. In short, Confucian democracy in a pluralist society should be understood as a kind of constitutional democracy.[49]

In the modern liberal political tradition, constitutional democracy is understood primarily in procedural terms such as individual rights, rule of law, and state neutrality. In fact, what characterizes recent liberalism (especially in the United States) is that the right has come to constitute the very content of the good. Thus, Michael Sandel, one of the strongest communitarian/republican critics of (rights-based) liberalism, calls the American constitutional democracy a "procedural republic," which to his Aristotelian moral sensibility is a contradiction in terms.[50]

While not refuting the importance of democratic proceduralism and democratic rights,[51] however, by constitutional unity in a Confucian

[49] Liberal democracy, too, is a kind of constitutional democracy, although there can be multiple variations of it, depending on how "liberalism" is understood and practiced. (The same is true for Confucian democracy.) Thus understood, what distinguishes a liberal democracy from a Confucian democracy is the nature of *constitution*, broadly understood, that governs the public affairs of the given society.

[50] Michael J. Sandel, *Democracy's Discontent: America in Search of a Public Philosophy* (Cambridge, MA: Belknap, 1996).

[51] By "democratic rights," I mean the political and civil rights that citizens in a democratic constitutional state are entitled to. They are qualitatively differentiated from human or natural rights that an individual person deserves morally *qua* human being. For the most elaborated statement of democratic rights, see Corey Brettschneider, *Democratic Rights: The Substance of Self-Government* (Princeton: Princeton University Press, 2007). I believe there is no reason for a Confucian democrat to oppose democratic rights, even if he or she may have a cultural or philosophical reason to be skeptical of the notion of natural rights.

pluralist democracy I do not mean a legal citizenship or the rule of law narrowly understood. I concur with Chaihark Hahm when he says, "[T]he success of a constitutional government depends on the disposition of its citizens. One might call this the 'political culture'; it might also be described as the civic virtue of citizens.... In other words, constitutionalism requires a certain type of citizens in order to function properly."[52] Inspired by Montesquieu, Tocqueville, and Clifford Geertz, Hahm understands constitution in terms of (civic) culture and mores, that is, "the constellation of contextual elements that can impede or enable the proper operation of legal ideas and institutions."[53] Law, in this understanding, is "a system of meaning, ... a distinctive grammar of the society according to which people make sense of the world and interact with one another."[54] A constitution that embodies the spirit of laws is "expressive of [a given] country's legal and political culture."[55]

What then is the core characteristic of Confucian constitutionalism? Once again, I share Hahm's conviction that ritual propriety (*li* 禮) "can provide a fruitful means of appropriating the Confucian cultural idiom for the project of establishing constitutionalism" in a Confucian democratic society.[56]

Philosophically, ritual propriety is inherently connected with *ren* 仁, the Confucian virtue par excellence, as clearly illustrated by Confucius in *Analects* 12:1 where he says, "To return the observance of the rites through overcoming the self constitutes benevolence (*ren* 仁)." Here both *li* and *ren* are presented as moral virtues – the virtues concerned with a person qua human being – and to that extent, they predicate the Confucian ethical system as a comprehensive and universalist moral and philosophical doctrine.

Therefore, to impose *li* of this kind on members of a democratic civil society, where they belong to different religious and (sub)cultural associations and thus are committed to different moral values, critically violates value pluralism. Indeed, in the modern context, it makes no sense to regard a person (say, a Korean Muslim) who does not subscribe to the comprehensive (or monistic) Confucian moral notion of ritual propriety as less authentic or less authoritative (according to Hall and Rosemont's translation of *ren*) as a human being.[57]

[52] Chaihark Hahm, "Constitutionalism, Confucian Civic Virtue, and Ritual Propriety," in Bell and Hahm, *Confucianism for the Modern World*, 33–4.

[53] Ibid., 38.

[54] Ibid., 39.

[55] Ibid., 41. This does not mean that (civic) culture is a static semiotic system. As Hahm admits, "culture is never a fully integrated, coherent, static, totalizing, seamless whole.... Culture always has room for subcultures and countercultures" (40). My third proposition (i.e., democratic contestability) is based on this dual nature of public/civic culture, which helps bind citizens horizontally and yet leaves (even makes) room for contestation with its totalizing reification. And this is the central feature of what I call "civil Confucianism" (see Chapter 2).

[56] Ibid., 43.

[57] Though I agree that Joseph Chan's moderate Confucian perfectionism can resolve many theoretical problems in making Confucianism a modern political philosophy, I still have strong reservations about it, particularly the state moral education that is integral to it. This is not to

In a Confucian pluralist democracy, both the nature and scope of the *li* is changed: its nature is primarily political (that is, constitutional) rather than moral and its scope is limited to political/civic culture, hence not concerned with human nature and moral perfection.[58] It is reinvented into a democratic civic virtue that transforms a private individual (in the market and his or her self-chosen private association) into a characteristically Confucian public citizen by helping him or her to restrain his or her unsocial passions and untrammeled self-interest, two major factors that are prone to exacerbate a toxic mode of identity politics and antidemocratic consumerism. From the standpoint of Confucian democratic pluralism, human moral perfectibility – whether or not one becomes an authoritative moral person (*junzi* 君子) or even a sage – is only a secondary question. What is more important is civic transformability through the practice of Confucian ritual (*fuli* 復禮).

In the pluralist democratic civil society I propose, *li* may not be able to resolve all social conflicts as traditional Confucians believed, for whom *li* (in tandem with music [*yue* 樂]) was the primary mechanism to achieve social harmony (*he* 和).[59] However, it can help bring citizens holding diverse values and identities to a shared political arena where they can codeliberate the problems that they commonly face.[60]

deny the importance of a certain educational mechanism through which citizens can be socialized into Confucian civics and mores. What I do not agree with (and reject) is that the principle agent for such a mechanism should be the state rather than social intermediaries in a democratic civil society, including schools, religious organizations, neighborhoods, community groups, and, most important, (extended) families. For Chan's moderate Confucian state perfectionism, see his *Confucian Perfectionism: A Political Philosophy for Modern Times* (Princeton: Princeton University Press, 2013). Also see Stephen C. Angle, *Sagehood: The Contemporary Significance of Neo-Confucian Philosophy* (Oxford: Oxford University Press, 2009), 204–9; Angle, *Contemporary Confucian Political Philosophy: Toward Progressive Confucianism* (Cambridge: Polity, 2012), 139–42.

58 On the danger of the politics aiming at moral perfection, see Michael Oakeshott, *The Politics of Faith and the Politics of Scepticism*, ed. Timothy Fuller (New Haven: Yale University Press, 1996).

59 See *Analects* 2:3; 13:3.

60 In saying this, I have in mind East Asian societies (such as South Korea, Taiwan, and China) that were traditionally Confucian and are now under staggering pressure to be Western-liberal democratized in both its political hardware and its public-civic cultural software. That is, my argument thus far is plausible only in the societies where Confucian rituals (and the mores and habits they generate) are still alive in the daily lives of ordinary citizens, however unconsciously. In this respect, my proposed Confucian pluralist democracy is mildly republican (in the sense it assumed one constitutional order and its background civic culture), but the same can be said about Galston's liberal pluralism whose pluralist constitutionalism heavily relies on a viable civic culture. Also, in the same respect, my book does not aim to propose Confucianism as a global philosophy, though I value such a proposal, provided that Confucianism understood as a *philosophical* system is adequately modified to be relevant in the modern societal context. For an attempt at such a conception of Confucianism, see Stephen Angle's works cited in note 57 in this chapter.

Thus understood, what is central to Confucian constitutionalism is the citizenry's willingness and capacity to maintain and reproduce an integrated (however democratically contested) Confucian political/civic culture. Confucian political/civic culture renders a given polity characteristically (if not essentially) Confucian, thus representing it as such to the outside world, which is increasingly culturally homogeneous and ethically monistic. At the same time, in civil society, Confucian political/civic culture, which binds the citizens horizontally, presents itself as the constitutional bulwark for (sub)cultural diversity and value pluralism by motivating and coordinating public deliberation across differences.[61] In this way, Confucian pluralist democracy attempts to strike a balance between international/global pluralism and domestic social pluralism.

2. *Confucian Virtues: Moral and Civic*

My first proposition entails two practical suggestions, which together constitute my second proposition: first, to differentiate (or pluralize) Confucian virtues into moral virtues concerned with a person's moral well-being qua human being and civic virtues related to the polity's *public character* and its reproduction; and second, to make only the latter relevant to the general public in a Confucian democracy. One may wonder how the second proposition can actually be worked out from Confucianism whose virtue ethics, just like Aristotelian ethics, is essentially monistic. For instance, Joseph Chan, who understands Confucianism as a theory of ethical perfectionism (monist ethics in other words), would be quite pessimistic about my apparently sanguine view on the possibility of Confucian pluralist democracy. Chan writes,

> As a theory of ethical perfectionism, Confucianism is inclined to view ethical disagreements as something regrettable, or something that is a result of human errors that can be overcome through proper ethical or rational training. As a theory of social and political perfectionism, Confucianism is inclined to suggest that disagreements should be removed as much as possible, and that the state should be led by the wise and the ethically better informed so as to resolve those conflicts and equip people with appropriate mental and ethical capacities.[62]

Here Chan is focused more on Confucianism than on pluralism and tries to accommodate the latter to the former while leaving Confucian perfectionist/

[61] Iris Marion Young points out "greeting" – whose gist she finds consisting of public acknowledgment – as one of the modes of inclusive communication (and public deliberation) because it offers the "communicative moment of taking the risk of trusting in order to establish and maintain the bond of trust necessary to sustain a discussion about issues that face us together" (*Inclusion and Democracy* [Oxford: Oxford University Press, 2000], 58). I think that once reconstructed as civic culture, Confucian ritual can fulfill what Young's "greeting" attains in civic cooperation and public deliberation.

[62] Joseph Chan, "Confucian Attitudes toward Ethical Pluralism," in *Confucian Political Ethics*, ed. Daniel A. Bell (Princeton: Princeton University Press, 2008), 115.

monist ethics intact. The social and political consequence of this strategy is political perfectionism assisted by meritocratic elitism, to which I will return later.[63] My position is quite the opposite – that Confucian ethics must be accommodated to the reality of value pluralism. While part of my goal in the previous section (my first proposition) was to offer a normative justification for the separation between Confucian moral and civic virtues, in this section I attempt to show the practical importance of this separation (as a way of accommodating Confucianism to value pluralism) from an empirical standpoint by paying attention to the social reality of East Asian post-Confucian societies, particularly South Korea.

When we call East Asian societies "Confucian," it is not because East Asians comprehensively subscribe to Confucianism (particularly Confucian ethics) by holding it as their self-chosen value system but because, often independently of their self-chosen value system (be it Protestantism, Catholicism, Buddhism, or Islam), they nevertheless live their lives largely in accordance with Confucian mores and habits, mostly informed by Confucian rituals and the ethical values associated with them. For example, according to Byung-ik Koh's empirical study on Confucianism in contemporary Korean society, fewer than 2 percent of Koreans self-consciously choose Confucianism as their religious faith, while about 20 percent choose Christianity.[64] Nevertheless, Koh, a sociologist, concludes that Korean society is culturally Confucian because Confucianism functions as habits of the heart of the Korean people, providing practical guidance to their daily social and political life. Put differently, most contemporary Koreans may not be "Confucian" in the comprehensive moral sense or in belief but they *are* still Confucian in practice – in the sense that Koreans, despite

[63] This does not mean that perfectionism is inherently at odds with pluralism. In fact, most contemporary perfectionists deny such an incompatibility thesis (see Joseph Raz, *The Morality of Freedom* [Oxford: Clarendon, 1986]; George Sher, *Beyond Neutrality: Perfectionism and Politics* [Cambridge: Cambridge University Press, 1997]; Steven Wall, *Liberalism, Perfectionism and Restraint* [Cambridge: Cambridge University Press, 1998]). Nor do I intend to say that monistic ethics is always oppressive of value pluralism. All I am saying here is that Chan's Confucian perfectionism is monistic and when tied with meritocratic elitism is likely to suppress value pluralism.

[64] Byung-ik Koh, "Confucianism in Contemporary Korea," in Tu, *Confucian Traditions in East Asian Modernity*. For the statistical data implying the similar observation, see Bae-ho Han, *Han'guk jeongchimunhwawa munjujeongchi* [Korean Political Culture and Democracy] (Seoul: Beopmunsa, 2003), 98. The key finding of Koh's research is not simply that a very small segment of Korean population is Confucian in the religious sense. Its far-reaching sociological and political message is that Koreans, while not self-consciously Confucian, are still "Confucian" in their cultural practice – good or bad. The importance of this finding should be appreciated against the background that in ordinary Korean *minds*, Confucian values are casually associated with antiliberal and antidemocratic norms such as patriarchy, gender discrimination, rigid hierarchy, and nepotism. In this regard, it is notable that virtually no political party or civic association (except Confucian clan associations) in Korea advocates Confucian values proactively.

all their religious and societal diversity, largely subscribe to Confucian ritual practice, which *constitutes* the civic/public culture in Korea.[65]

Considering the notable incongruence between belief/value and practice in East Asian societies,[66] therefore, Confucian democracy must be a morally circumscribed project, however vibrant it should be as social and political practice. That is, a Confucian democratic state should not promote Confucianism as a comprehensive moral doctrine with the presumption that those who do not conform to Confucian moral precepts are led morally astray, thus, by implication, needing "proper ethical and rational training" as Joseph Chan suggests. It would be indeed absurd to claim that more than 98 percent of Koreans are neither fully ethical nor fully rational because they are not a Confucian in the monist/perfectionist sense.

In a Confucian democracy, it is not problematic that citizens belong to different religious, ethnic, and cultural communities and associations, and hold different ethical values. Since virtually all contemporary Confucians emphasize the social dimension of the self and enthusiastically remind liberal democrats of the critical importance of what Will Kymlicka calls "societal culture" that makes personal life really meaningful,[67] it is even more plausible that Confucian democracy should respect a particular mode of social encumbrance experienced differently by individuals who nevertheless share one common *political* society. The fact that Confucian ethics is a monist or perfectionist ethics does not necessarily entail the conclusion that Confucian democracy ought to be a monist or perfectionist social and political practice. In a Confucian democracy, Confucianism constrains democracy, but it is simultaneously constrained by a democracy to which human plurality and collective self-determination are central.

[65] Surprisingly, according to Doh Chull Shin's survey research, the overarching Korean value system is still largely Confucian despite religious diversity and value pluralism among Koreans. See his *Confucianism and Democratization in East Asia* (New York: Cambridge University Press, 2012). Also see Chong-Min Park and Doh Chull Shin, "Do Asian Values Deter Popular Support for Democracy in South Korea?," *Asian Survey* 46 (2006), 341–61. Su-young Ryu's most recent empirical research on the Korean Confucian value system is worth special attention. First, Ryu extracted 113 items on the basis of content analysis of existing research results and newspaper articles from 1990 to 2006 that had dealt with Koreans' value system. Then she selected items reflecting typical Confucian values among those items through the Q-sort technique conducted by five experts on East Asian philosophy, thereby producing 37 statistically reliable and valid items. With these selected items, then, Ryu tested over 500 samples (age range from nineteen to fifty-seven years) by relying on common factor analysis and cross-validity testing. Her findings showed that Korean value systems mainly reflect collective values and emphasize rituals, family, and human relations. See Su-young Ryu, "Han'gukinui yugyojeok gachicheukjeongmunhang gaebal yeon'gu" [Item Development for Korean Confucian Values], *Korean Journal of Management* 15 (2007), 171–205.

[66] On this point, see Sungmoon Kim, "Confucianism in Contestation: The May Struggle of 1991 in South Korea and Its Lesson," *New Political Science* 31 (2009), 49–68.

[67] Will Kymlicka, *Multicultural Citizenship* (New York: Oxford University Press, 1995), 76.

Thus understood, what makes a democracy in a particular East Asian country a "Confucian democracy" is its Confucian public character embedded in the Confucian public/civic culture and the citizenry's resolve to maintain and reproduce it. In such a pluralist Confucian democracy, citizens have the constitutional right to become a member of a particular religious/moral/cultural community (i.e., freedom of association) and can subscribe to whatever value system they believe would make their life socially meaningful and morally flourishing. Confucian democracy, however, simultaneously stipulates that the value system, according to which people (qua members) choose to lead their lives, must be reasonable in light of Confucian public culture consisting of Confucian mores and habits that are widely shared and practiced in the civil society independently of the individual citizen's self-chosen value system. As democratic citizens, individuals in a Confucian democracy are *morally* required to vigorously and voluntarily embody the Confucian mores and habits that sustain and reproduce their public way of life. In other words, Confucian democratic citizens should be civically virtuous.

One may wonder about the nature of this "moral requirement" – that is, if individuals have a constitutional right to choose their personal moral value system within the civil society, what is the source and nature of this second-order *morality*, which, logically speaking, should be independently justified from the self-chosen moral value system? In other words, why should non-Confucians in civil society submit themselves to the Confucian political/civic culture, even when it is granted that the Confucianism at issue here is not a comprehensive moral doctrine?[68] My answer is twofold: first, because they are *citizens* of, say, Korean society – it is worth repeating that I do not make a universalist claim; my argument is specifically targeted at traditionally Confucian societies that remain Confucian at least in their public culture – in which their public reason is largely grounded in Confucian social habits and moral sensibility; second, as citizens they should not dismiss wholesale what they share in common at least in their public life, especially in the face of the ethically and culturally monistic force of globalization.[69] I agree Benjamin Barber when he says, "Biting the bullet, advocates of strong democratic civil society acknowledge that they are less than neutral; their conception of civil society is a rather restricted subset of all possible forms of association, and they limit it to forms that are at least nominally or potentially democratic and open."[70]

In other words, while democratic citizens should entertain the freedom of moral pluralism *within* civil society, they are simultaneously obligated to

[68] Whether it is possible to conceptually separate civic virtue from moral virtue in the Confucianism ethical system – which is purely a philosophical question – is a different issue. My second proposition is that this separation is necessary in modern East Asian societies that may wish to have both value pluralism and common citizenship in their civil society.

[69] See David Miller, *On Nationality* (Oxford: Oxford University Press, 1995).

[70] Benjamin R. Barber, *A Place for Us: How to Make Society Civil and Democracy Strong* (New York: Hill and Wang), 53.

maintain and reproduce the constitutional integrity, which is at once cultural and political, of their political regime. This obligation is constitutional-political in origin but is still a moral obligation in nature because it is deeply concerned with the democratic ideal of collective self-determination (and global pluralism).[71]

Before moving to my third proposition, let me recapitulate my core claim in this section: In a traditional Confucian society (say, Song-Ming China or Chosŏn Korea), Confucian virtue ethics was a universalist ethics focused on a person's moral well-being and development qua human being. The *junzi* 君子 (Confucian gentleman) was essentially a moral ideal. In a Confucian pluralist democracy, however, Confucian moral virtues associated with comprehensive moral ideas (or ideals) such as Dao 道, Heaven (*tian* 天), human nature (*xing* 性), and sagehood (*sheng* 聖) are relevant only to those who are self-conscious Confucians. For these people, Confucianism is not merely a public culture; it is their value/belief system that dictates their way of life in the morally comprehensive sense. According to Koh, approximately 2 percent of Koreans are Confucian in this sense (i.e., both in belief and in practice), most of whom are members of clan organizations, called *jungjong* 中宗 in Korean, whose internal affairs are strictly governed by the Family Ritual (*garye* 家禮, *jiali* in Chinese). While for Confucian democrats Confucianism is concerned with how to live a decent public life as a citizen, for Confucian believers Confucianism is about how to live a good life as a human being. Confucian pluralist democracy takes this distinction seriously.[72]

3. Confucian Civil Society and Democratic Contestation

I argued earlier that not any value system but only "reasonable" value systems in light of Confucian public culture deserve civic respect and constitutional protection. Now, both liberals (especially in the Kantian vein) and democrats may oppose my use of the term "reasonable," though for different reasons.

First, Kantian egalitarian liberals such as Brian Barry would claim that reasonableness can be discerned only in reference to *public reason*, which

[71] For an illuminating discussion on the importance of global pluralism and collective self-determination of a people, see John Rawls, *The Law of Peoples* (Cambridge, MA: Harvard University Press, 1999).

[72] In this regard, I strongly oppose the recent attempts by some Chinese Confucian scholars to promote the government by the community of Confucian scholars and make Confucianism a state religion in China. For such attempts, see Jiang Qing, *Zhengzhi Rujia: Dangdai Rujia de zhuanxiang, tezhi yu fazhan* [Political Confucianism: Contemporary Confucianism's Challenge, Special Quality, and Development] (Beijing: San lian shu dian, 2003); Kang Xiaoguang, *Renzheng: Zhongguo zhengzhi fazhan de disantiao daolu* [Humane Government: A Third Road for the Development of Chinese Politics] (Singapore: Global, 2005). For a critical engagement with Kang's and Jiang's political proposals, see Angle, *Contemporary Confucian Political Philosophy*, 41–7 and Sungmoon Kim, "Michael Oakeshott and Confucian Constitutionalism," in *Michael Oakeshott's Cold War Liberalism*, ed. Terry Nardin (New York: Palgrave Macmillan, forthcoming 2014), respectively.

is independent from any comprehensive moral doctrines and not necessarily grounded in a given society's public culture. Barry's strong liberal egalitarianism encourages him to berate cultural and value pluralists (whom he groups together as "multiculturalists") for failing to grasp the core democratic commitment that people who are different *ought to* be treated equally, the idea that is best inscribed in John Rawls's often misunderstood idea of the Original Position.[73]

In this view, Confucian mores and habits are too context-dependent, hence too malleable, to be able to provide a firm public ground for reasonableness. This charge, however, is based on rationalist presumption. The rationalist resolution (e.g., overlapping consensus) *may* be an attractive political option to deal with the intractable fact of pluralism in a radically diverse civil society such as the American civil society, though liberal pluralists like Galston oppose it, believing that such a resolution only undermines expressive liberty and associational freedom, but its plausibility in the Confucian democratic context is doubtful. Barry's understanding of "public reason" is particularly problematic from a Confucian standpoint. While Barry's public reason is completely detached (or uprooted) from what Rawls calls "the background culture" or "the culture of civil society,"[74] I believe that in the East Asian Confucian societies where institutional politics was traditionally predicated and operating on the moral-cultural-political semiotics of the *li* 禮 and the moral sentiment of *ren* 仁, the understanding of public reason as solely belonging to "a conception of a well-ordered constitutional (liberal) democratic society" is too narrow.[75]

Confucian pluralist democrats do not put constitutional politics beyond the background culture in civil society; nor do they refuse to allow public status to the background culture. They may not necessarily oppose an attempt to make constitutional essentials governed by principles of justice that are derived from public reason, but for them, public reason is neither pure rational faculty nor solely concerned with formal institutional politics. Being sensitive to the internal differentiation of democratic civil society – common public/civic culture where public reason is *cultivated* as well as exercised on one level and pluralist associational life on another – Confucian democratic pluralists are more attentive to the inextricable intertwinement between public culture and constitutional politics or the constitutional politics *of* public culture. As we have seen,

[73] Brian Barry, *Culture and Equality* (Cambridge, MA: Harvard University Press, 2001), 69.

[74] Rawls, *Law of Peoples*, 134.

[75] Ibid., 131. Also see Barry, *Culture and Equality*, 88. In my view, Sharon Krause's Humean (moral sentimental) understanding of public reason wound find strong resonance in the East Asian societies: "Public reasons reflect the shared horizons of concern that are implicit in the political culture of a particular community" (Sharon R. Krause, *Civil Passions: Moral Sentiment and Democratic Deliberation* [Princeton: Princeton University Press, 2008], 157).

Chaihark Hahm's "Confucian constitutionalism" lends support to this aspect of Confucian pluralist democracy.

In my view, a more serious challenge to my notion of "reasonableness in light of Confucian public culture" comes from the democracy school. Democrats would take issue with the communitarian element (however weak) implicated in Confucian pluralist democracy. From their point of view, the claim that citizens in a Confucian democracy should be civically committed to Confucian mores and habits is likely to do injustice to those who are non-Confucians, even in any weak sense. Immigrants (say Pakistan Muslims) and their Korean/Chinese/Taiwanese spouses, for instance, would likely protest the elevation of Confucian mores and habits as the public culture, precisely because they resist participating in the existing structure of shared meaning. In short, some members of Confucian democracy would raise a pressing question as to why the democracy that directly governs their social and political life should be a *Confucian* democracy.

But what is democracy? Is it merely "a system of ruled open-endedness, or organized uncertainty," as Adam Przeworski's formalistic definition says of it?[76] Is democracy simply about sharing and distributing power and interest as Ian Shapiro seems to claim?[77] But doesn't even Galston emphasize the fundamental importance of "liberal purposes" (not *any* civic purposes) as the public cultural underpinning of what he calls "pluralist constitutionalism" in American democracy?[78] Then, why not "Confucian purposes" composed of filial piety, fraternal love, respect of elders, moral legitimacy of political relationship, civic trust, and social harmony?[79]

Postmodernists and radical pluralists blame any form of social integration as (civic) totalitarian, and they hardly value the polity's public character as if it is a mere political ideology, failing to distinguish between the integration that promotes democratic citizenship and the integration (i.e., assimilation) that suppresses human plurality and fails to accommodate value diversity. But as Rogers Smith powerfully demonstrates, there is no civic constitutionalism as such that is completely free of any ideal of peoplehood.[80] Moreover, wholesale refusal to participate in the existing structure of shared meaning is not about

76 Adam Przeworski, *Democracy and the Market* (Cambridge: Cambridge University Press, 1991), 13.

77 Ian Shapiro, *The State of Democratic Theory* (Princeton: Princeton University Press, 2003).

78 See William A. Galston, "Pluralist Constitutionalism," *Social Philosophy and Policy* 28 (2011), 228–41.

79 By "social harmony" I mean dynamic social harmonization in the public space of civil society that involves not only public deliberation but also democratic contestation for more inclusionary public policies. For my understanding of harmony in a Confucian democratic civil society, see Chapter 2.

80 Rogers M. Smith *Stories of Peoplehood: The Politics and Morals of Political Membership* (Cambridge: Cambridge University Press, 2003).

pluralism but a signal of the "perils of pluralism," which drove early modern Western political theorists to search for the model of social contract as the legitimate form of social integration.[81]

Still, critics (including liberal pluralists) might find my emphasis of Confucian civics troubling on the assumption that the core issue for any intrinsically pluralist society is maintenance of equal constitutional status for each and every fundamentally different and contesting value system/life form in a certain universally justifiable political culture or public domain. I am not sure, however, that a respect for the intrinsic value of value pluralism necessarily entails a typically "liberal" mode of pluralist politics in which the characteristically liberal procedural values (i.e., the right), often considered universally justifiable, have become the substantive goods of liberal politics.[82] Value pluralism was never a part of traditional Confucian culture and it has rarely (almost never) been upheld in the public discourse of contemporary East Asian politics until very recently.[83] Even the heroic citizen-led democratization of East Asian countries (particularly South Korea and Taiwan) was not inspired by, nor intended for, value pluralism, although it was made possible by a political pluralism that differentiated democratic civil society, which was largely Confucian-originated and offered a citadel for popular will, from the authoritarian state.[84]

Thus understood, it is futile to think about, let alone advocate, value pluralism in modern Confucian societies without considering the societal and political context (i.e., Confucian civil society) that made democratization possible or even likely. At the same time, the ongoing struggle by ordinary East Asian citizens to strike a creative middle ground between maintaining their cultural identity as Confucian-Chinese/Korean/Taiwanese on one hand and respectfully accommodating value pluralism in their *existing* democratic or democratizing civil society on the other, should not be dismissed. As value pluralism is

[81] See Richard Boyd, *Uncivil Society: The Perils of Pluralism and the Making of Modern Liberalism* (Lanham, MD: Lexington Books, 2004).

[82] The uniquely liberal cultural fusion of procedural and substantive liberal political values is characteristic of many of civic liberals such as Amy Gutmann and Dennis Thompson, *Democracy and Disagreement: Why Moral Conflict Cannot Be Avoided in Politics, and What Should Be Done about It* (Cambridge, MA: Belknap, 1996); Stephen Macedo, *Liberal Virtues: Citizenship, Virtue, and Community in Liberal Constitutionalism* (Oxford: Clarendon, 1990); Richard Dagger, *Civic Virtues: Rights, Citizenship, and Republican Liberalism* (Oxford: Oxford University Press, 1997); Thomas A. Spragens, *Civic Liberalism: Reflections on Our Democratic Ideals* (Lanham, MD: Rowman & Littlefield, 1999). Galston's political position is unique because, unlike the civic liberals mentioned earlier, he derives the substantive liberal goods independently from liberal proceduralism. Of course, whether or not Galston's liberal goods are in fact independent of liberal proceduralism is a different story.

[83] Of course, free worship and tolerance were the norm in traditional China. But no traditional Confucians advocate the plurality of values as a distinct moral good.

[84] See, for instance, Namhee Lee, "The South Korean Student Movement: *Undongkwŏn* as a Counterpublic Sphere," in Armstrong, *Korean Society*; Geir Helgesen, *Democracy and Authority in Korea: The Cultural Dimension in Korean Politics* (Surrey: Curzon, 1998).

increasingly a social reality of East Asian Confucian societies, the respect of its intrinsic value should be pursued from within by modifying the Confucian public societal context that renders these societies characteristically Confucian – hence my first and second propositions.

What is more politically constructive in making a Confucian democracy a more pluralistic political practice is to allow minority groups the constitutional civil right to contest the existing public norms freely in civil society. That is, those who are not deeply soaked in Confucian mores and habits (such as immigrants and social minorities) should be able to contest the public reason cultivated in the public culture of Confucian democratic society as freely as possible, yet within the constitutional limit even when they are challenging that very limit.

For instance, same-sex couples and feminists should be able to contest the predominant Confucian public understanding of the "normal family." But they may do so without wholly refuting the value of the family as such and without accentuating their individual human rights in opposition to public interests and common democratic purposes.[85] Rather, they may be able to achieve their goal by actively appealing to the fundamental Confucian value of family relationships, though they would have to persuade the general public to be tolerant of nontraditional forms of the family. That is, without a direct recourse to the rights discourse, human rights can be effectively (even more effectively) promoted in ways that do not disrupt fundamentally the existing semiotics of social meaning that embody social affect and mutual concerns, if Confucian public reason is reasonably contested through its creative reappropriations in the service of minority rights.[86]

This suggestion may satisfy neither liberal democrats nor traditional Confucians, but I think it is an unavoidable price for Confucian pluralist democracy. To repeat, in Confucian democracy Confucianism and democracy are constraining each other. Confucian democracy is neither traditionally Confucian nor abstractly democratic. It is a realistic political practice that aims to be most suitable in the given cultural and sociopolitical context in East Asia.

[85] In saying this, I am by no means implying that human rights claim is inherently in opposition to public interest and democratic purposes. My point is that social minorities can claim their civil rights in a less adversarial and more politically productive manner if they are able to creatively reappropriate the existing cultural-moral-political semiotics in a Confucian society whose citizens are not yet very familiar with the discourse of human rights. In other words, my point is about the strategy of social struggle and moral contestation.

[86] A philosophical basis for this cultural reappropriation has been discussed by many so-called Confucian feminists. See, for instance, Li-Hsiang L. Rosenlee, *Confucianism and Women: A Philosophical Interpretation* (Albany: State University of New York Press, 2006) as well as essays in Chenyang Li (ed.), *The Sage and the Second Sex: Confucianism, Ethics and Gender* (Chicago: Open Court, 2000). I revisit this issue with more articulation in Chapter 11.

Concluding Remarks

In this chapter, I have justified the search of Confucian pluralist democracy on two grounds: first, by drawing attention to the reality that East Asian, traditionally Confucian, societies are rapidly becoming pluralist societies; and second, by challenging ethical monism implicit in the theorizations of Confucian democracy by those who present themselves as cultural and ethical pluralists when it comes to their critique of the global hegemony of Western liberal democracy. There is yet another reason, a more politically relevant one, that Confucian democracy must be a pluralist political theory and practice. Once again, I turn to the meritocracy thesis that I have critically examined in Chapter 3.

As we have seen, some Confucian democrats such as Daniel Bell, Tongdong Bai, and Joseph Chan have been increasingly attracted to the meritocratic justification of Confucian democracy.[87] Although they differ on detail, they share two baseline assumptions: (1) democracy understood as one person, one vote (or egalitarian distribution of political power) is highly susceptible to the whim of the "ignorant" or "uneducated" mass and (2) the idea of respect for rule by an educated elite – "the best and the brightest" in Bell's language[88] – is a dominant strand of Confucian political culture.

Confucian meritocratic democrats argue that the best government is attained when the morally virtuous (and knowledgeable) few rule the ordinary people who are more or less the petty men preoccupied with private interests. Here what is assumed is the traditional Confucian dichotomy between morality (*ren yi* 仁義) and self-interest (*li* 利), or, more accurately, the tension between morality that transforms self-interest into the common good and myopic self-interest. In traditional Confucianism, a *junzi* 君子 is one who has overcome one's egoistic self (*ke ji* 克己) and returned to ritual propriety (*fu li* 復禮), thereby realizing the moral virtue of *ren* (*wei ren* 爲仁), the Confucian virtue par excellence. What is central to the meritocracy thesis is that the *junzi* should be the political leader in contemporary East Asia.

This seemingly innocuous claim, however, is heavily problematic from the Confucian pluralist democratic viewpoint; for the traditional dualism between morality and self-interest that the advocates of meritocratic elitism uncritically embrace is no longer feasible in a pluralist society where the choice is not *only* between morality and self-interest (or immorality) but more frequently between multiple moral goods. In a pluralist society where the lexical hierarchy of *the* morality is impossible, who are the morally best and according to whose

[87] Daniel A. Bell, *Beyond Liberal Democracy: Political Thinking for an East Asian Context* (Princeton: Princeton University Press, 2006); Tongdong Bai, "A Mencian Version of Limited Democracy," *Res Publica* 14 (2008), 19–34; Joseph Chan, "Democracy and Meritocracy: Toward a Confucian Perspective," *Journal of Chinese Philosophy* 34 (2007), 179–93.

[88] Bell, *Beyond Liberal Democracy*, 157.

ethics? Or, is the Confucian meritocratic democrats' real intent to restore the lexical hierarchy of morality solely on the basis of Confucian ethics?[89]

It is far from my intention to deny the importance of the moral merit of political agents. My point, at least in our context, is that Confucian meritocratic democrats must take the theoretical and practical challenges arising from the fact of pluralism seriously or that they should clarify what they mean by "the (morally) best" in the pluralist societal context, let alone how to select them "democratically" as the political leader. As it currently stands, Confucian meritocratic democracy is uncritically founded on Confucian moral monism as if East Asian societies (particular China, the country of their major focus) are "Confucian" in the morally comprehensive sense, which, even more problematically, allows no room for reasonable moral conflicts and their democratic resolution.[90] While Confucian moral monism implicated in Confucian communitarian democracy results from insufficient attention to the intrinsic value of diversity, Confucian moral monism assumed in Confucian meritocratic democracy is the consequence of the disregard, even suppression, of the value of diversity. The results can be politically dangerous, to say the least.

[89] Therefore, in Chapter 7, I argue that in selecting good leaders in a representative democracy, goodness should be defined *extraneously* in reference to the candidate's *democratic civic integrity*, not according to his or her personal moral goodness, the meaning of which varies depending on which moral community he or she belongs to.

[90] Joseph Chan consciously differentiates moderate Confucian perfectionism from extreme Confucian perfectionism and presents the former as non-comprehensive (in the Rawlsian sense). However, considering that his preferred mode of leadership (or government) is, in Michael Oakeshott's language, "lordship," and given that a particular mode of the state (enterprise vs. civil) is postulated in a particular mode of leadership (managerial vs. ruling), I doubt that Chan's moderate Confucian perfectionism operating on managerial lordship (or state paternalism) can successfully keep the mode of the Confucian polity that he proposes from becoming a purposive enterprise association, which as Oakeshott powerfully shows is potentially oppressive of human plurality (see Michael Oakeshott, *On Human Conduct* [Oxford: Clarendon, 1975], 311–17). I admit that my proposed Confucian democracy, too, is moderately purposive (hence equally susceptible to the Oakeshottian criticism) but I find this much of purposiveness of the polity to be an ineluctable price *for* democratic coexistence and flourishing of human pluralities. Since Chan acknowledges only the instrumental value of democracy and for him the supreme political goal is to attain moral perfection, I am curious how his *Confucian* perfectionism, albeit moderate, can genuinely accommodate value pluralism in practice as long as *Confucianism* here remains a monistic ethical system.

5

Confucian Familialism and Public Reasoning

In Chapter 4, I argued that for Confucian democracy to be socially meaningful and politically practicable in increasingly pluralizing East Asian societies, both Confucianism and democracy must undergo dialectical transformations and constrain each other, thus creating the societal condition favorable for it. What was central to my argument was that as long as we understand Confucian democracy as a democracy operating on Confucian habits and mores that broadly constitute Confucian public reason, Confucian virtues must be differentiated into moral virtues concerned with a person's moral well-being qua human being and civic virtues related to the polity's public character and its reproduction and that only the latter should be relevant to the general public. I differentiated Confucian public reason from its liberal counterpart of the kind advocated by deontological liberals in terms of a freestanding conception of justice completely separate from the "background culture" in civil society, and argued that such an understanding of public reason as solely concerned with the standard for appraising the legitimacy of basic structures is too narrow to apply to a Confucian pluralist democratic society in which public reason (more accurately public reasons) derives from the background culture or the culture of civil society. In the Confucian democracy that I propose, public reason is *more than* what is required of judges, legislators, governmental officials, or the candidates for public office who are concerned with the constitutional essentials of the regime or who are dealing with basic constitutional structure in the (formal) *public political forum*. More important, public reason is what ordinary citizens appeal to in deliberating political questions and public policies in the public space of democratic civil society.[1]

[1] Compare my position to John Rawls's: "It is imperative to realize that the idea of public reason does not apply to all political discussions of fundamental questions, but only to discussions of

But, it may be objected, can we understand public reason this way? Can public reason be grounded in a civil society that is characterized with the fact of pluralism? After all, didn't John Rawls revivify this concept, first introduced by Thomas Hobbes to the modern political lexicon,[2] precisely because of the moral or value pluralism in modern civil society where citizens enjoy what Benjamin Constant called "the liberties of the moderns" such as freedom of conscience, freedom of religion, freedom of expression, and freedom of association? What exactly Rawls meant by public reason, or more generally, how public reason should be understood in a democratic polity, is an ongoing debate. For instance, scholars such as Steven Wall and Gerald Gauss understand the Rawlsian notion of public reason as a kind of *bracketing principle*, a principle of restraint that directs citizens "to set aside their controversial religious [or moral or philosophical] commitments when justifying their political activity."[3] According to this liberal-rationalist interpretation of public reason, public reason is a purely theoretical construct, having only a remote connection with what citizens actually believe.[4] It is morally *required* as an impartial arbiter standing free of the background culture, which is loaded with value pluralism, precisely because of the epistemological impossibility of resolving moral conflicts arising from the fact of pluralism in which reaching substantive moral agreement is virtually impossible. Therefore, public reason is necessary for public justification, and, as John Rawls puts it, the aim of the idea of public justification "is to specify the idea of justification in a way appropriate to a political conception of justice for a society characterized, as a democracy is, by reasonable pluralism."[5] Albeit from a different (i.e., more civic) angle from that which he employed in *A Theory of Justice* (especially in his discussion of the original position), the later Rawls still seems to resort to the notion of the unencumbered personhood when he says, "Since we are seeking public justification for political and social institutions – for the basic structure of a political and social world – we think of persons as citizens.... In giving reasons to all citizens we don't view persons as socially situated or otherwise rooted, that is, as being in this or that social class, or in this or that property and income group, or as having this or that

those questions in which I refer to as the public political forum" (*The Law of Peoples* [Cambridge, MA: Harvard University Press, 1999], 133).

2 Though it is commonly believed that Rawls picked up the idea of public reason from Immanuel Kant's short essay called "An Answer to the Question: 'What is Enlightenment?,'" the phrase "public reason" is first found in Thomas Hobbes's *Leviathan*, though Hobbes was referring to the judgment of the sovereign. See Michael Ridge, "Hobbesian Public Reason," *Ethics* 108 (1998), 538–68.

3 Steven Wall, "Perfectionism, Public Reason, and Religious Accommodation," *Social Theory and Practice* 31 (2005), 281–304, 281.

4 See Gerald F. Gauss, *Justificatory Liberalism: An Essay on Epistemology and Political Theory* (Oxford: Oxford University Press, 1996).

5 John Rawls, *Justice as Fairness: A Restatement*, ed. Erin Kelly (Cambridge, MA: Belknap, 2001).

comprehensive doctrine.... Rather, we think of persons as reasonable and rational, as free and equal citizens."[6]

Scholars such as Stephen Macedo and Soberts Skerrett, however, strongly disagree with this rationalist, overtly juridical, interpretation of Rawls's notion of public reason. Skerrett chastises Jeffrey Stout, who interprets Rawls's notion of public reason as deontic constraints,[7] by saying, "A political conception of justice is not freestanding in the sense that it might be deduced as an object of rational belief. Political conceptions of justice – Rawls acknowledges that there may be more than one – are based on a selection of norms implicit in historic democratic societies. These norms are ordered systematically and *presented* as freestanding, so that citizens can affirm the conception from irreducibly diverse comprehensive doctrines."[8] Macedo goes even further by fully exposing the civic and educative potential implicated in public reasonableness, thereby relabeling political liberalism as civic liberalism: "I will use the label 'civic liberalism' as a way of emphasizing the importance of the wider civic life of liberal democracy in practice, as well as liberalism's educative ambitions. Civic liberalism includes an account of the political institutions and social structures that help promote a publicly reasonable liberal community."[9] "Liberal public reason," Macedo continues, "invites us, therefore, to join with others who reject some of our (possibly true) beliefs for the sake of laying the groundwork for common political institutions."[10]

It is far beyond the scope of this book to resolve the exegetical question of whose interpretation of Rawls's notion of public reason is more accurate. That being said, in my view, the rationalist interpretation of public reason, concentrated on the *epistemological* impossibility of reaching substantive moral agreements under the fact of pluralism, is overstated even in the liberal social context in which political discourse is frequently mediated through rights claims. As I showed in Chapter 3, the greatest worry of the scholars who subscribe to this interpretation is that notions of political reasonableness are not readily available as Rawls assumes because they will be affected by our epistemic commitments. Gerald Gauss thus asserts that "there is little prospect of a consensus emerging on what is politically reasonable in a society that disagrees on what is religiously, morally, and epistemologically reasonable."[11] But (liberal) politics, which belongs to the realm of practice, cannot be reduced

[6] Rawls, *Law of Peoples*, 171.

[7] Jeffrey Stout, *Democracy & Tradition* (Princeton: Princeton University Press, 2004).

[8] K. Roberts Skerrett, "Political Liberalism and the Idea of Public Reason: A Response to Jeffrey Stout's *Democracy and Tradition*," *Social Theory and Practice* 31 (2005), 173–90, 177, emphasis in original.

[9] Stephen Macedo, *Diversity and Distrust: Civic Education in a Multicultural Democracy* (Cambridge, MA: Harvard University Press, 2000), 169.

[10] Ibid., 170.

[11] Gerald F. Gauss, "Reason, Justification, and Consensus," in Bohman and Regn, *Deliberative Democracy*, 222.

to or directly identified with (liberal) philosophy consisting of self-contained epistemic claims.[12] The fact that citizens subscribe to different moral, philosophical, and religious doctrines in modern society (namely, the fact of pluralism) does not necessarily establish the epistemological impossibility of reaching a reasonable public consensus, as if citizens are completely subsumed by the religious or philosophical value system to which they are committed as private individuals. It is certainly wrong to understand citizens in a liberal society, even when they take their philosophical, religious, cultural, or moral values seriously and strongly disagree with others on public matters, all as, say, the Amish people who claim that their lifestyle is incommensurable with the secular liberal-democratic life. What is obscured here is the dimension of common citizenship and democracy to which collective self-determination is central.

If it is agreed that the epistemological impossibility thesis does not hold strictly in the actual liberal social context in which it was originally raised, its applicability (as well as its rationale) to Confucian democracy is less compelling, given that in East Asia the fact of pluralism is not as intense as that which we find in the West (especially in North America). First of all, no East Asian society has ever experienced religious wars of the kinds that devastated Europe during the early modern period and thus is completely unfamiliar with what William Galston calls Reformation liberalism, a liberalism that cherishes the value of diversity more than the value of autonomy, which according to Galston is the hallmark of Enlightenment liberalism.[13] Second, while pluralism in the West is originally and still primarily related to religious freedom and religious groups' (or communities') associational freedom, in East Asia pluralism is closely associated with liberal individualization, particularly with rapidly growing social awareness of the importance of individual identity and individual rights. That is, Enlightenment liberalism and Reformation liberalism are being simultaneously introduced into East Asian societies without much awareness of the conceptual difference between the two, while these societies are also being democratized or, to say the least, becoming more democratic.[14] The challenge that pluralism (or pluralization) poses to East Asian Confucian societies is not so much how to adjudicate the clashing moral claims between membership and citizenship or how to *maximally* protect value diversity and associational freedom *in spite of* the democratic demand for common citizenship and duty of civility – what I call the Western liberal problematic. Instead, the East Asian challenge lies in how to respect the newly recognized intrinsic value of diversity *as much as possible* and legitimately without corroding the

[12] See Benjamin R. Barber, *The Conquest of Politics: Liberal Philosophy in Democratic Times* (Princeton: Princeton University Press, 1988).

[13] William A. Galston, "Two Concepts of Liberalism," *Ethics* 105 (1995), 516–34. Also see Chapters 4 and 9 in this book.

[14] Recently, pluralism has become a more salient social issue in East Asian societies in part because of the increasing number of immigrants and the ensuing multiculturalization. I will take up this issue in Chapter 11 with a special focus on South Korea.

societal culture that has underpinned the shared, characteristically Confucian, way of life.

In this chapter, I explore an alternative version of public reason that is best suitable in the Confucian democracy that I have developed in Chapter 4, without delving into the metaethical question of its epistemological possibility or its moral worth. Contra Kantian liberals who understand public reasons as "the considerations that are rationally accessible to all normal adult citizens of the state in question,"[15] I draw attention to the socially embedded character of public reason(ing) and its affective nature. Echoing the recent revival of Humean moral sentimentalism in political theory (particularly in deliberative democracy literature), I argue that public reasons are constituted by moral sentiments and social affects, or "civil passions" that *dispose* citizens who share common (yet publicly contestable) social, legal, and political institutions to have common (again contestable) concerns about things they all care about.[16] After revealing the affective nature of Confucian moral reasoning and then reconstructing Confucian public reason as "affective concerns" from a Mencian perspective, I argue that at the core of Confucian public reason are familial affectionate sentiments, especially what I call "critical affection," which makes public reason(ing) reflective, self-regulative, and inclusive.

Public Reason as a Horizon of Concern: A Humean Reconstruction

Though deliberative democracy has emerged as a powerful normative alternative to the long-dominant aggregative model of democracy in the past two decades, Confucian democrats have rarely engaged with the theories of deliberative democracy mainly because of their failure to appreciate (or identify) the crucial differences between the two models,[17] largely based on the assumption that deliberative democracy is just another version of "liberal democracy" that rationalizes rights-based individualism and emphasizes due procedure more than common good.[18] On the other hand, however, an equally important

[15] This is how Steven Wall understands public reason(s) ("Perfectionism, Public Reason, and Religious Accommodation," 287). Also see Joshua Cohen, "Procedure and Substance in Deliberative Democracy," in *Democracy and Difference: Contesting the Boundaries of the Political*, ed. Seyla Benhabib (Princeton: Princeton University Press, 1996).

[16] Though social affects are not necessarily overlapping with moral sentiments (as they can be both civil and uncivil), by them I mean the moral sentiments that have become socialized (or routinized) as the citizens' collective sociopsychological dispositions that orient them toward what *they* consider to be civil behaviors.

[17] For an illuminating survey of the critical differences between two models of democracy, see Ian Shapiro, *The State of Democratic Theory* (Princeton: Princeton University Press, 2003), chap. 1.

[18] Some critical exceptions include Baogang He, "Western Theories of Deliberative Democracy and the Chinese Practice of Complex Deliberative Governance," in *The Search for Deliberative Democracy in China*, ed. Ethan J. Leib and Baogang He (New York: Palgrave, 2006) and Baogang He and Mark E. Warren, "Authoritarian Deliberation: The Deliberative Turn in

reason for the lack of enthusiasm among Confucian democrats to make a constructive engagement with deliberative democracy seems to have a great deal to do with what Cheryl Hall calls the "endemic problem [of] deliberative theory," which "stems from the supreme value it places on calm rational discussion."[19] In fact, though Confucian ethics does not actively support "emotionally laden speech and passionate protests" – the critical exclusion of which critics of (the political theory of) deliberative democracy find heavily problematic[20] – because of its deep distrust in the power of speech and strong emphasis on the virtue of civility, moral sentimentalism which lies at the heart of Confucian (especially Mencian-Confucian) ethics is apparently at odds with strong rationalism embedded in deliberative democracy.

Recently, however, a group of scholars has challenged this rationalist presumption in the theories of deliberative democracy mainly by uncovering the sentimentalist elements implicit in them, that is, by pointing out that affect is already there in the very constitution of reason for it (reason) to have any motivational force in the actual process of deliberation.[21] For instance, taking issue with the purely Kantian-rationalist interpretation of John Rawls's *A Theory of Justice*, Michael Frazer draws attention to the influence of Scottish sentimentalists (particularly David Hume) on Rawls by focusing on his descriptive moral psychology. After thoroughly revisiting Rawls's arguably most Kantian work, Frazer then opposes the conventional approach that pits sentimentalism against rationalism and instead submits that "the contrast between rationalism and sentimentalism is best understood as the contrast between a hierarchical view of the moral soul, on one hand, and an egalitarian view, on the other – an egalitarian view in which normatively authoritative standards are the product of an entire mind in harmony with itself."[22]

Chinese Political Development," *Perspectives on Politics* 9 (2011), 269–89, though the deliberative democracy that the authors explore seem to be less democratically robust (but "some" plausibility given the existing political system in China).

19 Cheryl Hall, "Recognizing the Passion in Deliberation: Toward a More Democratic Theory of Deliberative Democracy," *Hypatia* 22 (2007), 81–95, 81.

20 Lynn Sanders, "Against Deliberation," *Political Theory* 25 (1997), 347–76; Michael Walzer, "Deliberation and What Else?," in *Thinking Politically: Essays in Political Theory*, ed. David Miller (New Haven: Yale University Press, 2007).

21 Sharon Krause, "Desiring Justice: Motivation and Justification in Rawls and Habermas," *Contemporary Political Theory* 4 (2005), 363–85; Susan M. Okin, "Reason and Feeling in Thinking about Justice," *Ethics* 99 (1989), 229–49. Amy Gutmann and Dennis Thompson, though primarily Kantian-rationalists, do not see the relationship between reason and passion in terms of stark opposition. See their *Why Deliberative Democracy?* (Princeton: Princeton University Press, 2004), 50–51. In addition to these points about motivation, recent work in cognitive science has shown that emotions are fundamentally part of the processes of cognition and thought. See, for instance, Antonio R. Damasio, *Descartes' Error: Emotion, Reason and the Human Brain* (New York: HarperCollins, 1994).

22 Michael L. Frazer, "John Rawls: Between Two Enlightenments," *Political Theory* 35 (2007), 756–80, 760.

What is important in our context is how this "Humean turn" in deliberative democratic theory has transformed our understanding of public reason and whether this renewed understanding of public reason can be reappropriated (not just copied) in the Confucian democratic context. Before attempting to answer the second question, let us first investigate how public reason is understood in deliberative democratic theory after the Humean turn. Sharon Krause's *Civil Passions: Moral Sentiment and Democratic Deliberation* offers one of the most compelling accounts of public reason reconceived with reference to Humean sentimentalism.[23]

According to Krause, theories of deliberative democracy in the Kantian-rationalist strand suffer from a *motivational deficit*: "The idea of reason as a faculty that abstracts from sentiment, which undergirds impartiality on this [rationalist] view, disconnects the deliberating subject from the motivational sources of human agency, which are found in the affective attachments and desires from which subjects are asked to abstract. The self as deliberator comes apart from the self as agent."[24] Kantian rationalists such as Joshua Cohen assert that the faculty of reason generates reasons for action independently of affective concerns or the passions that motivate action. Apparently, this radical disjuncture between norms and motives is intended to establish and protect the rationality as well as impartiality of public deliberation.[25] In Cohen's view, norms cannot depend on what one happens to be motivated to do; they should be firmly grounded in what one ought to do. Reason can motivate decisions because in the course of deliberation a moral agent is *sensitized* to reasons, understood as standards of criticism and guidance, and thus is able to develop or change affective concerns. Put differently, even when affect enters the deliberative forum, it is thought to come into being *endogenously* (as a sensitivity to the faculty of reason itself), not through the process of moral psychology involving passion.[26]

However, Krause finds this typical Kantian reasoning hopelessly circular and unconvincing and fails to come to grips with what is actually happening in the actual process of so-called rational reflection and deliberation: the agent is motivated to make a (public) decision because she "came to appreciate in a fuller, deeper way (with the help of reason) the range and implications of her

[23] Sharon Krause, *Civil Passions: Moral Sentiment and Democratic Deliberation* (Princeton: Princeton University Press, 2008).

[24] Ibid., 2.

[25] Ibid., 149.

[26] Ibid. It is important to note that recent Kantian deliberative democrats such as Cohen and Habermas do not dismiss completely the importance of affect in the "rational" deliberative process; they just make affect peripheral to moral reasoning by understanding it as an aid to reason but hardly as an integral element to it (because of their failure to see the soul and its operation holistically), without which reasoning is practically impossible. For a tacit importance of affect in Habermas's recent political theory, see Patchen Markell, "Making Affect Safe for Democracy? On 'Constitutional Patriotism,'" *Political Theory* 28 (2000), 38–63.

more settled desires, or reflective concerns [in the course of deliberation]."[27] Ultimately, contends Krause, what is at stake here is more than motivational significance. "It raises doubts about whether reason, conceived as a strictly cognitive faculty, can generate 'standards of criticism and guidance' without reference to at least some of the affective concerns that agents actually have."[28] Properly understood, reasons are constituted by the things we care about. By extension, "public reasons are constituted by the things we *all* care about – not by things that 'reason itself' tells us we *should* care about."[29] Krause gives a fuller account of public reason in the following:

> To engage the faculty of public reason in deliberation is essentially to frame one's arguments and make one's evaluations in terms of principles and evaluative standards that are constitutive of the polity and are therefore sources of common commitment, things that citizens *care* about. Public reasons reflect the shared horizons of concern that are implicit in the political culture of a particular community.... We have a conative, not merely a cognitive, orientation to public reasons, and as such they are forms of reflective desire. And ... there is a *good* reason to think that the principles of public reason must have this affective character if they are to be capable of motivating decisions and action.[30]

Thus understood, public reasons are not so much considerations that are rationally accessible to all adult citizens, but common concerns that are both caring and reflective. But how can public reasons that "*reflect* the shared horizons of concern that are implicit in the political culture of a particular community" be morally reflexive and politically impartial, thus legitimizing political decisions and public consensus given the fact of pluralism? Krause admits that while the rationalists suffer from a motivational deficit, the theorists of affect often suffer from a normative deficit, a failure to provide clear criteria for the legitimate incorporation of sentiment.[31]

To address a normative deficit in the sentimentalist approach, Krause then reconstructs what she calls "impartial moral sentiment" by drawing on Hume's moral psychology, which can undergird the democratic principles of reciprocity and equality. According to Krause, moral sentiment rests on two things: "the adoption of an impersonal perspective that incorporates, via the faculty of sympathy and the practice of perspective-taking, the reflectively endorsable sentiments of those affected; and attentiveness to human nature, conceived as a cluster of common, empirically verifiable human concerns."[32] Krause concludes that public reason as impartial yet socially grounded moral sentiment reflects what we have in common as public citizens and that this should not

[27] Krause, *Civil Passions*, 150.
[28] Ibid., 151.
[29] Ibid., emphases in original.
[30] Ibid., 157–8, emphases in original.
[31] Ibid., 4.
[32] Ibid., 17.

be obscured by the differences among us, however real they are. When moral conflicts arise, they should be "appropriately argued in terms of other elements in the public's horizon of concern, elements that are, for the moment, subject to agreement."[33] Otherwise stated, "in order for a new principle to revise public policy effectively and legitimately, it must connect up with some principles that are already subject to public agreement,"[34] by invoking familiar feelings and shared values.

The kind of impartiality that public reason makes possible may not satisfy those who are eager to find truly universal norms that are applicable with equal force to all of humanity. But Krause, contra Rawls and company, though quite plausibly in my view, maintains that however "capable of reflecting on particular elements in the background of values and concerns that give it content, public reason cannot ever transcend this background fully."[35] In Krause's judgment, rather than searching for a rationalist bracketing principle or a deontic constraint, it is much more politically legitimate and morally sound to "acknowledge the moral fallibility of public reason" and make every effort to maintain the norms of equal respect and reciprocity by "[leaving] room for sentiments that offer principled challenges to the status quo and hence contest certain parts of the public's horizon of concern, challenging the dominant view of public reason."[36]

In Chapter 4, I argued that as democratic citizens, individuals in a Confucian democracy are *morally* required to vigorously and voluntarily embody the Confucian mores and habits that sustain and reproduce their public way of life. I also explicated this "moral requirement" by making two points: first, because their public reasons are largely grounded in, even constituted by, Confucian social habits and moral sensibility, and second, as citizens they should not dismiss wholesale what they share in common at least in their public life *despite* their moral, cultural, or religious differences, especially in the face of an ethically and culturally monistic force of globalization. Of note, Krause's Humean account of public reason resonates remarkably well with what I call the moral requirement for Confucian democratic politics and citizenship.

In a sense, the strong resonance between pluralistically reconstructed Confucian democracy and Humean public reason is not so surprising considering the much noted similarities between Humean sentimentalism and Confucian (especially Mencian) virtue ethics of sentiments.[37] Moreover, when Krause appeals to Hume's insight into the intersubjective character of

[33] Ibid., 160.

[34] Ibid., 161.

[35] Ibid., 160.

[36] Ibid., 167.

[37] The phrase of "virtue ethics of sentiments" has been adopted from Philip J. Ivanhoe, "Virtue Ethics and the Chinese Confucian Tradition," in *The Cambridge Companion to Virtue Ethics*, ed. Daniel C. Russell (Cambridge: Cambridge University Press, 2013), 49. Also see Xiusheng Liu, "Mencius, Hume, and Sensibility Theory," *Philosophy East and West* 52 (2002), 75–97.

judgment, she does not embrace his substantive idea of justice which is far from democratic, being clearly aware of the danger of "be[ing] slaves to the sometimes limited vision of individual philosophers" when studying normative political theory through an interpretation of the history of political thought.[38] Krause stresses that affective impartiality alone is not sufficient in making a society just, though it can help legitimize political judgments and public policies based on it. To ensure the concurrence of democratic legitimacy and democratic justice, (liberal-)democratic politics is needed, which can achieve the great promise of an affectively engaged but impartial judgment. Thus Krause submits that "[i]mpartiality in affective judgment requires a political context of rights-supported activism and democratic contestation, which challenge prevailing power relations and incorporate the voices of excluded and marginalized members of the polity."[39]

Then two questions arise: How is my vision of Confucian democracy substantively different from the Humean liberal democracy advocated by Krause (or other liberal democrats who also incorporate Humean sentimentalism in their theorization of liberal democracy)? What is distinctively *Confucian* about public reason that is integral to the Confucian democracy that I proposed in previous chapters? In the remainder of this chapter, I attempt to illuminate, first, the sentimentalist character of Confucian moral reasoning from a Mencian-Confucian perspective and, second, the Confucian characteristic of public reason in Confucian democracy by democratic-politically extending Mencius's notion of extension, a method contrived by Mencius to explicate the moral psychological process of individual moral reasoning and judgment. My central claim is that Confucian-Mencian public reason is characteristically different from Humean public reason, despite their generic similarities. Though Confucian democracy, like Humean democracy, is institutionally reliant on liberal-democratic institutions for the purpose of democratic justice, Confucian public reason makes Confucian democracy more reflective, self-regulating, and inclusive than its Humean counterpart because it is working through what I consider the defining characteristic of Confucian public reason, namely, *critical familial affection.*

Affective Reasoning: The Mencian Perspective of Moral Judgment

In the *Analects*, Confucius defines *ren* 仁, the Confucian moral virtue par excellence (translated into English as benevolence or human-heartedness), in many different ways, yet quite often in relation to the practice of rituals (*li* 禮),[40]

[38] Krause, *Civil Passions*, 15. On the un-liberal-democratic nature of Hume's understanding of justice, see Michael L. Frazer, *The Enlightenment of Sympathy: Justice and the Moral Sentiments in the Eighteenth Century and Today* (New York: Oxford University Press, 2010), chap. 3.

[39] Ibid., 17.

[40] Most famously, in *Analects* 12:1, Confucius says, "Through self-disciple and observing ritual propriety (*li*) one becomes *ren*.... Do not look at anything that violates the observance of ritual

but at one point he presents it as loving others (*ai* 愛).[41] Unfortunately, however, Confucius never articulated what he meant by this statement – whether love here means impartial and universal (or inclusive) love, as the Mohists later understood it, or something qualitatively different in terms of scope or its moral psychological mechanism. Among later classical Confucians Mencius took this sentimentalist dimension of *ren* most seriously (while on the other hand advancing an Aristotelian-type virtue ethics that relates an innate human nature to the formation of moral character and human flourishing) and offered a sophisticated account of the moral psychology of *ren* as a moral sentiment in relation to moral self-cultivation.

Mencius famously argues that human nature is good (*xing shan* 性善). For him, however, the goodness of human nature does not mean moral perfection (as Buddhists believe). Nor does the uniqueness of Mencius's claim lie in his conviction about human moral perfectibility, the conviction that Xunzi, his archrival, also shares, who notoriously claims that human nature is bad (*xing e* 性惡). The kernel of Mencius's *xing shan* thesis consists in the belief that men are born with moral sensibilities, which incline them toward moral goodness. According to Mencius, men are endowed with four "sprouts" (*duan* 端) of virtue, which he describes in terms of moral sentiments.

Here is why I say that all human beings have a mind that commiserates with others. Now, if anyone were suddenly to see a child about to fall into a well, his mind would be filled with alarm, distress, pity, and compassion. That he would react accordingly is not because he would hope to use the opportunity to ingratiate himself with the child's parents, nor because he would seek commendation from neighbors and friends, nor because he would hate the adverse reputation [that could come from not reacting accordingly]. From this it may be seen that one who lacks a mind that feels pity and compassion would not be human; one who lacks a mind that feels shame and aversion would not be human; one who lacks a mind that feels modesty and compliance would not be human; one who lacks a mind that knows right and wrong would not be human. The mind's feeling of pity and compassion is the sprout of humanness (*ren* 仁); the mind's feeling of shame and aversion is the sprout of rightness (*yi* 義); the mind's feeling of modesty and compliance is the sprout of propriety (*li* 禮); and the mind's sense of

propriety; do not listen to anything that violates the observance of ritual propriety; do not speak about anything that violates the observance of ritual propriety; do not do anything that violates the observance of ritual propriety" (translation modified). Throughout this chapter, the English translations of the *Analects* (*Lunyu* 論語) are adopted from Roger T. Ames and Henry Rosemont Jr., *The Analects of Confucius: A Philosophical Translation* (New York: Ballantine Books, 1998). For a maximalist account of the inseparability between *ren* and *li*, see Herbert Fingarette, *Confucius: The Secular as Sacred* (New York: Harper, 1972). An increasing number of scholars, however, believe that there is a "creative tension" between *ren* and *li*. See Tu Weiming, "The Creative Tension between *Jen* and *Li*," *Philosophy East and West* 18 (1968), 29–39; Kwong-loi Shun, "*Jen* and *Li* in the *Analects*," *Philosophy East and West* 43 (1993), 457–79; Karyn Lai, "*Li* in the *Analects*: Training in Moral Competence and the Question of Flexibility," *Philosophy East and West* 56 (2006), 69–83.

[41] *Analects* 12:22.

right and wrong is the sprout of wisdom (*zhi* 智). Human beings have these four sprouts just as they have four limbs.[42]

Apparently, there is a logical disjuncture between the story of a child who is about to fall into a well and Mencius's conclusion that this story attests that every man has four sprouts of virtue because all this story tells us is that man has the feeling of pity and compassion, or the "unbearing heart," a heart that cannot bear to see the suffering of others (*bu ren ren zhi xin* 不忍人之心). Though it is unclear how the feeling of pity and compassion, the sprout of *ren*, is internally connected with other sprouts of virtue (thus making *ren* the Confucian virtue par excellence),[43] Mencius's core contention is clear enough: that is, truly human motive is not calculating or self-interested but is compassionate and the compassionate heart is the foundation of moral virtue.

As is well known, in the Western political philosophical tradition, compassion or pity has long been thought to be starkly opposed to reason. Even Rousseau, the first modern philosopher who emphasized the political virtue of pity and criticized (the then prevailing mode of) rationalism, never challenged the strict distinction between reason and passion itself (including moral sentiment). As a matter of fact, Rousseau was forced to invent his own version of *rationalism* in which passion (including compassion or pity) is tamed by reason because of what can be called the paradox of pity and the social pathologies it is likely to give rise to.

Pity is sweet because, in putting ourselves in the place of the one who suffers, we nevertheless feel the pleasure of not suffering as he does.[44]

If the first sight that strikes him is an object of sadness, the first return to himself is a sentiment of pleasure. In seeing how many ills he is exempt from, he feels himself to be happier than he had thought he was. He shares the sufferings of his fellows; but this sharing is voluntary and sweet. At the same time he enjoys both the pity he has for their ills and the happiness that exempts him from those ills.[45]

As Richard Boyd insightfully captured, pity, as conceived by Rousseau, "has less to do with a compassionate concern for the welfare of others than with the

[42] *Mencius* 2A6. Throughout this chapter, the English translations of the *Mengzi* 孟子 are adopted from Irene Bloom (trans.), *Mencius*, ed. Philip J. Ivanhoe (New York: Columbia University Press, 2009).

[43] Throughout the *Analects*, Confucius presents *ren* as the paradigm human virtue that encompasses all kinds of moral virtues including benevolence, righteousness, ritual propriety, and wisdom but he never articulates the internal connection among moral virtues or how other moral virtues are related to the virtue of *ren*. Mencius seems to argue that the virtue of *ren gives rise to* other moral virtues, but, unfortunately, he offers neither a philosophical/metaphysical account on the relationship among virtues nor a detailed psychological explanation as to how pity or compassion generates other moral sentiments.

[44] Jean-Jacques Rousseau, *Emile, or On Education*, trans. Allan Bloom (New York: Basic Books, 1979), 221.

[45] Ibid., 229.

even more elemental sentiment of self-preservation." When unaided by reason, pity, however conducive to virtue, is short of successfully moderating or regulating the activity of our self-love as it can easily collapse back into the more elemental Hobbesian faculty of self-preservation.[46]

Mencius's compassion is qualitatively different from Rousseau's pity because it involves (or more accurately, gives rise to) *reason* – what I call "affective reason." While Rousseau attributes pity to the natural quality that man shares with other animals, for Mencius compassion is what distinguishes human beings from animals, their inner quality (*qing* 情) that manifests their Heaven-given nature (*xing* 性, i.e., the propensity to moral goodness).[47] As Eric Hutton notes, compassion (and other sprouts of virtue) is not merely a latent capacity for goodness, which, being young and tender, can easily be overlooked, trampled, or uprooted. Rather, it is an *active impulse* that can "offer positive promptings and can, in unguarded moments and when [it is] not overwhelmed by desires to the contrary, move even uncultivated people toward proper behavior," although this spontaneous moral inclination should be further cultivated under proper education to apply to the precisely appropriate action.[48]

Put differently, in the Mencian moral perspective, there is neither pure reason nor unaided passion (including pity), either of which is susceptible to moral extremism and sociopolitical pathology.[49] As innate impulses, moral sentiments constitute the core of what we now call practical reason in the sense that they offer the basic direction for moral behavior. They provide a *reason* (although intuitively evoked rather than offered in the form of logical proposition) for one to respond to concrete situations in a morally appropriate way. More specifically, "one guides one's *qi* 氣 (the vital energies that fill the body) toward compassion when one perceives the immediate situation as giving rise to *a reason*" to think and behave appropriately, that is, morally.[50] This type of reason

[46] Richard Boyd, "Pity's Pathologies Portrayed: Rousseau and the Limits of Democratic Compassion," *Political Theory* 32 (2004), 519–46, 529.

[47] Compare *Mencius* 4B19 to Jean-Jacques Rousseau, *The First and Second Discourses*, ed. Roger D. Masters, trans. Roger D. Masters and Judith R. Masters (New York: St. Martin's, 1964), 130, where he says, "I speak of pity, a disposition that is appropriate to beings as weak and subject to as many ills as we are; a virtue all the more universal and useful to man because it precedes in him the use of all reflection; and so natural that even beasts sometimes give perceptible signs of it. Without speaking of the tenderness of mothers for their young and of the perils they brave to guard them, one observes daily the repugnance of horses to trample a living body underfoot. An animal does not pass near a dead animal of its species without uneasiness."

[48] Eric L. Hutton, "Moral Connoisseurship in Mengzi," in Liu and Ivanhoe, *Essays on the Moral Philosophy of Mengzi*, 174.

[49] While Rousseau reminds us of the danger of (unaided) pity's pathologies, Max Horkheimer and Theodor W. Adorno warn us of the danger of pure rationalism. See their *Dialectic of Enlightenment*, ed. Gunzelin S. Noerr, trans. Edmund Jephcott (Stanford: Stanford University Press, 2002).

[50] David B. Wong, "Reasons and Analogical Reasoning in Mengzi," in Liu and Ivanhoe, *Essays on the Moral Philosophy of Mengzi*, 194.

(or reasons) is qualitatively different from what David Wong calls "top-down reasoning," prevailing in the Kantian and the utilitarian rationalism, according to which ethical reasoning is governed from the top down by the most general and abstract principles. As *a* reason (or a host of *reasons*) emphatically aroused by our natural affective impulses, reason in Mencian sentimentalism has little (almost nothing) to do with a cognitive faculty of the mind as deontological liberals commonly understand it.

That Confucian reason arises from and is grounded on emotion, however, does not mean that it has no reflective component.[51] Quite the contrary. In fact, Mencius accentuates that to make a right judgment one is to reflect (*si* 思 in Mencius's own terminology) on whether the reasons sentimentally evoked are truly reflective of one's spontaneous (moral) feelings,[52] and whether one is experiencing a profound joy by doing what one is emphatically aroused or motivated to do.[53] I strongly agree with Hutton when he says, "The practice of reflecting on these feelings and delighting in the behavior they engender strengthens them and causes them to 'grow,' both in the sense that it increases the motivational force they possess, and in the sense of extending (*tui* 推) their guidance into new areas, i.e., broadening the range of moral judgment they provide."[54] Like Humean moral sentimentalism, in Mencian moral sentimentalism, too, there is no decoupling of the content of moral behavior from moral motivation. One is morally motivated by deepening one's sensitivity to one's spontaneous impulses and reflecting on what one truly delights in.

Mencius's notion of extension requires careful attention not only because it explicates the moral psychological process of *individual* moral judgment or deliberation in Mencian moral sentimentalism, but also, more important, because it can provide critical insight into the nature of public reason and the process of public reasoning in Confucian democracy (to which I will turn in the next section).

51 Rousseau, however, is persuaded that pity, if unaided by reason, has no reflective component in it: "He pities these miserable kings, slaves of all that obey them. He pities these false wise men, chained to their vain reputations. He pities these rich fools, martyrs to their display. He pities these conspicuous voluptuaries, who devote their entire lives to boredom in order to appear to have pleasure. He would pity even the enemy who would do him harm, for he would see his misery in his wickedness. He would say to himself, 'In giving himself the need to hurt me, this man has made his fate dependent on mine'" (Rousseau, *Emile*, 244).

52 According to Bryan W. Van Norden, even the process of *si* has an affective dimension. See his *Virtue Ethics and Consequentialism in Early Chinese Philosophy* (Cambridge: Cambridge University Press, 2007), 231–3.

53 For an importance of "joy" in Mencius's idea of moral self-cultivation, see Bryan W. Van Norden, "Mengzi and Xunzi: Two Views of Human Agency," in *Virtue, Nature, and Moral Agency in the Xunzi*, ed. T. C. Kline III and Philip J. Ivanhoe (Indianapolis: Hackett, 2000), 103–34; Philip J. Ivanhoe, "Confucian Self Cultivation and Mengzi's Notion of Extension," in Liu and Ivanhoe, *Essays on the Moral Philosophy of Mengzi*, 221–41.

54 Hutton, "Moral Connoisseurship in Mengzi," 175.

Mencius presents his notion of extension as a method of moral judgment in *Mencius* 1A7 where he (M) admonishes King Xuan of Qi (X), who is apparently attracted to the realpolitik of the kinds pursued by notable hegemons (*ba zhe* 霸者) such as Duke Huan of Qi and Duke Wen of Jin, with the Kingly Way (*wang dao* 王道), the ideal Confucian moral statecraft that relies on the rule by virtue (*dezhi* 德治). The conversation begins with King Xuan's inquiry about the nature of Confucian moral virtue (*de* 德).

X: What must one's Virtue be like in order to become a true king?

M: I have heard … that while the king was seated in the upper part of the hall someone led an ox past the hall below [in the courtyard]. On seeing this, the king asked where the ox was going and was told that it was being taken to serve as a blood sacrifice in the consecration of a bell. The king said, "Spare it. I cannot bear its trembling, like one who, though blameless, is being led to the execution ground…. [But h]ow could [the consecration of the bell] be dispensed with? Substitute a sheep instead." … With such a mind one has what it takes to become a true king.

This particular passage has been at the center of heated debate among students of Chinese philosophy, and it goes beyond the scope of this book to survey the debate in detail. What is worth noting is that here Mencius is not merely pointing out the king's logical inconsistency in failing to address the suffering of his people while sparing the ox out of commiseration as some scholars argue.[55] As Irene Bloom notes, in speaking of "such a mind," Mencius is referring not to the king's intellective or rational abilities but to his *capacity* for empathy.[56] This capacity, however, is not a full-blown innate emotive quality that needs *only* to be extended as it is. Rather, as David Wong notes, Mencian extension "involves significant alteration, expansion, or refinement of emotional capacities," for which a mere recognition of logical consistency cannot account.[57] But what exactly is going on in this process of extension? How can the king (or any person) develop, refine, or expand his innate capacity so that he can extend his compassion from X (ox) toward Y (people), if this process is not just about the correction of logical inconsistency? Philip J. Ivanhoe offers a powerful illustration about the moral psychological process implicated in Mencius's notion of extension in terms of "analogical resonance."

[Mencius] expects the king to experience a similar feeling of compassion in this second case (read: the case of the people), not because of some inherent need for consistency or in light of some recognition of a general imperative to relieve suffering, but because he believes the king simply will experience a similar reaction in this case – if only he will put forth some effort. The earlier experience has taught him what compassion feels like, what some of its general features are, and how to go about looking for, focusing on, and

[55] For a so-called logical extension interpretation, see David S. Nivison, *The Ways of Confucianism: Investigations in Chinese Philosophy* (Chicago: Open Court, 1996), 94–101.

[56] See note 21 in Bloom, *Mencius*, 7.

[57] Wong, "Reasons and Analogical Reasoning in Mengzi," 191.

appreciating such an emotional response. With such experience and reflection in hand, the king is now primed for compassion. The expectation is that the analogical resonance between these two cases will guide the king to look for, focus on, and appreciate the moral response in the second case. If he does so, he will have successfully extended his heart of compassion.[58]

Though Ivanhoe deliberatively avoids the word "reason" or "reasoning" when explicating the analogical resonance in Mencius's notion of extension for fear that it may suggest a crucial role for abstract rational reasons (of the kind that is assumed in the top-down reasoning),[59] I agree with David Wong that it is a kind of reasoning, precisely in the sense that "increased sensitivity to one's existing moral feelings works together with recognition of analogical resonance to produce extension of these feelings to new cases."[60] In my view, the point is not so much whether or not the process of extension and analogical resonance involves reason but whether *analogical reasoning* is motivated by reason's sensitization to reason itself (as claimed by Kantian rationalists), or motivated by "increased sensitivity" to one's affective moral feelings.

Thus far, I have illuminated the nature and process of moral reasoning in the Confucian ethical tradition from the perspective of Mencian moral sentimentalism. It should be clear that Confucian moral reasoning and judgment are affective, relying on analogical resonance, rather than rationalist. But, one may wonder, does this say anything directly about the nature of *public reason(ing)* in Confucian democracy? After all, what we have examined so far is the nature and the moral psychological process of *individual* moral reasoning and judgment in the Confucian ethical tradition, not public reason, which is concerned with collective self-determination and democratic legitimacy; although, as will be seen shortly, the character of public reason in Confucian democracy is strongly correlated with the affective nature of individual moral reasoning in Confucian ethics of moral sentiments. Therefore, before embarking on constructing public reason that is suitable in Confucian pluralist democracy, two points about Mencian moral sentimentalism should be addressed.

First, as Ivanhoe shows, Mencius presented his notion of extension not merely as a moral psychological method of moral judgment, but, more important, as a way of moral self-cultivation, which is ultimately concerned with one's moral flourishing as a human being. In the story, Mencius's point is not merely that the king should make a sound moral judgment as a *political leader*. He must be virtuous to be a true king (*wang* 王), the ruler who possesses the Heaven-given mandate (*tianming* 天命) to rule. As merely one of the moral qualities for being virtuous, therefore, sound moral judgment, however important in politics, is necessary but far from sufficient in making the ruler a true king, namely, a sage-king. Second, Mencius was never an advocate of democracy and thus never

[58] Ivanhoe, "Confucian Self Cultivation and Mengzi's Notion of Extension," 231.

[59] Ibid., 228–30.

[60] Wong, "Reasons and Analogical Reasoning in Mengzi," 199.

presupposed political equality between the ruler and the ruled (or among the people), even when he boldly reinterpreted the relationship between the ruler and the ministers as a moral relationship based on mutual reciprocity.[61]

These two points – the inextricable intertwinement between sound moral judgment and moral self-cultivation to become a sage and political inequality entwined with Mencius's idea of moral equality (in the sense that anyone, being endowed with Heaven-given nature, is capable of becoming a sage) – stand in the way of making Mencian moral sentimentalism compatible with Confucian pluralist democracy, central to which is strong citizenship, not so much sagehood (i.e., Confucian moral perfection). However, if we, as most contemporary moral philosophers do, focus on the affective process of moral reasoning without implicating it with the Confucian ideal of moral personhood, which is a comprehensive moral doctrine, and if we reject Mencius's own political assumptions and instead embrace the democratic ideal of political equality and reciprocal citizenship, Mencius's notion of extension can turn out to be not only compatible with value pluralism but also conducive to an overlapping consensus among citizens who, though sharing a public culture and participating in common sociopolitical and legal institutions, subscribe to different moral, religious, or philosophical doctrines. Of course, overlapping consensus conceived in this way has nothing to do with rationalist bracketing principles or deontic constraints completely decoupled from, or "freestanding" of, the background culture. Rather, it is deeply embedded in what people have in common as citizens in civil society in terms of common concerns. I now turn to public reasons in the Confucian democratic context by civically reconstructing Mencius's notion of extension.

Confucian Familialism, Critical Affection, and Public Reasoning

Because of their preoccupation with the formation of moral agency and individual moral judgment, students of Chinese philosophy have largely dismissed the political context in which Mencius's notion of extension is presented.[62] Though it is plausible to reconstruct Mencius's notion of extension as a coherent philosophical account in reference to his ideas of human nature and moral self-cultivation, applicable to *all* humans (then and now), a new insight can be gleaned if we consider that Mencius presented the method of extension to the king as a kind of statecraft, as a way to govern the people. Mencius's political message is clearly presented in the later part of his conversation with King Xuan in *Mencius* 1A7.

[61] See Tu Weiming, "Probing the 'Three Bonds' and 'Five Relationships' in Confucian Humanism," in *Confucianism and the Family*, ed. Walter H. Slote and George A. DeVos (Albany: State University of New York Press, 1998), 126.

[62] One important exception is found in Irene T. Bloom, "Mengzian Arguments on Human Nature (*Ren Xing*)," in Liu and Ivanhoe, *Essays on the Moral Philosophy of Mengzi*, 75–6.

[S]o the king's failure to be a true king is not in the category of taking Mount Tai under one's arm and jumping over the North Sea with it; his failure to be a true king is in the category of not bowing respectfully to an elder. By treating the elders in one's family as elders should be treated and extending this to the elders of other families, and by treating the young of one's own family as the young ought to be treated and extending this to the young of other people's families, the empire can be turned around on the palm of one's hand.... Thus, if one extends his kindness it will be enough to protect all within the four seas, whereas if one fails to extend it, he will have no way to protect his wife and children. The reason the ancients so greatly surpassed most people was nothing other than this: they were good at extending what they did. Now, your kindness is sufficient to extend to the animals but the benefits do not reach the people. Why do you make an exception in the case [of the people]?

Here Mencius pays special attention to filial sentiments, and his choice is not arbitrary given the general Confucian emphasis of the virtue of filiality. Most notably, Youzi, Confucius's disciple, says, "Exemplary persons (*junzi* 君子) concentrate their efforts on the root (*ben* 本), for the root having taken hold, the way (*dao* 道) will grow therefrom. As for filial and fraternal responsibility (*xiaodi* 孝弟), it is, I suspect, the root of *ren* 仁."[63] Confucius's own statement is more directly political, when he says, "Where the ruler (*junzi*) is earnestly committed to his parents [and other family members] (*qin* 親), the people will aspire to *ren*; where he does not neglect his old friends, the people will not be indifferent to each other."[64] Mencius's (M) emphasis of filiality as the sole "root" (*ben*) is most salient in his famous defense of the Confucian graded love (*cha deng ai* 差等愛) against Yi Zhi (Y), the Mohist.

Y: According to the Confucian Way, the ancients acted as if they were protecting an infant. What does this teaching mean? To me it means that one should love without distinctions but that the love begins with parents and extends from there.

M: Does Master Yi believe that a man's affection for his brother's child is just like his affection for the child of a neighbor? What he should have taken from the teaching [he cited] is that, if a child crawling toward a well is about to fall in, this is not the fault of the child. Heaven, in giving birth to living beings, causes them to have one root, while Master Yi supposes they have two roots.[65]

Interpreting this passage, David Nivison argues that the one root refers to the emotional capacity for love or the spontaneous inclinations of human nature (i.e., what we really want to do), and the second root refers to philosophical doctrine arrived at through rational reflection (i.e., what we ought to do and can rightly recognize we ought to do).[66] That is, as Eric Hutton nicely

[63] *Analects* 1:2 (modified).

[64] *Analects* 8:2 (modified). Note that the term *junzi* in this passage refers to the ruler, not an ideal moral person in a general sense.

[65] *Mencius* 3A5.

[66] David S. Nivison, "Two Roots or One," in *Ways of Confucianism*, 133–48, esp. 134. I also consulted with Hutton, "Moral Connoisseurship in Mengzi," 176.

summarizes, in Mencius's viewpoint, the Mohist approach "divorces moral motivation from the content of moral obligation and stretches the former to fit the latter."[67]

I believe this is a plausible philosophical interpretation of the passage that corresponds well with Mencius's notion of extension (as reconstructed by many contemporary moral philosophers) and his idea of human nature. That said, I am not sure whether the entwinement between moral motivation and the content of moral obligation was Mencius's own problem. Given the firm establishment of the "one root thesis" (that filiality is the root of *ren*) in the Confucian tradition and considering Mencius's unswerving faith in the foundational value of the virtue of filiality, Mencius's most eminent concern here seems to criticize the typical Mohist negligence of the moral significance of filiality in making humans authentically human as much as the notion of *ren* as the universal sentiment of compassion that is indiscriminate, hence unreflectively inclusive.[68] On this reading, Mencius's key point is that the Mohist notion of (undifferentiated) universal love (*jian ai* 兼愛), according to which our concern for all people should be equal, violates the well-established Confucian one root thesis, creating the problematic two roots thesis, according to which *ren* is rooted in both filial love, a kind of particular love, and compassion, the universal love that according to Mohism is motivated by concern about what is profitable for the people.[69]

This interpretation is supported by Mencius's criticism of Mo Di, the founder of Mohism, which says, "Mo holds for impartial care (*jian ai*), which entails denial of one's parents. To deny one's parents … is to be an animal."[70] More revealingly, while Mencius acknowledges the qualitative difference between love (*ai*) toward animals and love (*ren*) toward people, he further differentiates both kinds of love from filial love (*qin*): "The noble person (*junzi*) loves (*ai*) living things without being humane (*ren*) toward them and is humane toward the people without being filially affectionate (*qin*). That he is filially affectionate toward his family is what allows him to be humane toward the people and

[67] Hutton, "Moral Connoisseurship in Mengzi," 176.

[68] In this regard, Yi Zhi is not a typical Mohist because he acquiesces to the Confucian belief that universal love is extended from filial love and this acquiescence is hardly surprising given Yi Zhi's lavish burial of his parents, the very behavior for which Mohists leveled a poignant criticism against Confucians. As *a* Mohist, Yi Zhi's point is that no distinction should be allowed in loving people.

[69] Zhu Xi (1130–1200), the great compiler of Song Neo-Confucianism, discusses *Mencius* 3A5 as this: "One's birth must be rooted in one's parents alone, not in other people.… So one's love should also be established first of all in serving one's parents and then extended to other people with difference of degree. According to Yi Zhi, yet, one should treat one's parents like the strangers on the street, though [he acknowledges] the order of applying the love may start with one's parents" (quoted with modification from Qingping Liu, "Is Mencius' Doctrine of 'Extending Affection' Tenable?," *Asian Philosophy* 14 [2004], 79–90, 83).

[70] *Mencius* 3B9.

loving toward creatures."[71] That is, filial love (*qin*) is the single root of both love (*ai*) toward living things and love (*ren*) toward human beings.

If my interpretation of filial love is granted, in *Mencius* 1A7 Mencius's core message to King Xuan seems to be that the king should extend the filial and fraternal love for his own family members (and the moral responsibility that filial sentiments give rise to) toward his people, whom he should deem *as* his own children. The underlying assumption is that the state is modeled after the family and the political ruler is the (quasi-)father of the state-as-family (*guojia* 國家). Above anything else, what impels the king to be humane (*ren*) toward his people is his familial moral sentiments, not just any undifferentiated compassion. In other words, the king, who has attained his throne by hereditary right (thus is not necessarily virtuous), can be motivated to act humanely toward his people, de facto strangers, when his familial affectionate sentiments have been stimulated and politically expanded. Thus understood, Mencius's notion of extension, when extended to politics, is seen to be predicated on the assumption of *the familial as the political*, on which Confucian virtue politics (*dezhi*) is founded.[72] At the heart of the political extension of familial affectionate sentiments is the king's capacity to envisage the people *as if* they were his family members.

What is important is that despite Mencius's metaphysical account of filiality (as the root of *ren*) and his moral-cosmological understanding of the familial as the political (or of virtue politics, according to which the ruler is given the mandate to rule by Heaven), the capacity to envisage strangers as if they were (quasi-)familial members does not necessarily have to rely on the foundational metaphysical account of human nature and particular moral virtues inherently affiliated with it. This decoupling of Mencian familial moral sentimentalism and Mencius's own (moral-cosmological) idea of Confucian virtue politics provides us with an important insight into the nature of public reason and the process of public reasoning in a Confucian democratic civil society where individuals encounter each other primarily qua strangers, though as citizens they belong to the common political entity.

As I have argued in the previous chapters, Confucian civil society does not refer to a gemeinschaft of thick affect, in which members are socialized into

[71] *Mencius* 7A45 (slightly modified).

[72] *Shujing*'s 書經 (*The Book of Documents*) "Cannon of Yao" (*yao dian* 堯典) describes sage-king Yao's virtuous rule in terms of his filial virtue and affection: "He [Emperor Yao] was reverent, intelligent, accomplished, sincere and mild. He was genuinely respectful and capable of all modesty. His light spread over the four extremities of the world, extending to Heaven above and Earth below. He was able to make bright his great virtue and bring affection to the nine branches of the family. When the nine branches of the family had become harmonious, he distinguished and honored the great clans. When the hundred clans had become illustrious, he harmonized the myriad states. Thus the numerous peoples were amply nourished, prospered, and became harmonious" (reprinted from Wm. Theodore de Bary, *The Trouble with Confucianism* [Cambridge, MA: Harvard University Press, 1991], 1).

their proper social roles and maintain aesthetic harmony with one another, but rather a modern pluralist society, the Confucian characteristic of which is found in the public culture that citizens commonly share, though they subscribe to different moral, philosophical, and religious doctrines. While in a gemeinschaft relation, social affects function merely as *bonding capital* that cements the existing social fabric of moral community, in Confucian democratic civil society, social affects are *formed* through the social and political extension of familial affectionate sentiments cultivated by individual citizens to the public space of civil society, thus functioning as *bridging capital* that bonds citizens horizontally across their deep differences.[73]

Citizens in a Confucian civil society, their differences notwithstanding, are motivated to see themselves as belonging to "one family." This family, however, now institutionally housed in a democratic civil society, is neither the king's personal possession nor a Heaven-entrusted task but the place where every member (i.e., citizen) enjoys his or her civil freedom and political equality and whose membership is not fixed on a particular ethnicity or comprehensive moral doctrine. Public reasons here are norms that citizens have in common, citizens who, despite their awareness of the value of individual identity, individual rights, and value pluralism, nevertheless see themselves as related brothers and sisters or fathers and mothers, who have resolve to sustain their familial public norms and virtues. More specifically, Confucian public reasons are grounded in (but not fixed on) civic virtues such as filiality (*xiaoti* 孝悌), respect for the elderly (*jinglao* 敬老), respectful deference (*cirang* 辭讓), trustworthiness (*xin* 信), and social harmony (*he* 和), which define the polity as distinctively Confucian,[74] especially in comparison with liberal public reasons that are embedded in the core public values of the liberal-democratic polity such as the legal constraints of a constitution, a tradition of constitutional interpretation, and a set of basic rights.[75]

[73] For a more detailed discussion about how Confucian familism (or familialism) can help generate distinctively Confucian civility (viz., relational strangership) through the process of extension, see Sungmoon Kim, "Beyond Liberal Civil Society: Confucian Familism and Relational Strangership," *Philosophy East and West* 60 (2010), 476–98.

[74] In this regard, I strongly object to the views held by some contemporary Confucian scholars that because of the relational nature of the Confucian selfhood, Confucianism is fundamentally incompatible with rights-based individualism or any kind of individualism. This type of claim confounds the ontological account of individualism (what Charles Taylor calls "atomism") and the political account of individualism.

[75] Krause, *Civil Passions*, 19. Also see William A. Galston, *Liberal Purposes: Goods, Virtues, and Diversity in the Liberal State* (Cambridge: Cambridge University Press, 1991) and Stephen Macedo, *Liberal Virtues: Citizenship, Virtue, and Community in Liberal Constitutionalism* (Oxford: Clarendon, 1990). By "distinctively Confucian," however, I do not mean that Confucian and liberal public reasons are mutually exclusive or incommensurable. It is essentially a question of emphasis and valuation rather than fundamentally different moral epistemology.

The Confucian distinctiveness of public reasons (and public reasoning) in Confucian democracy, however, is not *only* derived from the Confucian attributes of familial norms and civic virtues. Equally important, the uniquely Confucian character of public reasons and public reasoning is also attributable to the familial nature of Confucian moral sentiments. Once again, Mencius offers a profound insight into the complex nature of familial affectionate sentiments.

Though Mencius emphasizes strenuously the moral value of familial affectionate sentiments and their naturalness, he does not present them as affection commonly understood in terms of positive attachment to the object one cares about. To understand Mencius's complex understanding of familial affectionate sentiments, let us revisit Mencius's interpretation of the chapter titled "Xiaopan (小弁)" in the *Shijing* 詩經 (*The Book of Poetry*), which I discussed, though briefly, in Chapter 2. Against the charge that the poem is of a small man (*xiao ren* 小人, i.e., a petty man) because of its resentful tone, Mencius defends the author of the poem as follows:

> There is a man here. A man of Yue draws his bow to shoot him. Were I to talk of this in a jocular manner, it would be solely because he is not a relative of mine. But if my older brother were to draw his bow to shoot him, I would shed tears when telling of it solely because he is my relative. The resentment (*yuan* 怨) in the "Xiaopan" is an aspect of the intimacy one feels with one's parents (*qin qin* 親親), and intimacy with one's parents is humaneness (*ren*).... In the "Xiaopan" the fault of the parent was great. When one is unresentful despite the fact that a parent's fault is great, the sense of estrangement is deepened. When one is resentful despite the fact that a parent's fault is small, an unwarranted obstacle is created. To deepen estrangement is to be unfilial and to create an obstacle is also unfilial. Confucius said, "Shun was consummately filial, yet at the age of fifty he still longed for his parents."[76]

As I argued in Chapter 2, resentment (*yuan*) in the "Xiaopan" is qualitatively different from resentment commonly understood as one of the strongest antisocial passions, driving men to a life-and-death struggle for recognition. The resentment in "Xiaopan" is a special kind of vehement passion that is often aroused in the intimate, mostly familial, relationships – hence "affective resentment." Contrary to the common communitarian depiction of the family as a haven of love and affection, family (including the Confucian family) is frequently filled with psychological tension and moral disagreement.[77] Shun's family is the case in point. Though Shun, who later became the legendary sage-king, succeeding Yao through abdication, is famous for his great filiality, he is recorded to have had morally despicable parents and a younger brother

[76] *Mencius* 6B3.

[77] For a revealing psychological study on psychological tensions in the Confucian family, see Bou-Young Rhi, "Mental Illness in Its Confucian Context," in Slote and DeVos, *Confucianism and the Family*, 285–310.

who constantly plotted to kill him.[78] But Mencius praised this moral hero not because he was single-mindedly obedient to his parents. In fact, Shun is seen to have revealed the same kind of emotion that we find in the "Xiaopan." When asked whether it was morally appropriate for Shun to be aggrieved about his violent parents and to weep and cry out to Heaven, Mencius responded that Shun's cry was from grief and longing and added that the mind of the filial son could not be so dispassionate as to not weep or cry out to Heaven and his parents (if he were in Shun's situation).[79]

What is important is Mencius's conviction that it was this very complex passion – what can be called *critical affection* in that it is not blindly positive, which would demand slavish obedience (*shun* 順), but *critical*, in the sense that it involves morally appropriate grief, longing, or resentment – that made Shun's filiality not just virtuous but greatly virtuous. The key here is the moral reflectivity that (familial) critical affection enables. Filiality that is motivated by critical affection, then, makes the agent a moral agent and his or her action moral behavior, not action propelled by his or her consanguinity, without involving any moral reflection.[80] Put differently, filiality is a moral virtue because it is an inner quality or character that has been cultivated through, or in spite of, relational upheavals with which one has been inevitably entangled throughout one's life, a tough process that involves both positive and critical affections.

Extending this Mencian-Confucian insight into critical affection to modern Confucian democratic politics, I now submit that the defining characteristic of affective civil passion in Confucian democracy, which constitutes the core of public reasons, is critical affection. As a concept, critical affection is counterintuitive because affection is generally positive in its character as an attachment. But in our actual psychological and social experience, affection is not always positive, and our political experience is no exception. For instance, people love their country, which they deem as an extended family (as *guojia*), but sometimes (quite often indeed) they hate or at least regret any injustice it did to others or even to its own people in the past (or even in the present). This is especially so for weak and small countries (or a large but weak one such as China in the late nineteenth and early twentieth centuries) that were once under foreign rule. In such countries, people's affection toward their country is, to say the least, ambivalent: they both love their country for republican, communitarian, or (liberal) nationalist reasons, but simultaneously, to varying degrees, they *hate* it because in the end it failed to protect their political liberty and could not prevent them from suffering individually and collectively. Still, it is important to note, people's critical attitude toward their beloved country

[78] *Mencius* 5A2.

[79] *Mencius* 5A1.

[80] On the view that interprets Confucian ethics in terms of mere consanguinity, see Qingping Liu, "Filiality versus Sociality and Individuality: On Confucianism as 'Consanguinitism,'" *Philosophy East and West* 53 (2003), 234–50.

is broadly nested in positive affection. They have developed critical feelings toward their country because they love it; hence critical *affection.*

If it is agreed that critical affection is neither a mere philosophical construct nor a conceptual oxymoron, I believe its constructive value as constitutive of public reasons can also be granted. The concept of critical affection holds political theoretical value as well because it can help break through the individual-collective dichotomy in liberalism on one hand and the entrenched republican contrast between natural/prepolitical passion and artificial/political passion on the other.[81]

First, that Confucian public reasons are grounded in (familial) critical affection (as well as constituted by familial norms and civic virtues) offers a new perspective on the individual-collective dichotomy. Many rights-based liberal individualists claim that moral capacity is possessed exclusively by a rational individual.[82] Since group identity is formed in mediation of passion, a group, by nature, cannot be capable of morality. When groups such as nation-states or organizations act morally, the moral agents are still the concrete *persons* who individually compose them.[83] In this perspective, public reason (of both Humean and Confucian kinds) sounds overbearing and collective morality seems like an oxymoron. Critical affection, however, helps us understand that collective passion encompasses certain reflective attitudes toward the entity to which it is positively attached. Granted that reflection or reflexivity is a quintessential moral quality or agency, critical affection makes collective morality (as distinct from individual morality) or public reason (as distinct from individual moral judgment) possible, though it is exercised by individual *citizens* (not only private individuals). Though strong liberal individualists such as Kateb or cosmopolitans like Martha Nussbaum may find it morally problematic,[84] reflective democratic citizenship on which Confucian democracy is predicated would make a democratic polity more politically robust (in the sense of better protecting citizens' public freedom and exercising collective self-determination) without violating individual citizens' democratic rights.

Second, critical affection rejects the stark republican distinction between a natural/prepolitical and an artificial/political passion. Just like most (individual and group) passion, critical affection is largely generated in prepolitical settings,

[81] According to Maurizio Viroli, political passion alone, which he also calls an artificial passion to differentiate it from a natural passion, is conducive to civic virtue, political liberty, and the common good, because natural passion is inherently affiliated with (ethnic) nationalism, which is the enemy of republican patriotism. See his *Republicanism*, trans. Antony Shugaar (New York: Hill and Wang, 2002).

[82] For one, see George Kateb, "Is Patriotism a Mistake?," in *Patriotism and Other Mistakes* (New Haven: Yale University Press, 2006), 3–20.

[83] See Dennis F. Thompson, "Moral Responsibility of Public Officials: The Problem of Many Hands," *American Political Science Review* 74 (1980), 905–16.

[84] Martha C. Nussbaum, "Patriotism and Cosmopolitanism," in *For Love of Country: Debating the Limits of Patriotism*, ed. Joshua Cohen (Boston: Beacon, 1996), 3–17.

in interpersonal relations, family relations, and/or associational or communal lives – namely, in civil societies. By solely focusing on its nonpolitical origin, however, republicans such as Maurizio Viroli would respond to it no differently than liberal individualists: both groups would see it as potentially dangerous and of no moral and political value. For instance, even if Viroli differs from Kateb in his valorization of political passion, for him there is no moral passion independent of political passion. However, Viroli (as well as Kateb) fails to realize that not only is critical affection a self-regulating – hence moral – passion, but it often transforms into political passion when extended to the public space of civil society, that is, in terms of public reasons. In democratic civil society critical affection reinvents itself into the citizenry's public concerns for political liberty and democratic justice. It allows citizens a moment for moral reflection to critically evaluate whether the state to which they are positively attached is indeed democratically legitimate and upholding democratic justice and offers them a space (i.e., civil society) for collective self-determination, thus opening a critical political distance between the state and themselves.

Conclusion

As a filial son or daughter becomes truly filial by undergoing moral reflection evoked by affective resentment, in Confucian democracy a citizen becomes civically empowered when he or she is reflective-critically attached to the polity. Critical affection that is deeply rooted in Confucian familialism plays a critical role in helping Confucian democratic citizens to care about what they, with all their differences, have in common and to be reflectively concerned about the problems facing them together.

In Confucian democracy, public reasons do not dictate individual lives or internal affairs of voluntary associations. Nor do they operate to serve the vested interests of the majority or those who are politically powerful by screening certain political agenda as nonpublic, as merely concerned with the private interests of some minority people, thereby systematically preventing minorities from accessing the public forum and freely participating in public decision-making processes. And in no case do they merely reflect what a group of political elites believe is good for all members of the political community. What they do instead is to facilitate public deliberations by cultivating in citizens a sensitivity to common concerns. In other words, they motivate citizens to extend their affective concerns for private affairs – whether material or ideational – to public affairs that commonly affect them. Most important, public reasons help citizens to emphatically engage with the sentiments of those who have been systematically excluded from political power so that their economic as well as cultural and religious interests (what Max Weber calls "ideal interests"[85]) can

[85] Max Weber, *From Max Weber: Essays in Sociology*, trans. and ed. Hans H. Gerth and C. W. Mills (New York: Oxford University Press, 1958), 280.

be fairly and equally represented in both constitutional essentials and public policies.

After all, as Krause rightly notes, political legitimacy is not synonymous with justice.[86] To make Confucian democracy not only culturally relevant and democratically legitimate but also just, especially under the fact of pluralism, public reasons must be open to democratic contestation. Though Mencian-Confucian familial moral sentimentalism can delineate the coherent, albeit not incontestable, parameter of public reasons in Confucian democracy, their substantive contents must not be fixed on singular, incontestable answers to specific questions of law and policy. Though advocates of thick Confucian communitarianism present Confucian democracy as largely free from moral uncertainty, conflicting interests, and competing goods, Confucian pluralist democracy embraces them as the ineluctable condition of common social life.

[86] Krause, *Civil Passions*, 168.

6

In Defense of Confucian Democratic Welfarism

In Chapter 3, I took issue with the sufficientarian interpretation of the Confucian perspective of social justice, not only because of its idiosyncratic attempt to draw sufficientarian implications from the Chinese term *zu* 足 (often translated in English into "sufficient") without much consideration of sufficientarianism's background ethics (evidenced in Harry Frankfurt's work),[1] but also because of the *negative thesis* implicated in sufficientarianism which rejects egalitarian and prioritarian reasoning at least above some critical threshold.[2] Indeed, given Confucianism's strong commitment to the (moral and material) well-being of the people, it is hard to dispute Joseph Chan's core contention that according to Confucianism, people who are worst off have first priority for care,[3] which is highly compatible with John Rawls's difference principle and his idea of social minimum.[4] My problem with Chan's view lies in his supplementary claim that inequalities of wealth and income beyond the threshold of sufficiency do not matter, a claim that he rationalizes primarily with reference to Xunzi, who

1 See Harry Frankfurt, "Equality as a Moral Ideal," *Ethics* 98 (1987), 21–43.

2 Paula Casal, "Why Sufficiency Is Not Enough," *Ethics* 117 (2007), 296–326, 299–300.

3 Among political philosophers, whether the principle of sufficiency is completely independent of the prioritarian principle is an unresolved question. For instance, while Frankfurt embraces no element of prioritarianism in his notion of the principle of sufficiency, Roger Crisp upholds a mixed thesis which stipulates that "absolute priority is to be given to benefits to those below the threshold (but not above it)" (Roger Crisp, "Equality, Priority, and Compassion," *Ethics* 113 [2003], 745–63, 758). Joseph Chan largely bypasses this controversy and simply assumes that the principle of sufficiency naturally incorporates prioritarianism below the threshold. See Joseph Chan, "Is There a Confucian Perspective on Social Justice?," *Western Political Thought in Dialogue with Asia*, ed. Takashi Shogimen and Cary J. Nederman (Lanham, MD: Lexington Books, 2008), 269–75.

4 On Rawls's idea of social minimum, see John Rawls, *A Theory of Justice* (Cambridge, MA: Belknap, [1971] 1999), 278–80.

singles out merit and contribution (as opposed to family background) as the only legitimate source of emolument.[5]

It is debatable whether the fact that Xunzi advocated the meritocratic emolument system, in the face of strong feudal aristocratic oppositions during the Warring States period, can be construed as an endorsement of inequalities beyond the threshold of sufficiency. But this interpretative issue, however important, is not my primary concern in the present chapter, nor am I interested in the philosophical investigation of which distributive principle Confucianism as an ethical system supports, between egalitarianism, prioritarianism, and sufficientarianism, all of which tend to favor less advantaged individuals when their interests conflict with those of more advantaged individuals.[6] Rather, my concern here is discovering the best way to realize the Confucian commitment to the people's material well-being in the given contemporary socioeconomic and political context of East Asian societies. In this regard, what commands our attention in Chan's sufficientarian claim is not so much its positive thesis, a point that is generally supported by all three distributive principles, but Chan's perfectionist justification of economic meritocracy beyond the threshold of sufficiency.

Though political meritocracy and economic meritocracy refer to categorically different things and therefore are not necessarily interrelated, advocates of Confucian political meritocracy (including Chan) largely subscribe to a modest version (or versions) of economic meritocracy, ascribing it to the Confucian conception of the good life. For instance, in the same vein with Chan, Chenyang Li asserts,

> If people perform different tasks in society on the basis of abilities and thereby make varied contributions, they should be rewarded accordingly. This recognition of differentiation in economic contribution is consistent with the principle of proportional equality. Xunzi's proportional distribution system is supplemented by a social welfare policy that the government would provide accommodations for orphans and the childless elderly and would subsidize the poor and needy (Wang, 1988: 152). As far as distribution policy is concerned, Xunzi strictly promoted a principle of proportional equality based on contribution.[7]

Here Li boldly claims (thereby making explicit what is only implied in Chan's advocacy of sufficientarianism) that it is not so much social welfarism as such

[5] Chan, "Is There a Confucian Perspective on Social Justice?," 274.

[6] For this judgment, see Casal, "Why Sufficiency Is Not Enough," 296. For my critique of the sufficientarian interpretation of and justification for Confucian social justice from both interpretive and normative standpoints, see Sungmoon Kim, "Confucianism and Acceptable Inequalities," *Philosophy & Social Criticism* (December 2013 , published online on October 15, 2013 as doi:10.1177/0191453713507015.).

[7] Chenyang Li, "Equality and Inequality in Confucianism," *Dao* 11 (2012), 295–313, 302. Wang's work in parenthesis refers to Wang Xianqian, *Xunzijijie* [Collected Interpretations of the *Xunzi*] (Beijing: Zhonghua shuju, 1988).

but proportional equality or economic meritocracy that is at the center of Confucian ethics and political theory.[8]

There are two problems in these related claims. First, even granting the meritocratic interpretation of ancient Confucian (especially Xunzi's) perspectives on socioeconomic distribution (though I find this interpretation largely mistaken because of its neglect of ancient China's unique socioeconomic and political context), it seems heavily problematic to directly apply this ancient Confucian position to contemporary East Asian societies that are suffering from ever-increasing socioeconomic inequalities and, more important, the hierarchical citizenship between the rich and poor that they create.[9] The reasoning that *because* there is some (sporadic and hardly systematic) textual support for a certain version of economic meritocracy in ancient Confucian classics, contemporary Confucian normative political philosophy must endorse a similar kind of economic meritocracy, is not only anachronistic but also absurd. Ancient Confucians never knew the modern capitalistic market system, not to mention the social problems it generates, the most serious of which includes the erosion of common citizenship and public-spiritedness. And when they (such as Xunzi) advocated the meritocratic emolument system,[10] their target was the feudal aristocrats who had maintained a privileged access to public posts and economic interests. In other words, ancient Confucians had no reason to be worried about the tyrannical force of money (or the market) that infiltrates into and dominates other social spheres such as the family, school, church, and the government, thereby violating what Michael Walzer calls "complex equality."[11]

Advocates of Confucian economic meritocracy (most of whom are also champions of meritocratic elitism), however, rarely pay attention to the tyranny of the capitalistic market and its devastating political implications.[12] Less

[8] Like Chan, Li, too, relies on Harry Frankfurt to reinforce his argument for economic meritocracy (ibid., 296). However, Li does so by only highlighting Frankfurt's central claim that equality is not intrinsically valuable, which he thinks is consistent with the Confucian view, without noticing the crucial difference between liberal-individualistic ethics that underpins Frankfurt's distributive principle and Confucian relational virtue ethics.

[9] For an illuminating discussion of the profound injustice involved in the translation (or transgression) of economic inequalities into political inequalities, see David Miller, *National Responsibility and Global Justice* (Oxford: Oxford University Press, 2007).

[10] As even Chan acknowledges (albeit implicitly), Xunzi never advocated economic meritocracy (alongside the principle of sufficiency) as his vision of *social justice*. His focus was mainly on the establishment of meritocratic bureaucracy, the idea that profoundly influenced his student, Han Fei, the famous Legalist.

[11] Michael Walzer, *Spheres of Justice: A Defense of Pluralism and Equality* (New York: Basic Books, 1983). Also see David Miller and Michael Walzer (eds.), *Pluralism, Justice, and Equality* (Oxford: Oxford University Press, 1995).

[12] On this point, see Benjamin R. Barber, *Consumed: How Markets Corrupt Children, Infantilize Adults, and Swallow Citizens Whole* (New York: Norton, 2007); Sheldon S. Wolin, *Democracy Incorporated: Managed Democracy and the Specter of Inverted Totalitarianism* (Princeton: Princeton University Press, 2008).

interested in equal democratic citizenship (see Chapter 3), they believe economic distribution is either a pure economic problem or a matter of philosophical principle, but hardly a political problem that defines the character of common social life. Though Chan's moderate economic meritocracy is less subject to this criticism, in the absence of an effective democratic control of the market, it would be practically impossible to generate both a social consensus on the content and level of sufficiency among citizens, who are differently situated and whose interests are diverse, and raise the threshold of sufficiency. Put differently, what is more important than identifying which distributive principle is consistent with the (ancient) Confucian view is how to realize such a principle democratically, namely, *democratic welfarism*, which is impossible without common and equal citizenship.[13]

Second, Confucian advocates of economic meritocracy understand "merit" in fixed and absolute terms. For them, concepts such as virtue, merit, desert, and contribution speak for themselves as if their meanings are universally agreed on or given a priori. However, as Amartya Sen argues, "meritocracy, more generally the practice of rewarding merit, is essentially underdefined, and we cannot be sure about its content – and thus about the claims regarding its 'justice' – until some further specifications are made (concerning, in particular, the objectives to be pursued, in terms of which merit is to be, ultimately judged). The merit of actions – and (derivatively) that of persons performing actions – cannot be judged independent of the way we understand the nature of a good (or an acceptable) society."[14] Of course, if the conceptualization of a good society includes the absence of serious economic inequalities, then it can be expected that putative merit will operate to lessen socioeconomic inequalities. This, however, is not what the Confucian advocates of (economic and political) meritocracy have in mind. Certainly, they are interested in the elimination of deprivation or absolute poverty, which they argue can be done by the wise public policies implemented by political elites, but as opponents of full-fledged democracy, they show less interest in social cooperation among citizens, which can be severely impaired by socioeconomic inequalities, though they frequently stress that harmony (*he* 和) is the prima facie Confucian social virtue.[15]

[13] Democratic welfarism is commonly thought to be affiliated with egalitarianism. However, this is not always the case if egalitarianism is understood mechanically to mean that "one outcome is to be preferred to another insofar as (undeserved) inequality is minimized" (Crisp, "Equality, Priority, and Compassion," 746). In my view, all three distributive principles (egalitarianism, prioritarianism, and sufficientarianism) can be connected with democratic welfarism as long as the distributive principle at issue is grounded in political equality or equal citizenship.

[14] Amartya Sen, "Merit and Justice," in *Meritocracy and Economic Inequality*, eds. Kenneth Arrow, Samuel Bowles, and Steven Durlauf (Princeton: Princeton University Press, 2000), 5–6. Also see Julian Lamont, "The Concept of Desert in Distributive Justice," *Philosophical Quarterly* 44 (1994), 45–64 for the claim that desert requires external values and goals to make it determinate.

[15] See, for instance, Chenyang Li, "The Confucian Ideal of Harmony," *Philosophy East and West* 56 (2006), 583–603. Famously, John Rawls defines political society as the fair system of

In this chapter, I present an alternative vision of Confucian social justice that is robustly democratic and morally justifiable in light of Confucian public reason, which embodies the citizens' collective vision of a good polity.[16] I argue that (1) the Confucian commitment to the people's material well-being or the ideal of people-centrism (*min ben* 民本) can be best achieved by the democratic welfare state and (2) Confucian familialism generates expanded responsibilities among citizens to the beneficiary's vulnerability, thus endorsing Confucian democratic welfarism. In making this claim, I will critically engage with Confucian family-oriented perspective on social justice (simply Confucian familism), according to which it is wrong for one to love strangers as one's core family members, and welfare financing is primarily a family responsibility rather than a state responsibility.[17] My central claim is that Confucian familism of the version that is nested in and justified by economic and political meritocracy must be revamped (or expanded) into Confucian familialism that puts vulnerability before merit.

Confucian Familism as a Distributive Principle?

Joseph Chan's sufficientarian interpretation of the Confucian perspective on social justice, though interesting and convincing (albeit partially), should leave normative Confucian political philosophers wondering about the nature of his argument – is he saying that the Confucian distributive principle is a kind of sufficiency principle (then what is there uniquely *Confucian*?) or that the sufficientarian rendition of Confucian distributive principle (assuming that there is such a thing) is most consistent with perfectionism, his preferred normative position (but if we have a different normative vision, say, democratic pluralism, the whole question is accordingly to be seen differently)?[18] Either way, there can be a criticism (though not here) regarding what is uniquely Confucian about Chan's sufficientarianism as a Confucian distributive principle.

cooperation and precisely on this ground he opposes meritocratic social justice, even if he allows the *ensuing* inequalities after meeting the basic needs of the worst off. See Rawls, *A Theory of Justice*, 91–2. More accurately, Rawls embraces a meritocratic society only of a democratic conception: "Thus a meritocratic society is a danger for the other interpretations of the principles of justice but not for the democratic conception. For, as we have just seen, the difference principle transforms the aims of society in fundamental respects" (91). One of my core arguments in this chapter is that Confucian public reason brings out a similar kind of transformation in the aims of the Confucian polity and in the concept of merit.

[16] For my idea of Confucian public reason, see Chapter 5.

[17] Most notably, see Ruiping Fan, *Reconstructionist Confucianism: Rethinking Morality after the West* (Dordrecht: Springer, 2010).

[18] See Joseph Chan, *Confucian Perfectionism: A Political Philosophy for Modern Times* (Princeton: Princeton University Press, 2013); Chan, "Legitimacy, Unanimity, and Perfectionism," *Philosophy and Public Affairs* 29 (2000), 5–42.

In this respect, Ruiping Fan's defense of Confucian familism as an alternative to existing distributive principles (particularly egalitarianism) is worth close attention because Fan presents it as a distributive principle that is most faithful to Confucian relational virtue ethics. In this section I will first present Fan's core argument and then explain why his view is limited in both capturing the core spirit of Confucian benevolent government (*ren zheng* 仁政) and realizing Confucian people-centrism in contemporary East Asia.

As a strong opponent of egalitarianism and an ardent follower of classical Confucianism, Fan begins to reconstruct a Confucian vision of distributive justice with a bold, anti-Aristotelian statement, that "[h]umans are by nature *familial animals*, possessing the potential to form appropriate families and pursue flourishing in familial relations."[19] On Fan's interpretation of Confucianism, humans are naturally disposed to love their family members and this natural disposition generates the morality of filial piety, which Confucians understand as the root of *ren*,[20] and accordingly, children's moral responsibility to take care of their (aged) parents. Rooted in human nature, therefore, filial responsibility is "a fundamental and comprehensive responsibility, including physical, mental, social, and spiritual care which can only be carried out at home."[21] Fan elaborates the centrality of filial piety to Confucian virtue ethics as the following:

> [F]or Confucians, filial piety is not only the source of perfect virtue, but is also the major manifestation of perfect virtue. An authentic human person must first be filial to his parents at home, be respectful to his elders abroad, and only if he still has time and opportunity after performing these duties, may he employ himself in the studies of other things (*Analects* 1:6).... [T]he true nature of general benevolence involves a natural hierarchy in which one's own parents must be cared for before one can care for other people.[22]

When Fan claims that humans are by nature familial animals and presents filial piety as the perfect and comprehensive human virtue, his aim is to contrast Confucian ethics to Western (a la Aristotelian) ethics, which understands human beings as fundamentally political animals, who by nature are disposed to live a political life by means of speech and action. In Fan's understanding, in Confucianism, filial piety holds the level of ethical (and political) significance commensurate with what both speech and action (and relevant virtues such as justice) have in (mainstream) Western politics, which together constitute the core of *vita activa*. In this reasoning, filial piety is not merely an inner disposition or natural sentiment that differentiates humans from animals, but rather the telos of human life, the virtue that makes man perfect and complete.

[19] Fan, *Reconstructionist Confucianism*, 76, emphasis added.

[20] *Analects* 1:2.

[21] Fan, *Reconstructionist Confucianism*, 96.

[22] Ibid.

Yet, the philosophical establishment of the moral significance of the family is only the beginning of Fan's normative political theorization. According to Fan, two ethical claims are derived from Confucian family-oriented ethics. First, since human beings are essentially familial animals and filial piety is the major manifestation of perfect virtue, to love all humans equally critically violates Confucian ethics, or more fundamentally, what it means to be an authentic human being. "Confucianism always requires that there ought to be a clear and definite order, distinction, and differentiation in the application of love.... This peculiar Confucian discrimination is aptly reflected in the Confucian slogan of 'love with distinction' or 'care by gradation' (*ai you cha deng* 愛有差等) in the process of Confucian self-cultivation (*xiu shen* 修身). It is wrong for one to love strangers as one's close family members," says Fan.[23] This further justifies Fan's normative claim that it is not transparent on what moral ground "I, as a stranger, [should] have a moral responsibility to pay tax in order to take care of others' parents" because "my existential status as a child of my parents assign[s] me a more significant moral responsibility for taking care of my parents."[24] In the end, Fan concludes, "unequals should be treated as unequals," and this is how Confucianism understands (or should understand) harmony and social justice.[25] Second, given the tremendous moral and metaphysical significance of the family in the Confucian ethical tradition, the family, contra liberal feminists such as Susan Okin,[26] cannot be understood as just another (contract-based) social institution but must be "distinguished outstandingly as an autonomous unit from the rest of society." "The autonomy of the family," therefore, "is the requirement that consensual relations within a given family governing the development of its children should not be coercively interfered with by the state."[27]

Ultimately, from these two claims (love with distinction and the autonomy of the family), which are premised on the foundational statement that humans are familial animals, Fan derives a Confucian family-oriented distributive principle (Confucian familism) and welfare policy (family care), and he does so by criticizing John Rawls – not only the Kantian liberal egalitarianism that Rawls subscribes to, which is the ethical basis of his two principles of justice, but also democratic welfarism as justified by Rawls's political and economic egalitarianism.

When the Rawlsian requirement of fair equality of opportunity has to use state-controlled measures to restrict or even prohibit the parents from pursuing better educational opportunities for their children, it violates the fundamental Confucian moral conscience of *ren*. Confucian social justice wants family-based opportunities autonomously

[23] Ibid., 53.

[24] Ibid., 97.

[25] Ibid., 55.

[26] Susan M. Okin, *Justice, Gender, and the Family* (New York: Basic Books, 1989).

[27] Fan, *Reconstructionist Confucianism*, 54.

provided by families, rather than the so-called "fair" equality of opportunity imposed by the state. For one thing, Confucians have always required that a government of *ren* make the taxes and levies light and leave resources to families for pursuing welfare for their family members as they see appropriate (see, e.g., *Mencius* 1A5). They strongly hold that welfare responsibility resides first with the family.[28]

Then, how is family care exercised in practice? Of note, Fan, who is otherwise highly skeptical about the compatibility between rights and Confucian relational virtues, appeals to a Confucian conception of rights by deriving it from the Confucian conception of filial virtue.

> Some obligations may be more important than others so that it can be taken as constituting a necessary requirement for exercising the virtue.... If such an obligation towards a person is thus identified, then an entitlement of that person entailed by this obligation can be set down as his/her right. Consider the Confucian children's virtue of filial piety (*xiao* 孝) as an example.... Suppose taking care of one's elderly parents' lives can be taken to be a necessary obligation for exercising the virtue of filial piety, then the entitlement of the elderly parents to receive such care can be set down as their right.[29]

I find Fan's presentation of filial piety and its supreme moral significance in the Confucian tradition largely convincing, given the ethico-religious and metaphysical implications of filial piety, especially in relation to *ren* and also to human nature, and his understanding of Confucian ethics as family-oriented acceptable.[30] What I find problematic is Fan's attempt to derive a Confucian distributive principle and welfare policy directly from this comprehensive philosophical understanding of filial piety, and the method in which he does this. There are at least four problems in Fan's normative claims.

First, there is a logical gap between the autonomy of the family and the moral significance of the family in the Confucian ethical tradition. Even if we accept Fan's controversial statement that humans are familial animals in the comprehensive moral sense, the idea of the autonomy of the family does not naturally derive from this foundational moral statement. Certainly, Confucians did acknowledge that there could be a tension between the family and the state but the nature of such a tension is essentially moral, in terms of one's filial obligation versus one's obligation to the state.[31] Confucians in no instance conceived of the family as a morally autonomous private domain that ought to

[28] Ibid.

[29] Ibid., 58–9.

[30] Also see Chenyang Li, "Shifting Perspectives: Filial Morality Revisited," *Philosophy East and West* 47 (1997), 211–32 for a similar argument. From a virtue ethics perspective, Philip J. Ivanhoe also articulates why filial piety in classical Confucianism cannot be reduced to an expression of a general virtue of gratitude or friendship. See his "Filial Piety as Virtue," in *Working Virtue: Virtue Ethics and Contemporary Moral Problems*, ed. Rebecca L. Walker and Philip J. Ivanhoe (Oxford: Oxford University Press, 2007).

[31] See *Analects* 13:18; *Mencius* 7A35. For an excellent investigation of this issue, see Sor-hoon Tan, "Between Family and State: Relational Tensions in Confucian Ethics," in *Mencius: Contexts and Interpretations*, ed. Alan K. L. Chan (Honolulu: University of Hawaii Press, 2002).

be vigilant of the state's (welfare) intervention as Fan claims. For Confucians, family held supreme moral significance not only because it is the realm for one's moral self-cultivation, which as Fan rightly claims begins with the cultivation of filial virtue, but also because the moral principles and virtues that govern the family are directly relevant to the governing of the state. Most tellingly, Confucius said, "It is all in filial conduct (*xiao* 孝)! Just being filial to your parents and befriending your brothers is carrying out the work of government."[32] There is nothing that can justify the autonomy of the family from the state in this statement. Instead, what we notice is the deep Confucian conviction that the political is extended from the familial. The *Great Learning*'s famous statement clearly vindicates this Confucian principle of the familial as the political: "[O]nly when families are regulated are states well governed; and only when states are well governed is there peace in the world."[33]

Second, Fan's thesis of the autonomy of the family is not so much Confucian but characteristically liberal, or closer to libertarian. Ironically, despite Fan's strenuous criticism of liberalism, his thesis of the autonomy of the family has much in common with one particular strand of liberalism – frequently observed among some radical Christian Americans – which is predicated on what Amy Gutmann calls the "theory of the state of families." The state of families places educational authority exclusively in the hands of parents, thereby permitting parents to predispose their children, through education, to choose a way of life consistent with their familial heritage.[34] When Fan asserts that "consensual relations within a given family governing the development of its children should not be coercively interfered with by the state," he clearly subscribes to the liberal theory of the state of families, thus upholding liberal pluralism,[35] not classical Confucianism, to which he is morally and normatively committed.

Of course, there is an appreciable difference between the liberal theory of the state of families and Fan's "Confucian" thesis of the autonomy of the family. While the former's focus is primarily on the moral-educational autonomy of the family vis-à-vis the state, the latter is ultimately concerned with the economic autarchy of individual family and social freedom it can

[32] *Analects* 2:21. The English translation is adopted from Roger T. Ames and Henry Rosemont Jr., *The Analects of Confucius: A Philosophical Translation* (New York: Ballantine Books, 1998).

[33] Wm. Theodore de Bary, Wing-tsit Chan, and Burton Watson (eds.), *Sources of Chinese Tradition*, vol. 1 (New York: Columbia University Press, 1960), 115. Mencius makes a similar claim, when he says, "The Empire (*tianxia* 天下) has its basis in the state, the state in the family, and the family in one's own self" (*Mencius* 4A5; unless otherwise noted, all English translations of the *Mengzi* 孟子 in this chapter are adopted from *Mencius*, trans. D. C. Lau [New York: Penguin, 1970]).

[34] Amy Gutmann, *Democratic Education* (Princeton: Princeton University Press, 1988), 28.

[35] From Gutmann's standpoint, William Galston's liberal pluralism is premised on the assumption of the state of families (ibid., 298–9). For Galston's position, see William A. Galston, *Liberal Pluralism: The Implications of Value Pluralism for Political Theory and Practice* (Cambridge: Cambridge University Press, 2002).

promise.[36] That is, while the former is wary of the state's moral paternalism, the latter's greatest fear is the likely intervention of the welfare state into private families.

> Evidently, families can give their children a great amount of advantage; private schools, culture in the home, a secure home environment, trips abroad, private lessons, an advantaged peer group, and successful role models. All of these can substantially enhance the children's opportunities for seeking offices and positions in society. Given that the existence of such advantageous family opportunities is unlikely to be beneficial to the least-favored children in society, Rawls' social justice, with its requirement of fair equality of opportunity, would have to restrict them in order to equalize life prospects for every child (or at least for those with similar natural endowments). But these family opportunities are permissible and even encouraged by the Confucian principle of *ren*.[37]

Here Fan rationalizes his "Confucian" defense of the state of families by appealing to the Confucian principle of *ren*, the essence of which (in his interpretation) lies in treating unequals unequally or love with distinction. I will examine whether Fan's understanding of *ren* is consistent with classical Confucianism shortly. For now, let me draw attention to the irony that the underlying theory of Fan's claim here is not so much Confucianism, according to which an ideal state is family-like (rather than starkly opposed to autonomous families), but libertarianism. The only difference between Fan's libertarian Confucianism and Nozickian libertarianism is that the former takes human society to be family-based, rather than individual-based.[38] The libertarian characteristic of Fan's family-oriented Confucianism is evident when he says that "[d]ue to its family-oriented characters, Confucianism views welfare financing (including health care payment) primarily as a family responsibility, rather than a state responsibility. Chinese families must save resources by themselves, rather than rely on the state, to support their family members' health care.... That is, it is basically every family's obligation to save resources in order to take care of their members' health care."[39]

[36] By way of comparison, it is important to note that Galston, who can be deemed as a proponent of the state of families, strongly opposes libertarianism. See William A. Galston, *Liberal Purposes: Goods, Virtues, and Diversity in the Liberal State* (Cambridge: Cambridge University Press, 1991).

[37] Fan, *Reconstructionist Confucianism*, 54.

[38] But even this difference is almost negligible because for Nozick "an individual" encompasses both an individual person and an individual (nuclear) family when it comes to property rights (involving taxation and inheritance). See Nozick's criticism of the ambiguity among the proponents of pattered principles of distributive justice (such as Rawls) toward the family as a social unit in Robert Nozick, *Anarchy, State, and Utopia* (New York: Basic Books, 1974), 167–74.

[39] Fan, *Reconstructionist Confucianism*, 78. Also see 64–5 where Fan argues that "the *free* market mechanism is virtually inevitable because of the natural inequality of things as well as the necessity of a division of labor.... [T]he Confucian principle of *ren* requires not only a free market, but also a privately-owned economic system ... [because] only the private-property economy, not the publicly owned regime, can embody the loving of humans.... Without a certain amount of private property, [the common people] would be motivated to act immorally" (emphasis in original).

Third, Fan's Confucian conception of rights with an economically minimalist state is too morally comprehensive to be practicable in modern East Asian societies. Apparently, Fan's strong emphasis of filial piety as the manifestation of perfect virtue has led him to conclude that the most fundamental *human right* is the right one possesses as a parent, namely, a right to be taken care of by one's (adult) child who owes to the parent a moral obligation of filial piety. Here the right to be taken care of is reciprocated with the moral duty of filial piety. In theory, this is not an implausible suggestion, if only it is agreed that (1) citizens in the given East Asian society (say, China) are all Confucians in a morally (even religiously) comprehensive sense, thus agreeing that filial virtue is the (manifestation of) perfect and complete human virtue and (2) the state is both a Confucian perfectionist state, the primary purpose of which lies in *making* people morally good (i.e., to become good sons and daughters),[40] and an economically minimalist state whose main role is to maintain the market as free as possible but has no (or only minimal) moral and political obligations to the general welfare of its citizens. The problem is twofold: not only are none of contemporary East Asian societies Confucian in the morally monistic sense,[41] but Fan's minimalist state thesis does not logically cohere with his own understanding of the Confucian state as the "family of families."[42] If an individual family is held morally responsible for the welfare of its members, then why is it that the state-as-family (*guojia* 國家) is exonerated from the same moral responsibility toward all families (and by implication all citizens)? Furthermore, and related, from the Confucian perspective of the familial as the political, in which the state is indeed rendered to be a family of families, Fan's minimalist state is neither familial nor benevolent.

Though I do not necessarily disagree with Fan's claim that a Confucian system of human rights would give emphasis to specific, agent-relative, and context-sensitive rights,[43] both the Confucian ideal of the familial and benevolent state and the modern (increasingly) pluralist social conditions of East Asia require a more politically inclusive and socioeconomically durable conception of rights, namely, Confucian democratic rights. These rights can be equally claimed by all citizens as equal members sharing and participating in the common political community, envisioned as an extended family, not toward the (abstract Weberian administrative) state as such, but as stipulated by Rousseau's general will, toward one another collectively comprising the body politic. The state or government is the agent that carries out the common will of democratic citizens, not the authoritarian enforcer of public policies that would only

[40] This is also Joseph Chan's position. See his "Confucian Attitudes toward Ethical Pluralism," in *Confucian Political Ethics*, ed. Daniel A. Bell (Princeton: Princeton University Press, 2008).

[41] See Chapters 3 and 4 of this book.

[42] Fan, *Reconstructionist Confucianism*, 106.

[43] Ibid., 59.

corrode the civic bond among citizens. In this Confucian democratic state, filial virtue is still cherished as a critical component of public reasons or as a *civic virtue*, but not necessarily as a perfect or complete human virtue. In the next section, I will discuss Confucian democratic rights in greater detail from the perspective of Confucian familialism.

Finally, as noted earlier, Fan's understanding of *ren* is not consistent with the Confucian vision of benevolent government (*ren zheng* 仁政). Indeed, there is no disagreement with Fan's core claim that in the Confucian tradition *ren* does not refer to indiscriminate love of all humanity (*jian ai* 兼愛 as Mohists call it) but care by gradation. But does *ren*, in practice, mean to treat unequals unequally? Does Mencius's defense of love with gradation give a justification to political inequality?

Admittedly, the notion of *ren* as care by gradation did not belong to Confucius but Mencius, which he presented during his critical engagement with Mohist philosopher Yi Zhi who challenged Confucianism with the notion of *ren* as universal impartial love. In Chapter 5, we have thoroughly examined *Mencius* 3A5 where the conversation between Mencius and Yi Zhi takes place and noted that Mencius's problem with Mohism was not so much inclusive care as such but the typical Mohist ignorance or dismissal of the moral importance of the virtue of filiality in making human beings truly human. Yi Zhi's core argument is that *ren*, rightly understood, refers to (universal) compassion, and compassion (which according to Mohism is motivated by the concern for what is profitable for the people) impels us to care for others equally or without distinctions. Mencius refutes Yi Zhi's claim by accentuating that compassion is rooted in filial love, making filial love the single source of moral sentiments, and that greater love for one's family members than strangers is natural and morally appropriate.

First of all, it is important to note that Mencius's concern here is primarily establishing the supreme moral value of the virtue of filiality, which is the root of *ren*, as the single source of ethical motivation. Second, though Mencius indeed believes love must be practiced differentially according to the degree of intimacy or relational closeness, he does not advance this view in terms of "natural inequality." More specifically, with the notion of *ren* as love with gradation, he never says that people are by nature unequal and accordingly should be treated unequally. To the contrary, as Irene Bloom forcefully shows, Mencius has a strong ethico-religious faith in common human nature (*xing* 性), the universal human endowment by Heaven, as a normative criterion, and therefore, for him, "moral development is accomplished through recognizing the likeness between ourselves and others, even though such recognition may take some effort."[44] From a slightly different angle, Donald Munro is also convinced that there is a common agreement among virtually all philosophical schools

[44] Irene T. Bloom, "Mengzian Arguments on Human Nature (*Ren Xing*)," in Liu and Ivanhoe, *Essays on the Moral Philosophy of Mengzi*, 93.

in China that men are naturally equal in terms of the common attributes or characteristics with which all men are born.[45]

Of course, as Munro cautions, both Bloom's normative conception of equality and Munro's descriptive sense of natural equality must be rightly differentiated from equality in the evaluative sense, which, according to Munro, "carries the suggestion that men are of similar 'worth' or deserve similar treatment."[46] But equality in this sense is concerned with desert or merit, not consanguinity as Fan claims.[47] For instance, the evaluative Confucian sense of equality would require us to treat a filial child and an unfilial child "unequally" based on the merit or demerit of their moral behavior in spite both of their natural and normative equalities as a person. Mencius's notion of care with gradation, however, is concerned with something categorically different: it aims to encourage us to be filial and extend our filial love toward other people, rather than uphold an abstract, emotionally hollow and morally unreflective, notion of *ren*. In short, what is at stake is the nature of *ren* as a moral sentiment and a moral motivation, not a justification of inequality or a family-oriented welfare policy.

In this section, I examined Ruiping Fan's normative argument for family care which he presents as an alternative to democratic welfarism (and to socialism), and I identified four problems in the way he derives his normative vision and policy suggestions from the comprehensive moral understanding of the virtue of filial piety. What is worth noting is Fan believes his normative vision, namely Confucian familism, is perfectly consistent with meritocratic elitism, particularly Daniel Bell's exam model.[48] The only difference between Fan and Bell is that while Bell presents his normative vision in terms of Confucian democracy, Fan calls his political vision, quite accurately in my view, "Confucian aristocracy."[49] In Chapter 3 I have critiqued meritocratic elitism from the perspective of Confucian democratic civil society, and in the next chapter I will explore a political meritocracy that is conducive to Confucian pluralist democracy. In the remainder of the current chapter, I will offer an idea of welfarism that can be supported by both the Confucian principle of the familial as the political (or Confucian familialism) and the democratic ideal of popular sovereignty.

Defending Democratic Welfarism

As Bernard Williams notes, one of our firmest moral intuitions is a strong sense of responsibility toward those who stand in some special relationship

45 Donald J. Munro, *The Concept of Man in Early China* (Stanford: Stanford University Press, 1969).

46 Ibid., 2.

47 Chenyang Li makes a similar claim as Fan's in "Equality and Inequality in Confucianism."

48 Fan, *Reconstructionist Confucianism*, 62–3. For my critique of Bell's exam model of meritocratic elitism, see Chapter 3.

49 Ibid., 56.

to us.[50] We naturally favor our own children over others', hence have stronger responsibilities to them than to others' children. Apparently, what bothered Mencius most was the Mohists' complete dismissal of this sheer psychological and sociological fact. Let's call this intuition WI (Williams's intuition).

Certainly, as Ruiping Fan has shown, Confucian familism is not a mere affirmation of WI. From a philosophical standpoint, what Mencius did was to give a moral-philosophical and metaphysical articulation to this intuition by affiliating it with a complex set of accounts of human nature, moral virtue, and moral self-cultivation. But then, an objection may be raised: even if we no longer subscribe to the moral metaphysics that underpins Mencius's theory of moral psychology and recast Confucian moral psychology (particularly the part involving filial love and virtue) in a way that it can lend support to the formation of civic virtue in a Confucian democratic society, the moral intuition about special responsibilities still remains unchallenged. Likewise, even if we reject Fan's libertarian-meritocratic appropriation of Confucian familism for the reasons I have offered earlier, it may still be claimed that as long as Confucianism is ethically committed to WI in terms of love with gradation (*cha deng ai*), family care, without necessarily invoking the thorny question of in/equality, should be taken seriously as one of the possible Confucian alternatives to dominant modes of welfarism including democratic welfarism.

This is a more moderate and reasonable suggestion than Fan's libertarian-meritocratic Confucian familism, but in my view, to derive normative political theory or public policy suggestions directly from WI is not without problems. WI seems to establish a moral claim that since we can't be intimate with our fellow citizens, who are de facto strangers, we *therefore* cannot (and according to Confucian relational ethics, should not) have the same degree of obligations to them that we have to our nearest and dearest, especially our family members. This is exactly how Fan (and other Confucian opponents of egalitarianism) interprets Mencius's notion of love with distinction. This assumption, however, is logically flawed, because to say that we have obligations to our fellow citizens is not to demand that we treat them as intimately as our family members. Pace some utilitarians, it is psychologically impossible to be sympathetic to our fellow citizens (and strangers in the world) as much as we naturally are to our intimate ones.[51] Democratic welfarism is not predicated on this impossible psychological demand, though it must still be nested in and motivated by affectionate moral sentiments or public reasons that are themselves grounded in moral sentiments.[52]

[50] Bernard Williams, *Moral Luck* (Cambridge: Cambridge University Press, 1981).

[51] For a revealing discussion on this point, see Kwame Anthony Appiah, *Cosmopolitanism: Ethics in a World of Strangers* (New York: Norton, 2006), 155–8.

[52] In this regard, my proposal parts company with John Rawls's overtly Kantian justification of democratic welfarism. As I have discussed in Chapter 5, however, it is increasingly being noted that Rawls's democratic welfarism cannot be adequately understood without appreciating a certain Humean element in it. See Michael L. Frazer, "John Rawls: Between Two Enlightenments," *Political Theory* 35 (2007), 756–80.

Democratic welfarism of the sort that I am proposing here is not derived from Kantian or utilitarian egalitarianism where egalitarianism is understood as a matter of (distributive) principle, nor is it concerned purely with economic equality. Rather, democratic welfarism is a socioeconomic expression of democratic citizenship, according to which citizens, while subscribing to different moral principles of distribution, share a common political fate as they share common legal, political, and (public) cultural institutions and values. Thus understood, democratic welfarism is neither a moral nor an economic principle, but a political principle that embodies the democratic ideal of popular sovereignty. Its political rationale arises from our *concerns* with the (material) well-being of our fellow citizens because their well-being is largely dependent on what we do and vice versa, and this mutual interdependence generates the moral and political condition of civility and democratic reciprocity. Without securing *our* well-being, it is impossible to form *our* collective will and to make public judgment (including policy decisions) for *us*. As Jack Knight and James Johnson rightly argue, democracy requires the government to treat citizens differently because "politically relevant capacities are beyond the control of individual citizens."[53] Put differently, "the development of cognitive capacities necessary for effective participation in democratic deliberation requires government expenditures to guarantee the social and economic prerequisites of effective participation."[54]

However, these concerns, which constitute the core of public reasons, are not motivated by rationalist imperatives (as most deliberative democrats including Knight and Johnson assume), nor do they operate on contractual obligations (as Thomas Scanlon claims).[55] Our concerns for the well-being of our fellow citizens stem from the peculiar vulnerabilities to which they (especially, those who belong to the lowest economic class) are helplessly exposed. Democratic welfarism is morally justified on this vulnerability model of welfare. In the vulnerability model, what is important is not so much egalitarianism as a moral (distributive) principle or economic equality as such, but the equal political standing of a citizen as a person. As Robert Goodin puts it, "It is their vulnerabilities, not our promises or any other voluntary act of will on our part, that imposes upon us special responsibilities with respect to them."[56]

The vulnerability model of democratic welfarism not only is consistent with the Confucian ideal of benevolent government, according to which the most important task of the government lies in the enhancement of the moral and

[53] Jack Knight and James Johnson, "What Sort of Equality Does Deliberative Democracy Require?," in Bohman and Rehg, *Deliberative Democracy*, 305.

[54] Ibid., 306.

[55] Thomas W. Scanlon, *What We Owe to Each Other* (Cambridge, MA: Belknap, 2000).

[56] Robert E. Goodin, "Vulnerabilities and Responsibilities: An Ethical Defense of the Welfare State," *American Political Science Review* 79 (1985), 775–87, 777.

material well-being of the people whom the ruler (i.e., the king) ought to deem as his own children, but at the same time it is remarkably well suited for the Confucian notion of the state as the family. While Western modern political theorists (particularly social contractarians) and contemporary political theorists profoundly influenced by them (such as Susan Okin and Carole Pateman) understand the family primarily as the legal-social institution formed by conjugal contract,[57] Confucians traditionally see the family as an entity naturally formed by parents and children, operating on the principle of filial affection and responsibility (*qin qin* 親親). If we bracket the moral-metaphysical connotation attached to the traditional Confucian notion of filiality (which makes it a supreme moral virtue in the comprehensive moral sense), the Confucian principle of filiality is premised on two sociological facts: (1) people cannot enter into the family voluntarily by choosing parents and siblings but rather are born into it, making the parent-child relationship more fundamental than the husband-wife relationship and (2) a child, especially in her first few years, is absolutely dependent on her parents' care. That is, it is the debt a child owes to her parents that gives rise to filial responsibilities on her part to her parents, including care for their material and physical well-being.

As we noted, Fan attempts to derive the Confucian conception of rights, that is, parents' right to be taken care of by their adult children, from sociological fact 2 and, based on this right, presents family care as an alternative to democratic welfarism. However, it is questionable whether relational reciprocity of this sort, which generates a moral obligation from one party and a welfare right for the other, can be called a *virtue* properly understood. The idea that parents should claim their welfare rights to their own children, not to the government, seems to turn the parent-child relationship, which according to Confucianism is and ought be based on the principle of filality (*qin qin*), into a contractual relationship. The underlying assumption is rather anti-Confucian: we (the parents) did you (the child) a favor and now it is our right to demand of you a filial duty to take care of us! Here the natural and voluntary nature that characterizes both parental care and filial virtue is difficult to appreciate.

Rather than generating a family-based welfare right, the two sociological facts about the family strongly support the vulnerability model of welfarism: the reciprocal duties of family life – of parents to their children, of children to their aged parents, and of spouses to each other – is the demonstration of mutual vulnerability.[58] Now, it is important to recall that parents typically do

[57] Pateman, however, calls the conjugal contract in modern contractualism "sexual contract," which justifies the civil dominion of women by men. See Carol Pateman, *The Sexual Contract* (Stanford: Stanford University Press, 1988). For a revealing overview of the conception of the family in Western political theory, see Hahm Chaibong, "Family versus the Individual: The Politics of Marriage Laws in Korea," in Bell and Hahm, *Confucianism for the Modern World*, 337–41.

[58] Goodin, "Vulnerabilities and Responsibilities," 778.

not care for their children because they *deserve* such care, though they surely praise or punish based on merit. That is to say, in the family, the strict sense of meritocracy does not apply in every case. If parental care is distributed based on what children deserve – say, in terms of academic achievement, athletic talent, or financial contribution to the household – it signals a critical violation of the meaning of the family. Likewise, we do not expect a child to exercise her filial virtue and responsibility by taking care of her aged parents *because* they deserve such care – some parents (such as Shun's) do not.[59] Nor do we typically believe that there should be (or that there even can be) a perfect symmetry between filial responsibilities to aged parents and the amount of care that the child has received from her parents. In a sense, it is the parents-children relation itself, which Confucianism regards as one of the cardinal human bonds, that generates both parental and filial responsibilities and care. And the essential feature of family relationship is interdependence and mutual vulnerability. Aid to vulnerable people, therefore, is morally justified on the same basis as aid rendered to our own parents and children.[60] By way of contrast to Fan's Confucian familism and corresponding to Confucian public reason, I would call this family-vulnerability model of democratic welfarism *Confucian familialism*.

Liberals (libertarians in particular) may raise a question about the feasibility of this family paradigm of the vulnerability model of welfarism. After all, the primary aim of modern liberal political theory (especially, John Locke's) was to critique the family model of the state, advanced most notably by Robert Filmer.[61] How to accommodate the family model within liberal political theory, therefore, does pose a critical challenge to liberals. This is not a challenge for Confucians, however. Unlike liberals, Confucians see the family as "the bedrock upon which sound political institutions and a well-ordered society could be built."[62] Put differently, to create the state modeled after the (good) family has been Confucianism's central political ideal and this ideal is still generally shared by most East Asian citizens.[63] This is not to say that there is no challenge for Confucian democrats regarding this ideal but the nature of the challenge is qualitatively different from that posed to liberal democrats. The challenge for

59 Shun is a legendary ancient sage-king who is hailed for his great filiality for his violent parents and fraternal love toward his younger brother who repeatedly plotted to murder him. See *Mencius* 5A2–3.

60 Goodin, "Vulnerabilities and Responsibilities," 782.

61 The central purpose of John Locke's *First Treatise of Government* is to criticize Robert Filmer's *Patriarcha*, in which Filmer justifies the king's entitlement to rule in terms of Adam's primogeniture.

62 Hahm, "Family versus the Individual," 341.

63 For the case of South Korea, for example, see Geir Helgesen, *Democracy and Authority in Korea: The Cultural Dimension in Korean Politics* (Surrey: Curzon, 1998), 94. According to Chong-Min Park and Doh Chull Shin's survey research, nearly three-fifths (59%) of the Koreans consider the family the prototype for government ("Do Asian Values Deter Popular Support for Democracy in South Korea?" *Asian Survey* 46 [2006], 341–61, 350).

Confucian democrats consists in making the family-state, traditionally ruled by the king by right of the mandate of Heaven (*tianming* 天命), democratically controlled and accordingly reconceptualizing welfare from the virtuous ruler's benefaction into a democratic right, a right citizens can claim from other citizens, who are politically equal to them, via the law and the state. I will show how this democratic reinvention of the Confucian family-state can be possible theoretically by reconstructing the text of the *Mencius* shortly. For now, let me consider one unresolved problem in justifying democratic welfarism on the family-vulnerability model – the question of the nature and scope of responsibility.

Conventionally, responsibility is understood in causal terms in the sense that one as a moral agent should be held responsible for the consequences of one's freely chosen actions. According to this causal definition of responsibility, responsibility is assigned "to particular agents whose actions can be shown as causally connected to the circumstances for which responsibility is sought." Iris Young calls this common model of assigning responsibility a "liability model."[64] As Young admits, this concept of responsibility is "indispensable [in the broad society] for a legal system and sense of moral right that respects agents as individuals and expects them to behave in respectful ways toward others."[65]

Certainly, it is naïve to posit the state literally as the family, replete with love and affection. In fact, no Confucian (either classical or contemporary) would insist that in the Confucian family-state family rituals replace law or that filial responsibility absolves the liability of an action or a choice.[66] The pressing question in our context is whether the family-vulnerability model of welfare absolves individual responsibility for decent economic life too easily. One may ask, why should I be held responsible for the poverty (and other miseries) of others, when I did not cause it, hence having no personal liability for it? Is it morally fair that I bear such a responsibility in the name of *we* and in terms of filial and fraternal responsibility? Already in the pre-Qin period, a similar challenge was raised by Hanfeizi, the famous Legalist, when he cast moral skepticism to the Confucian ideal of benevolent government.

> Now if men start out with equal opportunities and yet there are a few who, without the help of unusually good harvests or outside income, are able to keep themselves well supplied, it must be due either to hard work or to frugal living. If men start out with equal opportunities and yet there are a few who, without having suffered from some calamity like famine or sickness, still sink into poverty and destitution, it must be due to either to laziness or to extravagant living. The lazy and extravagant grow poor; the diligent and

[64] Iris M. Young, *Global Challenges: War, Self-Determination and Responsibility for Justice* (Cambridge: Polity, 2007), 172. For Young's more comprehensive democratic theory of responsibility, see her *Responsibility for Justice* (Oxford: Oxford University Press, 2011).

[65] Ibid., 174.

[66] See *Analects* 13:3 for Confucius's own position on the need of (penal) law.

frugal get rich. Now if the ruler levies money from the rich in order to give alms to the poor, he is robbing the diligent and frugal and indulging the lazy and extravagant.[67]

If men can really start off with equal opportunities as Hanfeizi assumes, the argument centering on individual responsibility would make sense.[68] The problem is that the fair socioeconomic conditions of equal opportunity are far from reality. In contemporary East Asia, where injustice is deeply imbedded in the socioeconomic and political structure itself, the feasibility of the liability model, with its strong emphasis on individual or family responsibility, is critically qualified. It is because of the increasing reality of structural injustice that Iris Young offers an alternative conception of responsibility, namely, *social connection model*.

According to Young, structural injustice exists "when social processes put large categories of persons under a systematic threat of domination or deprivation of the means to develop and exercise their capacities, at the same time as they enable others to dominate or have a wide range of opportunities for developing and exercising capacities."[69] The nature of structural injustice, then, calls for collective responsibilities. "Structural injustice occurs as a consequence of many individuals and institutions acting in pursuit of their particular goals and interests, within given institutional rules and accepted norms. All the persons who participate by their actions in the ongoing schemes of cooperation that constitute these structures are responsible for them, in the sense that they are part of the process that causes them. They are not responsible, however, in the sense of having directed the process or intended its outcomes."[70]

Though without attention to the structural nature of social injustice, Robert Goodin also makes a similar claim by separating task responsibility from causal responsibility, both logically and in practice. He says, "[I]n a great many cases, the agent best able to get a person out of a jam might well be someone other than the agent who got that person into it. Then, I would argue, task responsibility should be settled upon the former, even though that agent is in no way casually responsible.... This typically leads us to assign responsibility largely (and, on some analyses, almost exclusively) to people who were in no way causally responsible for the situations they are now being asked to remedy."[71]

[67] Burton Watson (trans.), *Han Fei Tzu: Basic Writings* (New York: Columbia University Press, 1964), 121.

[68] It may still not make *perfect* sense as long as the consideration of differing personal capabilities is ruled out. On the importance of personal capabilities in thinking about social justice, see Amartya Sen, *Commodities and Capabilities* (Oxford: Oxford University Press, 1999); Martha C. Nussbaum, *Women and Human Development: The Capabilities Approach* (Cambridge: Cambridge University Press, 2000).

[69] Young, *Global Challenges*, 170.

[70] Ibid., 170–71.

[71] Goodin, "Vulnerabilities and Responsibilities," 780.

What is worth noting is that in morally justifying collective responsibilities (i.e., task responsibilities assumed by the citizens in general) both Young and Goodin stress the relational character of the concepts of vulnerability and dependency.[72] Young even rejects the established liberal notion of a sovereign self and substitutes it with the notion of a relational self, which recognizes the constitution of selves by interaction with others and their interdependences.[73] Though Young draws on recent feminism for the concept of a relational self, the fundamentally relational character of the self has long been emphasized by contemporary Confucian scholars.[74] Indeed, as I noted in Chapters 1 and 2, the resurgence of Confucian democracy during the past two decades is mainly because of the Confucian discontent with the liberal conception of the sovereign autonomous self. While critiquing liberal individualism on levels of ontology and ethics, however, Confucian democrats have largely failed to develop a robust normative political theory from the relational conception of the self, which is at the same time consistent with Confucianism's family model of the state. In my view, Young's social connection model of responsibility is remarkably well suited for Confucian democracy, though Young does not ground her normative vision, which is global in scale, on the family model of democratic welfarism. Young's model helps us to see clearly why attention to vulnerability and dependency should enable us to separate task responsibility from causal responsibility, go beyond the liability model, and, most important, endorse collective responsibility for the welfare of the vulnerable people.

In this section, I have defended Confucian familialism, a family model of democratic welfare focused on vulnerability and (inter)dependency by critically engaging with Ruiping Fan's family care model and by implication libertarianism concentrated on an individual's (or an individual family's) responsibility for a decent economic life. In the next section, I present Mencius's idea of benevolent government as an ancient inspiration for this model and reconstruct it as consistent with democratic welfarism.

Mencius Revisited

Contra Fan, the following statement by Mencius, which he addresses to one of the feudal lords during the Warring States period, upholds the Confucian

[72] Ibid., 779.

[73] Young, *Global Challenges*, 33. For philosophical explorations of relational selfhood and autonomy, see Catriona Mackenzie and Natalie Stoljar (eds.), *Relational Autonomy: Feminist Perspectives on Autonomy, Agency, and the Social Self* (New York: Oxford University Press, 2000).

[74] In addition to works by Roger T. Ames, Henry Rosemont, and Sor-hoon Tan that I have examined in Chapters 1 and 2, see also Hwa Yol Jung, "Confucianism as Political Philosophy: A Postmodern Perspective," *Human Studies* 16 (1993), 213–30; Chaibong Hahm, "Postmodernism in the Post-Confucian Context: Epistemological and Political Considerations," *Human Studies* 24 (2001), 29–44.

principle of the familial as political or Confucian familialism, not Confucian familism narrowly understood. "By treating the elders in one's own family as elders should be treated and extending this to the elders of other families, and by treating the young of one's own family as the young ought to be treated and extending this to the young of other people's families, the empire can be turned around on the palm of one's hand."[75] As I noted in Chapter 5, most contemporary Confucian moral philosophers read this passage as conveying a general philosophical account of Mencius's notion of extension as a method of moral self-cultivation, applicable to *all humans*. While finding such interpretation plausible in the context of Mencius's moral philosophy, I proposed to pay close attention to the fact that the audience here is a political leader and the question in hand is statecraft with a view to making Mencius's notion of extension democratic-politically relevant to the conceptualization of Confucian public reason. Now, I propose that in the present context of the political theoretical exploration and articulation of Confucian democracy, this passage (and other passages that I will examine shortly) should be read as being addressed to ordinary citizens in a Confucian democratic civil society. It is a necessary step toward reconstructing classical Confucianism that had monarchy as its political backdrop into a civil Confucianism that can underpin the core assumptions of Confucian democracy, namely common citizenship and political equality among citizens. Then, Mencius's central message can be seen as a chastisement of Confucian familism (and family care as Fan understands it) rather than its endorsement. In my view, Robert Goodin's following statement best captures the essence of the democratically reconstructed Mencian-Confucian position: "My argument [for the welfare state] would seem to allow – indeed, to require – us to show *some* bias toward our own kind, however defined. But that bias must not be absolute. The vulnerability of others – be they needy fellow citizens, foreigners, heirs or hares – to our actions and choices may well be sufficiently large, and how we (and perhaps we alone) can help sufficiently clear, to require us to give their interests some substantial weight in reckoning our own responsibilities. Charity may indeed begin at home, but morally it must not stop there."[76]

According to Mencius, the best way to realize the Confucian ideal of benevolent government is to create and sustain the socioeconomic condition favorable to the welfare of the people because "[t]he people will not have constant heart (*hengxin* 恒心) if they are without constant means (*hengchan* 恒產) [and if they] lack constant hearts, they will go astray and fall into excesses, stopping at nothing."[77] If government fails to sustain socioeconomic conditions under which people can have sufficient means and thus are able to be self-reliant,

[75] *Mencius* 1A7. The English translation here is adopted from Irene T. Bloom (trans.), *Mencius*, ed. Philip J. Ivanhoe (New York: Columbia University Press, 2009).

[76] Goodin, "Vulnerabilities and Responsibilities," 783.

[77] *Mencius* 1A7.

and punishes them when they have violated the law, it is nothing but "setting a trap for the people."[78] Mencius's key point is not to exonerate those who "stopped at nothing" because of the lack of constant means as if an individual's criminal act should not be found culpable in the absence of decent socioeconomic conditions. What seems to bother Mencius most is the unreasonably strict application of a meritocratic standard with strong emphasis on individual responsibility to ordinary people whose miserable lives are deeply entangled in the unjust socioeconomic structure.

Thus understood, Mencius's focus is not so much on the people's problematic actions as such but on the socioeconomic conditions under which it is difficult to attribute social and political calamity solely to the individuals themselves. Let us call this a *condition requirement*, which stipulates that in the case of ordinary people under adverse socioeconomic conditions, the scope of their individual responsibility in both the socioeconomic and moral sense be reasonably *constricted*: not only must they not be found guilty in the strict legal sense for their immoral actions presumably necessitated by the harsh socioeconomic reality, but just as important, they should also not be held individually responsible for the entirety of their socioeconomic fate, which is inextricably compounded with their socioeconomic destitution. That is, *we* should not disregard the force of necessity to which an individual is helplessly vulnerable. In Mencius's judgment, treating a person under dismal socioeconomic conditions as if she were a perfectly free moral and social agent who is thus responsible for her freedom is indeed to disrespect her. Quite the contrary is the case: it is actually condemning her to the realm of necessity.

However, the condition requirement focused on socioeconomic conditions that hinder free and responsible actions and accordingly stipulate that individual responsibility be reasonably constricted in such circumstances must be qualified to avoid the misgiving that man's freedom of (moral and socioeconomic) action is wholly determined by material conditions. In fact, while constricting ordinary people's individual responsibility under harsh socioeconomic conditions, Mencius introduces another source of responsibility, a responsibility that falls on the government for the harsh socioeconomic conditions that drove or would drive people to immoral acts. Let us call this a *social responsibility requirement*. The following statement by Mencius to King Hui of Liang, one of the feudal lords of his time, helps us to understand what social responsibility requirement consists of.

Now when food meant for human beings is so plentiful as to be thrown to dogs and pigs, you fail to realize that it is time for garnering, and when men drop dead from starvation by the wayside, you fail to realize that it is time for distribution. When people die, you simply say, "It is none of my doing. It is the fault of the harvest." In what way is that different from killing a man by running him through, while saying all the time, "It

[78] Ibid.

is none of my doing. It is the fault of the weapon." Stop putting the blame on the harvest and the people of the whole Empire will come to you.[79]

While constricting the scope of ordinary people's responsibility for their presumably necessitous actions, Mencius is now *expanding* the ruler's (or the government's) social responsibility to the extent that it almost sounds unlimited. The social responsibility requirement, however, should not be misunderstood as upholding governmental paternalism that hardly allows room for individual moral and social agency. At issue here is not so much an expanded governmental intervention that is inherently in tension with individual freedom and responsibility, but a semilimited governmental responsibility that still enables individual moral and socioeconomic agency. Mencius's point is that when it comes to the destitution of the people's basic necessities, the responsibility falls on public authority, and in such cases trying to identify the proximate cause of the problem – even if it is a necessary endeavor in the case of identifying moral and legal responsibility – is not only practically futile, but more important, politically irresponsible as well, given its extensive public ramifications. As the supreme political agent, Mencius would argue, the government must take full social responsibility for *whatever* public consequences resulting from its public policies or lack thereof.[80]

Of course, Mencius's political thought itself, which is focused on monarchical benefaction and thus is strongly paternalistic, does not directly support democratic welfarism. After all, Mencius was never a democrat, committed to common citizenship and political equality. Once having been recast in light of responsibility and socioeconomic welfare, however, Mencius's political thought on benevolent government turns out to be remarkably consistent with democratic welfarism. Though Mencius never struggled to create a public space for the voices of socioeconomic underdogs, his astute attention to their vulnerabilities, which he found were often structurally originated, should encourage Confucian democrats to endorse the welfare state that supports "compulsory, collective provision for certain basic needs as a matter of right."[81]

This right, however, is not a social or economic right separate from civil or a political right as T. H. Marshall's taxonomy stipulates. It is itself a *political* right, which is justified by the very democratic ideal of popular sovereignty or collective self-determination. The political standing of this right is much more salient in a Confucian democratic society that is governed by and operates on the principle of the familial as the political, one of the core elements of Confucian public reason, according to which the state is, and ought

[79] *Mencius* 1A3.

[80] This and the preceding two paragraphs are based on Sungmoon Kim, "The Secret of Confucian *Wuwei* Statecraft: Mencius's Political Theory of Responsibility," *Asian Philosophy* 20 (2010), 27–42, 34–5.

[81] Goodin, "Vulnerabilities and Responsibilities," 784.

to be, envisioned as an extended family in which citizens are not sovereign individuals but related to one another in (quasi-)familial terms. Thus understood, in Confucian democracy, welfare rights gain a different meaning: they are not so much what a sovereign individual can claim as an entitlement but what I as a member of the political community receive as a gift from my fellow citizens who are politically equal to me, when I am in a deeply troubled situation.[82]

Concluding Remarks

In this chapter, I have defended democratic welfarism as an integral element of Confucian democracy by critically engaging with various New Confucian attempts to justify economic meritocracy on one hand and by reconstructing the Mencian-Confucian conception of benevolent government on the other. In closing, I emphasize that ultimately Confucian democratic welfarism finds its moral justification in the very conception of Confucian public reason: (Mencian) familial moral sentimentalism enables Confucian democratic citizens to extend (and expand) their care and aid to their fellow citizens, thus transforming their familial care into a civic concern and care. That is, even when they find *some* poor people not deserving their care and aid from the viewpoint of the ethic of individual responsibility, familial affections that they hold toward them, whom they see as quasi-family members, *nevertheless* enable them to focus on their vulnerabilities, most of which are structurally imbedded, and assume collective responsibilities to remedy them. This Confucian moral equilibrium is stimulated by critical affection that constitutes the core of Confucian public reason.

What is critically absent in the existing formulations of the Confucian perspective of welfarism and social justice is the articulation of the foundational importance of public reason or the polity's public character, against the backdrop of which the nature and scope of welfarism can reasonably be determined. Seen in this way, the problem with the sufficientarian interpretation of Confucian distributive principle is not so much its core argument that according to the Confucian perspective of social justice, there must be a social minimum for the worst off, but its endorsement of *unregulated* desert-oriented economic meritocracy beyond the threshold of sufficiency. I contend that the meaning of merit and the morally justifiable relation of desert to merit can be intelligible only after the content of Confucian public reason is first identified and morally defended, because the concept of merit is not freestanding of the political context but critically circumscribed by the public character and purpose of the Confucian political polity. In the Confucian democracy that I propose, economic inequalities among citizens, even after meeting the threshold of

[82] My position differs from that of Goodin, who understands welfare rights as a matter of entitlement: "[T]he welfare state allows beneficiaries to claim their entitlements as a matter of right" (ibid., 785).

sufficiency, must not be too great to the extent that they can erode familial-civic bonds and trust.

If merit in a Confucian democracy is context-specific and the context that is morally and politically relevant is circumscribed by Confucian public reason, how should we understand political meritocracy in a Confucian democracy? I now turn to this question by reconceiving political meritocracy from the perspective of Confucian public reason.

7

Rethinking Political Meritocracy: Selection Plus Two

As we have seen in Chapter 3, an increasing number of scholars who study East Asia have recently begun to argue that political meritocracy understood as rule by the wise and virtuous few is not only suitable for East Asian societies where there remains a strong Confucian tradition of respect for meritocratically chosen political elites, but more fundamentally offers a viable alternative to Western liberal democracy, which is often troubled by a variety of social problems that in their view germinate from liberalism's rights-based individualism.[1] Though these scholars disagree on how to implement political meritocracy, they concur on two points: the shortcomings of liberal representative democracy and the complexity of contemporary public affairs. First, advocates of political meritocracy argue that the policy of "one person, one vote (OPOV)," the political manifestation of rights-based individualism, ferments political irresponsibility and ultimately erodes the common good because of the unavoidable pressure

[1] Daniel A. Bell and Chenyang Li (eds.), *The East Asian Challenge for Democracy: Political Meritocracy in Comparative Perspective* (Cambridge: Cambridge University Press, 2013); Tongdong Bai, "A Mencian Version of Limited Democracy," *Res Publica* 14 (2008), 19–34; Chenyang Li, "Equality and Inequality in Confucianism," *Dao* 11 (2012), 295–313; Daniel A. Bell, *Beyond Liberal Democracy: Political Thinking for an East Asian Context* (Princeton: Princeton University Press, 2006); A. T. Nuyen, "Confucianism and the Idea of Equality," *Asian Philosophy* 11 (2001), 61–71; Ruiping Fan, *Reconstructionist Confucianism: Rethinking Morality after the West* (Dordrecht: Springer, 2010); Jiang Qing, *Zhengzhi Rujia: Dangdai Rujia de zhuanxiang, tezhi yu fazhan* [Political Confucianism: Contemporary Confucianism's Challenge, Special Quality, and Development] (Beijing: San lian shu dian, 2003); Jiang Qing, *A Confucian Constitutional Order: How China's Ancient Past Can Shape Its Political Future*, ed. Daniel A. Bell and Ruiping Fan, trans. Edmund Ryden (Princeton: Princeton University Press, 2012); Jiang, "From Mind Confucianism to Political Confucianism," in *The Renaissance of Confucianism in Contemporary China*, ed. Ruiping Fan (Dordrecht: Springer, 2011), 17–32; Kang Xiaoguang, *Renzheng: Zhongguo zhengzhi fazhan de disantiao daolu* [Humane Government: A Third Road for the Development of Chinese Politics] (Singapore: Global Publishing, 2005); Kang, "Confucianism: A Future in the Tradition," *Social Research* 73 (2006), 77–120.

on politicians, who are predominantly concerned with reelection, pandering to myopic popular opinion. Moreover, they assert that representative democracy, as long as it is OPOV based, is largely incapable of representing the interests of future generations and of the people living outside the national boundary. The second argument is independent of the ills or limitations of liberal representative democracy. Given the sheer complexity of public affairs, it is claimed, "a substantial amount of decision-making power must be placed in the hands of an intellectually agile elite, almost as a functional requirement of modern political societies.... [Hence] a pressing need for 'brains' in government."[2]

No doubt, liberal representative democracy is far from perfect, both as a political ideal and as a social practice.[3] Furthermore, from a practical standpoint, it may not be so prudential to transplant any particular mode of Western-style democracy (note: there are multiple modes of Western liberal democracies) in East Asian soil that is still deeply soaked in communitarian, characteristically Confucian, social mores and habits.

That being said, however, it is not even remotely clear why political meritocracy, which is understood by its Confucian advocates as the political system in which "political power [is] distributed according to merit, and merit is assessed in terms of the personal [moral] qualities,"[4] is at odds with liberal representative democracy. The main reason Confucian advocates of political meritocracy believe that political meritocracy can be a genuine political alternative to liberal democracy is that representative democracy allows no room for an individual political representative, who in principle *must* represent the voter's interest, to make an independent judgment that serves the well-being of the general public and even of future generations. But this is premised on a critical misunderstanding of how liberal representative democracy actually functions. As Nannerl Keohane argues, good character (consisting of sound judgment, decisiveness, integrity, intelligence, and commitment to public good), which according to supporters of political meritocracy constitutes the very core of political meritocracy, is indispensable to any political system, including a liberal democracy.[5]

In fact, if the problem with liberal democracy is unrestrained democratic populism as the supporters of political meritocracy claim,[6] then there is no inherent tension between political meritocracy and representative democracy,

[2] Bell, *Beyond Liberal Democracy*, 157.

[3] Famously, Benjamin Barber, one of the strongest advocates of participatory democracy (which he calls "strong democracy"), criticizes representative democracy as a kind of "political zoology" in that it tends to produce (economic and political) consumers rather than citizens who govern themselves. Benjamin R. Barber, *Strong Democracy: Participatory Politics for a New Age*, 20th anniversary ed. (Berkeley: University of California Press, 2003).

[4] Joseph Chan, "Democracy and Meritocracy: Toward a Confucian Perspective," *Journal of Chinese Philosophy* 34 (2007), 179–93, 188.

[5] Nannerl O. Keohane, *Thinking about Leadership* (Princeton: Princeton University Press, 2010).

[6] It is unclear whether these scholars oppose the democratic ideal of popular sovereignty itself.

because while stipulating and emphasizing the role of the people in selecting and dismissing their representatives and holding them accountable, representative democracy "does not depend upon – and may even preclude – robust popular participation in policy making.... There are constitutional or procedural limits on what 'the people' can decide, through a separation of powers, a bill of rights, judicial review, and other institutional features."[7] Representative democracy upholds popular sovereignty, which is the defining characteristic of democracy as political rule, but it stipulates that making and implementing policy decisions are delegated to leaders chosen by the people, thus limiting (if not preventing) popular participation. In representative democracy the ideal of popular sovereignty is realized by making leaders accountable to citizens.[8]

If misunderstanding what is meant by political representation in a representative democracy is the primary reason Confucian advocates of political meritocracy see political meritocracy and representative democracy as opposing terms, the second reason for this mistake is related to their infelicitous identification of political meritocracy with elite rule, as is clearly showcased in Bell's essay, "Taking Elitism Seriously" in *Beyond Liberal Democracy*. Certainly, political meritocracy of the kind Edmund Burke espoused, which operates on so-called trustee representation, is indisputably elitist because here, not only is a strong paternalistic assumption implied (that "the trustee knows better what is good for the trust's beneficiaries than do the beneficiaries themselves"), but more fundamentally, it is premised on skepticism of the people's capacities.[9] Political meritocracy, however, does not necessarily have to be elitist. Without alluding to political meritocracy, Jane Mansbridge has recently argued that the selection model of political representation, which, as "political meritocracy" stipulates, is focused on the agent's good character (such as public spiritedness), "need imply no more hierarchy than any representative process." In this model, "citizens select a 'citizen-candidate' from among themselves." That is, "when voters say they want to select a 'good man' or 'good woman' as a representative, they

[7] Ibid., 157.

[8] Barber levels strong criticism at the idea of representation, which in his view is incompatible with freedom (because it delegates and thus alienates political will at the cost of genuine self-government and autonomy), equality (because representation denies the existence of the self-governing community and in the absence of community, equality is a fiction that raises the specter of a mass society made up of indistinguishable consumer clones), and social justice (because among other things it impairs the community's ability to function as a regulating instrument of justice) (Barber, *Strong Democracy*, 145–6). Considering the debate among democratic theorists regarding the putative tension between democracy and leadership, it strikes me odd that Confucian advocates of political meritocracy take issue with representative democracy, into which political meritocracy or leadership is integral, not participatory democracy where leadership is found to have only a very limited role such as citizenship-facilitation (See Barber, *Strong Democracy*, 237–44). They seem to dismiss the much discussed distinction between these two types of democracy wholesale.

[9] Jane Mansbridge, "A 'Selection Model' of Political Representation," *Journal of Political Philosophy* 17 (2009), 386–7.

often seem to want someone like them, but with the interest, competence, and honesty to be a legislator."[10]

These two points – the misunderstanding of representation in a liberal representative democracy and the understanding of political meritocracy as an elite rule – render the recent call for political meritocracy less compelling as a political vision and practice, despite some initial appeal of its renewed emphasis on good character as the essential qualification of political leadership and political representation. As is currently formulated by its Confucian advocates, political meritocracy is likely to degenerate into a meritocratic elitism that is pitted not only against liberal representative democracy, but, and quite problematically, against democracy as such.[11] From a practical standpoint, what seems much more fruitful is to rethink the way in which meritocracy can be combined with democracy dialectically without denying popular sovereignty or limiting popular participation in collective decision making.

In this chapter, I explore a political meritocracy that is neither antiliberal democratic nor elitist and yet is fully consistent with the Confucian ideal of rule by virtue (*dezhi*).[12] My argument is threefold: (1) political meritocracy is highly compatible with, even integral to, representative democracy, if the selection model of political representation is preferred to the sanction model (the selection thesis); (2) political meritocracy can be *Confucian democratic* if representatives elected through the character selection process as well as high public officials (such as ministers, justices, public prosecutor general, and the police chief), whose appointment is recommended by the president (or its equivalent) and then ratified by the parliament, see themselves as public servants (*gongpu* 公僕), rather than as elitist rulers (the public servant thesis); and finally (3) if representatives exempt themselves from protection from public insult (which is legally permitted for ordinary citizenry in a Confucian democratic civil society), thus exposing themselves to open and free public criticism when they have failed to meet the standard of good character (what I call "democratic civic integrity"), thus breaching public faith (the no insult thesis).

What is important is that for these three theses to be realizable in any particular East Asian Confucian society, there should be a robust democratic civil society of the kind that I discussed in Chapter 3 – a public space where free citizens can boldly "insult" (that is, admonish, criticize, or even mock) political leaders and public officials who have gone astray from the Way (both democratic and Confucian-constitutional) and demand an explanation for

[10] Ibid., 387.

[11] This is problematic in that Bell and Bai, among others, never oppose democracy itself. Their goal is only to limit popular sovereignty. But, unlike liberal democrats, they want to do so not by means of liberal constitutionalism but by resorting to meritocratic elitism.

[12] As I discussed in Chapter 3, the recent formulation of political meritocracy by some new Confucians has seriously misappropriated the Confucian *dezhi* ideal, the main focus of which is not so much on who is entitled to rule but how to serve the moral and material well-being of the people.

their political judgment and public behavior. That is, in Confucian democracy, political leaders and public officials owe citizens not only (heavy) moral and political responsibility for the welfare of the people, which is the kernel of traditional Confucian virtue politics, but also *democratic accountability*. Committed to the moral and material well-being of citizens and upholding political leaders' and public officials' democratic accountability to citizens, the political meritocracy that I am proposing here is therefore more robustly democratic and morally demanding than the current formulations of Confucian political meritocracy, which promote strong paternalism and thus suffer serious democratic deficit.

The Selection Thesis

Representative democracy is premised on the belief that popular sovereignty is one thing and popular participation is another. Popular sovereignty is the defining characteristic of democracy and as the ideal of democracy it can never be compromised in any democratic political system, whatever mode it employs in practice. From a moral perspective, what distinguishes representative democracy from direct democracy is that it does not attempt a congruence (which is often deemed unrealistic in a modern nation-state) between popular sovereignty (a democratic ideal) and popular participation (a particular mode of governance – namely, self-government – to achieve popular sovereignty). In representative democracy, popular sovereignty is maintained vicariously through the election of representatives by free and equal citizens and by holding the former accountable to the latter. What is at stake here is not only different forms, but more fundamentally, different norms. Thus, Mansbridge says that "representation is, and is normatively intended to be, something more than a defective substitute for direct democracy. Constituents choose representatives not only to think more carefully than they about ends and means but also to negotiate more perceptively and fight more skillfully than constituents have either the time or the inclination to do."[13]

According to Ruth Grant and Robert Keohane, accountability implies that "some actors have the right to hold other actors to a set of standards, to judge whether they have fulfilled their responsibilities in light of these standards, and to impose sanctions if they determine that these responsibilities have not been met"[14] and accountability mechanisms are principally concerned with constraints on abuses of power. Unlike checks and balances mechanisms, which are "designed to prevent action that oversteps legitimate boundaries by requiring the cooperation of actors with different institutional interests to produce

[13] Jane Mansbridge, "Rethinking Representation," *American Political Science Review* 97 (2003), 515–28, 515.

[14] Ruth W. Grant and Robert O. Keohane, "Accountability and Abuses of Power in World Politics," *American Political Science Review* 99 (2005), 29–43, 29.

an authoritative decision," accountability mechanisms "always operate after the fact: exposing actions to view, judging and sanctioning them."[15]

In principle, democratic accountability is premised on the participation model in which power-wielders are viewed as instrumental agents of the public and the performance of power-wielders is evaluated by those who are affected by their actions. By contrast, in the delegation model of accountability, performance is evaluated by those entrusting them with powers and power-wielders are viewed as authorities with discretion.[16] What is important in our context is that the delegation model operates on *ex post* control and is more advantageous in a representative democracy than in a direct democracy because "representation allows for a separation or distance between the governed and their governors that allows the former to call the latter to account"[17] and also allows for discretionary judgment on the part of representatives. In political science, this type of political representation, undergirded on the delegation model, is called the "sanction model" and sees the relations between representatives and constituents in terms of principal-agent relations, which resemble economic models of employer-employee relations.[18] The traditional mode of political representation, which Mansbridge calls "promissory representation," is largely grounded in the sanction model, according to which "the representative is 'responsible to,' 'answerable to' [...] and even 'bound by' [the] voters."[19]

As noted, most Confucian advocates of political meritocracy find fault with representative democracy without clarifying precisely what is wrong with it. Not only do they fail to distinguish the delegation model from the participation model, but more problematically, their criticism of representative democracy is premised on the assumption of the participation model in which representatives reflect (or ought to reflect) their constituents' interests and beliefs and executive officers of government are mere instrumental agents of the legislature with little leadership role.[20] Without delving into the accountability problem,

[15] Ibid., 30.

[16] Ibid., 31. This is especially so in the "trustee model" of delegation. It is important to note that Grant and Keohane understand the trustee model and the "principal-agent" model (see note 18) as subcategories of the delegation model (32). By contrast, Richard Krouse distinguishes the trustee model, focused on an aristocratic principle of elite competence, from the delegation model (or the mandate model) upholding a democratic principle of mass participation. See Richard W. Krouse, "Two Concepts of Democratic Representation: James and John Stuart Mill," *Journal of Politics* 44 (1982), 510–11. In both cases, what is at stake is the distinction between representation with discretionary authority and popular participation.

[17] Grant and Keohane, "Accountability and Abuses of Power in World Politics," 32.

[18] Mansbridge, "'Selection Model' of Political Representation," 369. On the principal-agent model, see Mark A. Pollack, "Delegation, Agency and Agenda-Setting in the European Community," *International Organization* 51 (1997), 99–134. Also see Grant and Keohane, "Accountability and Abuses of Power in World Politics," 32.

[19] Mansbridge, "Rethinking Representation," 516. Here Mansbridge is focused on the capacity for imposing sanctions for past behavior (see note 2 in her essay).

[20] Grant and Keohane, "Accountability and Abuses of Power in World Politics," 31.

these Confucian critics of representative democracy (who actually are critical of democracy in toto) commonly complain about representative democracy's one person, one vote (OPOV) system, attributing to it all sorts of social problems that Western liberal democracies are currently struggling with. Tongdong Bai's following remark recapitulates the typical understanding of OPOV (by implication of liberal representative democracy) prevalent among the Confucian advocates of political meritocracy.

> At an institutional level, [in Western liberal democracy] political matters are to be decided ultimately by the policy of "one person, one vote" (OPOV), if we believe that the individual is the best judge of his or her interests. Some might also believe that a market economy – "one dollar, one vote" – is what represents these fundamental ideas on the level. This is why, for many people, the establishment of OPOV and a market economy is essential for a state to be democratic.... Confucianism, a dominant political philosophy in East Asia, seems to advocate ideas that are exactly opposed to the aforementioned liberal-democratic tenets. It is commonly believed that Confucianism gives priority to the state and the community over the individual, and advocates a kind of elitism or meritocracy which presupposes inequality (in political decision making) among human beings. This idea of the rule of the virtuous is sometimes considered to be implicated in Chinese authoritarianism, and strongly at odds with the idea of OPOV.[21]

I find numerous problems in this relatively short statement. But let me focus on what I consider to be the most serious problem – that is, there is a fundamental misunderstanding of the nature of OPOV and of political equality.[22] As Bai rightly notes, the underlying premise of OPOV is the belief that the individual is the best judge of his or her interests. But more fundamental than self-interest in modern representative democracy is political equality, the absence of which Bai (again rightly) characterizes as the defining feature of Confucianism as a political philosophy and a tradition.[23] Political equality represents democracy's moral commitment to popular sovereignty, the idea that power resides

[21] Bai, "A Mencian Version of Limited Democracy," 19–20.

[22] Another serious problem is found in the phrase "one dollar, one vote." In note 1 that accompanies the sentence involving this phrase (p. 20), Bai writes, "In fact, the economist Milton Friedman even argues that economic freedom, achievable only in a market economy, is simply a requisite for political freedom." I do not understand how Friedman's emphasis on the economic foundation of political freedom (a core thesis of John Locke's liberal constitutionalism) has anything to do with the regime of "one dollar, one vote," which is nothing but a timocracy.

[23] Chenyang Li, too, says that political equality "implies that every citizen having equal access to political decision-making process and to participation in government, including equal opportunity in selecting government officials, in making laws and policies, and in serving in the government. Confucianism does not endorse such philosophy" ("Equality and Inequality in Confucianism," 306). However, it is important to note that by "Confucianism" Li refers only to "ancient Confucianism." There is no reason to make this particular version of Confucianism, however foundational, represent or predetermine the direction or content of "modern Confucianism" that I argue must adapt to the modern societal condition. As I argued in the previous chapters, what is needed is to reconstruct Confucianism and Confucianism properly reconstructed can endorse the idea of political equality.

no longer in kings and aristocrats but in the people who are free and equal citizens. As private *individuals*, we radically differ from one another in terms of preference, aspiration, talent, interest, value, faith, and so on. Of course, as Confucians rightly claim, depending on the level of *personal* moral self-cultivation, some can be more virtuous than others. However, as *public* citizens, we are fundamentally equal in the sense that we share a common (yet internally contested) culture, a common (again, internally contested) history, and a common political and legal system.[24]

If the gist of political equality lies not in equal virtue, talent, or merit but in "common-sharing," Chenyang Li's following statements are equally problematic: that "in the Confucian view, the real question is not to have or not to have political inequality – which exists no matter what – but what kind of political inequality" and that "Confucian proportional equality in politics on the basis of talents and virtue comes with political inequalities."[25] Li's statements add only confusion precisely because his reference of "political equality" is to the Western political science lexicon (Li relies on Sidney Verba), which understands this concept in the republican or democratic sense as I did earlier.[26] For instance, the statement that "political inequality exists no matter what" fails to capture what is meant by political equality in both democratic political theory and practice.

Here both Bai and Li are confounding political equality, which is integral to both the democratic ideal of popular sovereignty and popular participation based on OPOV. In representative democracy, while political participation can be either vicariously exercised through representation mechanisms or not exercised at all if a voter so chooses (regrettably, from the viewpoint of participatory democracy), political equality can never be compromised. In politics, the antithesis of political equality is privilege of the few and political corruption.[27] Likewise, the opposite of democracy is not political meritocracy

[24] I admit that this apparently republican understanding of common citizenship may sound insensitive to our postmodern reality of difference and to the fact of pluralism. Here my point is that political equality is concerned with the institutions of common (contestable) citizenship and not with individual sameness or difference. On the common citizenship and its institutional underpinnings, see Maurizio Viroli, *Republicanism*, trans. Antony Shugaar (New York: Hill and Wang, 2002); David Miller, *On Nationality* (Oxford: Oxford University Press, 1995); Miller, *Citizenship and National Identity* (Cambridge: Polity, 2000); Yael Tamir, *Liberal Nationalism* (Princeton: Princeton University Press, 1993). On the compatibility between republicanism (republican democracy) and pluralism, see Philip Pettit, *Republicanism: A Theory of Freedom and Government* (Oxford: Oxford University Press, 1997), 143–6. Also see Chapter 11 for my own position on this issue.

[25] Li, "Equality and Inequality in Confucianism," 307–8.

[26] Of course, this is not to deny the possibility or existence of the (ancient) Confucian view of political (in)equality (see, e.g., *Xunzi* 4:12).

[27] In the republican and/or democratic polity, the very existence of political inequality signifies the corrupted nature of the regime. For more on this, see Maurizio Viroli, *For Love of Country: An Essay on Patriotism and Nationalism* (Oxford: Clarendon, 1995).

but aristocracy (or rather, oligarchy, its corrupted version) and/or kingship (or tyranny, its corrupted version).[28]

In short, OPOV is an institutional manifestation of the citizenry's political equality[29] and is by no means opposed to the idea of meritocratic government, according to which the virtuous should take leadership positions. As a matter of fact, political equality (by implication OPOV) is highly compatible with political meritocracy. Most tellingly, in Federalist No. 57, James Madison, who disagreed with Thomas Jefferson's more democratic ward system, wrote, "The aim of every political Constitution is or ought to be first to obtain for rulers, men who possess most wisdom to discern, and most virtue to pursue the common good of the society; and in the next place, to take the most effectual precautions for keeping them virtuous, whilst they continue to hold their public trust. The elective mode of obtaining rulers is the characteristic policy of republican government."[30] If it is agreed that (Confucian) political meritocracy and a nonelitist mode of representative democracy can be compatible, we Confucians should bring ourselves to a more productive task, that is, to find a way to turn this mutual compatibility into mutual reinforcement rather than being preoccupied with refuting so-called Western representative democracy. In this regard, the real problem for Confucians is the predominance of the sanction mode of political representation in the actually existing representative democracies including some East Asian democracies because it is far short of achieving a political meritocracy properly understood, despite its inevitability in the nonideal world.

[28] Some Confucian philosophers (like Li) tend to approach the question of political equality without giving an adequate consideration of the political regime it (or its denial) is tied to. By denying or resisting political equality, these scholars want to affirm a moderate form of inequality that they find inevitable in reality and, alternatively, endorse equity. This *may* be a sensible argument in dealing with the question of economic equality (as the advocates of the "principle of sufficiency" claim), but it is not the case when it comes to political equality. In politics, the denial of political equality implies the denial of democratic citizenship, which in turn implies the affirmation of an alternative form of political regime, be it an aristocracy or a kingship, or something else. Apparently, Li's preferred regime is close to an aristocracy by the virtuous and talented but this is only one particular mode of political meritocracy – that is, meritocratic elitism predicated on the trustee model of representation. Interestingly, however, later in his essay, Li proposes what he calls *general participation principle*, according to which "state leaders and legislators at all levels should be elected through general election [and] all citizens should have the opportunity to participate in [them]." But, ironically, this is exactly what *political equality* means. Although his second principle, namely, *qualification principle*, which stipulates that "[a] ll candidates for public offices must meet respective qualifications before they can be elected," is undemocratic because the "election" here involves no democratic competitive election, I wonder on what ground Li can support his first principle given his denial of political equality and popular sovereignty. See Li, "Equality and Inequality in Confucianism," 310–12.

[29] For a powerful statement for the dignity of legislation based on OPOV, see Jeremy Waldron, *The Dignity of Legislation* (Cambridge: Cambridge University Press, 1999).

[30] Alexander Hamilton, James Madison, and John Jay, *The Federalist Papers*, ed. Garry Wills (New York: Bantam Books, 1982), 289.

Obviously, the sanction model, which is an ex post facto measure centered on monitoring and controlling, is limited in realizing political meritocracy of the kind Madison espoused. According to Mansbridge, the benefits of selection are high "when agents will face unpredictable future situations, when agents must act speedily, creatively, flexibly, and adaptively, when they must dedicate their powers to an evolving goal and adopt different means as the need demands, when the goals are long-run rather than short-run, and when principles and agents prefer relationships based on mutual trust and common goals rather than instrumental relationship."[31] There is ample reason for Confucian advocates of political meritocracy to welcome the selection model given their deep interest in the quality of (long-term) public policy decisions and the fiduciary political relationship between political leaders and citizens.[32] Confucians would lend strong support to Mansbridge's claim that "[b]ecause both the sanction and the selection models are always mixed, it helps to think the selection model as having selection at its core and sanctions at its periphery."[33]

But how can we make sense of the selection model in a Confucian philosophical context? Can the selection model be supported by Confucianism? Confucius's following statements in the *Analects* are originally intended to illuminate how good government should be in a well-ordered Confucian society, but we can draw from them some important implications for the selection model of political representation.

A: Lead the people with administrative injunctions (*zheng* 政) and keep them orderly with penal law (*xing* 刑), and they will avoid punishments but will be without a sense of shame. Lead them with moral virtue (*de* 德) and keep them orderly through observing ritual propriety (*li* 禮) and they will develop a sense of shame, and moreover, will order themselves.[34]

B: [W]hen the observance of ritual propriety (*li* 禮) and the playing of music (*yue* 樂) do not flourish, the application of laws and punishments will not be on the mark; when the application of laws and punishments is not on the mark, the people will not know what to do with themselves.[35]

In statement A Confucius tells us that the essence of good government lies in a virtuous ruler's moral leadership, which relies on moral excellence and ritual propriety. Here, Confucius, who considered monarchy (ideally, sage-kingship)

[31] Mansbridge, "'Selection Model' of Political Representation," 370.

[32] For instance, Joseph Chan finds a "striking similarity" between Mansbridge's description of the quality of the constituent-representative relationship in the selection model and the Confucian ideal conception of ruler-ruled relationship. See his *Confucian Perfectionism: A Political Philosophy for Modern Times* (Princeton: Princeton University Press, 2013). Also see Bell, *Beyond Liberal Democracy*, 157–60.

[33] Mansbridge, "'Selection Model' of Political Representation," 370.

[34] *Analects* 2:3 (slightly modified). Unless noted otherwise, all English translations of the *Analects* of Confucius in this chapter are from Roger T. Ames and Henry Rosemont Jr., *The Analects of Confucius: A Philosophical Translation* (New York: Ballantine Books, 1998).

[35] *Analects* 13:3.

the only legitimate political system, does not mention *who* should rule or how to *select* a ruler (because for him a king is already and always there), but, apparently, he is deeply concerned about who is *qualified* to be a good ruler. Confucius's concern is *only* to distinguish good leadership from bad; the latter underpins political authority on a ruler's sanctioning power. Since sanctioning power is the ruler's exclusive political property, Confucius's ideal government works *only if* the ruler voluntarily brings himself to the moral precepts and principles articulated in the Confucian rituals, thereby constraining his power.[36] Put differently, the ruler owes no political accountability to the people, even though he is morally accountable to Heaven, who, in theory, can depose him from the throne. Confucius (and later Confucians) never allowed the people to hold the ruler directly accountable to them, nor did he advance institutional apparatuses that could realize a democratic idea of political accountability.[37]

That being said, statement A (and other assumptions implicated in it) can be creatively reappropriated to support the selection model of political representation in a more or less democratic society in today's East Asia, where ordinary people possess at least a considerable degree of political power, namely, the ability to sanction political leaders and public officials. In this reformulation of Confucian politics (now democratic politics), the direction of political sanction is from the people (citizens) to the political leaders. Here, a good democratic and meritorious leadership can be better achieved when people are concerned with how to select good representatives rather than how to sanction them. If the focus is on sanctioning, political leaders and public officials will not develop a sense of shame and only strive for reelection, and try to avoid responsibility at public costs. Likewise, statement B can be read equally anew in this democratic spirit: political sanction from the people is necessary because we are living in a nonideal world where there are more knaves than people of moral integrity but, nevertheless, political sanction should be at the periphery of democratic politics, not its core. The mainstay of democratic politics must

[36] Some scholars call this "Confucian constitutionalism." See Chaihark Hahm, "Ritual and Constitutionalism: Disputing the Ruler's Legitimacy in a Confucian Polity," *American Journal of Comparative Law* 57 (2009), 135–203; Hahm, "Constitutionalism, Confucian Civic Virtue, and Ritual Propriety," in Bell and Hahm, *Confucianism for the Modern World*; Jaeyoon Song, "The *Zhou* Li and Constitutionalism: A Southern Song Political Theory," *Journal of Chinese Philosophy* 36 (2009), 423–38; Sungmoon Kim, "Confucian Constitutionalism: Mencius and Xunzi on Virtue, Ritual, and Royal Transmission," *Review of Politics* 73 (2011), 371–99. Confucian constitutionalism, however, is not predicated on (nor upholds) democratic accountability.

[37] Later Confucians (especially Neo-Confucians) did develop political institutions that are politically accountable, thus being conducive to the welfare of the people. But the political accountability here is not so much democratic accountability (or vertical accountability) as horizontal accountability that helps maintain the mechanisms of checks and balances among the bureaucratic branches. See Jongryn Mo, "The Challenge of Accountability: Implications of the Censorate," in Bell and Hahm, *Confucianism for the Modern World*.

be filled with virtuous leaders who are genuinely committed to the moral and material well-being of the citizenry, particularly those citizens who deserve it.

Confucians should prefer the selection model of political representation to the sanction model, not only because the latter is likely to make political leaders and public officials shameless. For Confucians, the underlying assumption of the sanction model itself is heavily problematic, which stipulates that human beings are essentially self-interested and they almost never change.[38] Mencius leveled a poignant criticism at the common tendency to frame human behaviors and relationships in terms of self-interest.

> If a subject, in serving his prince, cherished the profit motive, and a son, in serving his father, and a younger brother, in serving his elder brother, did likewise, then it would mean that in their mutual relations, prince and subject, father and son, elder brother and younger brother, all cherished the profit motive to the total exclusion of morality (*ren yi* 仁義). The prince of such a state is sure to perish. If, on the other hand ... a subject, in serving his prince, cherished morality, and a son, in serving his father, and a younger brother, in serving his elder brother, did likewise, then it would mean that in their mutual relations, prince and subject, father and son, elder brother and younger brother, all cherished morality to the exclusion of profit. The prince of such a state is sure to a true King. What is the point of mentioning the word "profit"?[39]

Drawing on Dale Miller's psychological study, Mansbridge articulates the problem of describing most behavior in self-interested terms on three grounds: first, the image of human beings as self-interested leads to the creation of the kinds of social institutions that transform that image into reality; second, the implicit norm that one should act self-interestedly affects behavior because norms tend to change in the direction of the perceived majority's norms; third, thinking of oneself as one of the few non-self-interested people in a group implies that one's altruistic behavior will have only a miniscule potential effect.[40] Philip Pettit relates this (type of) psychological insight more directly to the selection model, which he calls the "screen model."

> Let us assume, then, that, however corruptible they are, people in power are not always actively corrupt; they have a natural, culturally supported tendency to think in public-spirited terms and to make their decisions on a public-spirited basis. This assumption invites us to consider the likely effects of deviant-centered sanctions [read: the conventional sanction model], not on actively corrupt deviants, but rather on those who have an independent disposition to comply with whatever are the public norms governing their behavior. It turns out that there are a variety of negative effects, and that these give us reason to wonder whether a deviant-centered strategy can do much or indeed

[38] Though Xunzi claims that human nature is originally bad, he, like Mencius, firmly believes in self-transformability of every human being.

[39] *Mencius* 6B4. The English translation is adopted from *Mencius*, trans. D. C. Lau (New York: Penguin, 1970).

[40] Mansbridge, "'Selection Model' of Political Representation," 379. For Miller's study, see his "The Norm of Self-interest," *American Psychologist* 54 (1999), 1053–60.

any good; they point us towards ways in which the strategy may be counterproductive. However successful it is with the natural deviants, it may cause natural compliers to do worse than we might otherwise have expected.[41]

Of course, there is a qualitative difference between Mencius and Pettit (and Mansbridge), besides the different political contexts in which they are writing. While Mencius's opposition to self-interest is grounded in his fundamental metaphysical assumption that human beings are inherently good, Pettit's qualified embracement of the sanction model at the periphery of republican/democratic politics assumes no such metaphysical foundation. On Pettit's account, the selection model can work independently of assumptions of human nature because what is at stake here is not an accurate description of human nature and the cultivation of *moral virtue* that is rooted in it but the cultivation of *civic virtue* (such as public-spiritedness), which unlike moral virtue, which is desirable for its own sake, is "valued instrumentally, for its contribution to sustaining a political community."[42] Since Confucian pluralist democracy, as I have reconstructed in Chapter 4, is based on the separation between one's moral virtue, which depends on the moral community one, as a private person, belongs to, and civic virtue, which is commonly and publicly shared by the citizenry, the selection model that Mansbridge and Pettit have in mind is highly recommendable and practicable in a Confucian democratic society.

The Public Servant Thesis I: Confucianism Revisited

In Chapter 3, I criticized Daniel Bell's exam model of political meritocracy because of its elitist implications. Bell offers various practical reasons to support this model as an alternative to full-scale democratic representation, but the strongest reason is based on the "success story" of premodern China: "Confucian societies institutionalized a stable mechanism capable of producing at least on occasion what was widely seen as a 'government of the best and brightest': China's famous two-thousand-year-old meritocratic civil examination system."[43] From a historical standpoint, however, there is much to doubt about the Confucian origin of the civil examination system, which was adopted in premodern Confucian countries to recruit (relatively high) public officials into the central government to assist the king, the sole ruler whose political legitimacy was in principle given by the "Mandate of Heaven" (*tianming* 天命). One of the main historical reasons for such skepticism has to do with the fact that the civil examination system was the outcome of a tension-ridden compromise between Legalism and Confucianism, between a doctrine that upheld a purely instrumental political meritocracy where merit was understood in terms

[41] Pettit, *Republicanism*, 217.

[42] William A. Galston, "Pluralism and Civic Virtue," *Social Theory and Practice* 33 (2007), 625–35, 625.

[43] Bell, *Beyond Liberal Democracy*, 154.

of military service or agricultural production and that promoting rule by virtuous man (*renzhi* 仁治 or *dezhi* 德治) to make the people morally good and economically content. Even if we grant partial Confucian credit for the civil examination system, it is still doubtful that it indeed created a political meritocracy of the kind that its contemporary espousers attribute to it, given that it was often entangled with various kinds of social and economic corruptions, thus inviting numerous criticisms from Confucian scholars who were genuinely dedicated to the study of the Way (*dao* 道).

It is important to note that not only did the civil examination system fail to offer any meaningful political alternative to monarchy (in fact, it was intended to facilitate the monarchical system), but, more important, no (classical or neo) Confucian (especially in China) proposed or supported the "government *of* the best and brightest" as Bell and company claim. If Confucians advocated government of the best and brightest, they meant a government of *one* best and brightest person, namely, "sage-kingship," the Confucian equivalent of philosopher-kingship, not the aristocracy of the best and brightest Confucian scholars.[44] From where does this misconception arise?

In my view, the mistake Confucian advocates of political meritocracy make in understanding the Confucian espousal of what I called "the aristocracy of Dao" in Chapter 3 as offering support for meritocratic elitism is the result of their complete dismissal of the importance of the Mandate of Heaven in Confucian political discourse. Among the ancient Confucian political thinkers, Mencius offers the most articulate account of the Mandate of Heaven. The following is a conversation between Mencius (M) and Wan Zhang (W), his student, regarding the abdication of the legendary sage-king Yao to Shun, his long-time minister who later became a legendary sage-king himself.

W: Is it true that Yao gave the *tianxia* (the world) to Shun?
M: No, the King [the Son of Heaven] cannot give the *tianxia* to another.
W: In that case who gave the *tianxia* to Shun?
M: *Tian* gave it him.
W: Does this mean that *Tian* gave him detailed and minute instructions?
M: No, *Tian* does not speak but reveals itself through its acts and deeds.

[44] Historically, only Chosŏn dynasty in Korea (particularly from the late sixteenth to the mid-eighteenth century) developed a political system close to aristocracy of the best and brightest Confucian scholars called the *sarim jeongchi* (士林政治, rule by the Neo-Confucian literati), but it was never sought as the alternative to the monarchical system (it pursued only the "combined rule by the king and ministers"), nor was it clear of social problems. In fact, this seemingly perfect political system generated and suffered from its own problems, no less serious and complicated than that we find in any other political system. To make a long story short, ceaseless struggles among the Confucian schools over the exclusive cultural and ethico-religious right to the orthodox lineage of the Confucian Way (*dao tong* 道統) simultaneously intensified the political struggles among the Confucian scholar-officials in the government who showed more interest in the glory of their own schools or families than in the welfare of the general public. See Sungmoon Kim, "Trouble with Korean Confucianism: Scholar-Official between Ideal and Reality," *Dao* 8 (2009), 29–48.

W: How does *Tian* do this?

M: The King can recommend a man to *Tian* but he cannot make *Tian* give this man the *tianxia*.... In antiquity, Yao recommended Shun to *Tian* and *Tian* accepted him; he presented him to the people and the people accepted him. Hence I said, "*Tian* does not speak but reveals itself by its acts and deeds."[45]

Mencius's key point can be recapitulated as this: (1) in the Confucian political tradition the right to rule comes only from Heaven, (2) the king, whose official title is the "son of Heaven" (*tianzi* 天子), alone has such a right based on the Mandate of Heaven, and (3) in reality the will of the people as a collective body vicariously *expresses* the Mandate of Heaven.[46] Based on the third point and mistaking the expression of the Mandate of Heaven as a form of political representation, many modern scholars have presented Mencius as a proto-democratic political thinker. However, as far as it is constrained by the second point, the third point alone cannot justify or establish democratic rule.[47] Unless the monarchical system is deconstructed (say, into the constitutional monarchy), the Heavenly mandate to rule is still held exclusively by the king, and the king's right to rule is not only symbolic but politically substantive. Thus understood, Mencius's political theoretical innovation in the Confucian political tradition lies not so much in his anticipation of democracy but in his more explicitly political reformulation of the Confucian notion of accountability: the ruler's moral accountability to Heaven should translate in practice into his heavy moral and political responsibility for the well-being of the people who as a collective vicariously express Heaven's content or discontent with the incumbent ruler or government.[48]

It is interesting that none of the recent advocates of political meritocracy pays attention to the tension between democratic rule and monarchy latent in Confucian (especially Mencian Confucian) political discourse, even when referring to Mencius, nor are they interested in developing Mencius's (arguably) nascent democratic idea into a robust democratic political theory.[49] Instead, they assert that ancient Confucianism supports political meritocracy understood as a government *of* the best and brightest and we moderns should replicate it in our own society. But, certain anachronisms in this claim aside, there is no such "of" in the Confucian political tradition because intellectual elites were never considered to be the possessors *of* the mandate or right to rule, even vicariously.[50]

45 *Mencius* 5A5.

46 For a detailed analysis of *Mencius* 5A5, see Kim, "Confucian Constitutionalism."

47 For a related argument, see Stephen C. Angle, *Contemporary Confucian Political Philosophy: Toward Progressive Confucianism* (Cambridge: Polity, 2012), 37–41.

48 On Mencius's political theory of responsibility see Sungmoon Kim, "The Secret of Confucian *Wuwei* Statecraft: Mencius's Political Theory of Responsibility," *Asian Philosophy* 20 (2010), 27–42.

49 Recall my critique of Bai's interpretation of the *Mengzi* in Chapter 3.

50 The only exception is when the regime is undergoing a critical constitutional crisis caused by regicide or its equivalents. According to Mencius, in such a political crisis a *tianli* 天吏 (Heaven's

When Confucian scholars entered the government, thus transforming themselves into bureaucrats and policymakers, their role was to *assist* (*xiang* 相) the king, not to make a decision for or on his behalf, which would practically mean usurpation.[51] Appointed by the ruler who is only accountable to Heaven, Confucian scholar officials owed political accountability only to their appointer, owing no political accountability to the people (hence the absence of vertical accountability), even though just like the ruler, they were morally responsible for the welfare of the people whose symbolic-moral-cosmological status, not their political status, was thought to be equivalent to that of Heaven.

Of course, Confucian scholars never thought of themselves as mere governmental functionaries. Especially after the rise of Neo-Confucianism in the twelfth century, most ardent Confucian scholars counted service for the Way as their Heaven-given mission and to that extent they shared with the ruler moral accountability to Heaven.[52] In other words, they saw themselves not merely as the king's servants but as Heaven's servants, *public servants* (*gongpu* 公僕) who should dedicate themselves not to increasing the ruler's private interest but the public's, that is, the welfare of the people who are morally equivalent to Heaven, the ultimate source of what is public (*gong* 公).[53]

Most East Asians are now living in a society where the moral cosmology of Heaven and the political metaphysics of the Mandate of Heaven have become completely obsolete.[54] In more or less democratic East Asian societies, the mandate to rule comes either directly or indirectly from ordinary citizens without any recourse to the moral authority of Heaven. In the absence of the Mandate of Heaven and after the total destruction of the Confucian monarchical system in which the king was presented as the son of Heaven, political leaders and public officials now owe both moral and political accountability directly to the

delegated official) should be appointed among the (virtuous) ministers in due course and his role as an interim ruler should end immediately after the next king is enthroned. See Justin Tiwald, "A Right of Rebellion in the *Mengzi*?," *Dao* 7 (2008), 269–82.

51 Doing so also violates the Confucian principle of "the rectification of the names" (*zhengming* 正名), according to which "the ruler must rule, the minister minister, the father father, and the son son" (*Analects* 12:11).

52 Wm. Theodore de Bary, *The Liberal Tradition in China* (New York: Columbia University Press, 1983); Peter K. Bol, *Neo-Confucianism in History* (Cambridge, MA: Harvard University Asia Center, 2008).

53 The Neo-Confucian "Heavenly servant" ideal traces back to Mencius's famous distinction between honors bestowed by Heaven (*tianjue* 天爵) and honors bestowed by man (*renjue* 人爵): "There are honors bestowed by Heaven, and there are honors bestowed by man. Benevolence, dutifulness, conscientiousness, truthfulness to one's word, unflagging delight in what is good – these are honors bestowed by Heaven. The position of a Ducal Minister, a Minister, or a Counsellor is an honor bestowed by man. [While] men of antiquity bent their efforts towards acquiring honors bestowed by Heaven, … [m]an of today bend their efforts towards acquiring honors bestowed by Heaven in order to win honors bestowed by man, and once the latter is won they discard the former" (*Mencius* 6A16).

54 An importance exception includes Jiang Qing who attempts to (re)construct Confucian constitutionalism on the basis of the scared legitimacy of Heaven.

people, the only legitimate source of sovereign authority. In short, they should be considered not so much as elitist leaders but as public servants committed to the moral and material well-being of the entire citizenry. In traditional Confucian regimes, Confucian public servants were often at a loss regarding what the public interest is because of the multilayered meanings of the public (*gong*) in Confucian ethical and political discourse and their dual commitments to Heaven and to the people, which were not necessarily congruent with each other because service to Heaven was often interpreted differently by different groups of scholar-officials.[55] In the post-Heaven era, there should be no such ambiguity in the public service of political leaders and public officials.

In the preceding section, I argued that modern Confucians should adopt the selection model of political representation to realize political meritocracy in a representative democratic system. I left one important point unresolved – who deserves electoral selection by the citizens. Most Confucian advocates of political meritocracy point to knowledge, ethics, experience, and skills,[56] but no one (including Joseph Chan who upholds the selection model explicitly) pays attention to the importance of selecting a representative who "already has policy goals much like the constituents,"[57] because of their elitist penchant. Much in the meritocratic spirit, James Fearon argues in favor of a selection model where "voters need not see elections as mechanisms that establish accountability: instead, they might understand elections as opportunities to choose a 'good type' of political leader, one who would act on their behalf independent of reelection incentives."[58] However, he then defines "good type" precisely in the democratic sense, as a politician "who (1) shares the voter's issue preferences, (2) has integrity, in that he or she is hard to bribe or otherwise induce to work against the voter's interests, and (3) is competent or skilled in discerning and implementing optimal policies for the voter."[59] In short, what is central to the good character of a political leader is what can be called "democratic civic integrity," an inner disposition to align his or her objective as a political

[55] For an excellent study of the multilayered Confucian concept of the public (*gong*), see Seung-Hwan Lee, "The Concept of *Gong* in Traditional Korea and Its Modern Transformations," *Korea Journal* 43 (2003), 137–63, esp. 140–49.

[56] See, for instance, Li, "Equality and Inequality in Confucianism," 306.

[57] Mansbridge, " 'Selection Model' of Political Representation," 374.

[58] James D. Fearon, "Electoral Accountability and the Control of Politicians: Selecting Good Types versus Sanctioning Poor Performance," in *Democracy, Accountability, and Representation*, ed. Adam Przeworski, Susan C. Stokes, and Bernard Manin (Cambridge: Cambridge University Press, 1999), 55–97, 56. It is important to note that when Fearon says that the selection model does not count elections as mechanisms that establish accountability, he has in mind traditional promissory accountability, not democratic accountability in general. According to Mansbridge's taxonomy of political representation, the selection model is closely related to what she calls "gyroscopic representation," in which voters "[select and place] in the political system representatives whose behavior is to some degree predictable in advance based on their observable characteristics" (Mansbridge, "Rethinking Representation," 521).

[59] Fearon, "Electoral Accountability and the Control of Politicians," 59.

representative with that of the voter whose interest he or she is supposed to represent.

In the selection model, meritocracy is realized when representatives employ their knowledge, experience, and skills to discern and implement optimal policies for the voter, not by going against the voter's "myopic" interest, as Confucian advocates of political meritocracy claim. In a sense, even the political judgment of what the optimal policies are is fundamentally circumscribed by what the voters collectively will and judge, however unrefined and rudimentary the outcomes may be, because for the representative's political judgment to be morally legitimate and politically effective, it must broadly reflect public judgment.[60] Although traditional Confucianism has little room for collective self-determination and/or public political judgment, which is indispensable to a viable democratic living, my reformed Confucianism, which integrates "the public servant thesis," as articulated in this section, is fully consistent with both the selection model of representation (hence nonelitist political meritocracy) and collective self-determination of the sovereign democratic citizenry.

The Public Servant Thesis II: Democratic Civic Integrity

Suppose we have selected "good" representatives who possess formidable character as well as experience, skill, and knowledge, through proper electoral channels. Again, the putative advantage of the selection model (and the gyroscopic representation it obtains) is deep predictability in the sense of "predicting an inner constellation of values that is, in important respects, like the constituent's own."[61] Put differently, after election, no scrupulous vigilance or monitoring is required as the representation mechanism is in a sense self-propelled.

However, it must be reminded that this advantage is only a *relative* advantage in comparison with the sanction model. That is, we may not have to be so scrupulously vigilant about every single move of our representatives since we have selected good types, but we as citizens should still remain vigilant of the possible corruption of our otherwise good representatives because power intoxicates even the good ones.

In political theory, *who guards our guardians?* has been a perennial dilemma. Surprisingly, however, none of the Confucian advocates of political meritocracy draw attention to the intoxicating nature of power while singularly highlighting the merits of meritocratic elitism (vis-à-vis the drawbacks of liberal democracy), as if political elites are immune from the indulgence in power. Of course,

[60] In this regard, I resist the tendency to see representative democracy as diametrically opposed to participatory democracy. On the central place of public judgment in the democratic practice, see Seyla Benhabib, *Situating the Self: Gender, Community and Postmodernism in Contemporary Ethics* (New York: Routledge, 1992), chap. 4; Benjamin R. Barber, *The Conquest of Politics: Liberal Philosophy in Democratic Times* (Princeton: Princeton University Press, 1988), chap. 8.

[61] Mansbridge, "Rethinking Representation," 521.

liberal democracy is not exempt from this problem of unchecked leadership (especially those based on the trustee model of political representation), but evidently, the Confucian models of meritocratic elitism presented so far (Bell's exam-based model, Bai's leveled model, and Li's test-recommendation model) are far more vulnerable to this problem than their liberal-democratic counterpart.[62] This is in part because Confucian models do not integrate the selection mechanism – be it a national exam, quality test, or committee recommendation – into the electoral representative system. But a more fundamental reason is that the Confucian advocates of political meritocracy do not understand *good character* in relation to the background political institutions.

Who are "good types"? Again, the Confucian proponents of political meritocracy single out experience, skill, talent, knowledge, moral character, and so on, as the relevant criteria. But can we trust that a good political leader will remain good throughout his or her tenure? Here our focus is on the selected leader's moral character. The conceivable response could be, "He or she is one of our 'best and brightest' and being morally good and intellectually superior, he or she won't turn out to be bad and if he or she does turn out to be bad, he or she should have not been selected because this proves ex post facto that he or she *was* not actually good. Then the blame goes to us who wrongly selected him or her, who failed to discern a good type from a bad one."[63]

The problem with this reasoning is obvious: unlike the moral judgment that we make as individuals in our private interpersonal settings, *political judgment* to determine who is good for a public post cannot be *endogenously* made in reference to the merit itself, on the assumption that there is a self-evident criterion of the good, and that the good, once identified, will prove to be good across all life spheres. The difficulty is that we no longer live in an ethically monist society, as we, as private individuals, subscribe to pluralist value systems. In the pluralist society, therefore, political judgment to identify who is good should be made *exogenously*, that is, in reference to the candidate's public or civic character – based on whether or not he or she is committed to the political principles that undergird *our* political system that we share together as *citizens*. When liberal democrats such as Fearon and Mansbridge define the good type in terms of ability to align the principal's and the agent's objectives, they do not suggest pandering with (uneducated) public opinion; their focus is precisely on this type of moral character, what I call *democratic civic integrity*.

[62] Chenyang Li's qualification principle upholds the model that mixes test and recommendation: "A non-partisan qualification committee may be in charge of the screening process. A candidate can be judged on the basis of his or her level of education, years of experience, and track records of success or the lack thereof, as well as moral character. Tests can be set up to prove candidates' knowledge and experience, as has been done in China since antiquity" ("Equality and Inequality in Confucianism," 310).

[63] This line of reasoning is evident in Chenyang Li's and Tongdong Bai's shared claim that human beings are morally and politically unequal and they should be treated according to what they deserve.

In a Confucian pluralist democracy, not only should citizens elect good types as their political representatives on the basis of their public character, but equally important, they must be able to demand that political leaders and public officials act according to political principles and public norms embedded in their shared public culture and the constitution that is (and ought to be) undergirded on it. Put differently, none other than citizens themselves should assume collectively the role of "the guardian" of their political representatives who may breach public trust on the basis of which they were initially selected. This is the natural corollary of the public servant thesis discussed in the previous section.

But how can citizens in a Confucian democracy effectively exercise this authority against political leaders and public officials who may abuse their power and betray public faith? Although there can be various indirect institutional mechanisms such as the Madisonian checks and balances and appeal to the constitutional court, let me suggest one way in which citizens can directly check the arbitrary exercise of political power by political leaders and public officials. In this way, we can recast representative democracy as more participatory and deliberative.[64]

The No Insult Thesis

My suggestion is that citizens in a Confucian democratic society should be able to remonstrate with, admonish, and criticize political leaders and public officials as freely as possible without fear. That is, the citizenry's *political* right to criticize political power and public authority should be maximally respected in Confucian democracy. Let me call this proposition the no insult thesis.

In Chapter 2, I justified and espoused the "virtue of incivility" particularly in political relations by extending the traditional Confucian political practice of remonstrance. There I showed that ancient Confucians not only encouraged the ministers to remonstrate with a ruler who had gone astray, but also exhorted the ruler to express civility and heed the subjects' loyal and faithful incivility, namely, their moral and political remonstrations. I found *Mencius* 4B3 particularly interesting. Recall that the following is what I said about this passage in Chapter 2:

> Mencius's reasoning is strikingly radical: if the ruler treats his subjects as an "enemy" by imposing docility on his subjects (and further by punishing them unrightfully), the righteous relationship (*yihe* 義合) between them becomes null and void. Not only that, upon the catastrophic dissolution of the relationship, the subject is morally entitled to regard his ruler as a stranger (that is, as "nobody" with whom he has no meaningful relational

[64] Following Mansbridge, I understand "deliberation" broadly as one that involves "everyday talk." See Jane Mansbridge, "Everyday Talk in the Deliberative System," in *Deliberative Politics: Essays on Democracy and Disagreement*, ed. Stephen Macedo (Oxford: Oxford University Press, 1999).

ties) and can even treat him as an enemy. Since there is no moral relationship, there is no moral obligation left for the subject to pay due ritual propriety (such as mourning) to the ruler. In extreme circumstances, subjects (particularly ministers of royal blood) can rightfully replace the ruler.

Mencius did not advocate democracy, and his fundamental faith in moral equality among human beings notwithstanding, he never upheld political equality. Despite his profound interest in the moral and economic well-being of the people, for Mencius, the only meaningful political relationship (as evidenced in his notion of five cardinal human relationships or *wulun* 五倫) was that between the king and his ministers. In Confucian democracy, this traditional Confucian assumption undergoes a radical transformation: now the king's subjects are all transformed into citizens who are politically equal to one another and there is no political hierarchy between the ruler and the ruled, as citizens themselves are the sovereign rulers. Here, citizenship is the most important and fundamental political relationship, but in the representative democratic system, a democratically legitimate relationship between citizens and their political representatives (and public officials appointed through the democratic procedure) is of equal importance and this relational legitimacy is maintained through various mechanisms of accountability. Ultimately, then, in Confucian democracy, the *right* to remonstrate with those who hold public positions and exercise political power goes to citizens.

However, traditional Confucian remonstrance, which was suggested originally on the assumption of political inequality between the ruler and the ruled, is too modest (or too "civil") to exert an expected political force in democratic society. In existing East Asian politics, Confucianism is still deeply associated with authoritarian habits and practices as its emphasis on social harmony and civility is occasionally exploited by shrewd politicians and state bureaucrats to serve their conservative, often antidemocratic, purposes.[65] Even in democratic Taiwan and South Korea, internal operations of political parties are far from democratic and important political decisions are frequently made in secret by a few so-called political leaders and elite bureaucrats. In these societies, "rule of law," government's favorite slogan, has little to do with protection of individual rights and promotion of the citizenry's public liberty; more often, it serves the opposite in the name of public security and the nation's international image.

The Confucian democracy that we want to have in East Asia cannot be a democracy with Chinese/Korean/Taiwanese characteristics, which often, as Fred Dallmayr criticizes Daniel Bell's political suggestion in China, turns out

[65] On the exploitation of Confucianism in democratic East Asia, see L. H. M. Ling and Chih-yu Shih, "Confucianism with a Liberal Face: The Meaning of Democratic Politics in Postcolonial Taiwan," *Review of Politics* 60 (1998), 55–82 for the case of Taiwan and Sungmoon Kim, "Confucianism in Contestation: The May Struggle of 1991 in South Korea and Its Lesson," *New Political Science* 31 (2009), 49–68 for the case of South Korea.

to be nondemocratic.[66] In our reconstructed Confucian democracy, citizens should actively demand political leaders and public officials of democratic civic integrity that they pledged during election campaigns and parliamentary confirmation hearings, and if they betray public faith, citizens should be emboldened to criticize them. Traditional Confucianism ascribed this type of political emboldenment solely to an individual scholar-official's personal virtue of courage, but in Confucian democracy it should enjoy an institutional protection and be valued as a core democratic right that safeguards the citizenry's public freedom.[67]

One practical way to protect the citizenry's right to criticize political leaders and public officials is to exonerate citizens who have actually exercised this right (freedom of speech) and as a result charged with deformation or insult, which is legally enforced in some East Asian countries such as China and South Korea. For instance, Article 311 of the Criminal Law of South Korea states, "[A] person who publicly insults another shall be punished by imprisonment or imprisonment without prison labor for no more than one year or by a fine not exceeding two million won [approximately two thousand U.S. dollars]." Here the "insult" is defined as an offense solely on the basis of the victim's subjective feeling, that is, based on an accusation that he or she has suffered damage from verbal, behavioral, or literal expressions of another's abstract judgment or derogatory expression, which depreciates his or her social value.

As I argue in Chapter 10, insult law is still socially relevant in Korean democratic society as it helps to moderate the vicissitudes of pluralist democratic life without suppressing the democratic right of expressive liberty. That is, in Confucian democratic civil society, insult law can be instrumental to cultivating the virtue of civility among free and equal citizens. However, its occasional exploitation by politicians and public officials to suppress the citizenry's rightful criticism of their compromise of democratic civic integrity and abuse of power is a different story. In Korea, insult charges arise very rarely among ordinary citizens who are keenly aware of the importance of civility in their daily social interactions with others. By contrast, insult and defamation charges are frequently invoked by members of the National Assembly and public officials (including members of the cabinet and presidential secretaries) against citizens who find fault with their public behaviors or public decisions, often by mocking (directly or through parody) in personal Internet blogs or online public debate cites. Insult charges of these sorts are absolutely

[66] Fred Dallmayr, "Exiting Liberal Democracy: Bell and Confucian Thought," *Philosophy East and West* 59 (2009), 524–30.

[67] For an excellent political theoretical investigation of public freedom, see Dana Villa, *Public Freedom* (Princeton: Princeton University Press, 2008).

unacceptable in a Confucian democracy that takes public liberty and freedom of speech seriously.[68]

The no insult thesis – no insult charge for the citizens who have "insulted" political leaders and public officials for their lack of democratic civic integrity and breach of public faith – is compatible with the selection model of political representation. According to Mansbridge, "In the selection model, the representative's accountability to the constituent will typically take the form of *narrative* and even *deliberative* accountability rather than accountability based on monitoring and sanctions."[69] In this understanding, accountability means that "the representative has an obligation to explain ('give an account for') his or her past actions, regardless of the system of sanctioning."[70] When political leaders and public officials have failed to account for their political decisions and public actions, citizens have every right to demand from them reasons for their decisions and actions.

It is not surprising that Confucian advocates of meritocratic elitism are completely silent about the citizenry's democratic right to social criticism (that may involve "insult") and the political obligation (not just moral obligation) on the part of political leaders and public officials to give an account for their public policy decisions and political actions. In fact, their elitist penchant is in no way compatible with what I have proposed here because, first, they (at least some of them) explicitly oppose the democratic ideal of political equality and, second, they do not think that ordinary citizens – ordinary because of their lack of moral and intellectual excellence and talent – *deserve* such a right. In their ideal Confucian meritocracy, all ordinary citizens can do when it comes to the breach of public faith is to opt for old-style Confucian remonstration with their "best and brightest" elite leaders who may or may not pay heed to it.

As I noted, however, remonstrance, which relies solely on personal moral courage, is far short of institutionalizing the accountability mechanisms, democratic or otherwise. In the absence of institutionalized mechanisms of political accountability, Confucian meritocracy absolutely depends for its success (understood in terms of regime stability but not of political/civic viability) on the elite leaders' so-called talent and paternalistic benefaction. Even though

68 This does not mean that politicians and public officials cannot appeal to the insult and defamation laws when their personal reputation and social value has been impaired by others, which makes the case a genuine civil dispute among private individuals in the civil society. My point is that social criticism (even involving mockery and derision) against political leaders and public officials should be maximally accommodated in a Confucian democratic society, if what is at stake are their public behaviors and speeches that owe accountability to citizens.

69 Mansbridge, "'Selection Model' of Political Representation," 369–70, emphases in original.

70 Mansbridge, "Rethinking Representation," 516n2. Here Mansbridge refers to Hannah F. Pitkin's classic, *The Concept of Representation* (Berkeley: University of California Press, [1967] 1972), 55ff.

the initial appeal of the recent proposals of Confucian meritocracy was the result of their realistic attention to the institutional configuration of the modern Confucian (semidemocratic) regime, what we now have is another form of rule by man (*renzhi* 人治), as they failed to articulate the institutional mechanisms of political accountability.[71] Do they rely, albeit implicitly, on the liberal constitutional mechanism of checks and balances? It is hard to tell.[72] But it is difficult to believe that Confucian meritocratic elitism can be a realistic political alternative to liberal democracy.

[71] On "rule by man" in the Chinese political context, see Leigh K. Jenco, "'Rule by Man' and 'Rule by Law' in Early Republican China: Contributions to a Theoretical Debate," *Journal of Asian Studies* 69 (2010), 181–203.

[72] Certainly not, in the case of Jiang Qing, according to whose Confucian constitutionalism, checks and balances mechanism operates only within the tricameral parliament (in the way to check popular sovereignty), but not across the branches of government.

PART III

CONFUCIAN DEMOCRACY IN PRACTICE – THE KOREAN CASE

8

Motivating and Legitimating Confucian Democracy: The Politics of *Chŏng*

If there is one thing that can tellingly distinguish Korean democracy from postcommunist democracies in Eastern and Central Europe, it is to be sure the extraordinary vibrancy of civil society in democratized Korea.[1] It is literally "extraordinary," because, among Western observers, it has been constantly reported that there is a salient contrast between a plethora of political actions and civil movements in democratizing postcommunist countries and a frustrating paucity of civic engagement in their democratized counterparts.[2] Considering the similar transitional experience – which political scientist Terry Karl termed a "mass-ascendant" mode of democratization[3] – in which "ethical civil society"[4] played a pivotal role in breaking down the (postcommunist or pseudo-democratic) bureaucratic authoritarian regime, the contrast in the viability of civil society between democratized Korea and its Eastern and Central European counterparts is quite remarkable.

[1] Sunhyuk Kim, "South Korea: Confrontational Legacy and Democratic Contributions," in Alaqappa, *Civil Society and Political Change in Asia.*

[2] Marc M. Howard, *The Weakness of Civil Society in Post-Communist Europe* (Cambridge: Cambridge University Press, 2003); Maria R. Markus, "Decent Society and/or Civil Society?," *Social Research* 68 (2001), 1011–30.

[3] Terry Karl, "Dilemmas of Democratization in Latin America," *Comparative Politics* 23 (1990), 1–21. For a detailed discussion of the mass-ascendant or civil society-led democratization, see Gullermo O'Donnell and Philip C. Schmitter, *Transitions from Authoritarian Rule* (Baltimore: Johns Hopkins University Press, 1986), esp. chap. 5; Vladimir Tismaneanu, *Reinventing Politics: Eastern Europe from Stalin to Havel* (New York: Free Press, 1992).

[4] This particular characterization originally referred to Polish civil society. See Juan L. Linz and Alfred Stepan, *Problems of Democratic Transition and Consolidation: Southern Europe, South America, and Post-Communist Europe* (Baltimore: Johns Hopkins University Press, 1996), 271. But it is now widely acknowledged that ethical civil society was the defining characteristic of the democratic transition in Eastern and Central European postcommunist countries. See Vladimir Tismaneanu, "Civil Society, Pluralism, and the Future of East and Central Europe," *Social Research* 68 (2001), 977–91.

For most comparative political scientists, the most eminent question has been, "Why such a sudden disappearance of civic energy in postcommunist Europe?" Most often, the inertial lifestyle that the previous rigid party-state has engendered over the past half century has been singled out as the most crucial source of the problem. That is, blame is placed on the citizenry's fundamental dependence on the party-state for virtually everything concerning their life: jobs, income, consumer goods, education, housing, health care, and social and geographic mobility.[5] According to Marc Howard, a lack of desire to participate in voluntary organizations in the postcommunist people follows from their past life experience under the ossified bureaucratic authoritarian regime that had widened the gap between authentic private and hypocritical public lives, deepened the mistrust of formal political organizations, and fostered friendship networks in the private sphere.[6]

Then, it should be asked, why is there such an interesting continuity between democratizing civil society and consolidating civil society in South Korea? Can the neo-institutionalist reasoning of the kind Valerie Bunce and Marc Howard adopt equally explain the political viability of Korean civil society in the consolidating stage of democratization? Moreover, given the social scientific truism that once democratized, mass-ascendant civil societies should go back to "normality" for democratic consolidation,[7] how can we make sense of Korea's postdemocratic civil society that is characterized by the national alliances of a multitude of large and small civic groups that together, as they profess, represent the voice of the (entire) people (i.e., the Korean public) and the public good, thus contending vigorously with the state for moral-political supremacy?[8] In this regard, the functional-institutional understanding of civil society as "a mediating conduit between the private sphere and the state," which is prevalent in the social science literature, is far short of capturing the essentially ethical nature of civil society as well as its normative value and force.

First of all, it should be noted, the ethical character of Korean civil society is qualitatively different from that found in postcommunist Europe. There, as Vaclav Havel famously noted, "living within a lie" confronted "living within

[5] Valerie Bunce, *Subversive Institutions: The Design and the Destruction of Socialism and the State* (Cambridge: Cambridge University Press, 1999), 24.

[6] Howard, *Weakness of Civil Society*, 26–9.

[7] For this argument, see Larry Diamond, *Developing Democracy: Toward Consolidation* (Baltimore: Johns Hopkins University Press, 1999); Steven Fish, "Rethinking Civil Society: Russia's Fourth Transition," *Journal of Democracy* 5 (1994), 31–42.

[8] In this respect, Korean civil society is distinguished from Japanese civil society as well, which is characterized with a plethora of small, local groups and a paucity of large, independent advocacy groups. See Robert Pekkanen, *Japanese Dual Civil Society* (Stanford: Stanford University Press, 2006). This does not mean that Korean civil society is a socially monolithic and ethically monistic unitary entity that only promotes conformism; quite contrarily, my point is that Korean civil society offers an incubator of common democratic citizenship and a powerful bulwark for public freedom.

the truth"; that is, the demands of the posttotalitarian system conflicted with the real aims of life.[9] So, in the truest sense, the revolution of 1989 had a liberating force, the energy of which was devoted to overcoming the system-induced alienation of the authentic private life from the hypocritical public life and that of the public self from the private self. Put differently, it was ethical in that it aimed at truly authentic and empowered individuality.[10]

Despite the similar confrontational legacy, however, Korean civil society seems to hardly be predicated on a philosophical humanism that purports to overcome self-alienation. This is not to say that such a concern is absolutely foreign to Korean civil society. The student-led protests and civil movements in the 1970s and 1980s indeed had such characteristics as many of them were guided in principle by left ideologies that are devoted to human emancipation.[11] But the civic energy that has been galvanizing Korean democratic civil society, which has become citizen-based and far more quotidian and spontaneous over the past two decades, seems to come from elsewhere. What is largely dismissed in mainstream political science is that the civic energy that invigorates civil society in postdemocratic Korea comes not so much from democratic values or principles as such, with which Koreans are culturally unfamiliar,[12] but from the traditional, characteristically Confucian, social mores or habits in which they are deeply imbedded.[13]

In this chapter, I argue that the extraordinary viability of Korean democratic civil society can be explained in terms of the social practice of *chŏng*, the Koreans' familial affectionate sentiments and the peculiar civic virtue – what I call "*uri* (we)-responsibility" – that it generates. That is, I present *chŏng* as a vital ethical force in invigorating Korean civil society and empowering

9 Vaclav Havel, "The Power of the Powerless," in *Living in Truth*, ed. Jan Vladislav (London: Faber and Faber, 1987), 36–122.

10 Timothy Ash states that the revolution of 1989 was "a springtime of nations, but not necessarily of nationalism; of societies, aspiring to be civil; and above all, of citizens." Timothy G. Ash, "The Year of Truth," in *The Revolutions of 1989*, ed. Vladimir Tismaneanu (London: Routledge, 1999), 119.

11 See Mi Park, "Organizing Dissent Against Authoritarianism: The South Korean Student Movement in the 1980s," *Korea Journal* 45 (2005), 261–89. But as I noted elsewhere, political dissenters in the 1980s were equally inspired by what can be called "radical Confucianism." See Sungmoon Kim, "Transcendental Collectivism and Participatory Politics in Democratized Korea," *Critical Review of International Social and Political Philosophy* 11 (2008), 57–77, 59–63.

12 Some Korean political scientists therefore assert that Koreans must be cognitively and conatively attuned to (West-originated) democratic values and principles. For such an argument see Doh Chull Shin and Chong-Min Park, "The Mass Public and Democratic Politics in South Korea: Exploring the Subjective World of Democratization in Flux," in Chu et al., *How East Asians View Democracy.*

13 For some illuminating discussions on this issue, see Geir Helgesen, *Democracy and Authority in Korea: The Cultural Dimension in Korean Politics* (Surrey: Curzon, 1998); Chaibong Hahm, "The Ironies of Confucianism," *Journal of Democracy* 15 (2004), 93–107.

Korean citizenship.[14] I am not, however, interested in merely demonstrating the democratic implications of the social practice of *chŏng*. My central purpose in this chapter is to make a normative claim that for it to be culturally relevant, socially practicable, and politically vibrant, Korean civil society must be *a* kind of Confucian civil society that operates on familial affectionate sentiments, because not only do they motivate civil and political actions, thus making Korean democracy more participatory, but more important, they constitute the core of public reason on which citizens can draw when they engage in public deliberation, thereby making Korean democracy "Confucian" in character. This chapter, therefore, serves as a case study that illustrates how familial affectionate sentiments (especially critical affection) can function as public reason in a particular Confucian-cultural and democratic political context.

The chapter consists of five sections. After this introductory section, the second section presents two civil action cases from the 2000s that show how *chŏng*-induced *uri*-responsibility can be creatively accommodated in and invigorate a democratic civil society in Korea, making it uniquely Korean and Confucian. The third section is mainly devoted to the conceptual clarification of key concepts like *uri* and *chŏng* from social-psychological and psychocultural perspectives as a preparatory step to construct *uri*-responsibility as a robust democratic civic virtue. Section IV explores the political implications of *uri* in civil society with reference to Rousseau's idea of general will and then articulates the cultural peculiarity of *uri*-responsibility by comparing it to two Kantian accounts of responsibility (moral responsibility and political responsibility). This chapter concludes by revisiting Korean *chŏng*ish civil society from the broader normative perspective of Confucian democracy.

Cases

Case 1: The Citizens' Alliance for the 2000 General Election (CAGE) (2000)

On 12 January 2000, nearly three months before South Korea's sixteenth general election for the National Assembly, about four hundred (later joined by an additional one hundred) small and large citizens' movement organizations nationwide formed the Citizens' Alliance for the 2000 General Election (CAGE). CAGE was formed to prevent the political parties from nominating "unqualified" candidates (rejection campaign), and then, ultimately, to defeat

[14] That is to say, I do not argue that Korean democratization is solely attributable to the politics of *chŏng*, nor do I attempt to demonstrate or establish the causal relationship between the politics of *chŏng* and democracy in Korea. My aim in this chapter is characteristically Tocquevillian, in the sense that I am exploring the democratic implications of *chŏng* as the Korean-Confucian habit of the heart. As I noted in Introduction (note 51), my methodology here (and in the following chapters) is what Stephen G. Salkever calls "explanatory evaluation," in which empiricality and normativity are entwined (see his *Finding the Mean: Theory and Practice in Aristotelian Political Philosophy* [Princeton: Princeton University Press, 1990]).

those who were nonetheless nominated to run in the election (defeat campaign). More generally, however, CAGE was formed to reform political society that, over a decade after democratization, was still rife with factionalism and nepotism based on chronic regionalism, a lack of democracy *within* political parties, money-based corruption, and insufficient accountability. Indeed, from the viewpoint of ordinary citizens, the period of democratic consolidation turned out to be a period of failure for political parties and elected representatives.[15]

On 24 January, as part of a plan to pressure political parties into withholding nominations from particular candidate, CAGE unveiled a list of sixty-seven unqualified candidates on its Internet home page (www.ngokorea.org).[16] In a nationwide opinion poll taken right after this revelation, more than 80 percent of Korean citizens supported CAGE's rejection campaign, while more than 60 percent said that they would not vote for these "unfit" candidates. On 30 January, despite the current election law that banned all citizens' organizations except labor unions from election campaigning activities (i.e., clauses 58, 87, 254), and with support from thousands of unaffiliated citizens, CAGE took to the streets to assert their constitutional right of freedom of association and assembly, which they claimed should trump election laws.[17]

On 2 February 2000, CAGE publicized a second list of forty-seven unqualified candidates, and began to pressure political parties to revise the election law to allow all citizens organizations to campaign. However, lawmakers of both the ruling and opposition parties collaborated across party lines to protect their vested interests by revising the law only minimally, leaving the clauses in question virtually intact (8 February 2000). Those who were uneasy with the grass-roots challenge to the national congress aligned themselves with the conservative news media, and hinted at a "conspiracy" between the citizens' organizations leaders and the incumbent government to stage the rejection campaign.[18]

Nevertheless, CAGE's rejection campaign greatly influenced the major political parties' nomination process. For instance, the opposition Grand National Party excluded a number of candidates who had allegedly used regional antagonisms to further their political careers. This caused a massive party defection, in which the new Democratic National Party emerged. This new Gyeongsang-province-based party made clear that it would compete with the Grand National

[15] Jangjip Choi, "Democratization, Civil Society and the Civil Social Movement in Korea: The Significance of the Citizens' Alliance for the 2000 General Elections," *Korea Journal* 40 (2000), 26–57, 42.

[16] The criteria were destruction of the democratic constitutional order through antihumanity activities (specifically, collaboration with the past authoritarian regimes), corruption, election law violation, instigation of regionalist sentiments, tax evasion, and conscription irregularities.

[17] The election law at issue was made in 1989 to prohibit such antidemocratic (un)civil organizations as those that mushroomed during the previous military authoritarian regimes from political activities.

[18] *OhmyNews*, 4 February 2000; 5 February 2000 (online).

Party for regional supremacy in Gyeongsang province to win the next presidential election over the incumbent Jeolla-province-based New Millennium Democratic Party, thereby further provoking regional antagonisms.

The reemergence of regional divides infuriated many, especially young, Koreans hoping for a new national and civic Korea above parochial regionalism. Korea's well-developed cyberspace provided an open and public outlet in which the ordinary, previously alienated Koreans could freely express their political opinions. During this period more than 900,000 netizens visited CAGE's home page, while more than 15,000 messages were posted.[19] A typical message read as follows:

As opposed to autocracy, the defining characteristic of democracy is that responsibility falls on the people. If there are corrupt politicians in democracy, it is the responsibility of the people who elected them. Frankly speaking, the quality of *our* politicians are very low; yet it is also true that *our* [democratic] quality is equally low because [after all] it is *we* who elected them on the grounds of regional attachment, nepotism, or *our* blind tendency to select the incumbent party. It is *our* inadvertent votes that have produced such corrupt politicians.... Therefore, *we* might not be entitled to criticize them. But *we* must take responsibility for *our* democracy. To be responsible for the democracy that *we* have corrupted, *we* must take action not to have such unqualified politicians in the political arena.... No one has done anything [about this situation]. *We* have just watched things happening.... [But] because of this very fact, the citizens' political reform movement that *we* are now engaging in is of great significance.[20]

Note the writer is appealing to a communal democratic sentiment transcending the individual Korean citizen: "*We* should take responsibility for something for which *we* are not directly accountable." "I" is never pronounced here; rather it is hidden behind "We." Furthermore, "We" is in no case a claim for a specific group's political right. Undoubtedly, the focus is on "responsibility" shared by all of *us*, Korean citizens, however tormenting it is, because *this* democracy is *our* democracy; because the corruption of *our* democracy falls on *us*. This very "fact" obligates us to collective political and moral responsibility, namely, *uri*-responsibility (*uri* being the Korean word for "we").

After the major political parties had announced their official nominations, CAGE's strategy shifted to the defeat of those who had been "wrongly" nominated. CAGE's *rejection-defeat* campaign proved a great success: of 86 candidates on CAGE's blacklist, 59 were defeated. Furthermore, 94 out of 207 incumbent congressmen who ran in the sixteenth general election failed to be reelected. Meanwhile, 112 new candidates ran successfully in the elections to enter the National Assembly, taking 41 percent of all seats. Perhaps most dramatically, CAGE's dual campaign successfully rearranged a political landscape that was previously structured on parochial regional interests.

[19] *Hangyeoreh Shinmun*, 15 May 2002 (online).

[20] Originally from http://www.peoplepower21.org/article/article_view.php?article_id=752, but this web page is no longer available. The English translation is mine.

Was CAGE's citizens' movement in 2000 a "civil revolution" or "the second June Uprising," as many Koreans call it? Korean scholars are cautious in their evaluations because they wonder whether CAGE's negative strategy of screening the unfit candidates did not, albeit unintentionally, help reinforce the existing conservative political landscape, thus failing to direct popular interest to such issues as labor problems, which a positive campaign could have mobilized.[21] More crucially, some scholars are skeptical about the impact it had on the democratization of party structures, in particular, and party politics, in general, a key indicator of democratic consolidation.[22] Nevertheless, from a normative perspective, the CAGE-led citizens' movement in 2000 was successful in revivifying a new type of national civil ethos,[23] which transcends parochial and uncivil regional attachments. In other words, the CAGE-led citizen's movement infused Korean citizens with *uri*-responsibility derived, as we shall see, from *chŏng*.

Case 2: The Civil Upheaval around Dual Citizen Military Dodgers (2005)

On 29 June 2005, the National Assembly in Korea roundly rejected a law that would strip those who abandoned their Korean citizenship to avoid the military draft of their status as overseas Koreans and deprive them of all rights as Koreans. Reacting to this decision, most Koreans raised a great uproar because the revision to the Act on the Immigration and Legal Status of Overseas Koreans had been regarded as a due follow-up to the May 2005 revision of the Nationality Law that bars dual citizens from giving up their Korean citizenship unless they complete mandatory military service. In fact, the revision was submitted by a lawmaker of the opposition party and was greeted with a landslide of popular support, as it had been observed that long lines of young dual nationals were forming at immigration offices to resign their Korean citizenship before the law went into effect.

Thousands of frustrated ordinary Korean citizens vehemently demanded that the names of those who voted against the bill be publicized – especially those "betrayers" who had rooted for the bill in the earlier stage of legislation and then withdrew their support. Some of them went further to organize a candlelight demonstration and launch new civic groups to press the legislature. Why such a fuss? Some liberals pointed out the danger of statism or nationalism that would threaten to thwart globalization. Others regretted the ordinary

[21] Choi, "Democratization, Civil Society and the Civil Social Movement in Korea," 53. Also see Dong-choon Kim, "Growth and Crisis of the Korean Citizens' Movement," *Korea Journal* 46, (2006), 99–128, 112.

[22] See Linz and Stepan, *Problems of Democratic Transition and Consolidation*, 8–10; Diamond, *Developing Democracy*; Jangjip Choi, *Minjuhaw ihuui Minjujuui* [Democracy after Democratization] (Seoul: Humanitas, 2005).

[23] Edward Shils understands civility in terms of "civil collective self-consciousness," and by "collective" he generally means "national" (*The Virtue of Civility: Selected Essays on Liberalism, Tradition, and Civil Society*, ed. Steve Grosby [Indianapolis: Liberty Fund, 1997], 71).

Koreans' ignorance of the modern principle of citizenship/nationality, that is, citizenship as a private right, hence a matter of personal choice. But does the liberal individualism on which these questions are tacitly grounded truly represent ordinary Koreans' view of citizenship?

Despite some liberals' framing the issue in terms of liberal individualism versus conservative nationalism, what complicated the issue was whether citizenship could be decoupled from social obligations.[24] What most Koreans could not understand was the so-called liberal idea that citizenship is a matter of the law and ultimately that of private choice. It was the concept of a pure individual right, or in Michael Sandel's words an "unencumbered" self's claim to the absolute right to private happiness that ordinary Koreans could not make sense of.[25] What infuriated them was not dual citizenship per se, but the fact that it was taken advantage of as a convenient means to circumvent civic obligations, thus making citizenship socially void and rendering the constitutional law to be only a matter of parchment.

At stake was not whether or not an individual's private right is bad or incompatible with Korean Confucian public culture. The real issue consisted in some dual citizens' lack of *uri*-responsibility, a collective (though exercised individually) moral responsibility of the kind proposed in one netizen's following proposal: "Let *us* make efforts, with sharp reason and calm judgment, to rebuild *our* mother country Korea on the right foundation and let a deserving leader lead it. [After all] the true patriots of this country are *us*, people, who silently yet assiduously do what is to be done. Shouldn't it then be none other than *us* who take responsibility to change *our* country?"[26]

Uri-responsibility is not a blind attachment to the nation, or patriotism of the kind George Kateb disparaged as "a commitment to the system of premature, violent death, inflicted and accepted."[27] *Uri*-responsibility works through *chŏng*, especially *miun chŏng* (literally, affectionate hatred) in this particular case. It was not that Koreans all love their country no matter what, but because, despite all the problems of which they are acutely aware and, for the most part, not individually responsible for incurring, they were *nevertheless* willing to take responsibility for them. Thus understood, *uri*-responsibility that

[24] On this question, see David Miller, *Citizenship and National Identity* (Cambridge: Polity, 2000).

[25] Michael J. Sandel, *Liberalism and the Limits of Justice* (Cambridge: Cambridge University Press, 1982).

[26] *OhmyNews*, 15 June 2005 (ID: jkrho777).

[27] George Kateb, "Is Patriotism a Mistake?," in *Patriotism and Other Mistakes* (New Haven: Yale University Press), 8. It is important to note that patriotism as a civic virtue is not incompatible with (civic-oriented) liberalism. See essays by Michael Walzer, Benjamin R. Barber, and Kwame Anthony Appiah in Joshua Cohen (ed.), *For Love of Country: Debating the Limits of Patriotism* (Boston: Beacon, 1996) and also Anna Stilz, *Liberal Loyalty: Freedom, Obligation, and the State* (Princeton: Princeton University Press, 2009). Therefore, the fact that Korean citizens upheld patriotism as a democratic civic virtue does not make them illiberal.

works on both *goun chŏng* (positive affection) and *miun chŏng* (critical affection)[28] constitutes the very meaning of the person's social right, and this special sense of collective moral responsibility underpins the national consciousness, which is the backbone of civil society and the matrix of citizenship according to Edward Shils.[29]

In the next section I will investigate the nature of *chŏng* and *uri* from social psychological perspectives and discuss how *chŏng*-induced *uri*-responsibility is distinguished from the liberal, particularly Kantian, accounts of responsibility, thus capable of buttressing the civic foundation of Korean-Confucian democracy.

The Social Psychology of *Chŏng*

In his rebuttal against Hein Cho who attributes the contemporary viability of Korean civil society to traditional Confucian culture,[30] David Steinberg chastises so-called we-ism, which is commonly found in Korean society, by asserting that it serves only to foster a "spirit of conformity," as the single greatest obstacle to the establishment of truly "civil" society in Korea.[31] Implicit in Steinberg's criticism is that the Korean "we" (*uri* in Korean) is so fundamentally and overbearingly a primordial and prepolitical group identity that it is incompatible with the basic requirements of the authentic civil society to which social and political pluralism is central.

However, Steinberg fails to distinguish the politically constituted we (we as citizens) from the social-psychological we by associating we exclusively with the latter, especially with its negative aspects. On the social-psychological level, Steinberg's claim could have *some* relevance because, as Sang-chin Choi's social psychological study shows, Koreans tend to think that *we* include as its inherent properties "identity, oneness, mutual dependence, mutual protection, and mutual acceptance" to the extent that "Korean's private self (or individual self) and social self (or collectivized self) overlap."[32] Admittedly (but arguably), the social-psychologically constituted *uri* in Korean society is qualitatively different from social groups (especially voluntary associations) in Western liberal societies wherein the personal identity of the independent, autonomous, and

[28] For the social psychological study of *goun chŏng* and *minun chŏng*, see Sang-chin Choi, Ji-young Kim, and Ki-bum Kim, "*Jeong* (*miun jeong goun jeong*)ui simlijeok gujo, haengwi mit gineungganui gujojeok gwangye bunseok [An Analysis of the Structural Relations between the Psychological Structure, Behaviors, and Functions of *Chŏng* (*minu chŏng, goun chŏng*)]" *Korean Journal of Social and Personality Psychology* 14 (2000), 203–22.

[29] Shils, *Virtue of Civility*, 207–9.

[30] Hein Cho, "The Historical Origin of Civil Society in Korea," *Korea Journal* 37 (1997), 24–41.

[31] David I. Steinberg, "Civil Society and Human Rights in Korea: On Contemporary and Classical Orthodoxy and Ideology," *Korea Journal* 37 (1997), 145–65, 151.

[32] Sang-chin Choi, "The Third-Person-Psychology and the First-Person-Psychology: Two Perspectives on Human Relations," *Korean Social Science Journal* 25 (1998), 239–64, 246.

individually distinctive self is preserved, because the Korean *uri* is normally accompanied by the group-specific self-transformation of individual participants, generating a unique group dynamic that is rarely found in liberal voluntary associations.[33]

That being said, the argument that social conformism that suppresses or even destroys individuality is the most salient feature of the group dynamic of *uri* is not only farfetched, but seriously misleading. What Steinberg overlooks is that the social formation of *uri* has nothing to do with "deindividuation" in which self-identity simply collapses within the group. What it entails is rather "depersonalization," in which individual self-identity is not only preserved but even developed.[34] To see the difference between deindividuation and depersonalization more clearly, it should be noted that the Korean self is hardly the entity-like, self-containing, and autonomously functioning "independent self" as customarily conceptualized in the Western scientific psychology and as naturalized in the modern liberal political theory (e.g., social contract theory). For the independent self, depersonalization is no different than deindividuation, which is tantamount to the total collapse of the self or the self's complete fusion with the group, which was the case with the ordinary Nazi soldiers.[35] In this psychological process, individual egos are enmeshed in the group ego, enabling the latter to be the only meaningful and lively, yet often immensely violent, agent.

In marked contrast, the "interdependent self" that constitutes the Korean "I" (*na*)[36] scarcely undergoes a total collapse of the self, which generates a massive fusion with the group self that forms a group ego. Since it does not attempt the containment of the pure self (a rationally controlled, self-sufficient self) from others and since it does not construe interdependence as pathetic dependence, the interdependent self seldom experiences a violent eruption of the group ego.[37] Instead, the personal empowerment of the interdependent self is made possible by forming *uri*-relationship with other equally interdependent selves. As such, *uri* is the fundamentally relation-centered group self, unlike the self-contained, power-seeking group ego, which emerges when the self becomes porous to itself and to others. Therefore, while the latter is the fusion of egos, the former refers *only* to the overlapping of egos. Pyong-choon Hahm, therefore, understands the Korean we in terms of "inter-ego relationship."

[33] Sang-chin Choi, *Han'gukin shimlihak* [The Psychology of the Korean People] (Seoul: Chung Ang University Press, 2000), 145.

[34] Ibid., 149. The concepts such as deindividuation and depersonalization are Choi's.

[35] Christopher R. Browning, *Ordinary Men: Reserve Police Battalion 101 and the Final Solution in Poland* (New York: Harper, 1992).

[36] Sang-chin Choi and Ki-bum Kim, "Han'gugin selpeuui teukseong: Seoguui selpeugaenyeomgwa daebireul jungsimeuro" [The Characteristics of the Korean Self: In Comparison with the Western Concept of the Self], *Korean Journal of Social and Personality Psychology* 13 (1999), 275–92.

[37] This partially explains why group psychology is underdeveloped and unpopular in Korea.

Where egos overlap and interlock however, there may be interpenetration and existential continuum, but no dependence. The shamanistic person would find a life in which egos are all autonomous, separate, discrete, and self-sufficient too cold, impersonal, lonely, and inhuman. It should be noted, however, that the overlap of egos in shamanistic culture does not signify a merger or fusion of ego. Rather, the overlapping egos interpenetrate one another, forming a commonly shared area, while leaving the remainder different and distinct. The resulting condition is neither a single ego nor two discrete egos, but something indeterminate which can only be described as something more than one but less than two.[38]

Quite often, both political scientists and social theorists tend to think of interdependent or relational self as an underdeveloped self – a primordial self that must be transformed into the independent "modern" self of the kind Ernest Gellner calls the "modular self."[39] The Korean interdependent self is, in Charles Taylor's words, "anti-structural," in that it is much closer to what he terms the "porous self" (of the earlier enchanted world) than to the "buffered self" – a clearly demarcated, self-coherent modern selfhood.[40] It is, however, unclear why we can't put both independent and interdependent, and porous and buffered selves on an equal footing, that is, view them as equally plausible types of developed selfhood in our contemporary moral and political life, especially given the observation that interdependent self is less susceptible to the deterioration into the pathological group ego.[41]

This is not to insist that *uri* is immune from its own problems. As Steinberg rightly points out, downward social conformism is one of its negative aspects. Nevertheless, the following must be remembered: First, *uri* as a social-psychological construct is not a pure primordial group identity as some critics assume; second, *uri* is primarily concerned with affectionate internal relations among the participants; and finally, heavy social conformism is *one* negative factor that sometimes accompanies *uri*, and not, by any means, its full essence. If *uri* cannot be identified as the all-encompassing group ego that is inherently dangerous, what then helps to prevent *uri* from deteriorating into it?

Chŏng is what makes the intersubjective overlapping possible in the formation of the Korean we by providing an emotional glue or, in a psychoanalytical language, a "transitional space," in and through which interdependent selves

38 Pyong-choon Hahm, *Korean Jurisprudence, Politics and Culture* (Seoul: Yonsei University Press, 1986), 323. For studies with a similar observation, see C. Fred Alford, *Think No Evil: Korean Values in the Age of Globalization* (Ithaca: Cornell University Press, 1999); Geung-Ho Cho, *Han'gukin ihaeui gaenyeomteul* [Reading Koreans Culturally: A Psychological Approach] (Seoul: Nanam, 2003).

39 Ernest Gellner, *Conditions of Liberty: Civil Society and Its Rivals* (New York: Penguin, 1996), 97–101. For a classical study on individual modernization, see Alex Inkeles, "Making Men Modern: On the Causes and Consequences of Individual Change in Six Developing Countries," *American Journal of Sociology* 75 (1969), 208–25.

40 Charles Taylor, *A Secular Age* (Cambridge, MA: Belknap, 2007), 37–8.

41 I raised this question in Sungmoon Kim, "On Korean Dual Civil Society: Thinking through Tocqueville and Confucius," *Contemporary Political Theory* 9 (2010), 434–57, 444.

can freely flow into each other.[42] Though *chŏng* is often spoken of in terms of a person's inner characteristic (*chŏng* as personality), its more significant and widely performed usage is as affectionate 'relationality' in ordinary social interactions among Koreans. However, this analytical distinction should not be too rigidly held because, in reality, the two are inextricably intertwined. That is, personal *chŏng* is what makes an otherwise privately encapsulated self into the interdependent self that is marked by a porous and relational *chŏng*. Then, *chŏng*, in turn, constantly situates the self in intersubjective *uri*-relationships, helps to internalize such intersubjective relationality within the self, and ultimately makes relationality integral to personality. In this sense, the Korean interdependent self is a *chŏng*ish self and as such the Korean self is fundamentally relational.

That *chŏng* is affectionate relationality, however, does not imply that any relationality is directly analogous to *chŏng*, just as any interdependent self could not be the Korean self.[43] For social relationality to be a *chŏng*ish relationality, it should be oriented to the creation of *uri*-relationship. Put differently, *chŏng* is a felt *uri*-ness and *uri*-ness is a realized *chŏng*.[44] This seemingly tautological explanation, however, is neither illogical nor irrational if we consider that the relational boundary that *uri*-ness (or *uri*-self) sets up is, in essence, a cultural-epistemological boundary as well. In other words, the social function of the *uri* boundary is not limited in separating *uri* from the other, which could entail the exclusive *uri*-ness. Its further-reaching social implication is that it produces its own verbal and nonverbal semiotic practices which those who are not immersed in Korean culture often find difficult (but not impossible) to master. *Chŏng* is the very key to such a semiotic cultural code. In short, *chŏng* is an emotionally cognitive *uri*-oriented relationality.

What then is the "cultural-epistemological boundary," after which *uri*-self is modeled and which is to be reproduced in broader social relations? Korean

42 Alford, *Think No Evil*, 49. Also see Sang-chin Choi and Jangju Lee, "Jeongui simlijeok gujowa sahoe: Munhwajeok gineung bunseok" [An Analysis of the Psychological Structure of Chŏng and Its Cultural Function], *Korean Journal of Social and Personality Psychology* 13 (1999), 219–34; Sang-chin Choi and Gyu-seok Han, "Gyoryuhaengwireul tonghaebon han'gukinui sahoesimli" [The Social Psychology of the Korean People from the Perspective of Interpersonal Relations], in *Han'gukmunhawwa han'gukin* [Korean Culture and the Korean People], ed. the Association of International Korean Studies (Seoul: Sagyejeol, 1998), 161–93; Yeong-ryong Kim, "Janjanhan jeongui nara han'guk" [Korea, a Serene Country of *Chŏng*], in *Chŏng, Chemyeon, Yeonjul geurigo hanguginui ingan gwangye* [*Chŏng*, Social Face, Network, and the Interpersonal Relationships of the Korean People], ed. Tae-seop Im (Seoul: Hannarae, 1995); Choi, Kim, and Kim, "*Jeong* (*miun jeong goun jeong*)ui simlijeok gujo, haengwi mit gineungganui gujojeok gwangye bunseok"; Cho, *Han'gukin ihaeui gaenyeomteul*, chap. 9.

43 It should be recalled that *chŏng* is the uniquely *Korean* phenomenon of (Confucian) familial affectionate sentiments. That is, familial affectionate sentiments (and interdependent selfhood) can be differently manifested in East Asian Confucian societies, depending on each society's particular geographical, social, and local-cultural context.

44 Choi and Lee, "Jeongui simlijeok gujowa sahoe," 224.

scholars widely agree that traditional Korean family relations present the prototype of *uri*-self, and they are strongly convinced that *chŏng* originates from them, particularly from a strong moral and psychological attachment between parents and children.[45] Though some scholars such as Pyong-choon Hahm and Sang-chin Choi cautiously ascribe the origin of *chŏng* to a pre-Confucian, indigenous Korean folk culture, many are increasingly persuaded that *chŏng* is a Confucian psychological phenomenon.[46] It is beyond the scope of this book to resolve the academic controversy on the origin of *chŏng* or to prove that *chŏng* is philosophically connected with Confucian virtue ethics. What is less controversial is that *chŏng* offers a powerful empirical case for the social psychological manifestation of Confucian familialism that I have investigated in Chapters 5 and 6.[47] It may not be accurate to call *chŏng* a moral sentiment as it is understood in the Mencian-Confucian ethical tradition, that is, as Heaven-endowed natural moral proclivity. But it is indisputable that *chŏng* is a civil passion (more accurately, it consists of a pack of civil passions) that is characteristically Confucian-familial.

What is important is that the (Confucian) family is the most important social metaphor of the Korean collective identity of all sizes. That is to say, when it is applied to the entire nation, the "family-relational we" constitutes the core of the "imagined community" of ordinary Koreans. Thus understood, Korea's *uri* imagined community is a *chŏng*-based ethico-cultural and cultural-epistemological entity.[48]

Having found that *chŏng* is an *uri*-building familial relationality, we can finally come to a better grasp of the internal structure of *chŏng*ish relationality. Since the family, except in the case of marriage, is a natural given in the sense

45 Ibid., 230.

46 Bong-yeong Choi, *Han'gukinui sahoejeok seonggyeok* [The Social Character of the Korean People] (Seoul: Neutinamu, 1994); Deuk-woong Han, "Han'gukyuhakui shimlihak" [A Psychological Study of Korean Confucianism], in *Dongyangshimlihak: Seogushimlihake daehan mosaek* [East Asian Psychology: In Search of an Alternative to Western Psychology], ed. Sang-chin Choi (Seoul: Jishiksaneopsa, 1999), 163–285; Cho, *Han'gukin ihaeui gaenyeomteul.*

47 It is worth noting that Su-young Ryu's empirical psychological study of Confucian values among the Korean people is premised on the assumption that in Korea, *chŏng* is the social manifestation of *ren*, the Confucian virtue par excellence (see her "Han'gukinui yugyojeok gachicheukjeongmunhang gaebal yeon'gu" [Item Development for Korean Confucian Values]," *Korean Journal of Management* 15 [2007], 171–205). In other work, I have suggested that "*chŏng* may be conceptualized as a de-metaphysicized, de-philosophized, de-individualized, and hence collectivized version of *ren*" (see Kim, "Transcendental Collectivism and Participatory Politics in Democratized Korea," 68).

48 For how this special cultural entity operates, see Sang-chin Choi, "Han'gukinui maeum" [The Mind of the Korean People], in Choi, *Dongyangshimlihak*, 377–479; Sang-chin Choi and Jeong-un Kim, "Jiphapjeok uimiguseonge daehan munhwashimlihakjeok jeopgeunuiroseoui munhwasimjeongshimlihak" ["Shim-Cheong" Psychology as a Cultural Psychological Approach to Collective Meaning Construction], *Korean Journal of Social and Personality Psychology* 12 (1998), 79–96; Choi, "Third-Person-Psychology and the First-Person-Psychology," 252–8; Choi, *Han'gukin shimlihak*, 102–20.

that one does not enter family relationships, choosing voluntarily his or her parents and siblings, *chŏng*ish relationality cannot be equated directly with positive affection (*goun chŏng*). We should not dismiss the reality that family (and familial) relations are frequently accompanied by immense psychological tensions, which can engender devastating mental illness. The chronic conflict between mother-in-law and daughter-in-law that is widely found in traditional Korean-Confucian families is a case in point.[49] What is interesting about the ordinary Koreans' social psychology is that, when it has been fairly long and constantly experienced, they count (and experience) negative feelings (such as hatred and resentment) toward their intimate ones, as another form of affection. Koreans call it "*miun chŏng*" (critical affection).[50] Miun *chŏng* is generated when the people have long experienced all aspects of human relationships (good or bad and joyful or painful) and maturely sublimated them into their relational, interdependent selfhood. It is, for example, a sort of mixed feeling that a daughter-in-law would feel after she has departed from her husband's family to start her own nuclear family: "I have come to have both *miun chŏng* and *goun chŏng* with my mother-in-law while having been entangled in all sorts of tensions and conflicts over the years."

Denser and deeper *chŏng* is one that has been steadily cultivated as a psychological and ethical complex that encompasses both *miun chŏng* and *goun chŏng*. If one looks at Korean family relations and, by extension, Korean *uri*-relations in terms of power relations, as some liberal feminists would be tempted to, the internal mechanism of *chŏng*, especially its *miun chŏng* aspect, can be easily eclipsed. Then, it would be impossible to properly make sense of *uri*-responsibility of the kind that we have seen in the cases presented earlier, because *uri*-responsibility is nourished on *chŏng* that includes not only *goun chŏng* but, more crucially, *miun chŏng*.

Thus far, we have examined *chŏng* and *chŏng*ish relationality from a social psychological perspective. The point is that *uri* as a complex social psychological construct cannot be identified with an overweening collective identity that simply promotes conformism. Nor can it be equated with the tyranny of majority or mob rule. To the contrary, as a set of tension-ridden familial-civil passions, *chŏng* is illustrative of the relational dynamic between Korean citizens and their hard-won democracy. In fact, the torment felt by the Korean netizen quoted in case 1 was essentially *miun chŏng* and his or her civic patriotism was based on the same logic: "I/We hate my/our democracy that I/We have now. *Nonetheless*, I/We, as a member of our political community, have a (task) responsibility for it, though I/We did not individually cause the problems." Here our (*miun*) *chŏng* seems to do injustice to us by shifting task

[49] Bou-young Rhi, "Mental Illness in Its Confucian Context," in Slote and DeVos, *Confucianism and the Family*, 285–310.

[50] Choi, Kim, and Kim, "*Jeong* (*miun jeong goun jeong*)ui simlijeok gujo, haengwi mit gineung-ganui gujojeok gwangye bunseok."

responsibility from them to *us* who have no task responsibility, thus letting those who are really responsible off the hook. But the real point is our deep concern for our body politic and our democracy. By saying "nonetheless," the netizen (and many Korean citizens) did not pessimistically affirm the reality as it is. In 2000, for instance, by *we* the (young) Koreans never meant a random collectivity. What they meant was a new Korean public or democratic citizenship, as opposed to the uncivil, parochial regionalism that had corrupted Korean politics for decades.

Thus understood, *uri* is not only a sociopsychological or psychocultural construct; when *uri*-responsibility, which is rooted in *chŏng*, is exercised in the public space of civil society, it is also a political practice. Of course, the political *uri* is profoundly predicated on the various levels, and types, of social practice of *uri*-formation. But the political practice of *uri*-formation is occasioned in the course of constructing the "*uri*-world," which is an open, deliberative, and contestatory public space. From this perspective, the recent invigoration of civil society in Korea cannot be approached in terms of a natural and unmediated extension of the psychocultural *uri*. The cases show another, namely, *political* dynamic of *uri*-formation that cannot plainly be reduced to social psychology alone.

Uri-World and General Will

How can we make political sense of *uri*-formation in civil society? Jean-Jacques Rousseau's controversial notion of general will can help here. "'Each one of us puts into the community his person and all his powers under the supreme direction of the general will; and as a body, we incorporate every member as an indivisible part of the whole.' Immediately, in place of the individual person of each contracting party, this act of association creates an artificial and collective body composed of as many members as there are voters in the assembly, and by this same act that body acquires its unity, its common ego, its life and its will."[51]

Rousseau's critics often point out that the general will featured in *The Social Contract* threatens a total dissolution of the self into collectivity or the complete negation of difference or human plurality, hence leading to the formation of a power-seeking, pathological group ego, ultimately to totalitarianism.[52] But, in *The Government of Poland*, in which Rousseau applies his social contract theory to Poland's actual political setting, we can see a far more pragmatic and democratic rendition of general will: "[T]he law, which is merely the expression of the *general will*, is certainly the product of the interplay of all sectional

[51] Jean-Jacques Rousseau, *The Social Contract*, trans. Maurice Cranston (Baltimore: Penguin, 1968), 61.

[52] J. L. Talmon, *Origins of Totalitarian Democracy* (New York: Praeger, 1960).

interests, combining with and balancing one another in all their variety."[53] If general will is "the product of interplay of all sectional interests," rather than the coercive annihilation of private interests, and if we understand interest as encompassing both material interest and interest in self-identity, it is problematic to see general will as starkly opposed to plurality.

Benjamin Barber, therefore, proposes to understand general will in the context of democratic legitimacy. According to Barber, what is important for Rousseau is not so much a schizophrenic splitting between individuality (private interests) and collectivity (common interests), but how to create legitimacy through a dialectical interplay between them. Barber says, "Legitimacy here is awarded not to the virtuous interest but to the general will, the will that incarnates a democratic community that is comprised in turn of the wills of autonomous citizens. The issue is not 'I want' versus 'you want' but 'I want' versus 'we will.' … But wills cannot all be equally legitimate in the same sense, because by willing one affects the world, and the world is finally one – our world – and can only be as legitimate as the process that willed it into being."[54] Here, the key word is "our world." What Barber (and Rousseau) tries to argue is that our world, to which the general will is directed, has nothing to do with the suppression of individual wills (and interests); to the contrary, it is the political construct resulting from collective will formation. The most critical problem of traditional liberal-democratic theory is that it does not take into account the possibility of self-transformation in democratic will formation processes. It claims that man is an inherently private individual, man's preference is fixed, man's natural right is absolute, and therefore the primary role of politics is to secure self-preservation by denying (anarchist democracy), or suppressing (realistic democracy), or merely tolerating (minimalist democracy) the conflict among self-seeking individuals.[55] But it can hardly come to terms with transforming the conflict. Democratic theories of self-transformation emphasize that the self as a willing agent can transform itself from a private individual to a public citizen by creating a public space (i.e., our world) in civil society in which all citizens can freely participate. Thus, by transforming the conflict, these theories mean to transform the self (often temporarily) to resolve the incumbent common problems, most important the problems of social injustice. Being essentially *political* in terms of scope and aim, democratic self-transformation is qualitatively different from aesthetic or spiritual self-transformation.[56]

[53] Jean-Jacques Rousseau, *The Government of Poland*, trans. by Willmore Kendall (Indianapolis: Hackett, 1985), 42, emphasis added.

[54] Benjamin R. Barber, *Strong Democracy: Participatory Politics for a New Age*, 20th anniversary ed. (Berkeley: University of California Press, 2003), 200–201.

[55] Ibid., 3–20. Also see Mark Warren, "Democratic Theory and Self-Transformation," *American Political Science Review* 86 (1992), 8–23 for a more qualified view on the transformative effects of democratic experiences.

[56] Deweyan Confucian democrats equally emphasize the importance of self-transformation. However, by self-transformation they rarely (almost never) mean political self-transformation

Our world, however, is not a rationalist discursive forum as most deliberative democrats conceive of it. As Benjamin Barber rightly notes, empathy or affection is indispensable to the creation of our world: "Empathy has a politically miraculous power to enlarge perspectives and expand consciousness in a fashion that not so much accommodates as transcends private interests and the antagonisms they breed.... Empathy ... as an artificial product of political talk, arouses feelings that attach precisely to 'strangers,' to those who do not belong to our private families or clubs or churches."[57] Thus understood, general will is a creative ensemble of both reason and emotions and, in the most profound sense, it consists of the citizenry's common public concerns.[58]

Can we call the Korean *uri* a kind of the Rousseauian general will? The answer, I suppose, is a qualified yes. The answer might be negative, if the *uri* in question is the *uri* formed on a prepolitical, psychocultural level because the overlapping of egos itself cannot be equated directly with the common interest created dialectically out of conflicting individual interests. Moreover, from the standpoint of the Korean (politically formed) *uri*, the Rousseauian conception of general will has its own problems: most likely, general will conceived as common interest can be susceptible to a sort of free-rider problem, as Rousseau himself acknowledges when he observes,

> For every individual as a man may have a private will contrary to, or different from, the general will that he has as a citizen. His private interest may speak with a very different voice from that of the public interest; his absolute and naturally independent existence may make him regard what he owes to the common cause as a gratuitous contribution, the loss of which would be less painful for others than the payment is onerous for him; and fancying that the artificial person which constitutes the state is a mere rational entity (since it is not a man), *he might seek to enjoy the rights of a citizen without doing the duties of a subject.*[59]

Uri-responsibility as a moral commitment to "doing one's own share" or "shouldering one's own burden," however, does not primarily mean an exercise of "interest," – be it general or private – against the state understood as a mere rational entity. Instead, *uri*-responsibility, which is exercised through palpable *chŏng*, is rooted in one's sense of shame, a shame that his or her lack of concern for the common world has helped injustice, or, at least, it is somewhat related with the unjust status quo.[60]

but aesthetic self-transformation, which may not always be able to enhance democracy as a political rule. See David L. Hall and Roger T. Ames, *The Democracy of the Dead: Dewey, Confucius, and the Hope for Democracy in China* (Chicago: Open Court, 1999); Sor-hoon Tan, *Confucian Democracy: A Deweyan Reconstruction* (Albany: State University of New York Press, 2003).

57 Barber, *Strong Democracy*, 189.

58 My understanding of general will is Humean rather than neo-Kantian. In (Confucian) democracy, general will and public reasons overlap.

59 Rousseau, *Social Contract*, 63–4, emphasis added.

60 On the Confucian importance of the sense of shame in making people live a virtuous life, see *Analects* 2:3.

That being said, if our focus is placed not on (common) interest but on a collectively shared responsibility, if it is admitted that political problems include moral issues as well as material questions,[61] and we are persuaded that private individuals can build citizenship not only by transforming the conflict, but also by sharing responsibilities,[62] the Korean *uri* – the political *uri* in the case – can be understood as a uniquely Korean-Confucian mode of general will. In short, in Korea, not only is collective will-formation related to the creation of the common interest (given the plurality of interest) but, more important, it is profoundly concerned with the creation of collective moral responsibility, namely *uri*-responsibility. The creation of collective moral responsibility is of critical importance particularly in a society like Korea in which almost every political issue is entangled in the question of moral justification unlike in Western societies wherein the separation between morality and politics has been firmly established at least on a public rhetorical revel. Our final question then is what exactly *uri*-responsibility is, to which I now turn.

Uri-Responsibility as Collective Moral Responsibility

As we have seen in the core cases, the defining characteristic of *uri*-responsibility is the task responsibility willingly assumed by citizens for the (moral and material) political predicaments that they as individuals might not have created or caused. In this section, I will articulate the unique character of *uri*-responsibility by comparing it with two Kantian-liberal accounts of responsibility – moral responsibility and political responsibility.

From a Kantian-liberal perspective, only a free agent can possess responsibility in a moral sense because she alone is responsible for the results of her actions. But Kant's understanding of freedom and responsibility is more complicated than this liberal account makes out because he explicates freedom in metaphysical terms while giving credit to Spinozian determinism. Though Kant fully develops his idea of freedom in his second *Critique*, it was a fundamental issue even in his first *Critique* when he grappled with the "third antinomy," a fundamental contradiction between theoretical reason and practical reason or between the law of nature (conditional causality) and freedom (unconditional/infinite causality).

> Now even if one believes the action to be determined by these causes [for a given natural effect], one nonetheless blames the agent, and not on account of his unhappy natural temper, not on account of the circumstances influencing him, not even on account of the life he has led previously; for one presupposes that it can be entirely set aside how that life was constituted, and that the series of conditions that transpired might not have

[61] Or, it can be argued that political problems are at once moral and material because the two cannot be clearly separated in reality.

[62] The two ways of self-transformation, however, are not mutually exclusive. Rather they are complementary in the actual political situation.

been, but rather that this deed could be regarded as entirely conditioned in regard to the previous state, as though with that act the agent has started a series of consequences entirely from himself.[63]

Specifically, the puzzle is this: if as empiricists (or eudaimonists) claim, a person is a purely theoretical (i.e., empirical) being only reacting on the sense data impressed or represented in his or her inner space (*res cogitans*) through the cognitive process of sense perception of the things-in-themselves in the external world (*res extensa*), and therefore his or her action, inherently reactive, is completely determined by the causality of nature, on what ground can he or she be called "free" and be held responsible for his or her action?[64] To resolve this puzzle, Kant submits that freedom *ought* to be approached from purely practical standpoint – that is, freedom *ought* to be thought to belong to the kingdom of the moral law, which in turn *ought* to be promulgated solely by the use of practical reason.[65] Psychological freedom predicated on a will, which is motivated by sensible impulses, can by no means be authentic freedom because it cannot avoid the infinite regress of the causality of action, which makes moral agency hardly identifiable. Such freedom is rather the freedom of a turnspit, which "when once it is wound up, also accomplishes its movement of itself." Therefore, freedom ought to be *transcendental* to the "whole chain of appearances" or to "the necessity of the connection of events in a time series." In other words, freedom ought to be independent of natural causality (causality as a phenomenon); instead it must be a *causa noumenon*.

Why Kant invents a noumenal definition of freedom is not difficult to tell; it is solely for the sake of autonomy, the quintessential core of an individual's moral agency. Kant thus says, "The sensible nature of rational being in general is their existence under empirically conditioned laws and is thus, for reason, heteronomy. The supersensible nature of the same beings, on the other hand, is their existence in accordance with laws that are independent of any empirical condition and thus belong to the autonomy of pure reason."[66]

Often, the distinction between the two worlds (noumenal and phenomenal) is seen to be an ontological one. But as Christine Korsgaard has wisely noted, the distinction is not between the two kinds of beings, "but between the beings of this world insofar as they authentically active and the same beings insofar as we are passively receptive to them."[67] Kojin Karatani, a renowned Japanese scholar, offers an illuminating explanation for this issue, when he rephrases

[63] Immanuel Kant, *Critique of Practical Reason*, trans. and ed. Mary Gregor (Cambridge: Cambridge University Press, 1997), 544.

[64] See ibid., 80.

[65] For a revealing discussion on this subject, see Christine M. Korsgaard, *Creating the Kingdom of Ends* (Cambridge: Cambridge University Press, 1996), esp. chap. 6.

[66] Kant, *Critique of Practical Reason*, 38.

[67] Korsgaard, *Creating the Kingdom of Ends*, 203.

Kant's antimony as, "From the beginning, neither freedom nor responsibility emerges out of the theoretical stance that queries the cause. According to Kant, the criminal's responsibility arises when the causality is bracketed, that is, when he is *a free agent*. In reality, he does not have freedom sensu strico. But he has to be deemed free in order for him to be responsible. Such is the *practical* standpoint."[68]

What is important is that Kant locates freedom of action only ex post facto, not ex ante facto. According to Karatani, the key concept in the lines quoted (and in Kant's famous notion of categorical imperative) is "as though," because it reveals that the most crucial point for Kant's ethic is responsibility, the responsibility for the result. That is, "[o]nly when we are considered free agents, though we are not at all in reality, do we become responsible."[69] In this view, one is to be held responsible for one's action, which could otherwise be claimed to have been occasioned because of the necessity of circumstances. Thus, responsibility is absolutely an individual responsibility.

In this respect, Hannah Arendt's concept of "collective responsibility" deserves close attention, because it provides a new type of responsibility, distinct from Kant's individualistic notion of responsibility, but still consistent with Kant's republican political philosophy.[70] According to Arendt, there are two types of (Kantian) responsibility. The first is *moral* responsibility. It is the Kantian individualistic responsibility that we have investigated so far. Since it is a responsibility to be held by a free agent for her willingly chosen action, it is essentially a causal responsibility. No doubt, the key to this particular notion of responsibility is the agent's moral autonomy or freedom.

The second is *political* responsibility. Political responsibility is a responsibility which a political community (normally, the state) is to hold for any political injustice it has inflicted on another political community (e.g., unjust war or international crimes). The best example is the collective responsibility the entire German nation had to assume for what it had done to other nations during WWII. Arendt also calls it *collective* responsibility to distinguish it from moral responsibility that is individualistic in nature. What is implicit in the notion of political responsibility is the Kantian republican conviction that the only legitimate collective moral agent is the state, the single most important role of which is to protect individual citizens. The Kantian notion of political responsibility, therefore, stipulates that in the political action of the nation, individuals are not to be held personally responsible not only because of the foundational idea of social contract by which the *body politic* is formed, but in practice because in most cases individuals cease to be rational persons, who

[68] Kojin Karatani, *Transcritique: On Kant and Marx*, trans. Sabu Kohso (Cambridge, MA: MIT Press, 2005), 118.

[69] Ibid., 117.

[70] Hannah Arendt, *Responsibility and Judgment*, ed. Jerome Kohn (New York: Schocken Books, 2003), 147–158.

can be morally responsible for his or her action, and become *nobodies* who do not think, thus fail to act.[71]

Thus understood, Arendt's twofold Kantian conception of responsibility is still firmly grounded in Kant's individualistic moral philosophy. For Arendt, collective responsibility is at best a residual category in her Kantian philosophy of morality, a concept contrived to make sense of the domain to which the traditional language of morality can hardly be applicable. In the end, even for Arendt, moral responsibility is always an individual responsibility. In her Kantian view, the nonpolitical (i.e., nonstatist) collective can in no way be a legitimate moral agent. Given the stark dualism between public and private, moral and political, and individual and collective, there is no room for what can be called *collective moral responsibility* that can navigate in between.

Korean *uri*-responsibility can hardly be grasped by either Kantian category. First, *uri*-responsibility defies a causal reasoning characteristic of the Kantian-liberal notion of moral responsibility. While in the Kantian account of moral responsibility what matters is a personal morality, and it is deemed as the question of an individual agent's volition, *uri*-responsibility enables citizens in civil society, which is institutionally separated from the state, to engage in a public deliberation to resolve collectively moral and political problems that have not been necessarily caused by them, while not exonerating the liability of those who have caused them.[72] Most important, unlike responsibility formulated in the Kantian liberal tradition, which is rationally motivated and justified ex post facto, *uri*-responsibility is motivated by civil passions broadly shared by the public. While Kantian responsibility, which is essentially a liability, cannot in principle be cultivated (because it is something to be rationally appropriated), *uri*-responsibility is a civic virtue that influences both personal character and the public character of the polity.

That *uri*-responsibility is a form of collective responsibility, however, does not make it a political responsibility as understood in the Kantian (liberal-republican) tradition. To Confucian Korean people who conceive of the political in terms of the familial, the kind of the political that Kant inherited from the British social contract tradition (especially from Thomas Hobbes) is completely unknown. If *uri*-responsibility can be called a *political* responsibility, it is so only in reference to the Confucian principle of the familial as the political, the core constituent of Confucian public reason. What this means is that since Confucian moral-politics does not separate the political from the familial and the political as the familial from the moral, *uri*-responsibility,

[71] For Arendt's notion of nobody, see Paul Formosa, "Moral Responsibility for Banal Evil," *Journal of Social Philosophy* 37 (2006), 501–20.

[72] But if those who are legally liable deserve *chŏng*, that is, if they have violated law for reasons that can be sympathized through *chŏng*, Koreans sometimes are willing to transfer part of responsibility to them by deeming the problems collectively or structurally caused at least partially.

which is rooted in Confucian familialism, can accordingly be understood as a moral responsibility. In the most proper sense, therefore, *uri*-responsibility is a collective moral responsibility.

Conclusion

Chŏng brings a multitude of otherwise separated and disjointed "I"s into a common public space, and motivates them to reflect on the sociopolitical problems that commonly confront them through various forms of talk, and, ultimately, helps them revitalize citizenship by reconstructing *our* world. This is the motivating effect of *chŏng*. *Chŏng*ish participation in the *uri*-world is *uri*-consciousness and *uri*-citizenship and it concomitantly empowers an individual citizen's moral and political agency as in Korean social psychology "We" (*uri*) is inextricably intertwined with "I" (*na*). Despite the title of "we," therefore, it is indeed "I" that actually exercises *uri*-responsibility. In my view, this is how Hegel's famous phrase of *an "I" that is "We" and "We" that is "I"* is practiced in the Korean Confucian democratic context. This is not a slavish submission of "I" to "We," but a creative dialectic between "I" and "We" in dealing with common problems. The voluntary will to create and join the *chŏng*ish *uri*-world in civil society offers the most viable way to maintain and empower a Korean democratic citizenship as facilitating the consolidation of a Korean democracy.

Motivating democracy is not the only role *chŏng* can play in Korean society, however. It can help to make socioculturally appropriate sense of and further legitimize new social discourses and practices that democratic institutions have introduced by providing public reasons to which ordinary Korean citizens can resort when they participate in public deliberation and contestations. In the following three chapters, I illuminate this legitimizing effect of *chŏng* in Korea's increasingly pluralist and multiculturalist democratic context.

9

Confucian Public Reason and the Liberalism of Human Rights

As far as its constitution is concerned, Korea is a liberal-democratic country. However, while its "democratic" character has been firmly affirmed in recent years,[1] its "liberal" character still remains ambiguous. Though there is notable dissatisfaction with the formal/procedural definition of democracy in terms of a free and regular election based on the principle of one person, one vote among Koreans (especially among the left who understand democracy in a more substantive sense), they believe democracy, for which they have shed blood, is irrevocable in Korea. At a minimum, there is wide consensus across the ideological spectrum that the June Uprising of 1987 is the landmark event that vividly separates the post-1987 regime from the previous ones, qualifying it to be *democratic*.[2] But what is the parallel event for Korean liberalism? Was the June Uprising a "liberal-democratic" revolution? Or does democracy naturally refer to liberal democracy?[3] If we grant that Korean democracy is a liberal democracy, what kind of liberalism does it imply?

For a long time, Koreans have equated democracy with liberal democracy, understanding liberalism in the Cold War context, namely, as the antithesis of the communism of the North.[4] For them, democracy is what they had (and still have) to fight for because it is about power and the common and equal

[1] Sunhyuk Kim, *The Politics of Democratization in Korea: The Role of Civil Society* (Pittsburgh: University of Pittsburgh Press, 2000); Chaibong Hahm, "South Korea's Miraculous Democracy," *Journal of Democracy* 19 (2008), 128–42.

[2] Even those who advocate a more substantive democracy in Korea do not deny the procedural democratic legitimacy of the post-1987 regime. See, for instance, Jangjip Choi, *Minjuhaw ihuui Minjujuui* [Democracy after Democratization] (Seoul: Humanitas, 2005).

[3] As we have seen in chapters in Part I of this book, many Confucian political theorists answer this question negatively.

[4] This type of negative definition of liberalism was strongly supported by Cold War liberals, most notably, Karl Popper, *The Open Society and Its Enemies* (London: Routledge, 2002) and Friedrich A. Hayek, *The Constitution of Liberty* (Chicago: University of Chicago Press, 1978).

sharing of power (i.e., collective self-government or popular sovereignty) had long been suppressed by earlier authoritarian regimes. However, in the popular understanding, Korea has always been (even under the authoritarian reigns) a *liberal* country, meaning opposed to, and often threatened by, communism. In fact, for some, because of the threat of communism, or to safeguard liberalism, human rights, the core value of liberalism, had to be suppressed at times. In short, in Korea, liberalism was not so much what the people had to fight for internally as what they had to guard against in the face of the external threat of communist forces. This strong ideological understanding of liberalism still deeply permeates Korean society.

The problem with this heavily ideological rendition of liberalism is that it makes it difficult to come to grips with the positive aspect of liberalism, the kind of liberalism that the early modern Europeans struggled to achieve, sometimes violently, by fighting absolutist monarchy, feudal aristocracy, and/or religious intolerance. In its positive sense, liberalism is a social and political *practice* (not merely a political ideology) that holds its own unique *moral* content such as the virtue of civility,[5] individual right,[6] and freedom of association,[7] and it is the underdevelopment of such liberal moral practices that characterizes Korean liberalism. Ironically, however, it is because of the lack of public interest in the moral content of liberalism or the hollowness of the substantive meaning of "being a liberal" in public discourse that "liberal democracy" has enjoyed uncontested political orthodoxy in Korea. Put differently, Korea has been a liberal country without having (or producing) many practicing liberals (in the Western sense) in its civil society.

Over the past decade, however, liberalism of a particular moral content, namely "liberalism of human rights" (hereafter LHR), has emerged and is now dominant in Korean society. Two new governmental entities, both established in 2001, have been instrumental in propagating this particular version of liberalism: the National Human Rights Commission and the Ministry of Gender Equality (now the Ministry of Gender Equality and Family).[8] Of importance are the drastic legal and social changes that both institutions have actually brought about in Korean civil society, which many Korean liberals acclaim as a gigantic step toward the realization of human rights. The abolition of the traditional Family Head System in 2008 is widely regarded as one of their crowning achievements.[9]

5 Edward Shils, *The Virtue of Civility: Selected Essays on Liberalism, Tradition, and Civil Society*, ed. Steven Grosby (Indianapolis: Liberty Fund, 1997).

6 Jeremy Waldron, *Liberal Rights* (Cambridge: Cambridge University Press, 1983).

7 Amy Gutmann (ed.), *Freedom of Association* (Princeton: Princeton University Press, 1998).

8 On the legal enactment, organization, and key tasks of the National Human Rights Commission, see Yong-whan Cho, "The National Human Rights Commission: Law, Reality, and Its Future Task," *Korea Journal* 42 (2002), 228–62.

9 For a detailed feminist critique of the Korean family head system, see Hyunah Yang, "Unfinished Tasks for Korean Family Policy in the 1990s: Maternity Protection Policy and Abolition of the Family-Head System," *Korea Journal* 42 (2002), 68–99.

In the recent valorization of LHR, however, it is rarely discussed that central to this version of liberalism is an interesting intertwinement between Kantian moral universalism and Millian ethical pluralism. The moral universalism implicated in liberalism insists that every man and woman is of equal moral worth and thus is equally entitled to human dignity and capable of personal moral autonomy.[10] It demands that every person be treated equally qua human being. In this universalist vision of liberalism, rights that a person entertains are *human* rights, a set of inalienable and inviolable rights that he or she is born with, whilst, liberal pluralism stipulates that every man and woman has distinctive and incommensurable personal traits (in terms of passions, preferences, choices, and lifestyles), and these radical individual differences must be fully respected and maximally accommodated within the reasonable constraints of liberal constitutionalism.[11]

Many Korean social and political theorists have tackled the Kantian universalist liberal presumption by exploring a uniquely Korean-style or Confucian-informed democracy and civil society.[12] However, it appears that their attitudes toward liberalism are far from coherent. None of them seem happy with the universalist presumption in the ideal of liberal democracy, but none seem able to proactively resist wholesale the universal value of human rights or to dismiss the fact of personal distinctiveness and the moral value of individuality (if not individualism), core tenets of liberal pluralism.

Thus, it is reasonable for Koreans (both political theorists and citizens) to ask the following questions regarding the liberal aspect of Korean liberal democracy: What is the *practical* meaning of the statement that Korea is a "liberal-democratic" country? Does that mean that Koreans should be moral universalists, treating each other (and strangers) qua human beings? Then what is the cultural and political meaning of being a "Korean"? Or, does "liberal-democratic" mean that Koreans should be value pluralists, maximally respecting others' different values, ideals, and lifestyles by resorting to negative liberty and/or the harm principle? What, then, happens to the positive conception of the common good affiliated with Korea's traditional (Confucian) ideal of good

[10] Immanuel Kant, *The Metaphysics of Morals*, trans. Mary J. Gregor (Cambridge: Cambridge University Press, 1996); John Rawls, *A Theory of Justice* (Cambridge, MA: Belknap, [1971] 1999); Charles Beitz, *Political Theory and International Relations* (Princeton: Princeton University Press, 1999).

[11] John Stuart Mill, *On Liberty* (New York: Penguin, 1974); George Kateb, *The Inner Ocean: Individualism and Democratic Culture* (Ithaca: Cornell University Press, 1992); Richard E. Flathman, *Pluralism and Liberal Democracy* (Baltimore: Johns Hopkins University Press, 2005).

[12] See, for instance, Hein Cho, "The Historical Origin of Civil Society in Korea," *Korea Journal* 37 (1997), 24–41; Chaibong Hahm, *Yugyo, jabonjuui, minjujuui* [Confucianism, Capitalism, and Democracy] (Seoul: Jeontong-gwa Hyeondae, 2000); Yunjae Chung (ed.), *Yugyolideoshipgwa han'gukjeongchi* [Confucian Leadership and Korean Politics] (Seoul: Baeksanseodang, 2002); Jin-deok Choi (ed.), *Jeontongyegyowa shiminyunli* [Traditional Rituals and Civic Ethics] (Seoul: Cheonggye, 2001).

government, which as many social scientists attest is still prevalent in Korean public discourse?[13] Should it be discarded as a sort of archaic traditionalism? Moreover and more fundamentally, what if Kantian universalism and Millian pluralism, both focused on human rights, are not necessarily compatible? What if they imply two distinct notions of "human rights"?

In this chapter, I tackle (if not resolve) this liberal conundrum in the context of Korea's given cultural (Confucian) and political (democratic) context from the perspective of the ordinary Korean-citizen.[14] Instead of positing liberal democracy as an internally coherent theory and practice and regarding liberal democracy as a universal normative ideal that ought to be fully transplanted in Korea, I anatomize the multiple strains implicated in the current Korean discourse of LHR and discuss what kind of liberalism is culturally relevant and socially practicable in Korean society.

The Conundrum of Liberalism in Theory and Practice

Many Koreans assume that liberalism is naturally associated with democracy as if they are two names for the same phenomenon. Thus, even if the Korean struggle for democracy before and during 1987 was primarily aimed at the common and equal sharing of power, and not necessarily at the liberalization of Korean society (and the individualization of the Korean people), the post-1987 endeavor toward further democratization of Korea seems to be concentrated more on liberalism or the consolidation of authentic liberalism that considers individual human rights the highest priority. In other words, where there seem to be no more salient authoritarian forces to be overcome, democracy in Korea is now being massively confounded with liberalism.[15]

However, there are two serious, theoretical and practical, problems in this confounding. First, in the public discourse of liberal democracy in Korea, it is rarely recognized that liberalism and democracy are distinctive moral practices

[13] See note 9 in the Introduction of this book for empirical and interpretive studies attesting to this observation.

[14] According to democratic theorists like Michael Walzer and Benjamin Barber, political theory addresses citizens, not philosophers or judges, so it should take the perspective of ordinary citizens in the given political community. Throughout this chapter, my primary focus will be not so much on liberalism that lawyers, judges, and/or philosophers idealize, but more on a particular kind of liberalism that ordinary Korean citizens would find most relevant and practicable in their daily cultural and social life. See Michael Walzer, "Philosophy and Democracy," *Political Theory* 9 (1981), 370–99 and Benjamin R. Barber, *The Conquest of Politics: Liberal Philosophy in Democratic Times* (Princeton: Princeton University Press, 1988).

[15] In a sense, this "confounding" between democracy and liberalism is deliberately pursued by the mainstream political science literature of democratic consolidation. Virtually all leading scholars in political science take for granted that consolidated democracy is a liberal democracy. For instance, see Juan L. Linz and Alfred Stepan, *Problems of Democratic Transition and Consolidation: Southern Europe, South America, and Post-Communist Europe* (Baltimore: Johns Hopkins University Press, 1996); Larry Diamond, *Developing Democracy: Toward Consolidation* (Baltimore: Johns Hopkins University Press, 1999).

and "liberal democracy" as a theory as well as practice is fraught with an internal tension between its liberal and democratic components, especially when liberalism is understood as the moral doctrine of human rights. Second, though Koreans understand LHR as a monolithic ethical and political tradition, there are indeed multiple versions of liberalism, most notably, Kantian moral universalism and Millian ethical pluralism. The problem is that though equally focused on the moral value of the human right, their understandings of human rights are not only qualitatively different but often conflicting.

Universalist Liberalism versus Democracy

As a universal moral doctrine of human rights, LHR has its intellectual roots in the Enlightenment. At the heart of this strain of LHR is moral individualism, which is internally tied with moral cosmopolitanism and by implication with cosmopolitan citizenship.[16] Seeing an individual qua human being and understanding the essence of morality (i.e., justice) as respecting human rights,[17] this particular version of liberalism prefers to bracket off the otherwise quintessential moral and political questions of national citizenship and territorial boundary from its ethical purview, by regarding them as contingent factors from the moral perspective.[18]

In contrast, the essence of democracy lies in citizen-formation, popular sovereignty, and collective self-determination. Because its major concern is with citizens, not individuals qua human beings, more specifically, with the economic, cultural, and sociopolitical contributions citizens bring to their political community through active civic and political participation over generations, democracy is *in practice* predicated on nationally bounded citizenship.[19] Though some individual-oriented democrats like Amy Gutmann find the notion of the "collective self" totalizing and thus dangerous,[20] many democratic theorists believe collective self-determination to be the core ideal of democracy.[21] According to these "strong" democrats, collective self-determination is attained by democratic means such as active civic and political participation in civil and

[16] Immanuel Kant, "Idea for a Universal History with a Cosmopolitan Purpose," in *Political Writings*, ed. Hans Reiss, trans. H. B. Nisbet (Cambridge: Cambridge University Press, 1991); Kok-Chor Tan, *Justice without Borders: Cosmopolitanism, Nationalism and Patriotism* (Cambridge: Cambridge University Press, 2004); Andrew Vincent, *Nationalism and Particularity* (Cambridge: Cambridge University Press, 2002), 191–224.

[17] Thomas Pogge, *World Poverty and Human Rights* (Cambridge: Polity, 2002); Beitz, *Political Theory and International Relations*.

[18] Thomas Pogge, *Globalizing Rawls* (Ithaca: Cornell University Press, 1989); Joseph H. Carens, "Aliens and Citizens: The Case for Open Borders," in *Theorizing Citizenship*, ed. Ronald Beiner (Albany: State University of New York Press, 1995).

[19] David Miller, *Citizenship and National Identity* (Cambridge: Polity, 2000), esp. 81–96.

[20] Amy Gutmann, *Democratic Education* (Princeton: Princeton University Press, 1988), 289.

[21] Benjamin R. Barber, *Strong Democracy: Participatory Politics for a New Age*, 20th anniversary ed. (Berkeley: University of California Press, 2003); Ian Shapiro, *Democratic Justice* (New Haven: Yale University Press, 1999); Sheldon S. Wolin, *The Presence of the Past: Essays on the State and the Constitution* (Baltimore: Johns Hopkins University Press, 1989).

political societies, which results in collective self-government. From this viewpoint, the liberal device of consent does not fully grasp the civic dimension of liberal democracy.[22]

Of course, the internal tension in the ideal of liberal democracy – between the universalism of human rights and the particularism of citizenship – does not necessarily end up in a practical dead-end. As Joseph Carens claims, if the core cultural and political value of the given society is indeed liberalism (understood as a doctrine of human rights) as is the case with many Western liberal democracies, democratic citizenship does not have to be (and should not be) nationally bounded or "closed" (as Rawls assumes in *A Theory of Justice*).[23] In fact, it is increasingly argued that an authentic liberal-democratic country is not morally justified to control its border unilaterally because the demos in such a country cannot be preconsensually given and culturally bounded. Quite the contrary: in liberal democracy, democratic boundary is perennially open to political contestation.[24] Citizenship, therefore, cannot be grounded in national identity; it is open to everyone (i.e., all actual and potential immigrants).

This sort of resolution, however, is not available in most non-Western democracies that are culturally unfamiliar with the Enlightenment ideal of the morally autonomous self and universal human rights, hence the practical difficulty of liberal democracy in those countries including Korea. In addition, I am not sure ordinary Koreans would accept the liberal resolution of the internal tension in the ideal of liberal democracy, if they were informed of this option. Nor am I sure that Korean liberal political theorists would actively pursue this line of reasoning.

Korea is still characteristically a Confucian society in the sense that the majority of the Korean people still subscribe to what I described in the previous chapters as *Confucian public reasons*. Though only few Koreans declare Confucianism as their self-consciously chosen value system, most Koreans (including immigrants) *practice* Confucian rituals in their daily life and these rituals play a significant role in making social and political communications among citizens affective, thus more effective.[25] Most tellingly, Koreans

[22] Thus, Benjamin Barber says, "The consent device skewed the relationship toward liberal individualism from the outset, however. It deprived liberals of the comforts of democracy as they tried to accommodate the communities produced by individuals (whom they recognized as such) with the individuals produced by communities (which they refused to recognize)" ("Liberal Democracy and the Costs of Consent," in Rosenblum, *Liberalism and the Moral Life*, 56–7).

[23] Carens, "Aliens and Citizens," 248–9.

[24] See Arash Abizadeh, "Democratic Theory and Border Coercion: No Right to Unilaterally Control Your Own Borders," *Political Theory* 36 (2008), 37–65. One way in which this tension can be resolved is by extending democracy globally, that is, by envisioning a global democracy whatever that means in practice, be it the EU model, world government, or global civil society.

[25] See Byung-ik Koh, "Confucianism in Contemporary Korea," in Tu, *Confucian Traditions in East Asian Modernity* and Kwang Kyu Lee, "Confucian Tradition in the Contemporary Korean Family," in Slote and DeVos, *Confucianism and the Family*.

still make sense of social relationships in family-relational terms by calling otherwise total strangers "brothers/sisters," "uncles/aunts," and "grandfathers/mothers."[26] In fact, the most important civic virtue in Korean Confucian culture, I believe, is the moral capacity to accommodate the Otherness of strangers into the intimacy of family relationships. This ability is primarily cultivated in the family as an ethic of filial and fraternal responsibility or simply "filiality" (Korean *hyoje*; Chinese *xiaoti*). Filiality, originally a family ethic, evolves into a civic virtue as its scope extends to broader social relations in civil society where strangers interact with each other.[27]

Furthermore, and in the same social psychological vein, Koreans continue to envision the state as a nationally extended family as the Korean term they use to refer to the state, *gukka* (literally "family-state"), denotes.[28] When they blame or criticize the government, they generally mean that the government has operated against the common mores of the Korean people, which they call *chŏng*, the familial affectionate sentiments, as well as against the common public interest or the law.[29] If we take Korean social psychology seriously, Korean nationhood and citizenship are not so much based on ethnocentrism as commonly claimed,[30] but on the relationality of *chŏng*. More than two decades ago, neo-Tocquevillians such as Robert Bellah famously submitted that the real engine that makes democracy work lies in the "habits of the heart" of the people.[31] In my view, filial virtue and *chŏng* constitute the core of the habits of the heart of the Korean people. In the most profound sense, they are not just habits, narrowly understood, but stances and standard that guide ethical reflection, especially on the state and public actors.

What is interesting is that while Korean democracy, when it has actually worked (and is working) with the Korean people, has always been operating on the habits of the heart of the Korean people, both during and after democratic transition,[32] no such liberal equivalent, which can be termed "Korean

[26] Hye-young Jeon, "Han'gukeoe banyeongdoen yugyomunhwajeok teukseong" [The Confucian Characteristics Reflected in Korean Language], in *Han'gukmunhwawa han'gukin* [Korean Culture and the Korean People], ed. the Association of International Korean Studies (Seoul: Sagyejeol, 1998), 235–58.

[27] See Chapter 5 for an elaboration of this civic extension of filial virtue and familial moral sentiments.

[28] Bong-yeong Choi, *Han'gukinui sahoejeok seonggyeok* [The Social Character of the Korean People] (Seoul: Neutinamu, 1994), 108–13. As noted in Chapter 6 (note 63), nearly three-fifths (59 percent) of Koreans consider the family the prototype for government (see Chong-Min Park and Doh Chull Shin, "Do Asian Values Deter Popular Support for Democracy in South Korea?," *Asian Survey* 46 [2006], 341–61, 350).

[29] On *chŏng* and its public implications in Korea, see Chapter 8.

[30] Gi-wook Shin, *Ethnic Nationalism in Korea: Genealogy, Politics, and Legacy* (Stanford: Stanford University Press, 2006).

[31] Robert N. Bellah et al., *Habits of the Heart: Individualism and Commitment in American Life* (Berkeley: University of California Press, 1985).

[32] See Geir Helgesen, *Democracy and Authority in Korea: The Cultural Dimension in Korean Politics* (Surrey: Curzon, 1998).

liberalism," has yet been created or even considered seriously as a practicable political theory. The result is an infelicitous situation, that universalist liberalism focused on human rights is at odds with the Korean democracy undergirded by uniquely Korean civic virtues and mores. The problem, however, is not this tension between universal liberalism and Korean democracy as such. The real problem is an ever-intensifying pressure for more liberalism in the name of democratic consolidation, which only helps erode, not reinforce, the cultural foundation of Korean civil society, which otherwise would make Korean democracy work better.

This is not to suggest that human rights are unimportant in making Korean democracy. Nor is it to argue that Korean democracy must be a parochial political vision, holding no universalist or inclusive outlook. I will discuss what should be gleaned from Kantian liberalism in making a Korean liberalism shortly. My point here is simply that liberal democracy cannot be imposed from outside as a sort of freestanding morality that *any* political community should or even can actively embrace at the expense of their local culture (mores, habits, and practices). Unfortunately, however, in Korea many champions of liberal democracy talk about it as if it is a freestanding, maximally universalist morality.[33] The political ramifications of this maximally universalist understanding of liberal democracy are immense: no meaningful civil and democratic communication between ordinary Koreans, for whom morality is an intersubjective value and civility is understood in the familial-relational terms on the one side,[34] and the liberal-minded intellectuals who understand morality ahistorically in terms of right, freedom/choice, and autonomy on the other.[35]

Many liberals in Korea who believe the core value of liberalism is human rights and that human rights are a universal value tend to disregard the fact that universalism rightly understood is neither objective nor unexpressive. From the standpoint of practice, however, universalism is always thin minimalism as Michael Walzer forcefully claims: "It is reiterative, particularist, and locally significant, intimately bound up with the maximal moralities created here and here and here, in specific times and places."[36]

[33] For instance, see Bumsoo Kim, "Minjujuuie isseo poyonggwa baeje" [How to Draw the Boundaries of Demos?], *Korean Journal of International Relations* 48 (2008), 173–98; Gooyong Park, "In'gwonui bopyeonjuuijeok jeongdanghawwa haemyeong" [The Universalist Justification of Human Rights], *Society and Philosophy* 7 (2004), 153–96.

[34] See C. Fred Alford, *Think No Evil: Korean Values in the Age of Globalization* (Ithaca: Cornell University Press, 1999); Chaihark Hahm, "Negotiating Confucian Civility through Constitutional Discourse," in Hahm and Bell, *Politics of Affective Relations*.

[35] I am not implying that autonomy/choice/right is starkly opposed to cultural practice. My point is that as Will Kymlicka argues, it is in the *societal culture* that an individual's autonomy/choice/right is meaningful and authoritative. I discuss this in greater detail in the "Liberal Democracy of 'Sound Common Sense and Legal Sentiment'" section. For Kymlicka's idea of "societal culture," see his *Multicultural Citizenship* (Oxford: Oxford University Press, 1995), 84.

[36] Michael Walzer, *Thick and Thin: Moral Argument at Home and Abroad* (Notre Dame, IN: University of Notre Dame Press, 1994), 7.

Thus understood, liberal democracy is not something to be imposed; it is rather something that ought to be developed locally. Only then can the internal tension between the universalism of liberalism and the particularism of democracy be resolved. Only then can human rights have a substantive cultural meaning and evolve into relevant social practice, the meaning and practice that any ordinary Korean citizen can understand and perform without embarrassment or self-alienation.

Personhood vs. Selfhood

But what is meant by "human rights"? When a Korean citizen claims that the Korean government is morally obligated to protect his or her human rights or when the Korean government intervenes in the family or other private associations when it deems they are oppressing the rights of its members, what right is being violated? As discussed earlier, in the Kantian strain of liberalism, what is being violated and the violation morally requiring governmental intervention is *personhood*. When a government recognizes human rights, "it is recognizing the equal human dignity of all persons – their status as human beings, rather than as things or materials or animals or prey or beasts of burden or children who are never able to grow up."[37] A criminal's right to fair judicial process or a child's right to be protected from domestic violence refers to the right a *person* as a human being (not a thing or an animal) possesses. Otherwise stated, it is a right not to be treated as "nobody" to use Hannah Arendt's famous concept.[38] The human rights that, for instance, the National Human Rights Commission is committed to, are in the main these sorts of rights, rights claimed by or on behalf of persons.

Now, let us turn to a particular human right enumerated in the Korean Constitution (Articles 18, 20, 21), namely, Freedom of Expression. Is this right concerned with personhood? The answer is yes and no – yes because it is only a human being that can possess and exercise it; no because what is at stake here is not a contrast between a person and a thing (or nobody) but the plurality/diversity of the selves. Though it is difficult to draw a sharp line between *personhood* and *selfhood*, Millian ethical (or value) pluralism is just about the plurality/diversity of selfhood. The following remark by George Kateb illuminates the significance of recognizing and respecting the plurality of selfhood in a liberal society. "Freedom of expression is not, then, properly conceptualized as a means or instrument for persons who exercise it.... The primary notion is that a lot of the time, one is one's expression, one lives to express, one lives by expressing. One does not merely use speech; one is one's speech; one's life is mostly speech. (That is why I do not wish to deny that it makes sense to claim intrinsic value for expression: identity is tied to expression.) ... Freedom of

[37] George Kateb, "The Value of Association," in Gutmann, *Freedom of Association*, 52.

[38] On the "person-nobody" distinction in Arendt's moral philosophy, see Paul Formosa, "Moral Responsibility for Banal Evil," *Journal of Social Philosophy* 37 (2006), 501–20.

expression is not the whole of freedom, but its soul."[39] Most Korean political theorists rightly capture liberalism in terms of individualism and their most favored reference in discussing modern individualism is Descartes' famous phrase "*cogito ergo sum*." Particularly those who are critical of modern liberalism almost always cite this phrase, intending to show that liberalism as individualism completely dismisses social relationships and community values and extols the purely rational mind as the epistemologically and politically sovereign authority.[40] No doubt, Cartesian epistemology profoundly influenced early modern liberals such as Hobbes, Locke, and Kant. It is even possible to present the history of modern liberal individualism as the evolution of the Cartesian rational mind into Kantian rational personhood.

Millian individualism is a liberalism of a different kind, however. Simply speaking, Millian individualism is not *about* rationalism; nor is it *about* universalism, though this does not mean that it contains no such elements. Millian individualism is primarily *about* the plurality of the self, the inevitable fact of diversity (even incommensurability) in passions, desires, values, preferences, ideals, lifestyles, and so on. In short, it is about individual identity. It is about what makes me *none other than* me.

Therefore, when we say that freedom of expression is a human right, our focus is not necessarily on personal dignity but mainly on the uniqueness of the self of the person who claims it. This implies that there are at least two different versions of LHR: while in one version universalism is directly derived from the dignity of *all human beings*, in another its alleged universalism only signifies that the moral value of the right to be recognized and respected as a unique individual is applied to *all individuals* within liberal-democratic constitutional boundaries. The problem is that these two versions of LHR are not always harmonious – more often, they are in tension. While the internal tension between liberalism (particularly universalist liberalism) and democracy stems from the tension between humanity and citizenship, the tension between Kantian liberalism and Millian pluralism consists in the tension between humanity (personhood) and individuality (selfhood).

Though Kantian liberals criticize utilitarianism for failing to take individuals singularly (as discrete persons), Kantian liberalism, being preoccupied with the distinction between person and thing/animal and identifying pure reason as the defining feature of the person, rarely pays attention to a person's individual uniqueness, her particular identity.[41] Moreover, in a real social setting,

[39] Kateb, "Value of Association," 53.

[40] Chaibong Hahm, *Talgeundaewa yugyo* [Postmodernity and Confucianism] (Seoul: Nanam, 1998).

[41] In saying this, I do not mean that for Kant, persons are just their rationality. For Kant, persons are also their autonomy, their ability to choose for themselves and forge their own conception of a good life. In this regard, Kant himself would disagree with my depiction of Kantianism. That said, many contemporary Kantians, particularly in non-Western societies (certainly in Korea), tend to interpret Kantianism simply in terms of rationality or rational personhood.

emphasis on the dignity of personhood can violate the plurality of selfhood. The ongoing debate among the leading liberal-democratic theorists on the in/congruence between internal life and practices of voluntary associations and the public culture of liberal democracy attests to the far-reaching public implications of the tension between personhood and selfhood. Let us revisit Mill's famous discussion of the moral value of freedom of association to understand its internal connection with freedom of expression.

> [The appropriate region of human liberty] comprises, first, the inward domain of consciousness, demanding liberty of conscience in the most comprehensive sense, liberty of thought and feeling, absolute freedom of opinion and sentiment on all subjects, practical or speculative, scientific, moral, or theological.... Secondly, the principle requires liberty of tastes and pursuits, of framing the plan of our life to suit our own character, of doing as we like, subject to such consequences as may follow, without impediment from our fellow creatures, so long as what we do does not harm them, even though they should think our conduct foolish, perverse, or wrong. Third, from this liberty of each individual follows the liberty, within the same limits, of combination among individuals; freedom to unite for any purpose not involving harm to others: the persons combining being supposed to be of full age and not forced or deceived.[42]

Mill's point is that while freedom of expression is essential to one's self-identity and freedom, freedom of association is indispensable (not merely instrumental) to freedom of expression. Put differently, in Millian pluralism freedom of association is logically derived from and intrinsically related to freedom of expression. Kateb clarifies the inextricable connection between freedom of expression (or selfhood/self-identity) and freedom of association by saying that "[w]e are not only one another's midwives, but inseminators also. Others are not merely instrumental to mental process, nor auxiliary to it. The process is the company. Mental life, of whatever level or quality, is a continuous movement between solitude and company, as between silence and utterance.... To put the point formally, the individual is the main (but not exclusive) beneficiary of constitutionally protected freedom of expression, but the associated individual is often the true bearer of the right (as with the free exercise of religion)."[43]

Here arise thorny questions: What if the internal life and practice of voluntary associations do not represent or reproduce the public (moral) principles of liberal democracy? Or, what if a voluntary association, while successfully empowering the individual identity and selfhood of its members, fails to reproduce autonomous persons (who are deemed analogous to liberal citizens in Kantian liberalism)? Is governmental intervention required in this case? Kantian liberal democrats like Susan Okin and Amy Gutmann support the congruence between internal life and the practices of voluntary groups and

[42] Mill, *On Liberty*, 71.

[43] Kateb, "Value of Association," 54.

the public (moral) principles of liberal democracy or the general congruence between selfhood and citizenship (as autonomous personhood).[44] That is, if the internal life and practice of voluntary groups or associations that are supposed to serve the expressive liberty of the freely associated individuals do not actually reproduce liberal-democratic values and citizenship, to which autonomous personhood is integral, the groups must be constrained (sometimes rectified) by the public principles of justice whose focus is the individual person.[45] In marked contrast, liberal pluralists like George Kateb, Nancy Rosenblum, and William Galston find such congruence overbearing and violating the spirit of liberalism (i.e., liberal pluralism).[46]

What is important in our context is to note, first, that Koreans are total strangers to the Kantian liberal-democratic notion of "citizen-as-person" (or autonomous citizen), which is a cultural product of the dialectical interplay between Kantian moral universalism and modern republicanism (or national-republican democracy),[47] and, second, that Koreans, who understand the self largely in family-relational terms, are equally unfamiliar with, even uncomfortable with, the idea of expressive selfhood.[48]

Certainly, Korean unfamiliarity with the core assumptions of LHR – citizenship-as-personhood and expressive selfhood – poses an important cultural obstacle to practicing liberalism in Korea. My problem with current Korean liberalism, however, is not that Koreans do not understand the core assumptions of liberalism, nor is it that Koreans must internalize the core assumptions of liberalism and ultimately realize authentic (Western-style) liberal democracy. As I will sketch at the end of this chapter, it is still possible (even desirable) to construct and practice "Korean liberalism" without embracing Western liberal assumptions and theoretical postulates. My problem, rather, is with the striking inconsistency in the way the Korean government (including the National Human Rights Commission) and the courts, allegedly committed to liberal democracy, understand and implement liberalism, thus raising more

[44] Susan M. Okin, *Is Multiculturalism Bad for Women?* (Princeton: Princeton University, 1999); Amy Gutmann, *Identity in Democracy* (Princeton: Princeton University Press, 2003).

[45] Gutmann argues that a liberal-democratic state should tolerate voluntary associations that do not respect core democratic moral principles such as equal liberty and civic equality but it must not support such associations as they violate democratic justice (see Gutmann, *Identity in Democracy*, 88–91). Though Gutmann appreciates the moral value of freedom of association (and freedom of expression that undergirds it), apparently, her primary concern is not so much with self-identity as such but with individual moral autonomy.

[46] Nancy L. Rosenblum, *Membership and Morals: The Personal Uses of Pluralism in America* (Princeton: Princeton University Press, 1998); William A. Galston, *The Practice of Liberal Pluralism* (Cambridge: Cambridge University Press, 2005).

[47] That the citizen is a morally autonomous person is the fundamental assumption of the mainstream Western (and Korean) democratic theory, most notably, deliberative democratic theory.

[48] This cultural unfamiliarity is rarely taken seriously by Korean social and political theorists, many of whom are ardent champions of liberal democracy.

confusion about liberalism among the Korean public. A recent court decision regarding religious freedom offers a useful perspective on the current state of liberal pluralism in Korea.

Liberal Pluralism in Korea: The Case

Having been assigned to Daekwang High School in 2002, Kang Ui-seok, then seventeen years old, was expelled in his third year (June 2004), when he held a one-person demonstration against the school's requirement that "all students must attend service, without exception." Kang subsequently won a court case to have his expulsion declared invalid. In 2003, when he entered college, Kang sued Daekwang High School and Seoul Metropolitan Office of Education (SOME) for the infringement of his constitutionally guaranteed religious and conscientious freedoms. In Korea, students are assigned to schools (including private schools established by religious groups) according to where they live, and this policy has been strictly maintained (with rare exceptions) in the democratic spirit of equal and standardized education irrespective of class difference among the students.

During the first trial, the court awarded Kang a partial victory by putting the student's religious freedom over the school's religious education. A court of appeals, however, overturned this verdict, saying, "The fact that Daekwang High School did not offer alternative courses to [Christian] religious courses [that students were required to take] does not mean that the school seriously violated a person's right to happiness and religious freedom." On 22 April 2010, the Korean Supreme Court overturned this ruling on the ground that religious schools must also guarantee religious freedom for students by seeking students' prior consent or offering alternative courses. Kang's case is the first ruling in Korea by the Supreme Court on compulsory religious education in private schools established by religious groups.[49]

It is not surprising that liberals and liberal-minded organizations welcomed the decision wholeheartedly by saying that Korea is now entering the true stage of liberalism in which freedom of an individual as a person is fully respected. For instance, one of the cochairmen of the Korean Institute for Religious Freedom, said, "[Even though] it will still take a long time for students' religious human rights and freedom to be fully ensured, it is high time that [more] public attention be given [to this fundamental human right]." The director of Institute of Religion and Culture in Korea went one step further by stressing the public character of the religiously founded private schools that are government-subsidized: "At the core of the [Supreme Court's] decision is the respect for the spirit of public education and the public character of religious faith and

[49] This summary of the Supreme Court's decision on Kang's case is adopted (with some modifications) from the English version of *Hangyeoreh Shinmun* (23 April 2010).

[therefore the decision implies that] the founding ideal of the private schools should serve the public [good or demand] of our time."[50]

What is interesting in these responses by Korean liberals (including Kang himself)[51] is the monolithic understanding of liberalism in terms of the respect of (universal) personhood, though what was truly at stake in Kang's case was Kang's distinctive selfhood. That is, Kang's core claim (to religious freedom) was not demanding to be treated as a rational human being but to be treated as a unique individual with his own values that cannot be trumped by any external authority. Viewing Kang's case as a question of personhood and taking the Kantian liberal congruence between personhood and selfhood for granted, however, few liberals in Korea were able to defend the freedom of association claimed by the religious private schools. Even the majority of voices in the Supreme Court, led by Justice Young-ran Kim, upheld the Kantian-liberal logic of congruence without acknowledging the difference between personhood and selfhood.[52]

> Even taking into account the freedom of private religious education, religious schools enjoy their basic rights within the bounds of establishing appropriate policies that take into consideration the basic rights of their students, including religious freedom.... There is therefore a limit to the acceptableness of a religious school providing particular and sectarian education that goes beyond the level of universal, religiously neutral, education to students that entered the school regardless of their own faith.... Daekwang High School, in contradiction to the officially announced policy of the Ministry of Education, Science and Technology, did not establish alternative subjects or seek the prior consent of its students.... As such, the school exceeded acceptable limits in terms of sound social common sense and legal sentiment and we acknowledge the illegality of this situation.[53]

A basic right of religious schools that the court acknowledged is freedom of association. According to the court's reasoning, however, this basic right must be constrained by "the appropriate policies that take into consideration the basic rights of students." Here we see a clash between two basic rights, namely, freedom of association and freedom of conscience (or religious freedom), and

[50] *Segye Ilbo*, 22 April 2010 (the English translations are mine).

[51] In an interview with a liberal-oriented Korean newspaper, Kang appealed his case to the Universal Declaration of Human Rights (*Gyeonghyang Shinmun*, 22 April 2010).

[52] In their dissenting opinions, Justices Young-chul Shin, Chang-soo Yang, and Dai-hee Ahan took the side of the school, saying that "[e]xcessively restricting religious education in religious schools and extending the definition of illegal behavior too broadly may result in infringement of the Constitutionally guaranteed freedom of religious education." However, this statement still fails to fully explain why freedom of religious education is a basic right, that is, how freedom of religion is derived from freedom of association and by extension from freedom of expression. Apparently, these dissenting justices wanted to deliberate the case solely from the legal perspective, but in doing so they failed to pay sufficient attention to the public purpose of the Korean Constitution, the fact that it is committed to liberal democracy.

[53] *Hangyeoreh Shinmun*, 23 April 2010.

the court gave precedence the latter over the former. The problem is that the court never clarified the meaning of basic rights that the students have – are they rights claimed by students as unique individuals or as human beings? If they are rights claimed by unique individuals who have their own values, why should priority be given to individual freedom, not associational freedom, which is essentially the individual freedom of members?

Without offering an appropriate explanation on this liberal conundrum, however, the court, nevertheless, came to the right decision. Why is the priority of religious freedom given over associational freedom *in this case*? It is because religious schools in Korea do not enjoy freedom of association because of the nonliberal public policy of equal and standardized education. Since students (and parents) do not have freedom to choose their (or their child's) school according to their religious faith, religiously founded private schools cannot claim expressive liberty of their membership fully. In fact, there cannot be any meaningful claim to religious membership, hence no compelling claim to associational freedom. Though the court never offered a reason why individual freedom is more essential than associational freedom,[54] it rightly concluded that in the absence of freedom of choice by individuals, freedom of association is almost meaningless.

But why didn't the court take issue with the absence of freedom of choice in the first place? The court reasoned that freedom of association must be constrained by the "appropriate [public] policies" that aim to protect individual freedom. But isn't freedom of choice an individual freedom?[55] What is most puzzling in the court's decision was that it never questioned Korea's nonliberal public education policy, according to which students (and parents) have no freedom to choose the school (including private schools) children must attend.

This is not to argue that there should be no constraint on individual freedom in a liberal-democratic society, but we should not forget the liberal constitutionalist stipulation that when government wants to put a constraint on individual freedom, it should be able to offer a compelling justification, which is the political meaning of negative freedom.[56] Most often, such justification is related to public security or the internal integrity of political community. The Supreme Court in Korea, however, offered no such justification. In its verdict, no *liberal-constitutional* justification was presented as to on what basis the

[54] Apparently, the court had no intention to engage with the broader issue of liberal constitutionalism, though it could have.

[55] Of course, freedom of choice is not a basic right. But freedom of choosing a particular religious education is intrinsically related to expressive freedom, which is a basic right.

[56] William A. Galston, *Liberal Pluralism: The Implications of Value Pluralism for Political Theory and Practice* (Cambridge: Cambridge University Press, 2002), 58. Also see Cass Sunstein, "On the Tension between Sex Equality and Religious Freedom," in *Toward a Humanist Justice: The Political Philosophy of Susan Moller Okin*, ed. Debra Satz and Rob Reich (New York: Oxford University Press, 2009).

public authority of the Korean government can trump freedom of association and individual freedom of choice. Thus understood, in Korea, liberalism is at once publicly promoted and curbed, often without public liberal constitutionalist justifications.

What is interesting, however, is the way the court rationalized "acceptable limits" on freedom of association (and implicitly individual freedom of choice and expressive liberty). Without alluding to any familiar liberal constitutional elements (such as more individual freedom or public liberty), the court did so in terms of "sound social common sense and legal sentiment." But what is the "social common sense and legal sentiment" in Korea that the court takes its existence for granted? We have no way of knowing what the court meant by it, but I suppose it is closely related to or even composed of Confucian public reasons, the central component of which is *chŏng*. But should liberal democracy take such a nonrationalist and collectivistic factor seriously?

Liberal Democracy of "Sound Common Sense and Legal Sentiment"

My answer is conditionally affirmative: yes, liberal democracy should take such a traditional, nonrationalist (if not irrational), and less-individualistic (if not anti-individualistic) factor seriously, *if* it is to be practiced effectively and legitimately, especially in the traditionally nonliberal, nonindividualistic, and non-Western social and cultural context.

According to William Galston, modern liberalism has two mutually independent historical roots – the Enlightenment and the Reformation.[57] Though rational autonomy and diversity are casually lumped together as if they are two interrelated faces of modern liberalism, rational autonomy is historically rooted in the Enlightenment (culminating in Kant's public reason), while diversity (along with tolerance and value pluralism) is a moral value discovered during and after the Reformation.

Neither of these historic events, however, took place in Korea and I think it is fruitless to try to extrapolate the liberal discourse of autonomy, (negative) freedom, diversity, and pluralism from its embedded social and cultural context, and implant it in Korean society without regard to its unique social and cultural condition, a society where ordinary people are still deeply soaked in Confucian habits of the heart and deliberate public affairs by drawing on Confucian public reasons. In a sense, it is quite natural that the Supreme Court in Korea showed no appreciation for the distinction between personhood and selfhood, presented no statement on the relation between individual freedom and associational freedom, and revealed puzzling inconsistency toward individual freedom, in that all these liberal elements, to which the court is officially committed, are of foreign provenance and thus have no social and cultural history or support in Korean society.

[57] William A. Galston, "Two Concepts of Liberalism," *Ethics* 105 (1995), 516–34.

I believe, however, that the very fact that the Korean Supreme Court (or any court in Korea for that matter) is struggling with liberalism, often with logical inconsistency and practical puzzlement, reveals ironically the resilience of traditional Confucian culture, thereby opening unexpected room to adapt liberalism to Korea's particular social and cultural context. To return to our case, the Korean government's equal and standardized education policy and its public acceptance is difficult to justify purely on liberal grounds. Why should individual freedom of choice yield to equal and standardized education policy when it obviously poses no imminent threat to the unity of the constitutional order of Korea? Or, what is the government's politically compelling and morally justifiable reason to constrain individual freedom on the matter of choosing schools? Of note, ordinary Koreans do not even raise these questions that beg peculiarly liberal-style moral justifications from the government.[58] Instead, they make use of their own cultural mechanism or semiotics, namely Confucian public reasons to make sense of these liberal conundrums.

As argued earlier, Koreans envisage the state as the family-state (*gukka*) and society as the extended family. Their interpersonal relations are largely guided by familial-relational language and they are endured by familial affectionate sentiments (*chŏng*). Even their collective actions in the public space of civil society are occasionally propelled by their shared familial affectionate sentiments, rather than by sheer ethnic nationalism or irrational populism. In my view, the Korean government's egalitarian yet nonliberal education policy and its general acceptance by the Korean people can be understood with reference to uniquely Korean social mores such as *chŏng*, which I believe the Supreme Court implicitly alluded to when it spoke of "sound social common sense and legal sentiment." Otherwise stated, the nonliberal Korean educational policy is publicly justifiable in light of the public, characteristically familial, moral sentiment, according to which no child should be discriminated against or left behind in the "family-modeled" Korean society.

Likewise, the Korean public's general sympathy toward Kang does not seem to be because of his liberal claim to human right or expressive liberty (Kang himself was not clear about the difference between these).[59] This does not mean that Koreans were against the freedom of association claimed by Kang's school. The fact of the matter is that most ordinary Koreans did not pay close attention to such liberal moral justifications as they were not yet familiar with the liberal language of human rights, expressive liberty, and freedom of association, let alone grasping its embedded social meaning, moral value, and practical implications for their social life. Rather, as far as I can see, public sympathy for Kang was generated by the observation that the school, which

58 In this regard, Kang is an exceptional *individual* in the Korean society.

59 It should be noted, however, that not a few Koreans (even those who were sympathetic to him) found Kang's action (suing his own school for example), which is reasonably liberal from the Western standpoint, as odd or even too extreme.

was supposed to act like a benevolent parent who is most concerned with the student's education and welfare, treated him ruthlessly by expelling him while offering him no alternatives, which would have allowed him to avoid transgressing the moral boundaries between him and the school (and teachers).

From the perspective of Confucian public reason, it was the school, not Kang, that transgressed relational moral boundaries, did not act according to its proper "name" (*ming* 名, *myeong* in Korean), and therefore failed to perform its expected role, when it forced Kang to take a particular religious course against his will. In other words, it was the school that first violated the important Confucian norm of "the rectification of names" or *zhengming* 正名 (*jeongmyeong* in Korean), according to which "the ruler must rule, the minister minister, the father be a father, and the son a son."[60] Thus understood, for Koreans, at issue was not so much the violation of individual rights (be it personhood or selfhood) but the violation of the proper moral boundary between the student and the school (and teachers). The school and teachers as surrogate parents failed Kang; they failed to take care of him as a good parent would.

Concluding Remarks

What is important is that by appealing to nonliberal moral sentiment and moral reasoning, the justices on the court (and Korean citizens who were sympathetic to Kang) were able to *practice* a Korean-style liberalism (though this implies that they failed to reproduce Western-style liberal individualism). Put differently, by creatively appropriating the "sound social common sense and legal sentiment" embedded in Confucian culture, particularly the Korean-Confucian *chŏng* culture, Koreans could localize liberalism. Although it is controversial, we may call this locally practiced liberalism *Korean liberalism*. Korean liberalism is a liberalism of a peculiar kind – it is a liberalism that is actually being practiced, albeit without theoretical and legal articulation, by the ordinary Korean people who are more Confucian than liberal (in the Anglo-American sense) in their mode of thinking and way of life. Therefore, I admit, as a theoretical concept, it still leaves much to be desired and improved.

However, it would be imprudent to dismiss the idea of Korean liberalism and instead seek to transplant Western-style liberal democracy in Korea because of its lack of theoretical and conceptual rigor and clarity. We tend to forget that there are multiple forms of liberal democracies even in the West and no modern Western liberal democracy emerged as a predesigned political *theory*. As Alexis de Tocqueville witnessed, American democracy, now extolled as the model liberal democracy, slowly evolved from a set of *practices* that were not necessarily internally coherent, hence his famous definition of democracy as a way of life. Liberalism, too, is a way of life.

[60] *Analects* 12:11.

As discussed earlier, from the viewpoint of practice, liberalism and democracy are not always harmonious. The potential tensions between personhood and citizenship, personhood and selfhood, and selfhood and citizenship perennially characterize what can be called the "paradox of liberal democracy." Korean liberalism, however, can mitigate (if not eliminate) these tensions not only because it is being developed simultaneously with Korean democracy but, more important, because both Korean democracy and Korean liberalism are mediated by Korea's Confucian public culture wherein a person is mainly defined in familial-relational terms. Liberal democracy in Korea, therefore, does not heavily rely on the core liberal distinctions between liberalism and democracy and between personhood and selfhood. Western liberals may be puzzled and wonder how liberalism is ever possible where there are no such distinctions and, more fundamentally, where there is no liberal conception of the self and its corresponding liberal individualism. The real challenge to Korean liberal democracy, therefore, will be to continue to practice liberal democracy in Confucian terms but without positing or implanting Western-style liberal individualism.

10

Confucian Civility and Expressive Liberty

As we have seen in previous chapters, many Confucian democrats argue not only that Confucianism is compatible with democracy as a political institution, but also that it can further invigorate a democratic way of life, which they count as essentially communitarian, because of its fundamental assumption of the self as a social self, and its faith in the harmony between individual and community and their mutual growth in mediation of Confucian rituals (*li* 禮). As we have seen in Chapters 1 and 2, however, this overly positive thesis on the possibility of Confucian democracy as a communitarian sociopolitical practice is vulnerable to and invites many challenging questions: What is meant by "social self"? Does the ontological claim that the Confucian self is a social self naturally (or always) support the ethical claim that it is a civil self? What exactly is meant by the "harmony" between individual and community? How can the relationship be immune to tyranny by the majority, to which democracy is highly susceptible, and what does it mean in the context of ethical pluralism, which is, according to John Rawls, the core characteristic of a modern democratic society?[1] Furthermore, if Confucian harmony is attained by participation in the *li* by the members of the community, what is the relation between *li* and law, or more specifically, how can we place *li* within the broader institutional framework of democratic constitutionalism? In short, precisely in what sense is Confucian democracy an alternative sociopolitical practice to liberal democracy in East Asian societies?

Of course, these questions cannot be answered adequately in the societal abstract. After all, how a person is "social" (or civil) cannot be evaluated without taking into account the sociopolitical and cultural context in which *his* or *her* society is embedded, and historically, each Confucian East Asian country – be it China, Taiwan, Vietnam, or Korea – has developed

[1] John Rawls, *Political Liberalism* (New York: Columbia University Press, 1993).

its distinct local Confucian civil and political culture. To borrow Alexis de Tocqueville's much celebrated language, Confucian East Asians may have a similar Confucian heart, but they have certainly cultivated and lived with different habits of the heart.[2]

Because of the predominant interest in the generic philosophical construction of Confucian democracy, however, normative political theorists and comparative philosophers have given less attention to the unique character of the existing (semi)democratic regimes in Confucian East Asia, such as Taiwan, South Korea, and, arguably, Hong Kong. Yet, the East Asian experiences of (or experiments with) democracy for the past two decades should encourage students of Confucian democracy to go beyond the question of the possibility of Confucian democracy – a question pertinent to mainland China – and grapple more with the particular mode of Confucian democracy that is suitable in a given society's cultural and democratic-political context. I believe this more contextualized political theoretical study of Confucian democracy can provide us with practically valuable insights into the prospect of Confucian democracy in yet-to-be-democratic East Asian countries such as China. At any rate, Confucian democracy as a political theory must prove practically useful in either democratizing authoritarian regimes or making an existing (non-liberal-individualistic) democracy work well (and hopefully better) in East Asia.

In this chapter, I will investigate how traditional Confucian culture and the new democratic way of life are mutually adapting to each other in today's Korean society. More specifically, I will discuss how social norms implicated in Article 311 of the Korean criminal law (namely, *moyokjoe*, which literally translates as insult law), which I argue undergirds a uniquely Korean Confucian communitarian mode of civility,[3] balances well with expressive liberty, a core democratic right which, according to liberals, holds *intrinsic* moral value.[4] My

[2] For instance, according to Su-young Ryu's empirical studies, though the Korean and Chinese value systems are quite similar, they are meaningfully different as Koreans are much more concerned with ritual propriety, whereas for the Chinese, the virtue of the "Middle Way" (*zhongyong* 中庸) is more crucial in their daily lives. For how she conceptualizes each of these concepts, see Su-young Ryu, "Han'gukinui yugyojeok gachicheukjeongmunhang gaebal yeon'gu" [Item Development for Korean Confucian Values], *Korean Journal of Management* 15 (2007), 171–205.

[3] The "existence" of insult law in Korea might have more do to with civil law jurisprudence (versus common law) than with Confucian culture as such as Koreans adopted their civil law during the Japanese colonial period. My argument in this chapter, though, is that not only is the way insult law is interpreted and socially practiced in Korea characteristically Confucian, but it undergirds and further reinforces the Koreans' Confucian habits of the heart.

[4] Freedom of expression is commonly regarded as one of the core "liberal" values that, according to many liberal political theorists, lack any evident connection to conditions of democratic procedure. Joshua Cohen, however, argues that religious, moral, and expressive liberties are integral to democratic ideal: "[A]bridgments of such liberties would constitute denials to citizens of standing as equal members of the sovereign people, by imposing in ways that deny the force of reasons that are, by the lights of their own views, compelling. The reasons for abridgment are unacceptably exclusionary, because they are unsuited to the ideal of guiding the exercise of

key argument is twofold. First, norms of Confucian civility in Korea, often considered at odds with ethical pluralism, underpin a democratic civil society that is internally pluralistic, thereby making Korean democratic civil society characteristically Confucian, thus qualitatively different from the prevailing mode of liberal-individualistic civil society characteristic of most Western democracies. Second, democratic socialization in turn has increasingly sensitized ordinary Korean citizens to the possibility that too much emphasis on civility by the government is likely to degenerate into docility, which works only to impair the regime's democratic vitality and political freedom.

This chapter consists of four sections including this introductory section. In the next section, I present the generic mode of liberal civility that norms associated with freedom of expression give rise to. This section will offer a cross-cultural comparative backdrop against which two generic features of Confucian civility, which I discuss in the third section, will be illuminated. Then, in the fourth section, I will draw attention to the uniquely Korean mode of Confucian communitarian civility in democratic Korean civil society and show how norms of Korean civility implicated in the insult law moderate expressive liberty. The fifth section serves as a conclusion in which I emphasize the critical importance of making Confucian communitarian democracy more responsive to increasing pluralism in Korean civil society and attempt to balance the Confucian communitarian value of Korean civility with the democratic right of expressive liberty.

Expressive Liberty and Liberal Civility

Freedom of expression, or expressive liberty, is considered a core human right, but why it is morally important is rarely discussed in non-Western societies. What is often said is that expressive liberty, which encompasses and/or entails freedom of thought, freedom of conscience, religious freedom, freedom of speech, and, more controversially, freedom of association, is a "modern liberty" as Benjamin Constant understood it and that its modern origin is closely linked to the Reformation and ensuing religious wars in early modern Europe. According to William Galston, expressive liberty is an essential component of what he calls "diversity liberalism," a version of liberalism that the Reformation gave rise to,[5] and he understands expressive liberty as "the absence of constraints, imposed by some individuals on others, that make it impossible (or significantly more difficult) for the affected individuals to live their lives in ways that express their deepest beliefs about what gives meaning or value to life."[6]

power by a process of reason-giving suited to a system of free and equal citizens" (Joshua Cohen, "Democracy and Liberty," in Elster, *Deliberative Democracy*, 207).

[5] William A. Galston, *Liberal Pluralism: The Implications of Value Pluralism for Political Theory and Practice* (Cambridge: Cambridge University Press, 2002), 20–24.

[6] Ibid., 28.

However, Galston's interpretation of expressive liberty as negative liberty is short of conveying its more positive moral dimension.[7] As we saw in Chapter 9, the positive moral value of expressive liberty is offered by George Kateb when he says that "freedom of expression is not the whole of freedom, but its soul."[8] Let us recall Kateb's core argument: (1) expressive liberty is a fundamental human right because it concerns one's self-identity (selfhood), because it is a right to express "who I am" as a unique individual; (2) since it is entwined with my self-identity and self-ontology (who I am), expressive liberty is an *intrinsic value* (i.e., a noninstrumental value) and hence it is a *human* right, a right every human being is entitled to possess simply by merit of his or her being human. Like Galston, Kateb believes expressive liberty is a negative liberty in that the absence of constraints is essential to its exercise. But for Kateb, emphasis is not so much on negative liberty as such but its maximal *exercise* by every individual citizen.[9] Thus understood, the practical essence of expressive liberty lies in self-realization.

Some are puzzled by the attempt to resuscitate value pluralism by maximally respecting expressive liberty and moral diversity in post-Reformation liberal politics (most saliently in the United States) because value pluralism often gives rise to identity politics in a democratic society,[10] and thus it is likely to reverse the liberal formula for the depoliticization of differences, thereby reigniting the "perils of pluralism," the evil of which Thomas Hobbes aptly portrayed in his remarkably violent account of the state of nature.[11] It is for this reason that Brian Barry criticizes multiculturalism (which he does not distinguish from diversity liberalism) for being oblivious to why modern liberal-democratic institutions were created in the first place.[12]

Though it is an intriguing and important question of political theory as to whether Barry's (and other civic liberals') concern is warranted, what is more important in our context is the point that expressive liberty is not harmless. In fact, one's expressive liberty is prone to harm others mostly by making them resentful (hence not necessarily physically). Following Joshua Cohen, we may

[7] In fact, Galston does talk about the positive moral dimension of expressive liberty in terms of "value pluralism." But he does not go further to discuss why value pluralism is morally important to a person.

[8] George Kateb, "The Value of Association," in *Freedom of Association*, ed. Amy Gutmann (Princeton: Princeton University Press, 1998), 53.

[9] Galston, too, takes the positive value of expressive liberty seriously, but, unlike Kateb, he does not think expressive liberty is essentially an individual right because he believes this right can be claimed by a group whose membership is ascriptive rather than self-chosen (i.e., the Amish people).

[10] On the inherent relation between value pluralism and identity politics in a democratic society, see Amy Gutmann, *Identity in Democracy* (Princeton: Princeton University Press, 2003).

[11] On the perils of pluralism and the origin of modern liberal constitutionalism, see Richard Boyd, *Uncivil Society: The Perils of Pluralism and the Making of Modern Liberalism* (Lanham, MD: Lexington Books, 2004).

[12] Brian Barry, *Culture and Equality* (Cambridge, MA: Harvard University Press, 2001), 24–5.

call harms accompanying freedom of expression the *costs* of expressive liberty.[13] What is interesting is Cohen's claim that in a liberal society protection of freedom of expression should not be repealed simply because of such costs.

Expression sometimes has unambiguous costs. It is sometimes offensive, disgusting, or outrageous; it produces reputational injury and emotional distress.... But ... the presence of such costs does not as a general manner suffice to remove protection from expression. Neither offense, nor cleanup costs for taxpayers, nor reputational injury, nor emotional distress, for example, suffice by themselves to deprive expression of protection.... [E]ven uncontested facts of reputational injury or emotional distress are not always sufficient to deprive expression of protection – as when the target of expression is a public figure or when the expression focuses on a subject of general interest.[14]

The ethical implications of Cohen's argument are not difficult to understand: free life is not cheap, and its costs are not insignificant; to live freely, I must be ready to put up with certain emotional distress and reputational injury caused by others' exercise of expressive liberty as they, on their part, must also tolerate my freedom. Cohen's view, however, goes beyond the reciprocal bearing of costs associated with expressive liberty and tolerance, which distinguishes him from strong liberal pluralists like Galston, who considers tolerance as the core democratic virtue in a liberal pluralist society; for Cohen's reciprocal justification of expressive liberty and its costs is fundamentally premised on the democratic ideal of collective decisions by free and equal citizens and the norms of justice (i.e., democratic justice) it entails. Thomas Scanlon offers one of the classic accounts on the inherent relation between expressive liberty and democratic justice:

Within certain limits, it seems clear that the value to be placed on having various kinds of expression flourish is something which should be subject to popular will in the society in question. The limits I have in mind here are, first, those imposed by considerations of distributive justice. Access to means of expression for whatever purposes one may have in mind is a good which can be fairly or unfairly distributed among the members of a society, and many cases which strike us as violations of freedom of expression are in fact instances of distributive justice.... Access to means of expression is in many cases a necessary condition for participation in the political process of the country, and therefore something to which citizens have an independent right.[15]

In the similar Kantian-Rawlsian vein, Cohen echoes Scanlon's maximalist justification of freedom of expression (of course within the constitutional limit) on the democratic principle of *deliberative inclusion*, when he says,

[13] Cohen's own understanding of "costs" is slightly different from mine because by the term he means, quite generically, "conditions that it is reasonable to want to avoid." Joshua Cohen, "Freedom of Expression," *Philosophy and Public Affairs* 22 (1993), 207–63, 214n23.

[14] Ibid., 214–15.

[15] Thomas Scanlon, "A Theory of Freedom of Expression," *Philosophy and Public Affairs* 1 (1972), 204–26, 223.

"[T]he deliberative conception requires more than the interests of all be given equal consideration in binding collective decisions; it requires, too, that we find politically acceptable reasons – reasons acceptable to others, given a background of reasonable differences of conscientious conviction."[16]

That said, however, both Cohen and Scanlon do not seem to take seriously enough the real and potential costs of expressive liberty. When Cohen says in a Kantian tone that citizens in a pluralistic society *ought to* subscribe to the democratic moral principle of deliberative inclusion, he does not explicate how they must come to terms with their emotional distress and reputational injury. Does democratic norm naturally dissolve psychological injury? Is reason itself its own motivational force? Scanlon's Millian justification for expressive liberty, however plausible politically, offers no better explanation. Scanlon's key argument is that citizens in a liberal democracy *ought to* put up with certain costs of expressive liberty because failure to do so implies more and frequent calls for governmental intervention in citizens' private affairs and such intervention is likely to happen without a compelling moral justification.[17] But how does the fear of unjustified governmental intervention help citizens deal with their emotional distress and reputational injury caused by others' exercise of expressive freedom in a pluralistic society? Evidently, something is missing in Cohen's and Scanlon's otherwise plausible normative political theories (deliberative inclusion and contractualism, respectively).

Nancy Rosenblum attributes this critical lacuna in mainstream democratic political theory to its typical understanding of democracy as moral norms or principles rather than as everyday social practice. Rosenblum's attention to the "democracy of everyday life" is inspired by Judith Shklar's insightful observation that "pluralism generates intended and unintended exclusions so that outsiders are inevitably rebuffed. Snobbery – 'the heart of making inequality hurt' – is a by-product of multiplicity."[18] Rosenblum's presentation of the picture of the democratic living of ordinary citizens is far more, sometimes disturbingly, realistic: "The democracy of everyday life does not attack the myriad distinctions based on styles of consumption, leisure activities, neighborhood, religion, race, or standard of living. It is not a promise of social equality. It would be wrong to see this democratic disposition as an adequate morality or

[16] Cohen, "Democracy and Liberty," 203.

[17] Of course, this does not mean that Scanlon opposes all kinds of government restrictions of freedom of expression. His position is much subtler: "The theory of freedom of expression which I am offering ... is based upon the Millian Principle, which is absolute but serves only to rule out certain justifications for legal restrictions on acts of expression. Within the limits set by this principle the whole range of governmental policies affecting opportunities for expression, whether by restriction, positive intervention, or failure to intervene, are subject to justification and criticism on a number of diverse grounds" (Scanlon, "Theory of Freedom of Expression," 224).

[18] Nancy L. Rosenblum, "The Democracy of Everyday Life," in Yack, *Liberalism without Illusions*, 26.

account of character. *The democracy of everyday life cannot even be taken as a sure sign of mutual respect.*"[19]

Rosenblum's point is that democratic living in actuality is in no way "orchestrated" by the principles of justice or democratic norms and ideals, that is, there should be no illusion of democracy. Again, free living in a democracy in which everyone is sovereign is not cheap, and the costs of free living are "ordinary vices," which include snobbery, misanthropy, betrayal, and hypocrisy, all having a great deal to do with mental distress and reputational injury.[20] What is vigorously avoided is cruelty, which is "the first vice" and the avoidance of cruelty (or "putting cruelty first" as Shklar calls it) should be at the heart of liberalism, namely, the *liberalism of fear*.

> This is a liberalism that was born out of the cruelties of the religious civil wars.... If the faith was to survive at all, it would do so privately. The alternative then set, and still before us, is not one between classical virtue and liberal self-indulgence, but between cruel military and moral repression and violence, and a self-restraining tolerance that fences in the powerful to protect the freedom and safety of every citizen, old and young, male or female, black or white. Far from being an amoral free-for-all, liberalism is, in fact, extremely difficult and constraining, far too much so for those who cannot endure contradiction, complexity, diversity, and the risks of freedom.[21]

In Rosenblum's (and Shklar's) viewpoint, the deliberative (or contractual-deliberative) model of democracy that Cohen and Scanlon put forward as most suitable in the social context of reasonable pluralism is far from adequate in coming to terms with ordinary vices in everyday democracy, despite their interest in expressive liberty and pluralism itself. To say the least, their accounts of liberal democracy in a pluralist society are incomplete. To begin with, Cohen's and Scanlon's account(s) of democracy, which represents mainstream democratic political theory, fails to do justice to the "vicissitudes of pluralist society,"[22] which stem in part from one's unique selfhood and the (expressive and associational) freedom that undergirds it. More important, however, what is lacking in mainstream democratic political theory is what mediates the vicissitudes of pluralist society (expressive liberty and its associated costs/risks) and

[19] Ibid., 30, emphasis added. In Rosenblum's view, the core characteristics of the democracy of everyday life that Shklar demonstrates are best shown in the social dynamic affiliated with freedom of association, the moral value of which is inherently tied with expressive liberty: "I suggest that affiliation with voluntary association in which we are wanted and willing members is a key source of self-respect; that discrimination may be safely contained in these groups; and that because associations often owe their origin to a dynamic of affiliation and exclusion resentment, and self-affirmation, liberal democracy is consistent with and even requires the incongruence between voluntary groups and public norms that always accompanies freedom of association" (Nancy L. Rosenblum, "Compelled Association: Public Standing, Self-Respect, and the Dynamic of Exclusion," in Gutmann, *Freedom of Association*, 76).

[20] Judith N. Shklar, *Ordinary Vices* (Cambridge, MA: Harvard University Press, 1984).

[21] Ibid., 5.

[22] Rosenblum, "Democracy of Everyday Life," 40.

inclusive democratic politics (equal opportunity and mutual respect) or what helps *individuals* struggling with the costs/risks of expressive freedom on a personal (mainly psychological) level present themselves as rational, free, and equal *citizens* in the public space of civil society. We can call this lack *liberal civility*, without which liberal-democratic living is practically impossible.

What, then, does liberal civility consist of? Shklar's statement clearly tells us that what is at the heart of liberal civility is a self-restraining tolerance. Here, however, the point is not so much tolerance as such but self-restraint that makes tolerance possible. Galston aptly elaborates what this liberal tolerance practically means when he says that "[it is] the conscientious reluctance to act in ways that impede others from living in accordance with their various conceptions of what gives life meaning and worth."[23]

Thus understood, tolerance, especially in the pluralist societal context, is a tension ridden virtue, which never deliberately aims for the complete psychological and political resolution of the costs of expressive liberty that is at once negative *and* positive.[24] After all, complete resolution of the costs of expressive liberty in a liberal pluralist society implies more unjustified governmental interventions and/or lack of firm selfhood. As such, expressive liberty (and the costs/risks accompanying it) always belies perfect equality among citizens in everyday democratic social settings. It is for this reason that the democracy of everyday life vitally hinges on the civilizing force of hypocrisy. "The democracy of everyday life, which is rightly admired by egalitarian visitors to America, does not arise from sincerity. It is based on the pretense that we must speak to each other as if social standings were a matter of indifference in our views of each other. That is, of course, not true. Not all of us are even convinced that all men are entitled to a certain minimum of social respect. Only some of us think so. But most of us always act as if we really did believe it, and that is what counts."[25]

If self-restraining tolerance makes up the inner disposition of liberal civility, hypocrisy is what facilitates civilized behaviors in a pluralistic democratic civil society, where citizens encounter one another primarily as strangers. Hypocrisy prevents one's mental distress or (minor) reputational injury from developing into uncivil behavior. By helping to build an internal wall between *private* (often negative) feelings toward others' expressive liberty and *public* civilities of tolerance and mutual reciprocity, hypocrisy achieves peaceful or civil coexistence of individuals subscribing to different comprehensive doctrines and secures democratic stability and constitutional order. In fact, deliberative cooperation and democratic participation that Cohen and Scanlon (and many

[23] Galston, *Liberal Pluralism*, 119.

[24] It is a negative liberty in the sense that its exercise is possible only in the absence of (unjustified) constraints, but it is essentially a positive liberty because its exercise is fundamentally concerned with one's self-realization.

[25] Shklar, *Ordinary Vices*, 77.

other civic liberals) cherish is not even conceivable without presupposing this apparently "thin" liberal baseline of civility that is not primarily aimed at a far more demanding democratic virtue of civic cooperation itself.[26]

Let me recapitulate what has been argued so far: (1) expressive liberty is a core democratic liberty, and its exercise in civil society is accompanied by some costs that are not cheap; (2) the costs of expressive liberty essentially render democracy to be a pluralistic way of life involving various modes of social vicissitudes; (3) in a liberal-democratic society the vicissitude of pluralism is civically moderated without losing its social vitality by means of the virtue of hypocrisy, a quintessential liberal virtue that is enabled by a self-restraining tolerance; and finally (4) hypocrisy as a liberal virtue is predicated on and reinforces the division between private emotions/passions and public appearance.[27]

What political theoretical implications can we draw from these findings for the study of Confucian democracy? Many Confucian democrats, mostly communitarian, have taken pains to show the incompatibility between Confucian ritual-based role ethics and liberal rights discourse and presented their vision(s) of Confucian democracy as an alternative to liberal democracy.[28] Therefore, core democratic rights such as freedom of expression and freedom of association have rarely, if ever, been discussed in, let alone integrated into, their theoretical/philosophical constructions of Confucian democracy by treating such rights in terms of "Western culture" – that is, by regarding such freedoms as *Western-liberal* rights rather than as liberties integral to a socially vibrant democratic living in *any* pluralist society, whether it be liberal or Confucian. In other words, Confucian communitarian democrats tend to assume Confucian society to be culturally monolithic and ethically monist, paying insufficient attention to existing intracultural plurality in East Asian societies and their rapidly increasing internal pluralization.

In the remainder of this chapter, I attempt to correct this problem by showing how citizens in democratized Korea grapple with pluralism, specifically focusing on their use of expressive liberty, *in* the societal context of their Confucian culture, without making their democratic way of life Western-style

[26] Though most deliberative democrats do not explicitly acknowledge the role of hypocrisy in the deliberative setting, Jon Elster insightfully notes how hypocrisy is integral to democratic deliberation. See his "Deliberation and Constitution Making," in Elster, *Deliberative Democracy*.

[27] For an insightful discussion about the kinds of deception, hypocrisy, and compromise that are morally and politically defensible, see Ruth W. Grant, *Hypocrisy and Integrity: Machiavelli, Rousseau, and the Ethics of Politics* (Chicago: University of Chicago Press, 1997).

[28] David L. Hall and Roger T. Ames, *The Democracy of the Dead: Dewey, Confucius, and the Hope for Democracy in China* (Chicago: Open Court, 1999); Sor-hoon Tan, *Confucian Democracy: A Deweyan Reconstruction* (Albany: State University of New York Press, 2003); Henry Rosemont, "Human Rights: A Bill of Worries," in de Bary and Tu, *Confucianism and Human Rights* and Craig K. Ihara, "Are Individual Rights Necessary? A Confucian Perspective," in Shun and Wong, *Confucian Ethics*. See Chapters 1 and 2 of this book for my critical engagement with these (and other related) works.

liberal individualistic. But before delving into the Korean case, let us briefly examine some defining features of Confucian civility, distinguishing Confucian civility from its liberal counterpart.

Confucian Civility: Generic Features

In this section I will discuss two generic features of Confucian civility. By "generic features," I mean the features that are generally found in the foundational Confucian classics, such as the *Analects of Confucius* (*Lunyu* 論語), the *Works of Mencius* (*Mengzi* 孟子), and the *Works of Xunzi* (*Xunzi* 荀子), the social manifestations of which may not have been identical in the actually existing Confucian societies in East Asia. The purpose of this section is, first, to discuss defining characteristics of Confucian civility in comparison with liberal civility discussed earlier and, second, to offer a cultural backdrop against which the unique features of Korean Confucian-democratic civility shall be illuminated.

1. Civility as Sincerity

As we have seen, one of the core elements of liberal civility, especially in the context of reasonable value pluralism, is hypocrisy, which, after all, is a species of deception, and thus a conventional vice. What makes hypocrisy a liberal virtue, particularly in a democratic societal context, though, is its remarkable social utility in avoiding the greater (perhaps the greatest) vice, namely, cruelty. While avoidance of cruelty is one of Confucianism's core concerns,[29] no classical (or later) Confucians ever encouraged people to utilize a vice to prevent a greater vice. Instead, Confucians consistently exhorted people to be sincere in every human relationship. So, the first generic feature of Confucian civility is sincerity, *cheng* 誠 in Chinese, which rejects a stark separation between one's private emotions and public behavior. Most tellingly, Mencius says, "There is in man nothing more ingenuous than the pupils of his eyes. They cannot conceal his wickedness. When he is upright within his breast, a man's pupils are clear and bright; when he is not, they are clouded and murky. How can a man conceal his true character if you listen to his words and observe the pupils of his eyes?"[30]

There is no clear distinction, let alone artificial separation, between inner and outer here: one's inner heart (*xin* 心) is unfailingly reflected in one's body (*shen* 身) and external behavior, for example, in the way one talks or in the kind

[29] This theme is most clearly presented in Mencius's political philosophy. See my discussion of Mencius's attitude toward the Hegemonic Rule (*ba dao* 霸道) in Sungmoon Kim, "Between Good and Evil: Xunzi's Reinterpretation of the Hegemonic Rule as Decent Governance," *Dao* 12 (2013), 73–92, esp. 76–9.

[30] *Mencius* 4A15. Throughout this chapter, all English translations of the *Mengzi* are adopted from *Mencius*, trans. D. C. Lau (New York: Penguin, 1970).

of words one uses when talking to others. Therefore, in the Confucian ethical tradition, self-cultivation (*xiushen* 修身) means the cultivation of both one's inner self and one's outer self. This simultaneous cultivation of the inner and outer self (*xin* and *shen*) is possible because, contra Descartes, Confucianism stipulates that both inner self and outer self are on a continuum, constituting a coherent social personhood. It is for this reason that Confucius imparted a tremendous moral value to rites (*li*), which was then widely deemed to be solely concerned with one's external behavior, and presented them as an indispensable vehicle for moral self-cultivation: "Deference unmediated by observing ritual propriety (*li*) is lethargy; caution unmediated by observing ritual propriety is timidity; boldness unmediated by observing ritual propriety is rowdiness; candor unmediated by observing ritual propriety is rudeness."[31] As Tu Weiming rightly claims, though *ren* 仁, Confucian moral virtue par excellence, and *li* are sometimes in (creative) tensions, "*li* can be conceived as an externalization of *ren* in a specific social context."[32]

Sincerity, therefore, is an essential feature of Confucian civility, which is typically mediated by the *li*.[33] To put on a mask of civil appearance to conceal one's true emotions for the sake of civil peace and social utility, which is what is meant by hypocrisy in the liberal tradition, directly goes against the spirit of Confucian civility. Confucian civility is what naturally results from the moral virtues (such as *ren* 仁, *yi* 義, *li* 禮, *zhi* 智) one has cultivated rather than what is artificially contrived against one's truest emotions for utilitarian consideration. Even Xunzi, who believed human nature is wicked and thus suggested what Philip J. Ivanhoe calls the "re-formation model" of moral self-cultivation,[34] stresses the critical importance of sincerity in Confucian civility.

[31] *Analects* 8:2.

[32] Tu Weiming, *Humanity and Self-Cultivation* (Berkeley, CA: Asian Humanities Press, 1979), 10.

[33] In their recent book, Adam Seligman and his colleagues make a powerful statement that what ritual (including Confucian ritual) does is constitute a "subjunctive world" in which "as-if" is a key modality, making sincerity the enemy of ritual (Adam B. Seligman, Robert Weller, Michael J. Puett, and Bennett Simon, *Ritual and Its Consequences: An Essay on the Limits of Sincerity* [Oxford: Oxford University Press, 2008]). I admit that there is indeed an important kind of room for not-full-sincerity in the Confucian practice of civility as pushing oneself to act in ways that one does not yet spontaneously feel motivated to do – which can be called "conscientious" behavior – is an integral part of the Confucian program of learning. After all, the social importance of face or *chemyeon* in Korean is widely acknowledged in traditionally Confucian East Asian societies. That being said, it is important to note that what makes keeping a face (or *chemyeon*) extremely important in such societies is the underlying premise of the inextricable intertwinement between one's inner and outer worlds, or, otherwise put, one's sincerity. That is, keeping face is important because one's external behavior is still assumed to manifest one's inner moral state and thus one *must* not reveal any chasm between one's inner state and outer behavior. For a psychological study of the ritual of keeping face in the Korean context, see Sang-chin Choi, *Han'gukin shimlihak* [The Psychology of the Korean People] (Seoul: Chung Ang University Press, 2000), 160–92.

[34] Philip J. Ivanhoe, *Confucian Moral Self Cultivation* (Indianapolis: Hackett, 2000), 29–42.

For the gentleman (*junzi* 君子) to nurture his mind, nothing is more excellent than sincerity (*cheng*). If a man has attained perfection of sincerity, he will have no other concern than to uphold the principle of humanity (*ren*) and to behave with righteousness (*yi*). If with sincerity of mind he upholds the principle of humanity, it will be (outwardly) manifested. Having been (outwardly) manifested, it becomes intelligent. Having become intelligible, it can produce transmutation (of the wicked human nature of the other people). (In other words,) if with sincerity of mind he behaves with righteousness, it will accord with what is naturally appropriate (*li* 理). According with what is naturally appropriate, it will become clear. Having become clear, it can transform (the people).[35]

The ultimate aim of Confucian civility is not so much civil peace or an avoidance of the state of nature, which is in actuality a state of war and cruelty. "Negative politics" of this kind is what characterizes the liberalism of fear.[36] Rather, Confucian civility is aimed at one's moral self-cultivation/transformation and social extension of the moral virtues thusly cultivated toward others, however imperfect one currently is. Extended from personal moralities such as benevolence, righteousness, and ritual propriety (thus far cultivated), civility is deeply entwined with one's moral character, and it is the virtue of sincerity that maintains the inextricable connection between civility and morality.

From the Confucian ethical standpoint, the liberal preoccupation with appearance and reliance on "deception" (which enables the virtue of hypocrisy) is likely to produce a "village-worthy" (*xiang yuan* 鄉愿) whose inner self and public persona are polarized: "As for the person who give the outward appearance of being stern while being pulp inside, if we were to look to petty people for an example of this kind of deceit, it is the house burglar who bores holes in walls or scales over them."[37] Certainly, the village-worthy is not equivalent to a petty man (*xiaoren* 小人) found in a pre-*li* state, whom Xunzi presents as the polar opposite of the Confucian gentleman (*junzi* 君子). While a petty man is both immoral and uncivil, a village-worthy is immoral but appears civil in his speech and behavior, thus making his civility only specious and his inner self polarized. In Confucius's own language, the village-worthy is the "thief of virtue."[38]

[35] *Xunzi* 3:9a (modified). The English translation is adopted from John Knoblock, *Xunzi: A Translation and Study of Complete Works*, 3 vols. (Stanford: Stanford University Press, 1988, 1990, 1994).

[36] Michael Walzer, "On Negative Politics," in Yack, *Liberalism without Illusion*.

[37] *Analects* 17:12. Throughout this chapter, all English translations of the *Analects* of Confucius are adopted from Roger T. Ames and Henry Rosemont Jr., *The Analects of Confucius: A Philosophical Translation* (New York: Ballantine Books, 1998).

[38] *Analects* 17:13. Also see *Mencius* 7B37. For a more detailed discussion of the village worthy from a comparative perspective, see Sungmoon Kim, "Self-Transformation and Civil Society: Lockean vs. Confucian," *Dao* 8 (2009), 383–401, 394–5.

2. Civility as the Extension of Filiality

The second general characteristic of Confucian civility is that it is rooted in and extended from filiality (*xiaoti* 孝悌). In the preceding subsection, we have seen that Confucian civility is extended from moral virtues, however imperfect they may be currently. What is now important to note is that in the Confucian ethical tradition, *ren* is understood as the supreme (or generic) moral virtue that encompasses all other virtues such as righteousness (*yi*), ritual propriety (*li*), faithfulness (*xin* 信), and moral and intellectual judgment (*zhi*), and it is said to be rooted in filial and fraternal responsibility, or simply filiality. Most famously, Youzi, one of Confucius's disciple, said, "[e]xemplary persons (*junzi*) concentrate their efforts on the root, for the root having taken hold, the way (*dao* 道) will grow therefrom. As for filial and fraternal responsibility (*xiaodi* 孝弟), it is, I suspect, the root of *ren*."[39]

Being extended from moral virtues, therefore, Confucian civility is also rooted in filiality. In saying this, I mean two things. First, generally speaking, Confucian civility is attained by extending filiality that one has cultivated in one's family relationships to others. The Mencian-Confucian theory of extension (about which I elaborated in Chapter 5), especially in the formation of civility from filiality, lends support to the first generic characteristic of Confucian civility, namely, sincerity. It is neither premised on the stark separation between private and public and/or inner and outer, nor calls for the virtue of hypocrisy as modus operandi in forming and maintaining civility. One's self remains coherent throughout all life spheres, and the quality of one's moral character is tightly connected with one's capacity for sociability. In short, what undergirds the actual moral psychological process of extension is sincerity.

My second point about Confucian civility being rooted in filiality is concerned with the character of Confucian civility: not only does filiality help generate Confucian civility, but it renders Confucian civility as essentially familial. That is, by virtue of Confucian civility, one is enabled to envision the state (or society) as an extended family – in the Confucian tradition state is called the "state-family" (*guojia* 國家) – and see others *as if* they were a member of one's (extended) family.[40]

For instance, in the *Analects*, Zixia, a student of Confucius, admonishes Sima Niu who laments that he has no brother: "Since the *junzi* is respectful and impeccable in his conduct, is deferential to others and observes ritual propriety, everyone in the world is their brother. Why would a *junzi* worry over having no brothers?"[41] This passage is commonly interpreted to mean either that a *junzi*

[39] *Analects* 1:2.

[40] In this regard, I oppose Joseph Chan's rigorous distinction between *civil virtues* and *relational virtues* in Confucian ethics, which attributes only to the former a disposition "to behave in a civil manner to everyone" (Joseph Chan, "Exploring the Nonfamilial in Confucian Political Philosophy," in Hahm and Bell, *Politics of Affective Relations*, 61–74, 67–8).

[41] *Analects* 12:5 (modified).

will be naturally loved by everyone in the world or that a *junzi* ought to treat everyone in the world as his brothers. In my view, however, a more plausible interpretation is that being morally cultivated and civically sociable, a *junzi* is able to (rather than *ought to*) regard everyone in the world *as* his family members, regardless of whether or not he is loved by them. Put differently, what is at stake is one's moral capacity to regard others (including total strangers) as one's family members, namely, Confucian civility. By regarding others as one's family members, one overcomes (or dissolves) such antisocial passions as enmity and resentment that one would have harbored toward them. While liberal civility is focused on a "strangership" enabled by rational self-control and an art of appearance (or the virtue of hypocrisy), Confucian civility is fundamentally a *relational strangership*.[42]

In this section, I have discussed two generic features of Confucian civility in reference to core Confucian philosophical classics and showed how they make Confucian civility distinct from its liberal counterpart. I now turn to Confucian civility in democratic Korea whose civil society is increasingly pluralistic – more specifically, how Korean citizens exercise their constitutional right to freedom of expression in a context of which norms are heavily informed by the general features of Confucian civility discussed in this section.

Insult Law and Its Implications for Contemporary Korean Society

In political science, it is a truism that democratization refers to the change of a regime from authoritarian to democratic, where "regime" is understood chiefly in terms of political institutions. Therefore, factors such as societal culture and social psychology and the norms of civility that seem to lie outside the formal political institutions are rarely taken seriously in the political science literature on democracy. Even when political scientists pay attention to such factors (especially social psychology), their focus is on the cognitive and affective elements of individual respondents – by "social psychology" they commonly refer to *aggregated* results from individuals' surveys, but not the psychology of the *people*.[43] The social psychology of the people may not be so germane to a multiethnic, multicultural, or radically pluralistic society, but it is highly relevant to an ethnically and culturally homogeneous democracy like Korea that, albeit arguably, has long maintained its nation-statehood.[44]

[42] For a more detailed discussion of Confucian civility as relational strangership, see Sungmoon Kim, "Beyond Liberal Civil Society: Confucian Familism and Relational Strangership," *Philosophy East and West* 60 (2010), 476–98.

[43] See for instance, Doh Chull Shin, *Confucianism and Democratization in East Asia* (New York: Cambridge University Press, 2012); Yun-han Chu, Larry Diamond, Andrew J. Nathan, and Doh Chull Shin (eds.), *How East Asians View Democracy* (New York: Columbia University Press, 2008).

[44] For studies on Korean social psychology in contemporary Korea, see Sang-chin Choi's and his collaborators' works cited in Chapter 9 of this book. For an excellent philosophical

As we have seen in the previous chapter, in Korea, democratization is not limited to a regime change. In a most profound sense, democratization in Korea entails a drastic change in folk psychology, civility, and ultimately societal culture. More specifically, as democratization progresses, citizens in Korea are under increasing pressure to adapt to liberal-democratic societal culture as well as to their new liberal-democratic sociopolitical institutions. And they are under equal pressure to adopt liberal civility as a new mode of social living. In the next section I will discuss how Korean citizens can accommodate liberal civility without giving up traditional Confucian civility in an increasingly pluralistic civil society. In the present section, I illustrate the Confucian communitarian character of Korean democratic civil society by focusing on the way Confucian civility moderates expressive liberty and reduces its costs. Special attention will be given to the "insult law" in the Korean criminal code, which, I argue, has offered a critical institutional bulwark for Confucian civility in contemporary Korea.

Article 311 of the Criminal Law of Korea states, "a person who publicly insults another shall be punished by imprisonment or imprisonment without prison labor for no more than one year or by a fine not exceeding two million won [approximately two thousand U.S. dollars]." While the defamation charge in Article 307 defines an offense in terms of public exposure of a specific fact (with an intention to defame other person) or the fabrication of a fact (which thereby defames other person), the "insult charge" in Article 311 defines an offense solely on the basis of the victim's subjective feeling, that is, based on an accusation that he or she has suffered damage from verbal, behavioral, or literal expressions of another's abstract judgment or derogatory expression, which depreciates his or her social value. In other words, a case of "insult" is constituted without involving representation or fabrication of a fact.

Defamation is a crime that can be prosecuted without the explicit agreement of the victim: except in the case of the victim's death, the accusation will be subject to criminal or civil prosecution unless the victim clearly expresses the desire not to prosecute the one who defamed him or her. In contrast, with the insult law, the one who insulted will not be prosecuted without an explicit complaint from the victim (or the victim's family members, who can succeed the victim's legal right) since the criminality of insult does not involve a fact (whether its public exposure or fabrication); the criminality of insult is constituted solely by the victim's subjective feeling and its (legal) complaint. What is important here is that under the insult charge, though it is quite difficult to prosecute the insulting conduct because of its eligibility requirements (including the victim's explicit complaint), it is relatively easy to impose the prosecution once the victim proceeds with a complaint – not only because it is

anthropological study of the Korean people in a postdemocratic Korea, see C. Fred Alford, *Think No Evil: Korean Values in the Age of Globalization* (Ithaca: Cornell University Press, 1999).

prosecutable as long as the expression indicates an abstract judgment which depreciates the reputation of a person in light of the common norms of society, but also because the expression in question does not need to be as specific as in the defamation case.

Apparently, the existence of insult law and the heavy criminal punishment of its violation is one of the distinctive characteristics of the Korean criminal law and, by extension, Korean law and society in general. First, barring a few exceptions such as Germany and France, almost all Western liberal-democratic countries have either scrapped insult law from their criminal codes or do not count private insult, the criminality of which is completely based on the victim's reputational (and psychological) injury, as an object of public, especially criminal, legal jurisdiction. In the United States, for instance, not only is private insult not a crime, but even defamation, which involves either public exposure or fabrication of a fact with an intention to impair the public reputation of other person, does not necessarily create a criminal case.[45] Among democratic countries in East Asia, only Japan, whose civil society is most Western and liberal among East Asian countries, has an insult law in the criminal code, but the degree of punishment for the accused is far less severe than is the case in Korea. China, a communist state according to its constitution, maintains insult law in its criminal code (Article 246), but compared to Korean insult law, the Chinese law is ambiguous about what constitutes criminality in the conduct of insult and largely confounds insult with libel or defamation. Comparatively speaking, Korean insult law is the most articulate in content and comprehensive in scope.

In the present context the sociopolitical and cultural implications of the criminality of private insult for Korean democratic civility are important, and I argue that norms presupposed in the Korean insult law show, albeit vicariously, the Confucian communitarian character of Korean civility and its lasting importance in Korean civil society. Three points can be made in this regard.

First, the criminalization of private insult and its general endorsement by the Korean public represents the lower enthusiasm on the part of ordinary Korean citizens to live with the "vicissitudes of pluralism" (if not pluralism itself) or their unease with the costs caused by others' exercise of expressive freedom, such as reputational injury and emotional distress. As noted, one of the central reasons that liberals (of fear) are attracted to the civil virtue of hypocrisy is that they fear more likelihood of arbitrary governmental intervention in private affairs. Otherwise stated, liberals are far more troubled by the (potential) violation of individual human rights than by the polarization of the self, which remains as a psychological injury, however negligible. According to Confucian moral sensibility, however, self-polarization critically impairs one's coherent moral selfhood/character and hampers moral growth. By criminalizing private

[45] But even in the United States "intentional inflictions of emotional stress" is punishable by the civil law.

insult, Koreans seem to be less concerned with governmental intervention in private affairs than with mental distress and, especially, reputational injury. They are less culturally familiar with the art of hypocrisy and, accordingly, find that *virtue* (*virtù*) is morally unpalatable. In their view, self-polarization should be avoided by all means as it denotes not merely a psychological burden, but fundamentally, a moral failure.

Second, the fact that Korean citizens are not gravely (compared to Western liberal citizens) concerned with state/government involvement in their private affairs especially when it comes to cases of insult reveals that their understanding of the state is still deeply informed by Confucian culture. In Korea, the image of the state as the "family-state" has never been seriously challenged and ordinary Korean citizens largely subscribe to the traditional Confucian notion of the state as the *gukka* (the Korean equivalent of the Chinese *guojia*), which, according to Kyung Moon Hwang's excellent historical study, was never abandoned during the Korean enlightenment period in the late nineteenth century when most creative minds in Korea were absorbed in the building of the modern Korean nation-state.[46] Being envisaged as the extended family, the state in Korea is expected to take care of the welfare of the people, where welfare includes both economic and civil (especially social-reputational) welfare, rather than a necessary evil the involvement of which (read: intervention) in private affairs must be minimized. Therefore, the distinction between state and society is not clearly delineated, nor is the distinction between public and private.[47]

Third, and most important, the strong hold of insult law in Korean society reveals its Confucian communitarian character. According to Fred Alford's research, Koreans do not define evil independently of who is relating to whom because the relationship defines what is good or evil in a particular context. Alford thus concludes that "[i]f 'tell me the relationship and I'll tell you what's evil' defines evil, then the real evil must be the evil that cannot be spoken: unrelatedness, the dread of absolute alienation and unconnectedness, pure loneliness, absolute difference."[48] Why is relationship so important to Koreans? As many Korean social psychologists confirm, Koreans see social relationships as a sort of (extended) family relationship. Accordingly, it is also important to note that "to see every relationship in terms of family relationships is a value choice, a decision that makes the world meaningful, a richly woven human web."[49] Unrelatedness is unthinkable, not because Confucian ethics teaches that relationship is everything and Confucian ethics is a role ethics as some

[46] Kyung Moon Hwang, "Country or State? Reconceptualizing *Kukka* in the Korean Enlightenment Period, 1896–1910," *Korean Studies* 24 (2000), 1–24.

[47] This does not mean that such distinctions are not recognized and respected in contemporary Korea. My point is that, comparatively speaking, the line between private and public and between state and society is much more permeable in Korea, and this permeability has a great deal to do with the Korean Confucian understanding of the state.

[48] Alford, *Think No Evil*, 11.

[49] Ibid., 99.

New Confucians believe. Rather, it is because unrelatedness means no relationship with one's family members. In Korea, therefore, insult is more than a psychological injury because it destroys family (or familial) relationships. Insult drives one (and those whom one is related to) to what is unthinkable and/or unspeakable, namely, what is evil.

Though it is difficult to prove scientifically that the Korean "habits of the heart" to see social relationship in terms of family relationship is formed by Confucian ethics,[50] it is indisputable that it is deeply imbedded in the Confucian ethical tradition. For instance, Confucius famously said, "Glib speech, an obsequious countenance, and excessive solicitude – Zuoqiu Ming thought this kind of conduct shameless, and so do I. To seek out someone's friendship while harboring *ill will toward them* – Zuoqiu thought this kind of conduct shameless, and so do I."[51] (Civil) friendship that harbors ill will or resentment (*yuan* 怨), according to Confucius, is only hypocrisy; it is what the village-worthy would do. But Confucius's point is not merely to blame hypocrisy. His supreme concern is to make sure that ill will or a sense of resentment does not arise in social relationships, because its presence signifies bad relationships, thus being detrimental to one's moral growth.[52] The Korean habits of the heart are, to use Max Weber's terminology, a *routinized* mode of Confucian ethics in the everyday life of ordinary Korean citizens: they do not tell us much about an individual Korean citizen's personal morality, which is the central concern of Confucian ethics, but, as social mores, they are highly relevant in appreciating the moral character of Korean society.

The three points I have discussed so far together offer us an important insight into the nature of democratic citizenship in Korean society. Koreans, who have long maintained ethnic homogeneity and common cultural identity, rarely see their fellow citizens as *political equals*, those who share the same constitution or subscribe to the same principles of justice. Rather, the strong egalitarian sentiment commonly found among Koreans has a great deal to do with their understanding of citizenship as a kind of family relationship. Just as in a good Confucian family, certain reasonable social hierarchies (especially between the old and the young) are still maintained in Korea's democratic civil society.[53] For most Koreans, the highest goal of democracy is to achieve and maintain social harmony.

[50] In most social scientific research on Confucian values (most recently, Doh Chull Shin's cited earlier), this connection between what is Korean (or Chinese, etc.) and what is Confucian is often just assumed rather than scientifically demonstrated, and I do not know whether such demonstration is possible in "scientific" language and methodology.

[51] *Analects* 5:25, emphasis added.

[52] See Kim, "Self-Transformation and Civil Society."

[53] Swedish political scientist Geir Helgesen conducted surveys in 1990 and 1995 to study the political culture of democratic Korea and close to 90 percent of the respondents on average in both surveys accepted that democracy is seeking harmonious social relations and the ideal society is the family. Geir Helgesen, *Democracy and Authority in Korea: The Cultural Dimension*

Here equality among citizens or *civic equality* has a different meaning than what we see in a liberal-democratic society. It is not so much about the equal political standing of free citizens (the importance of which is increasingly acknowledged in public discourse though) but primarily about the entitlements one can expect and claim as a legitimate family member. The gist of democratic civility, then, lies in the avoidance of insulting others, which turns family relationships into cold, hostility-suppressed, strangership, and being insulted, which implies being treated as *nobody*. Therefore, in Korea, democratic equality is maintained to the extent that none is insulted in a family-like civil society that may not be "egalitarian" as Western liberals understand the term. Likewise, democratic inclusion is attained not necessarily by deliberative inclusion but by extending familial affectionate sentiments (*chŏng*) to other members of civil society.[54] Or, more accurately, in Korean practice, deliberative inclusion, if it were to happen, is not a purely rational process (as Cohen understands it to be) but is always mediated by Confucian public reasons stimulated by familial affectionate sentiments.

Where society is deemed to be an extended family, democracy is understood as instrumental to social harmony, and civility (and civil language) is practiced primarily in familial terms,[55] freedom of expression is exercised differently from the way it is exercised in Western liberal democracies. Though it is well-received public knowledge that expressive liberty is one of the core democratic rights, as is also stipulated in the Korean constitution, very few Koreans seem to believe that insult law is incompatible with their expressive liberty. To the contrary, many seem to believe that expression of one's earnest personal feelings, religious faith, and/or political ideas can be best protected only when there is a social (and legal) guarantee that the line between expressive liberty and private insult is clearly maintained. That is, under no circumstances can expressive liberty undermine the self-respect of another whose recognition of one's moral worth and social standing is essential to one's own self-esteem. A recent decision by the Korean Constitutional Court affirms this public knowledge and

in Korean Politics (Surrey: Curzon, 1998), 94. A similar finding is attested by Chong-Min Park and Doh Chull Shin's more recent survey research. See their "Do Asian Values Deter Popular Support for Democracy in South Korea?," *Asian Survey* 46 (2006), 341–61. Of note, Stephen C. Angle says, "even while contemporary Confucians identify and criticize oppression, they should not reject all forms of hierarchy and deference, both of which are sometimes mistakenly identified with oppression" (*Contemporary Confucian Political Philosophy: Toward Progressive Confucianism* [Cambridge: Polity, 2012], 128).

54 This is not to say that deliberation is unimportant in Korean democratic civil society. As shall be argued shortly, deliberation in Confucian democracy must be grounded in the familial affectionate sentiment as well as in reason (also see Chapters 5 and 8).

55 On the Confucian influence on the language practice among ordinary Koreans, see Hye-young Jeon, "Han'gukeoe banyeongdoen yugyomunhwajeok teukseong" [The Confucian Characteristics Reflected in Korean Language], in *Han'gukmunhwawa han'gukin* [Korean Culture and the Korean People], ed. the Association of International Korean Studies (Seoul: Sagyejeol, 1998), 235–58.

provides us with an important clue to understanding how insult law is compatible with expressive liberty in democratic Korean civil society.

In February 2009, a forty-three-year-old man, arrested on charges of insulting a police officer using profanity under the influence of alcohol and subsequently ordered by the district court to pay a fine of 1 million won (then approximately one thousand U.S. dollars), filed a petition with the Constitutional Court. He argued that Article 311 of the criminal code not only defines the offense ambiguously but also violates the constitutional principle of proportionality. Turning down the petition unanimously, the court's nine justices echoed a shared and articulate sentiment:

> (a) Since "publicity" in the context of a charge of insult means a condition which can be recognized by the unspecified or the multitude, its precise meaning must be determined on a case by case basis. Considering the lawmaking environment, it is either impossible or significantly difficult for lawmakers to set every criterion to delineate the conditions of "publicity" since the criteria of "publicity" and "insult" should be defined in a specific and individual manner according to general norms of society and common sense, not in an abstract and general manner.
>
> (b) ... Considering the legislative purpose, Article 311 does not violate the principle of precision in the context of legal principle since it is deemed that general individuals with healthy common sense and reasonable sense of law can easily predict what conduct is prohibited in this Article and there is also no concern that a law enforcement agency would make an arbitrarily expanded interpretation....
>
> (c) As a means of sanction, a criminal penalty after the victim's accusation is not deemed arbitrary. If derogatory expressions against person's dignity are made in public, this not only damages the person's social value, but, [moreover,] this damage can be easily propagated in a modern society in which its recovery is getting more difficult.
>
> (d) It is deemed that there is no considerable imbalance between public and private interests since the public interests achievable by this Article are significantly important, whereas what is prohibited is [merely] the expressions of abstract judgment or derogatory sentiment toward others, which would hurt the social value of an individual in public [cite]. Therefore, Article 311 applied to this case does not violate the principle of excessive regulation.[56]

In paragraphs a and b, the court refutes the charge of ambiguity in Article 311 (particularly terms such as "publicly" and "insult") by appealing to "healthy common sense and a reasonable sense of law," yet without clarifying what constitutes its content. I suppose that by common sense and reasonable sense of law the court meant what I have characterized above as Korean civility, which is broadly Confucian in nature, or Confucian public reason.[57] What

[56] Constitutional Court 2011.06.30. 2009 *heonba* 199 (the alphabetical numbering is given by the author).

[57] For a similar observation, see Chaihark Hahm, "Disputing Civil Society in a Confucian Context," *Korea Observer* 35 (2004), 433–62; Hahm, Negotiating Confucian Civility through Constitutional Discourse," in Hahm and Bell, *Politics of Affective Relations*, 277–308.

the court's decision (and the insult law as the court understands it) implies is that insult law (or legal code in general) is de facto nested in the public norms of civility that ordinary Korean citizens generally share and expressive liberty as a constitutional right is equally circumscribed by them.

What is surprising from a liberal standpoint is that the court sees no considerable tension between expressive liberty and insult law. The court claims that the "public good" (Korean *gong'ik* 公益), which the insult law secures, cannot be superseded by the "private interest" (Korean *saik* 私益) accompanying the right to freedom of expression, and this is what the court means by "balance." Once again, however, the court offers no explanation as to what public interest consists of. From paragraph c, we can infer only that from the court's viewpoint, a person's social value (outer/social reputation) is a public interest. But then a question arises: why does the court regard one's social value as public interest, which is commonly understood as a private interest in the liberal political tradition, while seeing expressive liberty as a private interest? In the absence of the court's explication, it is difficult to unravel this conundrum with certainty. That said, if my cultural and social psychological analysis of Korean civility is not wrong, it is still possible to make sense of the underlying assumption in the court's reasoning.

As we have seen, Korean Confucian civility is a kind of communitarian virtue and no clear distinction between one's inner private self and outer social self is assumed. In Korean, fundamentally "relational," selfhood,[58] one's outer social self is closely related to, even thought to reflect, one's inner self. Since Korean society is deemed as an extended family, Korean relational selfhood is essentially familial, and Korean civility is extended from Confucian filiality, what concerns the value/reputation of one's outer social self becomes a "public" concern. Otherwise stated, what is violated in the conduct of insult is not merely a victim's social value but his or her legitimate family membership in a democratic civil society deemed as a family-community. In this sense, we can say that in Korea *the political is familial*. Again, my claim is largely speculative, but I believe it can enable us to make sense of the court's attitude toward expressive liberty.

To be sure, the court affirms the constitutional basis of the right to freedom of expression. But the court does not seem to appreciate the *intrinsic* value of expressive liberty, a moral value deriving directly from the distinctiveness of one's self-identity and its status as a *democratic right*, a right that is essential for democratic inclusion, when it says, "the public interests achievable by this Article are significantly important, whereas what is prohibited is [merely] the expressions of abstract judgment or derogatory sentiment toward others, which would hurt the social value of an individual in public [cite]." Here the court is exclusively focused on the "costs" of expressive liberty and attempts to weigh them with the public interests to be gained by implementation of the

[58] On the Korean relational selfhood, see Choi, *Han'gukin shimlihak*, 121–39.

insult law. However, again from a liberal standpoint, this is an unfair assessment because, logically speaking, we cannot uphold expressive liberty without embracing *certain* costs that inevitably accompany this fundamental human and democratic right. From this viewpoint, when the court declared that the public interests gained by the insult law outweigh the costs of expressive liberty (i.e., the harm done to the victim's social selfhood), it seems to have resolved the tension between insult law and expressive liberty too easily.

What is worth noting, however, is the very nonliberal reasoning by the Korean Constitutional Court and its public acceptance. That is, in democratic Korean civil society, expressive liberty has a different legal and sociopolitical standing than in Western liberal democracies. Insufficient attention to the intrinsic moral value of expressive liberty and less appreciation of its status as a fundamental democratic right is not a result of the underdevelopment of Korean democracy or the intolerance of the Korean people toward difference. Rather, it reveals the Confucian communitarian character of Korean democracy, which is oriented toward social harmony, where an ideal society is still deemed to be a form of family. Just as distinctive selfhood is less important (if not unimportant) than a harmonious relationship in the family in which one's self-identity is massively fused with other family members', in Korea, as the court acknowledged, the private interest of expressive liberty is less valued than the public good of social harmony, despite its constitutional standing as a right.

Conclusion: Toward Confucian Pluralist Democracy

In the previous section, I have discussed how Korean Confucian civility is qualitatively differentiated from liberal civility by focusing on the way insult law and expressive liberty, seemingly at odds with each other, are simultaneously upheld in the democratic civil society. My key argument has been that insult law reflects Korean Confucian communitarian civility and that expressive liberty, while being respected as a constitutional right, is moderated by insult law, which is itself circumscribed by Confucian public reason(s). In this concluding section, I discuss the challenge that further democratization of Korean society poses to Korean civility and then explore a mode of Confucian democracy that is most suitable in light of such a challenge. Let me revisit the court's decision as analyzed earlier.

From a political perspective, I believe the court made the right decision when it affirmed the constitutionality of Article 311 of the Korean Criminal Law. First of all, I agree that law is (and should be) grounded in common sense and public reason generally shared by the citizens. Second, given the Confucian societal culture in which Korean civilities are embedded, I think it is reasonable to uphold insult law, a predemocratic legacy, even in a democratic civil society, and strive to balance it with expressive liberty, a core democratic right. Perhaps this is the most practicable way to balance Confucian communitarianism and democratic pluralism, though in reality it implies more about the latter's accommodation to the former than the other way around.

The problem is that Korea is no longer a Confucian communitarian society in any culturally monolithic and ethically monistic sense. In fact, in the past two decades, democratic civil society in Korea has rapidly diversified internally along religious, cultural, and political lines, and, more recently, the increasing number of immigrants (particularly foreign spouses from other, less well-to-do Asian countries) has rendered Korea no longer an ethnically and culturally homogeneous nation-state. The result is the erosion of the ideal of the family-state and of attendant civic virtues that have undergirded democratic civil society and semifamilial democratic citizenship. In a sense, Korean democracy is undergoing a crisis; as its civil society is rapidly being pluralized and multiculturalized, it is spending down the bonding social capital that it used to be able to draw on for sustenance. Does this change make insult law and Korean Confucian civility on which it is publicly justified no longer relevant in Korean society? Or, should Korean citizens strive to reinforce their traditional Confucian civility to overcome social pluralization because it threatens to disrupt their otherwise family-like civil society? How can Korean citizens continue to strike a middle ground between insult law (and Confucian civility) and expressive liberty in a pluralistic societal context? Here I have two suggestions aimed at breaking through this dilemma.

My first suggestion is that democratic civil society in Korea should be approached on two different levels. First, as a social bulwark for democratic citizenship in which citizens are free and equal vis-à-vis the state, civil society should be understood as a home for collective self-determination and public freedom, an incubator of public sentiment and reason. Civil society thus understood should be able to bond together citizens, who otherwise subscribe to different comprehensive moral doctrines and belong to different cultural and religious communities and associations, horizontally and impart to them a common political identity as Korean citizens. In this democratic civil society, Korean Confucian civility is still relevant not as *bonding* social capital, as it used to be, which draws on common ethnic national identity, but as *bridging* social capital that aims at social integration across cultural, ethnic, and religious difference.[59] In this regard, insult law should be reconstructed as a vehicle for democratic inclusion and mutual respect, more than a conservative means to maintain social order and harmony. It is not difficult to imagine that as Korean society becomes more multicultural, there will be more incidents of insult in everyday life because one's free expression of one's utmost religious convictions and cultural values is likely to provoke others who do not necessarily share them. Insult law and, more important, the norms implicated in it

[59] For an illuminating discussion of the difference between bonding social capital and bridging social capital, see Robert D. Putnam, *Bowling Alone: The Collapse and Revival of American Community* (New York: Touchstone, 2000), 18–24.

will turn out to be of great help in inculcating civic virtues in Korean citizens who are internally diverse. Ultimately, Korean citizens, whose differences have been bridged by Korean civility, can effectively protect and exercise their public liberty and democratic right to collective self-determination against the potentially intrusive state.

My second suggestion is that while functioning as a bulwark for collective self-determination and public freedom, democratic civil society in Korea must simultaneously offer itself as a home for, what John Rawls calls "reasonable pluralism." Norms implicated with the Korean insult law, or Korean civility more broadly, should in no case be exploited to oppress new voices or expressions and expressive liberty must be understood (and respected) as a core democratic right, which cannot be violated without a *compelling* moral justification from the state. What I find problematic in the court's decision is that in this important decision on the constitutionality of Article 311, the article that is profoundly concerned with public norms and civility in Korea, the court did not grapple sufficiently with the democratic importance of expressive liberty.[60] Certainly, as the court rightly claimed, the petitioner's libel case did not present a strong case of expressive liberty as a democratic right. But when the court gave more weight to social norms that the insult law underpins by calling them "public interests" than to expressive liberty, which it deemed as a private interest, it undoubtedly did not do full justice to the democratic importance of that right.

I concede that there is no clear and definitive way to strike a middle ground between Korean civility and expressive liberty or Korean communitarian democracy and value pluralism. But there is no other way than striving to balance the two in democratic, yet internally diverse, Korean civil society. Making Confucian communitarian democracy more responsive to pluralism is a daunting task, but ongoing social changes in Korean society since democratization are putting enormous pressure on Korean citizens and policymakers to struggle with it. This chapter can be considered *a* response to this pressure from a political theoretical standpoint.

[60] Liberals would encourage the court to consider the intrinsic moral value of expressive liberty in addition to its status of democratic right.

11

Confucianizing Multiculturalism

In Korea, "multiculturalism" (*damunhwa* or *damunhwajuui* in Korean) is one of today's hottest topics both in academia and in civil society.[1] According to Dong-Hoon Seol's recent article, the number of published scholarly articles containing *damunhwa(juui)* as a key word or a title word amounted to 810 as of November 2010, and the number of articles in the Korean news media on *damunhwa(juui)* has dramatically increased in recent years – from 137 in 2000 to 14,437 in 2009.[2] Most tellingly, in 2006, as the total number of foreign residents (immigrants and migrant workers combined) approached one million, amounting to approximately 2 percent of the entire Korean population, and as the number of international marriages sharply increased (especially in rural areas), President Roh Moo Hyun publicly declared that Korea is moving toward a multicultural society and this trend is irreversible.

As a result, in the past five years, scholars, consisting mainly of sociologists and anthropologists, have actively discussed (1) the various factors contributing to a multicultural Korea – demographic change, economic demands, and, more directly, periodic immigration policy reforms in each democratic government since 1992,[3] (2) the current state or character of Korean

[1] In the existing body of literature in Korea, the distinction between multiculturalism as *a fact about certain societies* and multiculturalism as *a response to this fact* is often obscure, rendering the English word "multiculturalism" to be both *damunhwa* (multiculturalism as a fact) and *damunhwajuui* (multiculturalism as a response) in Korean. Unless otherwise noted, in this chapter, "multiculturalism" is used in the former sense, especially in the phrase "the logic of multiculturalism." Also, since the main cause of the multiculturalization of Korean society is immigration, by multiculturalism (both as a social fact and as a political response to it) I mean "immigrant multiculturalism."

[2] Dong-Hoon Seol, "Which Multiculturalism? Discourse of the Incorporation of Immigrants into Korean Society," *Korea Observer* 41 (2010), 593–614, 597–8.

[3] Byoungha, Lee, "The Development of Korea's Immigration Policies: Security, Accumulation, Fairness, and Institutional Legitimacy," *Korea Observer* 40 (2010), 763–99; Hye-Kyung Lee,

multiculturalism,[4] and (3) both normative-theoretical and policy-oriented practical suggestions on how to create a more decent multicultural society in Korea.[5]

Although these studies have certainly encouraged us to grapple with a plausible way to conceptualize multiculturalism in the Korean society and seek policy measures, insufficient attention has been given to the broader political question – that is, how to conceive of Korean multiculturalism and how to implement multicultural policies in the existing societal context that has enabled Korean democracy.

Arguably, many Korean multiculturalists (both academics and activists) do not consider this normative political theoretical question to be their core philosophical concern because they casually regard multiculturalism as an inherent component of liberal democracy, to which Korea is constitutionally committed, or as a stage at which Korean democracy ought to reach for it to be morally (not only politically) valid. More specifically, many assume that multiculturalism can be best attained by making Korean society more liberal, that is, by making it open and, more important, fair to "strangers" (foreign immigrants and even illegal residents such as undocumented migrant workers)[6] and by fully respecting their individual human rights, their rights qua human beings (if they are temporary residents) or qua Korean citizens (if they have

"International Marriage and the State in South Korea: Focusing on Governmental Policy," *Citizenship Studies* 12 (2008), 107–23; Yoonkyung Lee, "Migration, Migrants, and Contested Ethno-Nationalism in Korea," *Critical Asian Studies* 41 (2009), 363–80; Kyoung-hee Moon, "Gukjeijuyeoseong'eul gyegiro salpyeoboneun damunhwajuuiwa han'gukui damunhwahyeonsang" [Making Multicultural Korea: Can Multicultural Politics Help Foreign Brides to Fully Integrate into Korean Society?], *21st Century Political Science Review* 16 (2006), 67–93.

4 Nora H. J. Kim, "Korean Immigration Policy Change and the Political Liberals' Dilemma," *International Migration Review* 42 (2008), 576–96; Nam-Kook Kim, "Multicultural Challenges in Korea: The Current Stage and a Prospect," *International Migration* (advance online publication, October 2009); Ian Watson, "Multiculturalism in South Korea: A Critical Assessment," *Journal of Contemporary Asia* 40 (2010), 337–46; Injin Yoon, "Han'kukdamunhwajuuiui jeon'gaewa teukseong" [The Development and Characteristics of Multiculturalism in South Korea], *Korean Sociological Review* 42 (2008), 72–103.

5 Nam-Kook Kim, "Shimui damunhwajuui: Munhwajeok gwonliwa munhwajeok saengjon" [Deliberative Multiculturalism: A Path to Cultural Rights and Cultural Survival], *Korean Political Science Review* 39 (2005), 87–107; Bumsoo Kim, "Minjujuuie isseo poyonggwa baeje" [How to Draw the Boundaries of Demos?], *Korean Journal of International Relations* 48 (2008), 173–98; Jun-hyeok Kwak, "Damunhwa gongjon'gwa sahoejeok tonghap" [Multicultural Coexistence and Social Integration], *Korean Journal of Political Science* 15 (2007), 23–41.

6 For this argument, see Kim, "Minjujuuie isseo poyonggwa baeje" and for the critique of this radical liberal suggestion, see Seol, "Which Multiculturalism?" Bumsoo Kim supports an open-border policy purely from a normative standpoint implicated in liberalism (of the Habermasian strand) but, according to some observers, full human rights should be granted even to undocumented migrant workers because their illegal status was often created by the illiberal foreign labor policies pursued by the Korean government. On this point, see Lee, "The Development of Korea's Immigration Policies" and Lee, "Migration, Migrants, and Contested Ethno-Nationalism in Korea."

been naturalized).[7] That is, even when multiculturalism is discussed in political theoretical terms, it is often done in reference to the moral/normative ideal of liberal democracy focused on *individual* human or citizen rights, but rarely (almost never) by giving a consideration to the societal, political, and (public-) cultural conditions on which Korean democracy (and Korean democratic citizenship) is predicated.

Certainly, justifying, devising, and developing government programs and civic activities aiming to grant (low-skilled) migrant workers, foreign spouses, and Chinese denizens certain rights are important parts of multiculturalism in Korea, a country still entertaining an impressively high degree of ethnic homogeneity. The three groups have often been treated unjustly by native Koreans and the Korean government, hence the key objects of multicultural studies and policies in Korea – full human rights (as the moral ideal of liberal democracy dictates) and citizen rights (as the Korean constitution stipulates) are valid priorities. And to the extent that a decent multicultural society can be attained by earnestly employing the liberalism of human rights, the assumption that multiculturalism is an integral component of liberal democracy is well warranted.[8]

However, this individual rights-centered approach fails to give adequate attention to the political implications of the claim to cultural rights by immigrants, rights that are individually possessed but often exercised collectively. As I will show, cultural rights generate a so-called logic of multiculturalism, or cultural pluralism, and this likely puts multiculturalism at odds with liberal-democratic values upholding individual rights. Multiculturalism, expressed as cultural pluralism and morally justified in terms of value pluralism, can harm a liberal democracy, if the individual's and the cultural/identity group's claim to expressive liberty is presented in an absolutist manner and thus is

[7] Most feminist multiculturalists in Korea are critical of the current Korean multicultural policies precisely because of the Korean government's failure to fully respect women's (i.e., foreign spouses') human/citizen rights. For instance, Hyun-mee Kim claims that "the government's efforts simply reinforce prevailing attitudes in Korea of using women as uniform objects to achieve the state-building project" (Hyun-mee Kim, "The State and Migrant Women: Diverging Hopes in the Making of 'Multicultural Families' in Contemporary Korea," *Korea Journal* 47 [2007], 100–122, 105). For a similar view, see Seon-young Chun, "Damunhwasahoe damlonui han'gyewa yeokseol" [The Limit and Paradox of the Discourse on "Multicultural Society"], *Handoksahoegwahaknonchong* 14 (2004), 363–80; Moon, "Gukjeijuyeoseong"; Jung-hye Yang, "Sosuminjok ijuyeoseongui jaehyeon" [Representing Migrated Women], *Midieo, jendeo, munhwa* 7 (2007), 47–77. In the same vein but with a different focus, Hye-kyung Lee criticizes the "2006 Grand Plan" – the most progressive and comprehensive multicultural social integration policy in Korean history – because its "overemphasis on 'family' highlight[s] their roles as 'wives' and 'daughter-in-laws' instead of their more important role as 'independent human beings'" ("International Marriage and the State in South Korea," 120).

[8] In my observation, this is how majority (if not all) Korean multiculturalists understand "Korean multiculturalism" as distinct from multiculturalism in more ethnically, religiously, and culturally diverse Western countries.

difficult to put into a dialectic balance with other important social goods. As long as Korean multiculturalists rely on rights-based liberalism, they cannot avoid the logic of multiculturalism implicated in the claim to cultural rights, even if they do not want to be embroiled in it.

If it is agreed that (1) the logic of multiculturalism consists of cultural pluralism, (2) there are potential tensions between multiculturalism and liberal democracy, and (3) these tensions raise the important political question of how a democratic political authority can reasonably come to terms with the cultural rights and cultural/identity politics that emerge without suppressing cultural pluralism and obstructing democratic justice, it is imperative to search for a way to accommodate the fact of multiculturalism to the context of Korean democracy.[9] This requires us to develop a normative framework of multiculturalism that can serve the public purposes of Korean democracy that substantiate the practical meaning of democratic justice in Korea.[10]

In this concluding chapter, I construct a normative framework of Korean multiculturalism in the Confucian societal context of Korean democracy by focusing on the political implications of the claim to cultural rights and cultural pluralism that is likely to emerge in Korean democracy. After examining the logic of multiculturalism that often puts multiculturalism in tension with liberal democracy, I turn to Will Kymlicka's political theory of multiculturalism (particularly immigrant multiculturalism) that resolves this potential tension. Then, I construct a normative framework of Korean multiculturalism, such that a decent multicultural society can be established on the same public-cultural ground on which Korean democracy has matured in the past two decades. My central claim is that the two seemingly mutually opposing goals of democratic empowerment and multicultural coexistence can be attained in Korea if two conditions are met – democratic pluralism and Confucian-democratic citizenship.

[9] This is not to argue for a one-way accommodation. I harbor no illusion that the cultural and sociopolitical character of today's Korean democracy reveals or fully represents the normative ideal of "liberal democracy" to which Korean citizens aspire. I, however, am not persuaded that there is an ultimate form of liberal democracy that has to be consolidated (or imposed) in Korea, independently of Korea's given sociopolitical and cultural context. In the concluding section of this chapter, I will discuss how Korean democracy should be reasonably modified by the fact of multiculturalism within the parameter set by Korean democratic purposes.

[10] Amy Gutmann famously defines democratic justice in a multicultural society in three terms: civic equality, equal freedom and fair opportunity. See her *Identity in Democracy* (Princeton: Princeton University Press, 2003). But as Michael Walzer and David Miller remind us, the meanings of the key components of democratic justice are always context-dependent and context-specific. See Michael Walzer, *Spheres of Justice: A Defense of Pluralism and Equality* (New York: Basic Books, 1983) and David Miller, *On Nationality* (Oxford: Oxford University Press, 1995).

The Logic of Multiculturalism and Its Liberal-Democratic Discontents

In this section, I will briefly introduce a formidable theoretical critique of multiculturalism from the liberal-democratic position primarily with reference to George Kateb's liberal individualism, which we have examined in the previous two chapters, and discuss its implications for a new liberal democracy in a non-Western, characteristically Confucian society. My aim in this section is to provide an important vantage point for exploring a mode of multiculturalism that is socioculturally plausible and politically practicable in today's democratic and pluralist Korea.

George Kateb criticizes the recent fascination with multiculturalism – or, as he calls it, "cultural pluralism" – from the perspective of democratic individuality that is predicated on rights-based individualism. According to Kateb, in a liberal democracy, freedom of association as the logical extension of freedom of expression should be maximally respected,[11] and therefore, all kinds of associations or groups, even cultural/identity groups that are not liberal-democratic in their internal operations, deserve liberal toleration unless they vitally impede others' equal right to freedom of expression. He writes, "In any case, neither the freedom to associate nor the general freedom to live as one likes, of which free association is an indispensable part, is to be tolerated only when the quality of uses to which it is put is admirable."[12]

But toleration should not be understood as support.[13] Although Kateb does not offer a clear statement as to whether all voluntary associations, which he believes are internally coherent with democratic individuality and rights-based individualism, deserve governmental support, he strongly opposes governmental support (not merely financial subsidies) for cultural groups that are formed on the basis of ascriptive elements such as race, ethnicity, religion, and, to a lesser degree, language.[14]

Kateb, however, is not a champion of cultural (ascriptive) groups' expressive freedom as are some liberal pluralists, such as William Galston and Nancy Rosenblum, according to whom pluralist politics should be maximally accommodated within a liberal-democratic constitutional boundary, unless a group's behavior harms others, providing a "compelling reason" for the state to intervene.[15] Rather, Kateb's intent is to insist that certain vices are intrinsic

[11] For Kateb's position regarding freedom of association, see George Kateb, "The Value of Association," in Gutmann, *Freedom of Association*.

[12] George Kateb, "Notes on Pluralism," in *Patriotism and Other Mistakes* (New Haven: Yale University Press, 2006), 24.

[13] Also see Gutmann, *Identity in Democracy*, 88.

[14] Kateb, "Notes on Pluralism," 24–5.

[15] Galston and Rosenblum justify the maximal accommodation of pluralist politics within a liberal constitutional democracy in similar terms: value pluralism (Galston) and the morality of pluralism (Rosenblum). For Galston's position, see William A. Galston, *Liberal Pluralism: The Implications of Value Pluralism for Political Theory and Practice* (Cambridge: Cambridge University Press, 2002); *The Practice of Liberal Pluralism* (Cambridge: Cambridge University

in any strong claim to group identity and such vices not only destabilize the liberal-democratic constitutional order, which is a typical Madisonian or Hobbesian concern, but more fundamentally, they actively harm, even demolish, a human being's status as a person. In Kateb's observation, the vices that cultural/identity groups engender are essentially mental vices that "damage the basic moral personality."[16] Kateb presents six particular vices arising from cultural pluralism but here the focus will be on one of them, "self-mystification," as it serves to summarize well Kateb's core idea.

> A person's *uniqueness* is what he or she can bring forth, the special work one can do, the unprecedented sentences one can say and write. It is unpredictability growing out of infinitude. Uniqueness is taking the next steps in one's own direction, a refusal to be distracted or diverted.... The balance to a sense of one's uniqueness is not a feeling of indebtedness and allegiance to a cultural group (or even any particular society) but an ever deepening conviction of a *common humanity* shared by all human beings.... Strong group identity and membership enfeeble the ability to imagine oneself in the situation of another or in an analogous situation; or to imagine how it would feel to be like another. The imagination of sameness, which is fairness, and the imagination of otherness, which is empathy, are both actively discouraged.[17]

Kateb's key argument is twofold. First, while democratic individuality (and liberal democracy that is ethically committed to this ideal) is founded on pluralism (each person's uniqueness), democratic individuality is incompatible with (strong) group pluralism (or cultural pluralism) because the ascriptive identity that it promotes is not a person's genuine identity. Second, in the deep psychological sense, an individual of a democracy is not necessarily confined to a particular democratic community, which is nothing but another cultural group, but ought to define himself or herself qua human being, as a member of an infinite and common humanity.[18] For Kateb, ascriptive group identity or cultural pluralism is the antithesis of both individuality and humanity, thereby violating the ethical core of liberal democracy, the unbound respect of human dignity.

Kateb's critique of multiculturalism provides us with an important insight into the "logic" of multiculturalism, particularly in a liberal democracy that respects individual and associational pluralism. First, in a liberal democracy, cultural rights (including religious rights) are core components of the right to

Press, 2005); and for Rosenblum's, see Nancy L. Rosenblum, *Membership and Morals: The Personal Uses of Pluralism in America* (Princeton: Princeton University Press, 1998); "Compelled Association: Public Standing, Self-Respect, and the Dynamic of Exclusion," in Gutmann, *Freedom of Association*, 75–108.

[16] Kateb, "Notes on Pluralism," 30.

[17] Ibid., 33–4.

[18] For this reason, Kateb berates patriotism as the single greatest obstacle to cosmopolitan humanity and rights-based individualism. While Kateb reluctantly tolerates cultural pluralism, he flatly refutes patriotism (and nationalism which he practically equates with patriotism) by calling it a totalizing ideology. See George Kateb, "Is Patriotism a Mistake?," in *Patriotism and Other Mistakes*, 3–20.

freedom of expression. Second, even if the right to freedom of expression is essentially an individual right, it is often exercised collectively in mediation of the freedom of association. Third, when freedom of association is adopted to promote cultural/religious/ethnic identities, it is likely to give rise to dangerous cultural pluralism that not only destabilizes the liberal-democratic constitutional order, but also, more fundamentally, suppresses an individual's unique identity and further violates his or her human rights.

Although Kateb does not discuss the logic of multiculturalism (or the potential perils of cultural pluralism) in the context of immigrant multiculturalism, his argument is just as relevant to immigrant multiculturalism because Kateb helps us clearly see that the logic of multiculturalism is integral to the core liberal-democratic rights to freedom of expression and freedom of association. Therefore, the logic of multiculturalism raises an important practical question: which is more important between cultural/religious/ethnic associational membership and common democratic citizenship, should they conflict? And how can this (actual or potential) conflict be dealt with reasonably in a liberal-democratic society? Staunch liberal pluralists like Rosenblum and Galston place more value on membership than on citizenship, believing that certain social vicissitudes are unavoidable (even necessary) costs for a viable pluralist coexistence of individuals and groups in a liberal-democratic society.[19] But is this type of strong multicultural pluralism the only mode of multiculturalism that is compatible with a liberal democracy?

Will Kymlicka offers a more moderate way to come to terms with multiculturalism (particularly immigrant multiculturalism) without compromising his liberal commitment to individual rights. In the following section, I first examine Kymlicka's notion of polyethnic rights and his civic liberal resolution of the "logic" of multiculturalism, and then discuss how Kymlicka's account of immigrant multiculturalism is nevertheless exposed to some critical logical and practical problems.

Kymlicka's Immigrant Multiculturalism and Its Liberal *Aporia*

Unlike strong liberal pluralists, Kymlicka supports a cultural group's "group-differentiated citizenship" not for the sake of the ethical value of the expressive value of a group's cultural identity itself but mainly out of respect for individual rights, even when he believes that collective rights are often accorded to the

[19] For instance, Rosenblum says, "[A]ffiliation with voluntary associations in which we are wanted and willing members is a key source of self-respect; that discrimination may be safely contained in these groups; and that because associations often owe their origin to a dynamic of affiliation and exclusion, resentment and self-affirmation, liberal democracy is consistent with and even requires the incongruence between voluntary groups and public norms that always accompanies freedom of association" ("Compelled Association," 76). Again, unlike strong liberal pluralists, Kateb embraces pluralism *if only* it secures individual self-identity and individual human rights.

group as a whole. According to Kymlicka, while "'collective rights' [casually] refer to the rights accorded to and exercised by collectivities, where these rights are distinct from, and perhaps conflicting with, the rights accorded to the individuals who compose the collectivity, ... many forms of group-differentiated citizenship are in fact exercised by individuals."[20]

It is important to note that for Kymlicka, the "culture" that deserves survival and respect is so-called societal culture, which "provides its members with meaningful ways of life across the full range of human activities, including social, educational, religious, recreational, and economic life, encompassing both public and private spheres."[21] In other words, societal culture is of critical importance because it provides individual members with a context of choice.[22] "For meaningful individual choice to be possible, individuals need not only access to information, the capacity to reflectively evaluate it, and freedom of expression and association. They also need access to a societal culture. Group-differentiated measures that secure and promote this access may, therefore, have a legitimate role to play in a liberal theory of justice."[23] According to Kymlicka, immigrants who have left their native national communities and voluntarily entered a new national political community are still entitled with cultural rights called "polyethnic rights," through which they can access their own societal culture. Polyethnic rights include public funding for ethnic associations, magazines, and festivals. More controversially, they include an accommodation of ethnic groups' demand for exemptions from laws and regulations that disadvantage them, given their cultural (often religious) practices.[24]

For polyethnic rights to be claimed, two stipulations must be met. First, since polyethnic rights are intended to "help ethnic groups and religious minorities [consisting of voluntary immigrants] express their cultural particularity and pride without it hampering their success in the economic and political institutions of the dominant society,"[25] they are legally and politically obliged to respect the authority of such institutions. Put differently, (voluntary) integration is the legitimate "price" for polyethnic rights. Second, albeit arguably, polyethnic rights are intended for culturally vibrant immigrant "communities." Recall that in Kymlicka's view, individual autonomy can best be realized in societal culture and is constituted by a shared identity of the members of minority (immigrant) communities. That is, even if polyethnic rights are exercised by the individual members of immigrant communities, these rights are

[20] Will Kymlicka, *Multicultural Citizenship* (Oxford: Oxford University Press, 1995), 45.

[21] Ibid., 76.

[22] Galston criticizes Kymlicka for this valorization of individual autonomy and choice, thus failing to understand that "[m]any cultures or groups do not place a high value on choice and (to say the least) do not encourage their members to exercise it" (*Liberal Pluralism*, 21).

[23] Kymlicka, *Multicultural Citizenship*, 84.

[24] Ibid., 31.

[25] Ibid.

difficult to realize in reality in the absence or underdevelopment of culturally self-conscious immigrant communities in the first place.

Central to Kymlicka's account of immigrant multiculturalism is a "new logic" of multiculturalism that involves "accepting the principle of state-prescribed integration, but renegotiating the terms of integration."[26] Unlike national minorities or indigenous communities within a multinational/multi-ethnic state, immigrants (and immigrant communities) cannot (and should not) claim self-government rights because they forfeited such rights when they voluntarily came to (and integrate into) the dominant society. Therefore, for immigrant multiculturalism, what is at issue is not so much whether integration as such is just but whether the societal integration of immigrants takes place *on fair terms* so that immigrant groups are able to equally participate within the mainstream – academic, economic, and political – institutions of the dominant society. Kymlicka thus counters his critics, who blame him for promoting "separatism," that "public affirmation and recognition of immigrants' ethnic identity occurs *within common institutions*."[27]

Seen in this way, Kymlicka's political theory of (immigrant) multiculturalism has more in common with civic liberalism that accommodates centrifugal social diversity and cultural/religious/ethnic membership to liberal-democratic civic purposes and common democratic citizenship, than strong liberal pluralism that cherishes membership more than citizenship.[28] Kymlicka writes, "[In many Western democracies,] multicultural accommodations operate within the context of an overarching commitment to linguistic integration, respect for individual rights, and inter-ethnic co-operation."[29]

Then, is Kymlicka's account of immigrant multiculturalism directly applicable to Korea, where the public culture is still predominantly Confucian communitarian, and thus less embedded in the liberalism of human rights? My answer is only partially affirmative. Although I appreciate Kymlicka's rendition of the societal integration of immigrants in terms of democratic fairness and justice as opposed to top-down assimilation or a nationalizing process,[30] and see its general applicability to Korean society,[31] there is still good reason to be

[26] Will Kymlicka, *Politics in the Vernacular: Nationalism, Multiculturalism, and Citizenship* (Oxford: Oxford University Press, 2001), 169.

[27] Ibid., 165.

[28] On civic liberalism, see Stephen Macedo, *Diversity and Distrust: Civic Education in a Multicultural Democracy* (Cambridge, MA: Harvard University Press, 2000).

[29] Kymlicka, *Politics in the Vernacular*, 174.

[30] On top-down assimilation and nationalization, see Heather Rae, *State Identities and the Homogenisation of Peoples* (Cambridge: Cambridge University Press, 2002) and Rogers Brubaker, *Nationalism Reframed: Nationhood and the National Question in the New Europe* (Cambridge: Cambridge University Press, 1996), respectively.

[31] As noted earlier, most Korean multiculturalists, while being critical of Korea's state-led multiculturalism and the Korean government's instrumentalist mindset, generally support a fair integration of immigrants with full respect of their individual human rights. I guess many (if not all) of these scholars would agree with Kymlicka's suggestions.

cautious about the wholesale employment of Kymlicka's suggestions to Korean society.

Though Kymlicka consciously seeks to distinguish between immigrant multiculturalism and cultural pluralism (the kind that worries liberal individualists like George Kateb and egalitarian liberal democrats like Brian Barry)[32] by proposing a new logic of multiculturalism, there is no guarantee that immigrant multiculturalism, simply because of the voluntary nature of immigration, will not turn into strong immigrant communitarianism. Kymlicka's second (albeit implicit) stipulation reveals that what is assumed in polyethnic rights as one type of group-differentiated rights is the existence of self-conscious immigrant communities, and in a liberal democracy where freedom of association is valued, immigrant communitarianism is highly conceivable – in fact, its emergence (even its flourishing) is quite natural.[33]

Certainly, as Kymlicka rightly claims, immigrant communitarianism is qualitatively distinguished from immigrant nationalism that aims at self-government, but a variety of forms of local immigrant communitarianism can be fully materialized in a liberal-democratic society, especially when associational freedom is expressed in strong cultural/religious terms, giving rise to the tension between group membership and democratic citizenship *within* common institutions. Put differently, as long as freedom of expression and freedom of association remain integral to liberal democracy that cherishes pluralism, the "logic" of multiculturalism (and the potential perils of cultural pluralism affiliated with this logic) is hardly avoidable, let alone resolvable, even after a fair societal integration of immigrants. After all, freedom of association is one of the essential components of fairness that Kymlicka advocates.[34] Let us call this problem the "liberal *aporia*."

The liberal *aporia* found in Kymlicka's account of immigrant multiculturalism brings us back to the "logic" of multiculturalism. Again, one way to deal with this logic is to "live with it" by virtue of tolerance and by means of liberal constitutionalism, as Rosenblum's liberal realism suggests. In the remainder of this chapter, I explore a way to come to terms with the logic of multiculturalism in Korea's Confucian communitarian societal context that has successfully undergirded Korean democracy, but without neglecting core liberal-democratic principles (such as respect of human rights, political liberty, and the autonomy of civil society) to which Korean democracy is constitutionally committed.

[32] For Brian Barry's egalitarian liberal critique of multiculturalism, see his *Culture and Equality* (Cambridge, MA: Harvard University Press, 2001).

[33] In Korea, for instance, foreign immigrants especially from China and Southeast Asian countries have formed their own local, strongly communitarian, communities (most saliently, Joseonjok [Korean-Chinese] towns) in downtown Seoul and in many other middle-sized cities in the Seoul metropolitan area.

[34] See Kymlicka, *Multicultural Citizenship*, 84.

Confucian Public Culture and Korean Democracy

My discussion so far leads us to confront the following questions: To what extent can Korean democracy accommodate the claim to cultural rights by immigrants and immigrant multiculturalism it generates in face of the logic of multiculturalism? More specifically, what are the proper multiculturalist response(s) to increasing migrant workers and multicultural/multiethnic families in the context of Korean democracy that is culturally embedded in Confucian communitarianism but institutionally built in the idea of liberal democracy? This and the following sections aim to answer these questions first by illuminating Confucian public culture as the facilitating societal condition of Korean democracy and second by developing a normative framework of Korean multiculturalism with respect to Confucian public culture.

Like most third-wave democracies, Korean democracy was sought by ordinary people in civil society as an alternative way of life to an authoritarian regime. Arguably, though, what galvanized the general Korean public (if not self-conscious political activists) were their embodied Confucian moral sensibilities. During the turbulent period of Korean democratization in the mid- and late 1980s, democracy was understood as "anything but military dictatorship."[35] Yet, in the minds of the Korean people, democracy was envisioned in terms of the ideal Confucian benevolent government (*in-jeong* 仁政) as opposed to autocracy (*pok-jeong* 暴政) by military dictators who viciously violated the traditional norm and ideal of good government.[36] In this public social imagination, student deaths resulting from militant protests against the authoritarian regime were represented not only as political murders, but, more compellingly, as martyrdoms. During the most pivotal period of Korean democratization in 1987, Confucian moral martyrdom was reproduced in terms of a "democratic martyrdom," exemplified by slogan "Down with the Military Authoritarian Regime and Up with Civil Government."[37]

It is, therefore, not surprising to find that the positive ideal of liberal democracy pivoted around individual human rights was rarely articulated

[35] Geir Helgesen, *Democracy and Authority in Korea: The Cultural Dimension in Korean Politics* (Surrey: Curzon, 1998), 72. Helgesen's work insightfully captures the Confucian moral-political dynamic of Korean democratic politics during and after democratization. For another interesting study of the Confucian cultural dimension of Korean political discourse and practice, see Chaibong Hahm, "The Confucian Political Discourse and the Politics of Reform in Korea," *Korea Journal* 37 (1997), 65–77. For empirical studies on the pervasiveness of Confucianism as cultural practice and value system in Korea (and beyond), see the works cited in note 9 in the Introduction of this book, especially Byung-ik Koh, "Confucianism in Contemporary Korea," in Tu, *Confucian Traditions in East Asian Modernity*; Chong-min Park and Doh C. Shin, "Do Asian Values Deter Popular Support for Democracy in South Korea?," *Asian Survey* 46 (2006), 341–61.

[36] See Helgesen, *Democracy and Authority in Korea*, 84.

[37] Sungmoon Kim, "Transcendental Collectivism and Participatory Politics in Democratized Korea," *Critical Review of International Social and Political Philosophy* 11 (2008), 57–77, 61.

during (or even after) the heroic democratic transition in ordinary Korean public discourse. In fact, as I argued in Chapter 9, Korean democratization unfolded independently of a social and political awareness of the ethics of liberalism. For most Korean citizens, democracy was equivalent, in practice, to *collective self-determination in the civil society* and the ideal of the democracy they struggled for was centered on communitarian-egalitarian democratic citizenship.[38]

What clearly differentiates Korean democracy from other third-wave democracies is the political viability of a national civil society that contends with the state without being accompanied by flourishing associational life at the local level. Though this semirepublican mode of Korean democracy is hardly "liberal" in the sense that most liberal individualists understand the term, I argue that a firm institutional separation and the institutionalized tension between the state and civil society still qualifies Korean democracy as "liberal" particularly in the political sense, for democratic civil society in Korea – Confucian communitarian both in its public character, and albeit arguably, in its historical origin[39] – has established itself as a formidable bulwark for political liberty or public freedom.

This is not to claim that Korean democratic civil society, which is culturally Confucian communitarian and yet politically liberal, is ethically monistic, allowing no room for ethical pluralism. Quite the contrary, while maintaining its unified political power, thus successfully consolidating democracy, Korean civil society has simultaneously offered itself as a home to many different moral doctrines, religious faiths, and philosophical perspectives. In fact, the remarkably peaceful "multicultural" (particularly multireligious) coexistence among Korean citizens, which often amazes Western observers, is precisely the result of the Confucian public culture commonly shared by Koreans, despite their differing personal moral and/or religious beliefs. But still, what exactly is meant by Confucian public culture, particularly in contemporary Korean society? The nature and political significance of Confucian culture in Korea can be explained on two accounts – its civic power to bind Korean citizens horizontally, given all their internal diversity, and its opposition to ethical monism and patriarchal worldview and practice.

First of all, however pluralistic Korean citizens have become as a private individual (or a member of a particular association) in terms of moral value and religious faith, Korean society, which has long maintained a common public Confucian communitarian culture, has hardly been multicultural until recently, as there have been virtually no "cultural associations" strongly

[38] Helgesen, *Democracy and Authority in Korea*, 73.

[39] In his quite polemical essay, Hein Cho argues that the development of Korean civil society that was immensely instrumental to the democratization of Korean society has an indigenous origin in Korean Confucian culture. Hein Cho, "The Historical Origin of Civil Society in Korea," *Korea Journal* 37 (1997), 24–41.

claiming identity-based associational freedom against the general public interest by directly appealing to the Korean constitution.

Moreover, having only recently been introduced to a liberal-democratic way of life, many Koreans are struggling with a new set of liberal "habits of the heart" to recognize a person as a morally autonomous individual and respect his or her rights that he or she allegedly possesses qua human being. As Helgesen's research based on survey date demonstrates, an absolute majority (90 percent on average in both the 1990 and 1995 surveys) of Koreans believe the ideal society is like a family.[40] Moreover, many Koreans still tend to see their conationals as a member of their cultural-political community called *gukka* (國家, namely "family-state") in which the state is envisioned in the image of a large harmonious (Confucian) family and civic relationships in heavily (Confucian) familial terms.[41]

As most Korean citizens are still soaked in Confucian public culture and have yet to embody the new liberal-democratic civility,[42] astute social attention to, let alone active social practice of, freedom of expression, which is apparently at odds with the social norms embedded in Korea's Confucian familial-relational habits of the heart, is very rare.[43] Therefore, though it is preposterous to say that contemporary Korea has an ethically monistic society, as it once had (albeit arguably) under Neo-Confucianism during the Chosŏn dynasty (1392–1910),[44] it is less disputable that Koreans still largely share a Confucian-grounded public culture.

In this regard, it is not surprising that a wholehearted constitutional claim to freedom of association (whether voluntary or ascriptive), which is built on the freedom of expression, is very rare in Korean democratic civil society. Accordingly, the "multicultural problems" resulting from the tension between ascriptive group identity and liberal-democratic justice or between cultural membership and liberal-democratic citizenship that we have investigated earlier are not politically pronounced in democratized Korea. In the same vein, in the scholarly and public discourse on multiculturalism in Korea, what is at issue is not so much the expressive freedom of cultural groups but the human/citizen rights of individual migrant workers or foreign spouses, their individual rights to be treated equally.

Respecting a right to be treated as an equal human being (in the case of migrant workers) or as an equal citizen (in the case of foreign spouses), however,

[40] Ibid., 94. Also see Park and Shin, "Do Asian Values Deter Popular Support for Democracy in South Korea?," 350–51.

[41] Bong-young Choi, *Han'gukinui sahoejeok seonggyeok* [The Social Character of the Korean People] (Seoul: Neutinamu, 1994), 267.

[42] Chaihark Hahm, "Negotiating Confucian Civility through Constitutional Discourse," in Hahm and Bell, *Politics of Affective Relations.*

[43] For more on this point, see Chapter 10.

[44] Martina Deuchler, *The Confucian Transformation of Korea: A Study of Society and Ideology* (Cambridge, MA: Council on East Asian Studies, Harvard University, 1992).

is a supreme moral and political concern for any decent liberal democracy (including Korean democracy), not a typical moral demand of multiculturalism. Certainly, there is a law to protect the pluralist exercise of expressive and associational freedom in Korean democratic society, but its politicization has been culturally discouraged by commonality-enhancing Confucian public culture focused on family-like social harmony and mutual cooperation.

Thus understood, although Confucianism has lost its monolithic and all-encompassing power as an ethical system in contemporary Korea, it is still alive in civil society in the form of a public culture that horizontally binds individuals, who are socially and culturally diverse, as *citizens*. And it is the Confucian civic culture that sustains Korea's internally pluralistic and increasingly liberal democracy. Precisely in this public-cultural sense, we may call Korean democratic citizenship a "Confucian democratic citizenship."[45]

Confucian public culture's civic power to bind Korean citizens horizontally cannot be possible if the essential characteristics of Confucianism were patriarchal (hence violating gender equality), rigidly hierarchical, and/or sociopolitically exclusive. Therefore, it is of critical importance to note that the second feature of Confucian public culture in contemporary Korean society is its opposition to ethical monism and patriarchal worldview and practice. Here we need to pay heed to the distinction between Confucian *public* culture and Confucian culture in the ethically monistic sense.[46]

As noted, during the Chosŏn dynasty Confucianism was an all-encompassing moral and sociopolitical ideology in Korea, and its monistic ethic penetrated into every nook and cranny of Korean society. At the heart of the monistic ethic of Confucianism (more accurately Cheng-Zhu Neo-Confucianism), which allowed no room for ethical pluralism, was the patriarchal social hierarchy undergirded on clan law (Korean *jongbeop* 宗法) and family rituals (Korean *garye* 家禮). Most modern Koreans reject this monistic and socially rigid mode of Confucianism, but Confucianism of this kind is not completely obsolete in contemporary Korea. Those who belong to Confucian clan organizations such as *jungjong* 中宗 or maintain an extended family governed by Confucian family rituals (Korean *munjung* 門中) still cherish this monistic Confucianism.

Confucian public culture is qualitatively differentiated from ethically monistic and socially patriarchal Confucianism. Certainly, organizations and families guided by monistic/patriarchal Confucianism are (and should be) constitutionally protected in Korean democratic society on the basis of freedom of association and expressive freedom unless they vitally violate the constitutional

[45] It is important to emphasize that I do not see Confucian democracy (and Confucian democratic citizenship) as diametrically opposed to liberal democracy (and liberal-democratic citizenship). It must be clearly understood that while the former is focused on the public-cultural character of Korean democracy and citizenship, the latter is with reference to the political orientation of Korean democracy. For a similar argument, see Stephen C. Angle, *Contemporary Confucian Political Philosophy: Toward Progressive Confucianism* (Cambridge: Polity, 2012).

[46] For a more detailed discussion on this point, see Chapter 4.

order of the Korean polity. However, Confucianism of this type is only a *private* Confucianism, one of many religious and cultural associations found in Korean society. Religious Confucianism does not (and should not) constitute the core of Confucian public culture, which is concerned with Korean citizens in general. Instead, Confucian public culture consists of Confucian moral sentiments and social practices that any reasonable Korean, regardless of her private value system, can empathetically resonate with, with a right to democratically contest its public nature. *Chŏng* is at the heart of Confucian public culture in Korea as it constitutes the core of Confucian public reason, but a multitude of social practices, such as filial and fraternal love and responsibility, respect of elders, moral criticism and rectification of government, and social harmony, underpin Confucian public culture.[47] I believe these values and practices, albeit attenuated, are broadly found and even upheld in contemporary Korean society. According to Helgesen's observations, these Confucian public values and practices, though often unarticulated in the official political discourse, made a critical contribution to democratization and subsequent democratic consolidation in Korea.

In the following section, I attempt to construct a normative framework for Korean multiculturalism with respect to Confucian public culture as articulated in this section. In doing so, I pay special attention to recent demographic changes caused by the increasing number of migrant workers.

Developing a Normative Framework of Korean Multiculturalism

Multiculturalist critics in Korea rightly draw attention to the fact that Korea is no longer ethnically homogeneous. Indeed, a significant increase in the number of migrants, particularly migrant workers over the past ten years, who were vigorously imported to supplement the labor shortage in so-called 3D (difficult, dirty, and dangerous) industries after the 1997 financial crisis, has brought about a notable demographic change in Korean society.[48]

Critics' core argument is that for Korean society to be genuinely multicultural as the Korean government publicly claims it to be, and more important, as the norm of liberal democracy dictates, prevailing legal, social, and political discriminations against migrants must be eliminated. More specifically, they insist (again rightly) that any remnants of the notorious "trainee system" introduced by the Korean government in 1991, be completely abolished under which migrant workers were often exploited while being denied full access to labor

[47] Brooke Ackerly recommends the Confucian values of benevolence, good human nature, moral criticism as the core resources to develop an indigenous form of democracy, namely Confucian democracy in East Asian societies. See Brooke A. Ackerly, "Is Liberalism the Only Way toward Democracy? Confucianism and Democracy," *Political Theory* 33 (2005), 547–76.

[48] As of 2007, there were 393,331 migrant workers in Korea, and they have been increasingly coming from South or Southeast Asian countries (Lee, "Migration, Migrants, and Contested Ethno-Nationalism in Korea," 361).

rights and, more fundamentally, without respect for human rights.[49] According to these scholars, every migrant worker should be treated equally as a human being regardless of his or her particular occupation, religion, race, or national origin. In this regard, the Korean government's contrasting treatment of and semilegal endorsement of a hierarchy between high- and low-skilled migrant workers – a phenomenon that was exacerbated during the Lee Myung Bak administration (2008–13), which enthusiastically sought "foreign high skills and brains" in the name of the nation's global competitiveness – is especially problematic. In short, for many multiculturalists in Korea, multiculturalism as public policy and social program should protect migrants' (especially low-skilled migrant workers') individual human rights on fair terms.

While these scholars' liberal-democratic commitment to individual human rights and social justice is admirable and the Korean government's tendency to regard migrant workers as merely the vital "resources" for the continuous development of the Korean economy is morally problematic, it is highly dubious that their proposed "multiculturalism," understood as respect for migrants' individual human rights, fully comes to grips with the logic of multiculturalism and the potential perils of cultural pluralism affiliated with it. Moreover, it is debatable that their prescription of multiculturalism, once fully implemented, would make Korea democracy more viable, as they wish.

First of all, while it is important to concern the individual human rights of migrant workers (i.e., labor-related rights and other basic socioeconomic rights), it is equally, especially with regard to Korean democracy, important to draw attention to and adequately deal with the increasing permanent or semipermanent settlement of migrant workers in Korea, mainly from China and increasingly Southeast Asian countries. What the current literature glosses over is the more eminently "multiculturalist" question of whether or not broad civil rights that are integral to the ideal of liberal democracy such as freedom of expression and freedom of association should be granted to migrant workers and their families who have become de facto citizens of Korea, and if so, to what extent. As we have seen, ultimately, multiculturalism is predicated on the claim to cultural rights, and as our examination of polyethnic rights reveals, cultural rights are group rights, even when they are exercised by individual members against the broader political community.

Indeed, all immigrants residing in Korea are social beings (not just abstract beings whose moral autonomy and sociopolitical rights could be maximally respected according to the universal principle of liberal democracy) who want to reproduce their cultural and religious practices in Korea and who wish to educate their children according to their own cultural values and religious

[49] Kim, "Korean Immigration Policy Change and the Political Liberals' Dilemma"; Lee, "Development of Korea's Immigration Policies"; Lee, "Migration, Migrants, and Contested Ethno-Nationalism in Korea."

precepts.[50] And this is exactly what multiculturalism as a social program and political practice stands for. The question, then, is how to accommodate the claim to cultural rights by immigrants (and by long-term or semipermanent migrant residents).

Kymlicka's suggestion informs us that the dominant society is morally obligated to make such an accommodation with a view to fairness. There is no disagreement with this claim. However, Kymlicka's reference of "fairness" is clearly to the liberal public culture underpinning Western liberal-democratic societies. It should be recalled that earlier, I identified Kymlicka's suggestions with regard to immigrant multiculturalism as a kind of civic liberalism. The content of "civic," though, is neither culturally neutral nor simply dictated a priori by universal moral principles (i.e., respect of human rights) of liberalism.[51] To be sure, Kymlicka demands more than mere toleration in favor (a la Rawls) of the fair societal integration of immigrants. He is silent, however, when it comes to associational freedom of immigrant communities *after* the fair integration of immigrants into the institutions of a dominant society. There is good reason, though, to suspect that Kymlicka would support immigrant communitarianism (but not immigrant nationalism) if it is reasonable in light of liberal public culture.[52]

As we have seen, however, Confucian public culture in contemporary democratic Korean society is qualitatively different from liberal public culture pivoted around the discourse of human rights in which the right to expressive and associational freedom holds supreme moral value. Cultural pluralism, which accompanies the "logic" of multiculturalism, has never been salient in Korean society, but not because Korean democracy suppresses ethical pluralism or the Korean people have no constitutional right to freedom of association. Rather, it is because the Korean people rarely exercise their associational freedom, such as religious associational freedom, in such politically volatile terms as cultural pluralism or expressive freedom of group identity. Rather, they largely exercise their liberal-democratic civil rights in ways that allow

[50] Recently, *Hangyeoryeshinmun*, a progressive daily newspaper in Korea, covered extensively on how Muslim immigrants and their families are struggling with reproducing their cultural and religious life in Korean society especially in the areas of marriage and child education (16 May 2011, 17 May 2011). Virtually all Muslim immigrants interviewed, most of whom came to Korea initially as a migrant worker, no doubt see themselves as legitimate Korean citizens and want to fully integrate into the mainstream Korean society, but in no way want to abandon their way of religious/cultural life. Once again, what we see here is the tension between cultural/religious membership and identity and Korean democratic citizenship.

[51] See Rogers M. Smith, *The Stories of Peoplehood: The Politics and Morals of Political Membership* (Cambridge: Cambridge University Press, 2003).

[52] Political theorists and policy makers tend to approach public reason purely in rationalist (a la Kant) terms. Sharon Krause corrects this rationalist presumption by saying that "[p]ublic reasons reflect the shared horizons of concern that are implicit in the political culture of a particular community." See Sharon R. Krause, *Civil Passions: Moral Sentiment and Democratic Deliberation* (Princeton: Princeton University Press, 2008), 157.

them to be in harmony with the Confucian social mores and public reasons embedded in Korean civil society.[53]

Then, what is a fair way to accommodate immigrant multiculturalism with reference to Confucian public culture and with a view to Korean democracy? I have three general suggestions.

First, Confucian public culture should be the reference through which the public good is identified and deliberated. We have already seen what Confucian public culture consists of and why subscribing to it is reasonable in the Korean democratic context. Second, however, since what constitutes the public good is open for debate, both citizens and foreign residents who are (and are likely to be) adversely affected by the existing concept of the public good and public policies based on it should be able to contest it in the public space of civil society. Indeed, Korean democratic civil society is full of public debates between the left and right and among relevant social groups and organizations regarding the concept and the content of the public good, but, unfortunately, immigrants (let alone foreign residents such as migrant workers) are often excluded from them. I propose that this be rectified. Third, that being said, the shared public culture or public reason(s) that makes individuals residing in Korea the "Korean citizens" broadly understood must be able to prevent any particular cultural or religious group – be it Confucian, Protestant, Catholic, Buddhist, or Islamic – from dominating the public forum and political institutions.

The claim to democratic contestation with the public good, however, should meet two stipulations. First, in politically contesting the public good, the relevant concern of the contestant should be only with individual members' basic interests, but not with their best interests. Without delving into a complicated philosophical discussion about what constitutes basic interests and how to distinguish them from best interests,[54] let us revisit freedom of expression and association to see the Confucian democratic relevance of this distinction. No one will contest that freedom of expression and association are basic interests for *any* member of the political community, and it is on this ground that I have argued that long-term and semipermanent migrant workers should be granted the democratic right

[53] This claim is empirically tested. For instance, in the United States, it is generally assumed that freedom of expression and association, being a constitutional right notwithstanding, is not costless, and as Rosenblum shows, the cost involves an injury or insult to one's identity to whom the freedom of expression is addressed or resentment against whom freedom of association is exercised. It is for this reason that at the core of liberal civility is toleration. In marked contrast, in Korea, citizens rarely proactively exercise freedom of expression and association precisely because they do not want to live with such injury/insult/resentment, which, in their view, is the very sign of lack of harmony, or even of social anomie. If they feel insulted by others' exercise of such freedoms, they even appeal to the court (even including the constitutional court) to demand public apology from a person or an association that has exercised such a right (for instance, see Hahm, "Negotiating Confucian Civility," 285–8). In most liberal societies, the court order of public apology is almost inconceivable because of the danger of violating individual freedom.

[54] For a philosophical articulation of this distinction, see Ian Shapiro, *Democratic Justice* (New Haven: Yale University Press, 1999), 85–96.

to enjoy this freedom. However, the claim to this freedom is always respected within the boundary set by Confucian public culture, and the general democratic public is obligated to strive to accommodate other citizens' basic interests, but not their best interests, which morally require a maximal accommodation. In the actual Korean democratic political setting, the liberal-democratic constitution obligates Korean citizens to respect any Korean (both legal and de facto) citizen's democratic claim to the (basic) rights to freedom of expression and association, but these rights should not be exercised in absolutist liberal terms, and their scope should be mediated through Confucian public reason(s).

My second stipulation concerns the effectiveness of democratic contestation with the public good. As we have seen, Kymlicka's reference for the fair social integration of immigrants is the liberalism of individual human rights or liberal public reasons and most multicultural critics in Korea rely mainly on rights discourse to redress injustices in government policies and social practices. This direct recourse to rights-based individualism, however, is limited in practice to achieve the intended liberal-democratic justice for reasons that we already have investigated, that is, the general Korean public's cultural unfamiliarity with the ethics of liberal individualism or the different nature of public reason in Korean civil society. Therefore, a cultural group's contestation with the public good generally accepted in Korean society purely in terms of cultural rights is likely to give rise to anxiety, resentment, and even social and political backlash among and from majority Korean citizens.[55]

To avoid this kind of social cost and potential political danger, cultural groups are better advised to take advantage of Confucian public discourse and appeal to Confucian public reasons to advance their cultural rights. For instance, rather than directly appealing to their cultural "rights" to educate their children according to their religious precepts and practices, Muslim families and groups may contest the dominant notion of the public good in Korean society by referring to the Confucian values of a loving family, moral development of a person, and benevolence. Of course, for this to be *reasonable* to the general Korean public, Muslim families and groups, in their turn, may have to embrace the Confucian values of filial love, fraternal responsibility, and benevolence that may prevent them from oppressing women without fundamentally revamping their cultural practices (say, polygamous marriage).[56] Whether

[55] I fully agree with Jacob Levy that a political theory of multiculturalism should be "centrally concerned neither with preserving and celebrating ethnic identities nor with overcoming them," but instead it should focus on "mitigating the recurrent dangers such as state violence toward cultural minorities, inter-ethnic warfare, and intra-communal attacks on those who try to alter or leave their cultural communities" (Jacob T. Levy, *The Multiculturalism of Fear* [New York: Oxford University Press, 2000], 12–13).

[56] This strategy can be useful to other types of cultural groups, such as gay and lesbian groups (the so-called sexual minorities). Rather than protesting against the illegalization of same-sex marriage by direct recourse to the Korean constitution or the University Declaration of Human Rights, they can appeal to the general public's moral sensibility by stressing the Confucian importance of developing intimate relationships and a loving family.

the dominant Korean society will accommodate Muslim families and groups' *reasonable* requests is subject to empirical test. But passing this test will verify the maturity of the Korean democratic polity.

What is essential in these suggestions is that there should be a general public commitment among Korean citizens to the reproduction of Confucian public culture that binds Korean citizens (again broadly/inclusively understood) horizontally and civically. In this way, we can avoid what is now bedeviling many Western European countries that once actively pursued multiculturalism – namely, the dangerous politics of multiculturalism that puts culture and religion on the frontline of political struggle, eroding public purposes and common democratic citizenship.

Conclusion

My final claim therefore is as follows: multiculturalism can be most effectively practiced in Korea if two conditions are met – (1) democratic civil society is internally liberal-pluralistic (democratic pluralism) while being a unified bulwark for political liberty or public freedom *and* (2) democratic pluralism safeguarded by the citizens' collective self-determination is reasonably constrained by their shared Korean-Confucian public culture (Confucian-democratic citizenship). Radically liberal Korean multiculturalists may not like my conclusion. But then it is their burden to show a more plausible way to realize a multicultural society that is democracy-enhancing without the invocation of perilous cultural politics between immigrants and native Koreans, and among different groups of immigrants.

Bibliography

Abizadeh, Arash. 2008. "Democratic Theory and Border Coercion: No Right to Unilaterally Control Your Own Borders." *Political Theory* 36: 37–65.

Ackerly, Brooke A. 2005. "Is Liberalism the Only Way toward Democracy? Confucianism and Democracy." *Political Theory* 33: 547–76.

Alaqappa, Muthiah (ed.). 2004. *Civil Society and Political Change in Asia: Expanding and Contracting Democratic Space*. Stanford: Stanford University Press.

Alford, C. Fred. 1999. *Think No Evil: Korean Values in the Age of Globalization*. Ithaca: Cornell University Press.

Ames, Roger T. 1988. "Rites and Rights: The Confucian Alternative." In Rouner, *Human Rights and the World's Religions*, 199–216.

2003. "Confucianism: Confucius (Kongzi, K'ung Tzu)." In *Encyclopedia of Chinese Philosophy*, edited by Antonio S. Cua. New York: Routledge, 58–63.

2011. *Confucian Role Ethics: A Vocabulary*. Honolulu: University of Hawaii Press.

Ames, Roger T. and Henry Rosemont Jr. 1998. *The Analects of Confucius: A Philosophical Translation*. New York: Ballantine Books.

Angle, Stephen C. 2009. *Sagehood: The Contemporary Significance of Neo-Confucian Philosophy*. Oxford: Oxford University Press.

2012. *Contemporary Confucian Political Philosophy: Toward Progressive Confucianism*. Cambridge: Polity.

Appiah, Kwame Anthony. 2006. *Cosmopolitanism: Ethics in a World of Strangers*. New York: Norton.

Arendt, Hannah. 1958. *The Human Condition*. Chicago: University of Chicago Press.

2003. *Responsibility and Judgment*, edited by Jerome Kohn. New York: Schocken Books.

Armstrong, Charles K. (ed.). 2002. *Korean Society: Civil Society, Democracy, and the State*. London: Routledge.

Ash, Timothy G. 1999. "The Year of Truth." In *The Revolutions of 1989*, edited by Vladimir Tismaneanu. London: Routledge, 108–24.

Bai, Tongdong. 2008. "A Mencian Version of Limited Democracy." *Res Publica* 14: 19–34.

2011. "Against Democratic Education." *Journal of Curriculum Studies* 43: 615–22.

Balazs, Etienne. 1964. *Chinese Civilization and Bureaucracy*, translated by H. M. Wright and edited by Arthur F. Wright. New Haven: Yale University Press.

Barber, Benjamin R. 1988. *The Conquest of Politics: Liberal Philosophy in Democratic Times*. Princeton: Princeton University Press.

1989. "Liberal Democracy and the Costs of Consent." In Rosenblum, *Liberalism and the Moral Life*, 54–68.

1992. *An Aristocracy of Everyone: The Politics of Education and the Future of America*. Oxford: Oxford University Press.

1998. *A Place for Us: How to Make Society Civil and Democracy Strong*. New York: Hill and Wang.

2003. *Fear's Empire: War, Terrorism, and Democracy*. New York: Norton.

2003. *Strong Democracy: Participatory Politics for a New Age*, 20th anniversary ed. Berkeley: University of California Press.

2007. *Consumed: How Markets Corrupt Children, Infantilize Adults, and Swallow Citizens Whole*. New York: Norton.

Barry, Brian. 2001. *Culture and Equality*. Cambridge, MA: Harvard University Press.

Beiner, Ronald. 1992. *What's the Matter with Liberalism?* Berkeley: University of California Press.

Beitz, Charles. 1999. *Political Theory and International Relations*. Princeton: Princeton University Press.

Bell, Daniel A. 1999. "Democratic Deliberation: The Problem of Implementation." In Macedo, *Deliberative Politics*, 70–87.

2000. *East Meets West: Human Rights and Democracy in East Asia*. Princeton: Princeton University Press.

2003. "Constraints on Property Rights." In Bell and Hahm, *Confucianism for the Modern World*, 218–35.

2006. *Beyond Liberal Democracy: Political Thinking for an East Asian Context*. Princeton: Princeton University Press.

2008. *China's New Confucianism: Politics and Everyday Life in a Changing Society*. Princeton: Princeton University Press.

2010. "Reconciling Socialism and Confucianism? Reviving Tradition in China." *Dissent* 57: 91–9.

Bell, Daniel A. and Chaibong Hahm (eds.). 2003. *Confucianism for the Modern World*. Cambridge: Cambridge University Press.

Bell, Daniel A. and Chenyang Li (eds.). 2013. *The East Asian Challenge for Democracy: Political Meritocracy in Comparative Perspective*. Cambridge: Cambridge University Press.

Bellah, Robert N. 2006. "Civil Religion in America." In *The Robert Bellah Reader*, edited by Robert N. Bellah and Steven M. Tipton. Durham, NC: Duke University Press, 225–45.

Bellah, Robert N., Richard Madsen, William M. Sullivan, Ann Swidler, and Steven M. Tipton. 1985. *Habits of the Heart: Individualism and Commitment in American Life*. Berkeley: University of California Press.

Benhabib, Seyla. 1992. *Situating the Self: Gender, Community and Postmodernism in Contemporary Ethics*. New York: Routledge.

Berlin, Isaiah. 1969. "Two Concepts of Liberty." In *Four Essays on Liberty*. Oxford: Oxford University Press, 118–72.

Berman, Sheri. 1997. "Civil Society and the Collapse of the Weimar Republic." *World Politics* 49: 401–29.

Bloom, Irene T. 2002. "Mengzian Arguments on Human Nature (*Ren Xing*)." In Liu and Ivanhoe, *Essays on the Moral Philosophy of Mengzi*, 64–100.

(trans.). 2009. *Mencius*, edited by Philip J. Ivanhoe. New York: Columbia University Press.

Bohman, James. 2000. *Public Deliberation: Pluralism, Complexity, and Democracy*. Cambridge, MA: MIT Press.

Bohman, James and William Rehg (eds.). 1999. *Deliberative Democracy*. Cambridge, MA: MIT Press.

Bol, Peter K. 2008. *Neo-Confucianism in History*. Cambridge, MA: Harvard University Asia Center.

Boyd, Richard. 2004. "Pity's Pathologies Portrayed: Rousseau and the Limits of Democratic Compassion." *Political Theory* 32: 519–46.

2004. *Uncivil Society: The Perils of Pluralism and the Making of Modern Liberalism*. Lanham, MD: Lexington Books.

Brettschneider, Corey. 2007. *Democratic Rights: The Substance of Self-Government*. Princeton: Princeton University Press.

Browning, Christopher R. 1992. *Ordinary Men: Reserve Police Battalion 101 and the Final Solution in Poland*. New York: Harper.

Brubaker, Rogers. 1996. *Nationalism Reframed: Nationhood and the National Question in the New Europe*. Cambridge: Cambridge University Press.

Bunce, Valerie. 1999. *Subversive Institutions: The Design and the Destruction of Socialism and the State*. Cambridge: Cambridge University Press.

Carens, Joseph H. 1995. "Aliens and Citizens: The Case for Open Borders." In *Theorizing Citizenship*, edited by Ronald Beiner. Albany: State University of New York Press, 229–53.

Carter, Stephen L. 1998. *Civility: Manners, Morals, and the Etiquette of Democracy*. New York: Basic Books.

Casal, Paula. 2007. "Why Sufficiency Is Not Enough." *Ethics* 117: 296–326.

Chan, Joseph. 1999. "A Confucian Perspective on Human Rights for Contemporary China." In *The East Asian Challenge for Human Rights*, edited by Joanne R. Bauer and Daniel A. Bell. Cambridge: Cambridge University Press, 212–37.

2000. "Legitimacy, Unanimity, and Perfectionism." *Philosophy and Public Affairs* 29: 5–42.

2002. "Moral Autonomy, Civil Liberties, and Confucianism." *Philosophy East and West* 52: 281–310.

2004. "Exploring the Nonfamilial in Confucian Political Philosophy." In Hahm and Bell, *Politics of Affective Relations*, 61–74.

2007. "Democracy and Meritocracy: Toward a Confucian Perspective." *Journal of Chinese Philosophy* 34: 179–93.

2008. "Confucian Attitudes toward Ethical Pluralism." In *Confucian Political Ethics*, edited by Daniel A. Bell. Princeton: Princeton University Press, 113–38.

2008. "Is There a Confucian Perspective on Social Justice?" In *Western Political Thought in Dialogue with Asia*, edited by Takashi Shogimen and Cary J. Nederman. Lanham, MD: Lexington Books, 261–77.

2012. "On Legitimacy of Confucian Constitutionalism." In Jiang Qing, *A Confucian Constitutional Order: How China's Ancient Past Can Shape Its Political Future*, edited by Daniel A. Bell and Ruiping Fan and translated by Edmund Ryden. Princeton: Princeton University Press, 99–112.

2013. *Confucian Perfectionism: A Political Philosophy for Modern Times*. Princeton: Princeton University Press.

Chandler, Marthe and Ronnie Littlejohn (eds.). 2008. *Polishing the Chinese Mirror*. New York: Global Scholarly Publications.

Chang, Yu-Tzung and Yun-han Chu. 2007. "Traditionalism, Political Learning and Conceptions of Democracy in East Asia." *Asian Barometer Working Paper Series No. 39*. Taipei: National Taiwan University.

Chang, Yu-Tzung, Yun-han Chu, and Frank Tsai. 2005. "Confucianism and Democratic Values in Three Chinese Societies." *Issues & Studies* 41: 1–33.

Chen, Albert H. 2003. "Mediation, Litigation, and Justice: Confucian Reflections in a Modern Liberal Society." In Bell and Hahm, *Confucianism for the Modern World*, 257–87.

Chen, Ming. 2012. "Modernity and Confucian Political Philosophy in a Globalized World." In *Contemporary Chinese Political Thought: Debates and Perspectives*, edited by Fred Dallmayr and Zhao Tingyang. Lexington: University Press of Kentucky, 110–30.

Cheng, Chung-ying. 2004. "A Theory of Confucian Selfhood: Self-Cultivation and Free Will in Confucian Philosophy." In Shun and Wong, *Confucian Ethics*, 124–47.

Ching, Julia. 1997. *Mysticism and Kingship in China: The Heart of Chinese Wisdom*. Cambridge: Cambridge University Press.

1998. "Human Rights: A Valid Chinese Concept?" In de Bary and Tu, *Confucianism and Human Rights*, 67–82.

Cho, Geung-Ho. 2003. *Han'gukin ihaeui gaenyeomteul* [Reading Koreans Culturally: A Psychological Approach]. Seoul: Nanam.

Cho, Hein. 1997. "The Historical Origin of Civil Society in Korea." *Korea Journal* 37: 24–41.

Cho, Yong-whan. 2002. "The National Human Rights Commission: Law, Reality, and Its Future Task." *Korea Journal* 42: 228–62.

Choi, Bong-yeong. 1994. *Han'gukinui sahoejeok seonggyeok* [The Social Character of the Korean People]. Seoul: Neutinamu.

Choi, Jangjip. 2000. "Democratization, Civil Society and the Civil Social Movement in Korea: The Significance of the Citizens' Alliance for the 2000 General Elections." *Korea Journal* 40: 26–57.

2005. *Minjuhaw ihuui Minjujuui* [Democracy after Democratization]. Seoul: Humanitas.

Choi, Jin-deok (ed.). 2001. *Jeontongyegyowa shiminyunli* [Traditional Rituals and Civic Ethics]. Seoul: Cheonggye.

Choi, Sang-chin. 1998. "The Third-Person-Psychology and the First-Person-Psychology: Two Perspectives on Human Relations." *Korean Social Science Journal* 25: 239–64.

(ed.). *Dongyangshimlihak: Seogushimlihake daehan mosaek*. Seoul: Jishiksaneopsa.

1999. "Han'gukinui maeum" [The Mind of the Korean People]. In Choi, *Dongyangshimlihak*, 377–479.

2000. *Han'gukin shimlihak* [The Psychology of the Korean People]. Seoul: Chung Ang University Press.

Choi, Sang-chin and Gyu-seok Han. 1998. "Gyoryuhaengwireul tonghaebon han'gukinui sahoesimli" [The Social Psychology of the Korean People from the Perspective of Interpersonal Relations]. In *Han'gukmunhawwa han'gukin* [Korean Culture and the Korean People], edited by the Association of International Korean Studies. Seoul: Sagyejeol, 161–93.

Choi, Sang-chin and Jeong-un Kim. 1998. "Jiphapjeok uimiguseonge daehan munhwashimlihakjeok jeopgeunuiroseoui munhwasimjeongshimlihak" ["Shim-Cheong" Psychology as a Cultural Psychological Approach to Collective Meaning Construction]. *Korean Journal of Social and Personality Psychology* 12: 79–96.

Choi, Sang-chin, Ji-young Kim, and Ki-bum Kim. 2000. "*Jeong* (*miun jeong goun jeong*)ui simlijeok gujo, haengwi mit gineungganui gujojeok gwangye bunseok" [An Analysis of the Structural Relations between the Psychological Structure, Behaviors, and Functions of *Chŏng* (*miun chŏng, goun chŏng*)]. *Korean Journal of Social and Personality Psychology* 14: 203–22.

Choi, Sang-chin and Ki-bum Kim. 1999. "Han'gugin selpeuui teukseong: Seoguui selpeugaenyeomgwa daebireul jungsimeuro" [The Characteristics of the Korean Self: In Comparison with the Western Concept of the Self]. *Korean Journal of Social and Personality Psychology* 13: 275–92.

Choi, Sang-chin and Jangju Lee. 1999. "Jeongui simlijeok gujowa sahoe: Munhwajeok gineung bunseok" [An Analysis of the Psychological Structure of *Chŏng* and Its Cultural Function]. *Korean Journal of Social and Personality Psychology* 13: 219–34.

Chu, Yun-han, Larry Diamond, Andrew J. Nathan, and Doh Chull Shin (eds.). 2008. *How East Asians View Democracy*. New York: Columbia University Press.

Chun, Seon-young. 2004. "Damunhwasahoe damlonui han'gyewa yeokseol" [The Limit and Paradox of the Discourse on "Multicultural Society"]. *Handoksahoegwahaknonchong* 14: 363–80.

Chung, Yunjae (ed.). 2002. *Yugyolideoshipgwa han'gukjeongchi* [Confucian Leadership and Korean Politics]. Seoul: Baeksanseodang.

Cline, Erin M. 2008. "Rawls, Rosemont, and the Debate over Rights and Roles." In Chandler and Littlejohn, *Polishing the Chinese Mirror*, 77–89.

Cohen, Joshua. 1993. "Freedom of Expression." *Philosophy and Public Affairs* 22: 207–63.

(ed.). 1996. *For Love of Country: Debating the Limits of Patriotism*. Boston: Beacon.

1996. "Procedure and Substance in Deliberative Democracy." In *Democracy and Difference: Contesting the Boundaries of the Political*, edited by Seyla Benhabib. Princeton: Princeton University Press, 95–119.

1998. "Democracy and Liberty." In Elster, *Deliberative Democracy*, 185–231.

Creel, H. G. 1960. *Confucius and the Chinese Way*. New York: Harper & Row.

Crisp, Roger. 2003. "Equality, Priority, and Compassion." *Ethics* 113: 745–63.

Cua, Antonio S. 1984. "Confucian Vision and Human Community." *Journal of Chinese Philosophy* 11: 227–38.

Dagger, Richard. 1997. *Civic Virtues: Rights, Citizenship, and Republican Liberalism*. Oxford: Oxford University Press.

Dallmayr, Fred R. 2002. "'Asian Values' and Global Human Rights." *Philosophy East and West* 52: 173–89.

2004. "Confucianism and the Public Sphere: Five Relationships Plus One?" In Hahm and Bell, *Politics of Affective Relations*, 41–59.

2009. "Exiting Liberal Democracy: Bell and Confucian Thought." *Philosophy East and West* 59: 524–30.

Damasio, Antonio R. 1994. *Descartes' Error: Emotion, Reason and the Human Brain.* New York: HarperCollins.

de Bary, Wm. Theodore. 1983. *The Liberal Tradition in China.* New York: Columbia University Press.

1991. *The Trouble with Confucianism.* Cambridge, MA: Harvard University Press.

1998. *Asian Values and Human Rights: A Confucian Communitarian Perspective.* Cambridge, MA: Harvard University Press.

de Bary, Wm. Theodore, Wing-tsit Chan, and Burton Watson (eds.). 1960. *Sources of Chinese Tradition*, vol. 1. New York: Columbia University Press.

de Bary, Wm. Theodore and Tu Weiming (eds.). 1998. *Confucianism and Human Rights.* New York: Columbia University Press.

Deneen, Patrick J. 2005. *Democratic Faith.* Princeton: Princeton University Press.

de Tocqueville, Alexis. 2000. *Democracy in America*, edited and translated by Harvey C. Mansfield and Delba Winthrop. Chicago: University of Chicago Press.

Deuchler, Martina. 1992. *The Confucian Transformation of Korea: A Study of Society and Ideology.* Cambridge, MA: Council on East Asian Studies, Harvard University.

1999. "Despoilers of the Way – Insulters of the Sages: Controversies over the Classics in Seventeenth-Century Korea." In *Culture and the State in Late Chosŏn Korea*, edited by JaHyun K. Haboush and Martina Deuchler. Cambridge, MA: Council on East Asian Studies, Harvard University, 91–113.

Dewey, John. 1954. *The Public and Its Problems.* Athens, OH: Swallow Press.

1969. "The Ethics of Democracy." In *John Dewey: The Early Works*, vol. 1, edited by George E. Axetell and Jo Ann Boydston. Carbondale: Southern Illinois University Press, 227–49.

Diamond, Larry. 1999. *Developing Democracy: Toward Consolidation.* Baltimore: Johns Hopkins University Press.

Dryzek, John S. 2000. *Deliberative Democracy and Beyond: Liberals, Critics, and Contestations.* Oxford: Oxford University Press.

Dunn, John. 2001. "The Contemporary Political Significance of John Locke's Conception of Civil Society." In Kaviraj and Khilnani, *Civil Society*, 39–57.

Eisenstadt, Shmuel N. 1985. "This Worldly Transcendentalism and the Structuring of the World: Max Weber's 'Religion of China' and the Format of Chinese History and Civilization." *Journal of Developing Societies* 1: 168–86.

Elman, Benjamin A. 2000. *A Cultural History of Civil Examinations in Late Imperial China.* Berkeley: University of California Press.

Elster, Jon. 1998. "Deliberation and Constitution Making." In Elster, *Deliberative Democracy*, 97–122.

(ed.). 1998. *Deliberative Democracy.* Cambridge: Cambridge University Press.

Fan, Ruiping. 1997. "Self-Determination vs. Family-Determination: Two Incommensurable Principle of Autonomy." *Bioethics* 11: 309–22.

2010. *Reconstructionist Confucianism: Rethinking Morality after the West.* Dordrecht: Springer.

Fan, Yun. 2004. "Taiwan: No Civil Society, No Democracy." In Alaqappa, *Civil Society and Political Change in Asia*, 165–90.

Fearon, James D. 1999. "Electoral Accountability and the Control of Politicians: Selecting Good Types versus Sanctioning Poor Performance." In *Democracy, Accountability, and Representation*, edited by Adam Przeworski, Susan C. Stokes, and Bernard Manin. Cambridge: Cambridge University Press, 55–97.

Fingarette, Herbert. 1972. *Confucius: The Secular as Sacred*. New York: Harper.

Fish, Steven. 1994. "Rethinking Civil Society: Russia's Fourth Transition." *Journal of Democracy* 5: 31–42.

Flathman, Richard E. 2002. *Thomas Hobbes: Skepticism, Individuality, and Chastened Politics*. Lanham, MD: Rowman & Littlefield.

2005. *Pluralism and Liberal Democracy*. Baltimore: Johns Hopkins University Press.

Formosa, Paul. 2006. "Moral Responsibility for Banal Evil." *Journal of Social Philosophy* 37: 501–20.

Fox, Russell A. 1997. "Confucian and Communitarian Responses to Liberal Democracy." *Review of Politics* 59: 561–92.

2008. "Activity and Communal Authority: Localist Lessons from Puritan and Confucian Communities." *Philosophy East and West* 58: 36–59.

Frankfurt, Harry. 1987. "Equality as a Moral Ideal." *Ethics* 98: 21–43.

Frazer, Michael L. 2007. "John Rawls: Between Two Enlightenments." *Political Theory* 35: 756–80.

2010. *The Enlightenment of Sympathy: Justice and the Moral Sentiments in the Eighteenth Century and Today*. New York: Oxford University Press.

Fukuyama, Francis. 1992. *The End of History and the Last Man*. New York: Free Press.

Galston, William A. 1991. *Liberal Purposes: Goods, Virtues, and Diversity in the Liberal State*. Cambridge: Cambridge University Press.

1991. "Toughness as Political Virtue." *Social Theory and Practice* 17: 175–97.

1995. "Two Concepts of Liberalism." *Ethics* 105: 516–34.

2002. *Liberal Pluralism: The Implications of Value Pluralism for Political Theory and Practice*. Cambridge: Cambridge University Press.

2005. *The Practice of Liberal Pluralism*. Cambridge: Cambridge University Press.

2007. "Pluralism and Civic Virtue." *Social Theory and Practice* 33: 625–35.

2011. "Pluralist Constitutionalism." *Social Philosophy and Policy* 28: 228–41.

Gauss, Gerald F. 1996. *Justificatory Liberalism: An Essay on Epistemology and Political Theory*. Oxford: Oxford University Press.

1999. "Reason, Justification, and Consensus." In Bohman and Rehg, *Deliberative Democracy*, 205–42.

Gellner, Ernest. 1996. *Conditions of Liberty: Civil Society and Its Rivals*. New York: Penguin.

Ginsburg, Tom. 2002. "Confucian Constitutionalism? The Emergence of Constitutional Review in Korea and Taiwan." *Law & Social Inquiry* 27: 763–99.

Glendon, Mary A. 1991. *Rights Talk: The Impoverishment of Political Discourse*. New York: Free Press.

1995. "Forgotten Questions." In *Seedbeds of Virtue: Sources of Competence, Character, and Citizenship in American Society*, edited by Mary A. Glendon and David Blankenhorn. Lanham, MD: Madison Books, 1–15.

Goodin, Robert E. 1985. "Vulnerabilities and Responsibilities: An Ethical Defense of the Welfare State." *American Political Science Review* 79: 775–87.
Grant, Ruth W. 1997. *Hypocrisy and Integrity: Machiavelli, Rousseau, and the Ethics of Politics.* Chicago: University of Chicago Press.
Grant, Ruth W. and Robert O. Keohane. 2005. "Accountability and Abuses of Power in World Politics." *American Political Science Review* 99: 29–43.
Gutmann, Amy. 1988. *Democratic Education.* Princeton: Princeton University Press.
(ed.). 1998. *Freedom of Association.* Princeton: Princeton University Press.
2003. *Identity in Democracy.* Princeton: Princeton University Press.
Gutmann, Amy and Dennis Thompson. 1996. *Democracy and Disagreement: Why Moral Conflict Cannot Be Avoided in Politics, and What Should Be Done about It.* Cambridge, MA: Belknap.
2004. *Why Deliberative Democracy?* Princeton: Princeton University Press.
Habermas, Jürgen. 1996. *Between Facts and Norms: Contributions to a Discourse Theory of Law and Democracy*, translated by William Rehg. Cambridge, MA: MIT Press.
Hahm, Chaibong. 1997. "The Confucian Political Discourse and the Politics of Reform in Korea." *Korea Journal* 37: 65–77.
1998. *Talgeundaewa yugyo* [Postmodernity and Confucianism]. Seoul: Nanam.
2000. *Yugyo, jabonjuui, minjujuui* [Confucianism, Capitalism, and Democracy]. Seoul: Jeontong-gwa Hyeondae.
2001. "Postmodernism in the Post-Confucian Context: Epistemological and Political Considerations." *Human Studies* 24: 29–44.
2003. "Family versus the Individual: The Politics of Marriage Laws in Korea." In Bell and Hahm, *Confucianism for the Modern World*, 334–59.
2004. "The Ironies of Confucianism." *Journal of Democracy* 15: 93–107.
2008. "South Korea's Miraculous Democracy." *Journal of Democracy* 19: 128–42.
Hahm, Chaihark. 2003. "Constitutionalism, Confucian Civic Virtue, and Ritual Propriety." In Bell and Hahm, *Confucianism for the Modern World*, 31–53.
2004. "Disputing Civil Society in a Confucian Context." *Korea Observer* 35: 433–62.
2004. "Negotiating Confucian Civility through Constitutional Discourse." In Hahm and Bell, *Politics of Affective Relations*, 277–308.
2009. "Ritual and Constitutionalism: Disputing the Ruler's Legitimacy in a Confucian Polity." *American Journal of Comparative Law* 57: 135–203.
Hahm, Chaihark and Daniel A. Bell (eds.). 2004. *The Politics of Affective Relations: East Asia and Beyond.* Lanham, MD: Lexington Books.
Hahm, Pyong-choon. 1986. *Korean Jurisprudence, Politics and Culture.* Seoul: Yonsei University Press.
Hall, Cheryl. 2007. "Recognizing the Passion in Deliberation: Toward a More Democratic Theory of Deliberative Democracy." *Hypatia* 22: 81–95.
Hall, David L. and Roger T. Ames. 1999. *The Democracy of the Dead: Dewey, Confucius, and the Hope for Democracy in China.* Chicago: Open Court.
2003. "A Pragmatic Understanding of Confucian Democracy." In Bell and Hahm, *Confucianism for the Modern World*, 124–60.
Hamilton, Alexander, James Madison, and John Jay. 1982. *The Federalist Papers*, edited by Garry Wills. New York: Bantam Books.

Han, Bae-ho. 2003. *Han'guk jeongchimunhwawa munjujeongchi* [Korean Political Culture and Democracy]. Seoul: Beopmunsa.

Han, Deuk-woong. 1999. "Han'gukyuhakui shimlihak" [A Psychological Study of Korean Confucianism]. In Choi, *Dongyangshimlihak*, 163–285.

Havel, Vaclav. 1987. "The Power of the Powerless." In *Living in Truth*, edited by Jan Vladislav. London: Faber and Faber, 36–122.

Hayek, Friedrich. A. 1978. *The Constitution of Liberty*. Chicago: University of Chicago Press.

He, Baogang. 2004. "Confucianism versus Liberalism over Minority Rights: A Critical Response to Will Kymlicka." *Journal of Chinese Philosophy* 31: 103–23.

2006. "Western Theories of Deliberative Democracy and the Chinese Practice of Complex Deliberative Governance." In *The Search for Deliberative Democracy in China*, edited by Ethan J. Leib and Baogang He. New York: Palgrave, 133–48.

He, Baogang and Mark E. Warren. 2011. "Authoritarian Deliberation: The Deliberative Turn in Chinese Political Development." *Perspectives on Politics* 9: 269–89.

Held, Virginia. 2006. *The Ethics of Care: Personal, Political, Global*. New York: Oxford University Press.

Helgesen, Geir. 1998. *Democracy and Authority in Korea: The Cultural Dimension in Korean Politics*. Surrey: Curzon.

Herr, Ranjoo S. 2008. "Cultural Claims and the Limits of Liberal Democracy." *Social Theory and Practice* 34: 25–48.

Holmes, Stephen. 1989. "The Permanent Structure of Antiliberal Thought." In *Liberalism and Moral Life*, edited by Nancy L. Rosenblum. Cambridge, MA: Harvard University Press, 227–53.

1996. *The Anatomy of Antiliberalism*. Cambridge, MA: Harvard University Press.

Horkheimer, Max and Theodor W. Adorno. 2002. *Dialectic of Enlightenment*, edited by Gunzelin S. Noerr and translated by Edmund Jephcott. Stanford: Stanford University Press.

Hourdequin, Marion. 2010. "Engagement, Withdrawal, and Social Reform: Confucian and Contemporary Perspective." *Philosophy East and West* 60: 369–90.

Howard, Marc M. 2003. *The Weakness of Civil Society in Post-Communist Europe*. Cambridge: Cambridge University Press.

Huntington, Samuel P. 1991. *The Third Wave: Democratization in the Late Twentieth Century*. Norman: University of Oklahoma Press.

Hutton, Eric L. 2002. "Moral Connoisseurship in Mengzi." In Liu and Ivanhoe, *Essays on the Moral Philosophy of Mengzi*, 163–86.

2008. "Han Feizi's Criticism of Confucianism and its Implications for Virtue Ethics." *Journal of Moral Philosophy* 5: 423–53.

Hwang, Kyung Moon. 2000. "Country or State? Reconceptualizing *Kukka* in the Korean Enlightenment Period, 1896–1910." *Korean Studies* 24: 1–24.

Ihara, Craig K. 2004. "Are Individual Rights Necessary? A Confucian Perspective." In Shun and Wong, *Confucian Ethics*, 11–30.

Inkeles, Alex. 1969. "Making Men Modern: On the Causes and Consequences of Individual Change in Six Developing Countries." *American Journal of Sociology* 75: 208–25.

Ivanhoe, Philip J. 2000. *Confucian Moral Self Cultivation*. Indianapolis: Hackett.

2002. "Confucian Self Cultivation and Mengzi's Notion of Extension." In Liu and Ivanhoe, *Essays on the Moral Philosophy of Mengzi*, 221–41.

2002. *Ethics in the Confucian Tradition: The Thought of Mengzi and Wang Yangming*. Indianapolis: Hackett.

2007. "Filial Piety as Virtue." In *Working Virtue: Virtue Ethics and Contemporary Moral Problems*, edited by Rebecca L. Walker and Philip J. Ivanhoe. Oxford: Oxford University Press, 297–312.

2007. "Heaven as a Source for Ethical Warrant in Early Confucianism." *Dao* 6: 211–20.

2008. "The Shade of Confucius: Social Roles, Ethical Theory, and the Self." In Chandler and Littlejohn, *Polishing the Chinese Mirror*, 34–49.

2013. "Virtue Ethics and the Chinese Confucian Tradition." In *The Cambridge Companion to Virtue Ethics*, edited by Daniel C. Russell. Cambridge: Cambridge University Press, 49–69.

Jenco, Leigh K. 2010. "'Rule by Man' and 'Rule by Law' in Early Republican China: Contributions to a Theoretical Debate." *Journal of Asian Studies* 69: 181–203.

Jeon, Hye-young. 1998. "Han'gukeoe banyeongdoen yugyomunhwajeok teukseong" [The Confucian Characteristics Reflected in Korean Language]. In *Han'gukmunhwawa han'gukin* [Korean Culture and the Korean People], edited by the Association of International Korean Studies. Seoul: Sagyejeol, 235–58.

Jiang, Qing. 2003. *Zhengzhi Rujia: Dangdai Rujia de zhuanxiang, tezhi yu fazhan* [Political Confucianism: Contemporary Confucianism's Challenge, Special Quality, and Development]. Beijing: San lian shu dian.

2011. "From Mind Confucianism to Political Confucianism." In *The Renaissance of Confucianism in Contemporary China*, edited by Ruiping Fan. Dordrecht: Springer, 17–32.

2012. *A Confucian Constitutional Order: How China's Ancient Past Can Shape Its Political Future*, edited by Daniel A. Bell and Ruiping Fan and translated by Edmund Ryden. Princeton: Princeton University Press.

Jung, Hwa Yol. 1993. "Confucianism as Political Philosophy: A Postmodern Perspective." *Human Studies* 16: 213–30.

Kang, Xiaoguang. 2005. *Renzheng: Zhongguo zhengzhi fazhan de disantiao daolu* [Humane Government: A Third Road for the Development of Chinese Politics]. Singapore: Global Publishing.

2006. "Confucianism: A Future in the Tradition." *Social Research* 73: 77–120.

Kant, Immanuel. 1991. "Idea for a Universal History with a Cosmopolitan Purpose." In *Political Writings*, edited by Hans Reiss and translated by H. B. Nisbet. Cambridge: Cambridge University Press, 41–53.

1996. *The Metaphysics of Morals*, translated and edited by Mary Gregor. Cambridge: Cambridge University Press.

1997. *Critique of Practical Reason*, translated and edited by Mary Gregor. Cambridge: Cambridge University Press.

Karatani, Kojin. 2005. *Transcritique: On Kant and Marx*, translated by Sabu Kohso. Cambridge, MA: MIT Press.

Karl, Terry. 1990. "Dilemmas of Democratization in Latin America." *Comparative Politics* 23: 1–21.

Kateb, George. 1992. *The Inner Ocean: Individualism and Democratic Culture*. Ithaca: Cornell University Press.

1998. "The Value of Association." In Gutmann, *Freedom of Association*, 35–63.
2006. "Is Patriotism a Mistake?" In *Patriotism and Other Mistakes*. New Haven: Yale University Press, 3–20.
2006. "Notes on Pluralism." In *Patriotism and Other Mistakes*. New Haven: Yale University Press, 21–40.
Kaviraj, Sudipta and Sunil Khilnani (eds.). 2001. *Civil Society: History and Possibilities*. Cambridge: Cambridge University Press
Keohane, Nannerl O. 2010. *Thinking about Leadership*. Princeton: Princeton University Press.
Kim, Bumsoo. 2008. "Minjujuuie isseo poyonggwa baeje" [How to Draw the Boundaries of Demos?]. *Korean Journal of International Relations* 48: 173–98.
Kim, Dong-choon. 2006. "Growth and Crisis of the Korean Citizens' Movement." *Korea Journal* 46: 99–128.
Kim, Hyun-mee. 2007. "The State and Migrant Women: Diverging Hopes in the Making of 'Multicultural Families' in Contemporary Korea." *Korea Journal* 47: 100–122.
Kim, Nam-Kook. 2005. "Shimui damunhwajuui: Munhwajeok gwonliwa munhwajeok saengjon" [Deliberative Multiculturalism: A Path to Cultural Rights and Cultural Survival]. *Korean Political Science Review* 39: 87–107.
2009. "Multicultural Challenges in Korea: The Current Stage and a Prospect." *International Migration* (advance online publication, October 2009).
Kim, Nora H. J. 2008. "Korean Immigration Policy Change and the Political Liberals' Dilemma." *International Migration Review* 42: 576–96.
Kim, Sangjun. 2002. "The Genealogy of Confucian *Moralpolitik* and Its Implications for Modern Civil Society." In Armstrong, *Korean Society*, 57–91.
Kim, Sungmoon. 2004. "Confucian Charisma and the True Way of the Moral Politician: Interpreting the Tension between Toegye and Nammyeong in Late Sixteenth-Century Joseon." *Review of Korean Studies* 7: 201–30.
2008. "The Origin of Political Liberty in Confucianism: A Nietzschean Interpretation." *History of Political Thought* 29: 393–415.
2009. "Confucianism in Contestation: The May Struggle of 1991 in South Korea and Its Lesson." *New Political Science* 31: 49–68.
2009. "Self-Transformation and Civil Society: Lockean vs. Confucian." *Dao* 8: 383–401.
2008. "Transcendental Collectivism and Participatory Politics in Democratized Korea." *Critical Review of International Social and Political Philosophy* 11: 57–77.
2009. "Trouble with Korean Confucianism: Scholar-Official between Ideal and Reality." *Dao* 8: 29–48.
2010. "Beyond Liberal Civil Society: Confucian Familism and Relational Strangership." *Philosophy East and West* 60: 476–98.
2010. "Confucian Citizenship? Against Two Greek Models." *Journal of Chinese Philosophy* 37: 438–56.
2010. "On Korean Dual Civil Society: Thinking through Tocqueville and Confucius." *Contemporary Political Theory* 9: 434–57.
2010. "The Secret of Confucian *Wuwei* Statecraft: Mencius's Political Theory of Responsibility." *Asian Philosophy* 20: 27–42.
2011. "Confucian Constitutionalism: Mencius and Xunzi on Virtue, Ritual, and Royal Transmission." *Review of Politics* 73: 371–99.

2012. "Before and After Ritual: Two Accounts of *Li* as Virtue in Early Confucianism." *Sophia* 51: 195–210.

2013. "Between Good and Evil: Xunzi's Reinterpretation of the Hegemonic Rule as Decent Governance." *Dao* 12: 73–92.

2013. "Confucianism and Acceptable Inequalities." *Philosophy & Social Criticism*. Published online on October 15, 2013 as doi:10.1177/0191453713507015.

forthcoming. "John Dewey and Confucian Democracy: Toward Common Citizenship." *Constellations*.

forthcoming (2014). "Michael Oakeshott and Confucian Constitutionalism." In *Michael Oakeshott's Cold War Liberalism*, edited by Terry Nardin. New York: Palgrave Macmillan.

Kim, Sunhyuk. 2000. *The Politics of Democratization in Korea: The Role of Civil Society*. Pittsburgh: University of Pittsburgh Press.

2004. "South Korea: Confrontational Legacy and Democratic Contributions." In Alaqappa, *Civil Society and Political Change in Asia*, 138–63.

Kim, Yeong-ryong. 1995. "Janjanhan jeongui nara han'guk" [Korea, a Serene Country of *Chŏng*]. In *Chŏng, Chemyeon, Yeonjul geurigo hanguginui ingan gwangye* [*Chŏng*, Social Face, Network, and the Interpersonal Relationships of the Korean People], edited by Tae-seop Im. Seoul: Hannarae, 13–34.

Kloppenberg, James T. 1998. *The Virtues of Liberalism*. Oxford: Oxford University Press.

Knight, Jack and James Johnson. 1999. "What Sort of Equality Does Deliberative Democracy Require?" In Bohman and Rehg, *Deliberative Democracy*, 279–319.

Knoblock, John. 1988, 1990, 1994. *Xunzi: A Translation and Study of Complete Works*, 3 vols. Stanford: Stanford University Press.

Koh, Byung-ik. 1996. "Confucianism in Contemporary Korea." In Tu, *Confucian Traditions in East Asian Modernity*, 191–201.

Korsgaard, Christine M. 1996. *Creating the Kingdom of Ends*. Cambridge: Cambridge University Press.

Krause, Sharon R. 2005. "Desiring Justice: Motivation and Justification in Rawls and Habermas." *Contemporary Political Theory* 4: 363–85.

2008. *Civil Passions: Moral Sentiment and Democratic Deliberation*. Princeton: Princeton University Press.

Krouse, Richard W. 1982. "Two Concepts of Democratic Representation: James and John Stuart Mill." *Journal of Politics* 44: 510–11.

Kwak, Jun-hyeok. 2007. "Damunhwa gongjon'gwa sahoejeok tonghap" [Multicultural Coexistence and Social Integration]. *Korean Journal of Political Science* 15: 23–41.

Kymlicka, Will. 1995. *Multicultural Citizenship*. Oxford: Oxford University Press.

2001. *Politics in the Vernacular: Nationalism, Multiculturalism, and Citizenship*. Oxford: Oxford University Press.

Lai, Karyn. 2006. "*Li* in the *Analects*: Training in Moral Competence and the Question of Flexibility." *Philosophy East and West* 56: 69–83.

Lamont, Julian. 1994. "The Concept of Desert in Distributive Justice." *Philosophical Quarterly* 44: 45–64.

Lau, D. C. (trans.). 1970. *Mencius*. New York: Penguin.

Lee, Byoungha. 2010. "The Development of Korea's Immigration Policies: Security, Accumulation, Fairness, and Institutional Legitimacy." *Korea Observer* 40: 763–99.

Lee, Hye-Kyung. 2008. "International Marriage and the State in South Korea: Focusing on Governmental Policy." *Citizenship Studies* 12: 107–23.

Lee, Kwang Kyu. 1998. "Confucian Tradition in the Contemporary Korean Family." In Slote and DeVos, *Confucianism and the Family*, 249–64.

Lee, Namhee. 2002. "The South Korean Student Movement: *Undongkwŏn* as a Counterpublic Sphere." In Armstrong, *Korean Society*, 132–64.

Lee, Seung-Hwan. 1992. "Was There a Concept of Rights in Confucian Virtue Based Morality?" *Journal of Chinese Philosophy* 19: 241–61.

2003. "The Concept of *Gong* in Traditional Korea and Its Modern Transformations." *Korea Journal* 43: 137–63.

Lee, Yoonkyung. 2009. "Migration, Migrants, and Contested Ethno-Nationalism in Korea." *Critical Asian Studies* 41: 363–80.

Levy, Jacob T. 2000. *The Multiculturalism of Fear*. New York: Oxford University Press.

Li, Chenyang. 1997. "Confucian Value and Democratic Value." *Journal of Value Inquiry* 31: 183–93.

1997. "Shifting Perspectives: Filial Morality Revisited." *Philosophy East and West* 47: 211–32.

(ed.). 2000. *The Sage and the Second Sex: Confucianism, Ethics and Gender*. Chicago: Open Court.

2006. "The Confucian Ideal of Harmony." *Philosophy East and West* 56: 583–603.

2012. "Equality and Inequality in Confucianism." *Dao* 11: 295–313.

Ling, L. H. M. and Chih-yu Shih. 1998. "Confucianism with a Liberal Face: The Meaning of Democratic Politics in Postcolonial Taiwan." *Review of Politics* 60: 55–82.

Linz, Juan L. and Alfred Stepan. 1996. *Problems of Democratic Transition and Consolidation: Southern Europe, South America, and Post-Communist Europe*. Baltimore: Johns Hopkins University Press.

Liu, Qingping. 2003. "Filiality versus Sociality and Individuality: On Confucianism as 'Consanguinitism.'" *Philosophy East and West* 53: 234–50.

2004. "Is Mencius' Doctrine of 'Extending Affection' Tenable?" *Asian Philosophy* 14: 79–90.

Liu, Xiusheng. 2002. "Mencius, Hume, and Sensibility Theory." *Philosophy East and West* 52: 75–97.

Liu, Xiusheng and Philip J. Ivanhoe (eds.). 2002. *Essays on the Moral Philosophy of Mengzi*. Indianapolis: Hackett.

Macedo, Stephen. 1990. *Liberal Virtues: Citizenship, Virtue, and Community in Liberal Constitutionalism*. Oxford: Clarendon.

(ed). 1999. *Deliberative Politics: Essays on Democracy and Disagreement*. Oxford: Oxford University Press.

2000. *Diversity and Distrust: Civic Education in a Multicultural Democracy*. Cambridge, MA: Harvard University Press.

MacIntyre, Alasdair. 1984. *After Virtue: A Study in Moral Theory*. Notre Dame, IN: Notre Dame University Press.

Mackenzie, Catriona and Natalie Stoljar (eds.). 2000. *Relational Autonomy: Feminist Perspectives on Autonomy, Agency, and the Social Self*. New York: Oxford University Press.

Manin, Bernard. 1997. *The Principles of Representative Government*. Cambridge: Cambridge University Press.

Mansbridge, Jane. 1980. *Beyond Adversary Democracy*. Chicago: University of Chicago Press.

1999. "Everyday Talk in the Deliberative System." In Macedo, *Deliberative Politics*, 211–39.

2003. "Rethinking Representation." *American Political Science Review* 97: 515–28.

2009. "A 'Selection Model' of Political Representation." *Journal of Political Philosophy* 17: 386–7.

Markell, Patchen. 2000. "Making Affect Safe for Democracy? On 'Constitutional Patriotism.'" *Political Theory* 28: 38–63.

Markus, Maria R. 2001. "Decent Society and/or Civil Society?" *Social Research* 68: 1011–30.

Metzger, Thomas A. 2001. "The Western Concept of Civil Society in the Context of Chinese History." In Kaviraj and Khilnani, *Civil Society*, 204–31.

Mill, John Stuart. 1974. *On Liberty*. New York: Penguin.

Miller, Dale. 1999. "The Norm of Self-interest." *American Psychologist* 54: 1053–60.

Miller, David. 1995. *On Nationality*. Oxford: Oxford University Press.

2000. *Citizenship and National Identity*. Cambridge: Polity.

2007. *National Responsibility and Global Justice*. Oxford: Oxford University Press.

Miller, David and Michael Walzer (eds.). 1995. *Pluralism, Justice, and Equality*. Oxford: Oxford University Press.

Mills, Chris. 2012. "Can Liberal Perfectionism Generate Distinctive Distributive Principles?" *Philosophy and Public Issues* 2: 123–52.

Mo, Jongryn. 2003. "The Challenge of Accountability: Implications of the Censorate." In Bell and Hahm, *Confucianism for the Modern World*, 54–68.

Moon, Kyoung-hee. 2006. "Gukjeijuyeoseong'eul gyegiro salpyeoboneun damunhwajuuiwa han'gukui damunhwahyeonsang" [Making Multicultural Korea: Can Multicultural Politics Help Foreign Brides to Fully Integrate into Korean Society?]. *21st Century Political Science Review* 16: 67–93.

Mouffe, Chantal. 1993. *The Return of the Political*. London: Verso.

Munro, Donald J. 1969. *The Concept of Man in Early China*. Stanford: Stanford University Press.

Neville, Robert C. 2000. *Boston Confucianism: Portable Tradition in the Late-Modern World*. Albany: State University of New York Press.

Nivison, David S. 1996. "Two Roots or One." In *The Ways of Confucianism: Investigations in Chinese Philosophy*, edited by Bryan W. Van Norden. Chicago: Open Court, 133–48.

Nozick, Robert. 1974. *Anarchy, State, and Utopia*. New York: Basic Books.

Nussbaum, Martha C. 1996. "Patriotism and Cosmopolitanism." In Cohen, *For Love of Country*, 3–17.

2000. *Women and Human Development: The Capabilities Approach*. Cambridge: Cambridge University Press.

Nuyen, A. T. 2001. "Confucianism and the Idea of Equality." *Asian Philosophy* 11: 61–71.

2009. "Moral Obligation and Moral Motivation in Confucian Role-Based Ethics." *Dao* 8: 1–11.

Oakeshott, Michael. 1975. *On Human Conduct*. Oxford: Clarendon.

1991. *Rationalism in Politics and Other Essays*. Indianapolis: Liberty Fund.

1996. *The Politics of Faith and the Politics of Scepticism*, edited by Timothy Fuller. New Haven: Yale University Press.

O'Donnell, Gullermo and Philip C. Schmitter. 1986. *Transitions from Authoritarian Rule*. Baltimore: Johns Hopkins University Press.

O'Dwyer, Shaun. 2003. "Democracy and Confucian Values." *Philosophy East and West* 53: 39–63.

Okin, Susan M. 1989. *Justice, Gender, and the Family*. New York: Basic Books.

1989. "Reason and Feeling in Thinking about Justice." *Ethics* 99: 229–49.

1999. *Is Multiculturalism Bad for Women?* Princeton: Princeton University.

Palais, James B. 1984. "Confucianism and the Aristocratic/Bureaucratic Balance in Korea." *Harvard Journal of Asiatic Studies* 44: 427–68.

Park, Chong-Min and Doh Chull Shin. 2006. "Do Asian Values Deter Popular Support for Democracy in South Korea?" *Asian Survey* 46: 341–61.

Park, Goo-yong. 2004. "In'gwonui bopyeonjuuijeok jeongdanghawwa haemyeong" [The Universalist Justification of Human Rights]. *Society and Philosophy* 7: 153–96.

Park, Mi. 2005. "Organizing Dissent Against Authoritarianism: The South Korean Student Movement in the 1980s." *Korea Journal* 45: 261–89.

Pateman, Carol. 1988. *The Sexual Contract*. Stanford: Stanford University Press.

Pekkanen, Robert. 2006. *Japanese Dual Civil Society*. Stanford: Stanford University Press.

Pettit, Philip. 1997. *Republicanism: A Theory of Freedom and Government*. Oxford: Oxford University Press.

Pines, Yuri. 2009. *Envisioning Eternal Empire: Chinese Political Thought of the Warring States Era*. Honolulu: University of Hawaii Press.

Pitkin, Hannah F. [1967] 1972. *The Concept of Representation*. Berkeley: University of California Press.

Pocock, J. G. A. 1971. "Ritual, Language, Power: An Essay on the Apparent Political Meanings of Ancient Chinese Philosophy." In *Politics, Language and Time: Essays on Political Thought and History*. New York: Atheneum, 42–79.

Pogge, Thomas. 1989. *Globalizing Rawls*. Ithaca: Cornell University Press.

2002. *World Poverty and Human Rights*. Cambridge: Polity.

Pollack, Mark A. 1997. "Delegation, Agency and Agenda-Setting in the European Community." *International Organization* 51: 99–134.

Popper, Karl. 2002. *The Open Society and Its Enemies*. London: Routledge.

Przeworski, Adam. 1991. *Democracy and the Market*. Cambridge: Cambridge University Press.

Putnam, Robert D. 2000. *Bowling Alone: The Collapse and Revival of American Community*. New York: Touchstone.

Pye, Lucian W. 1985. *Asian Power and Politics: The Cultural Dimensions of Authority*. Cambridge, MA: Belknap.

Rawls, John. 1993. *Political Liberalism*. New York: Columbia University Press.

1999. *The Law of Peoples*. Cambridge, MA: Harvard University Press.

[1971] 1999. *A Theory of Justice*. Cambridge, MA: Belknap.

2001. *Justice as Fairness: A Restatement*, edited by Erin Kelly. Cambridge, MA: Belknap.

Rae, Heather. 2002. *State Identities and the Homogenisation of Peoples*. Cambridge: Cambridge University Press.

Raz, Joseph. 1986. *The Morality of Freedom*. Oxford: Clarendon.

Rhi, Bou-Young. 1998. "Mental Illness in Its Confucian Context." In Slote and DeVos, *Confucianism and the Family*, 285–310.

Ridge, Michael. 1998. "Hobbesian Public Reason." *Ethics* 108: 538–68.

Rosemont, Henry. 1988. "Why Take Rights Seriously? A Confucian Critique." In Rouner, *Human Rights and the World's Religions*, 167–82.

1991. "Rights-Bearing Individuals and Role-Bearing Persons." In *Rules, Rituals, and Responsibility*, edited by Mary I. Bockover. Chicago: Open Court, 71–101.

1998. "Human Rights: A Bill of Worries." In de Bary and Tu, *Confucianism and Human Rights*, 54–66.

Rosemont, Henry and Roger T. Ames. 2009. *The Chinese Classic of Family Reverence: A Philosophical Translation of the Xiaojing*. Honolulu: University of Hawaii Press.

Rosenblum, Nancy L. (ed.). 1989. *Liberalism and the Moral Life*. Cambridge, MA: Harvard University Press.

1996. "The Democracy of Everyday Life." In Yack, *Liberalism without Illusions*, 25–44.

1998. "Compelled Association: Public Standing, Self-Respect, and the Dynamic of Exclusion." In Gutmann, *Freedom of Association*, 75–108.

1998. *Membership and Morals: The Personal Uses of Pluralism in America*. Princeton: Princeton University Press.

Rosenlee, Li-Hsiang L. 2006. *Confucianism and Women: A Philosophical Interpretation*. Albany: State University of New York Press.

Rouner, Leroy S. (ed.). 1988. *Human Rights and the World's Religions*. Notre Dame, IN: University of Notre Dame Press.

Rousseau, Jean-Jacques. 1964. *The First and Second Discourses*, edited by Roger D. Masters and translated by Roger D. Masters and Judith R. Masters. New York: St. Martin's.

1968. *The Social Contract*, translated by Maurice Cranston. Baltimore: Penguin.

1979. *Emile, or On Education*, translated by Allan Bloom. New York: Basic Books.

1985. *The Government of Poland*, translated by Willmore Kendall. Indianapolis: Hackett.

Ryu, Su-young. 2007. "Han'gukinui yugyojeok gachicheukjeongmunhang gaebal yeon'gu" [Item Development for Korean Confucian Values]. *Korean Journal of Management* 15: 171–205.

Salkever, Stephen G. 1990. *Finding the Mean: Theory and Practice in Aristotelian Political Philosophy*. Princeton: Princeton University Press.

Sandel, Michael J. 1982. *Liberalism and the Limits of Justice*. Cambridge: Cambridge University Press, 1982.

1996. *Democracy's Discontent: America in Search of a Public Philosophy*. Cambridge, MA: Belknap.

Sanders, Lynn. 1997. "Against Deliberation." *Political Theory* 25: 347–76.

Scanlon, Thomas W. 1972. "A Theory of Freedom of Expression." *Philosophy and Public Affairs* 1: 204–26.

2000. *What We Owe to Each Other*. Cambridge, MA: Belknap.

Schak, David C. 2009. "The Development of Civility in Taiwan." *Public Affairs* 82: 447–65.

Schak, David C. and Wayne Hudson (eds.). 2003. *Civil Society in Asia*. Burlington, VT: Ashgate.

Schmidt, James. 1998. "Civility, Enlightenment, and Society: Conceptual Confusions and Kantian Remedies." *American Political Science Review* 92: 419–27.

Schwartz, Benjamin I. 1985. *The World of Thought in Ancient China*. Cambridge, MA: Harvard University Press.

1996. "The Age of Transcendence." In *China and Other Matters*. Cambridge, MA: Harvard University Press, 64–8.

Seligman, Adam B. 1992. *The Idea of Civil Society*. Princeton: Princeton University Press.

Seligman, Adam B., Robert Weller, Michael J. Puett, and Bennett Simon. 2008. *Ritual and Its Consequences: An Essay on the Limits of Sincerity*. Oxford: Oxford University Press.

Sen, Amartya. 1999. *Commodities and Capabilities*. Oxford: Oxford University Press.

2000. "Merit and Justice." In *Meritocracy and Economic Inequality*, edited by Kenneth Arrow, Samuel Bowles, and Steven Durlauf. Princeton: Princeton University Press, 5–16.

Seol, Dong-Hoon. 2010. "Which Multiculturalism? Discourse of the Incorporation of Immigrants into Korean Society." *Korea Observer* 41: 593–614.

Shapiro, Ian. 1999. *Democratic Justice*. New Haven: Yale University Press.

2003. *The State of Democratic Theory*. Princeton: Princeton University Press.

Sher, George. 1997. *Beyond Neutrality: Perfectionism and Politics*. Cambridge: Cambridge University Press.

Shils, Edward. 1996. "Reflections on Civil Society and Civility in the Chinese Intellectual Tradition." In Tu, *Confucian Traditions in East Asian Modernity*, 38–71.

1997. *The Virtue of Civility: Selected Essays on Liberalism, Tradition, and Civil Society*, edited by Steve Grosby. Indianapolis: Liberty Fund.

Shin, Doh Chull. 1994. "On the Third Wave of Democratization: A Synthesis and Evaluation of Recent Theory and Research." *World Politics* 47: 135–70.

2012. *Confucianism and Democratization in East Asia*. New York: Cambridge University Press.

Shin, Doh Chull and Chong-Min Park. 2008. "The Mass Public and Democratic Politics in South Korea: Exploring the Subjective World of Democratization in Flux." In Chu et al., *How East Asians View Democracy*, 39–60.

Shin, Gi-wook. 2006. *Ethnic Nationalism in Korea: Genealogy, Politics, and Legacy*. Stanford: Stanford University Press.

Shklar, Judith N. 1984. *Ordinary Vices*. Cambridge, MA: Harvard University Press.

1990. *The Faces of Injustice*. New Haven: Yale University Press.

Shun, Kwong-loi. 1993. "*Jen* and *Li* in the *Analects*." *Philosophy East and West* 43: 457–79.

Shun, Kwong-loi and David B. Wong (eds.). 2004. *Confucian Ethics: A Comparative Study of Self, Autonomy, and Community*. Cambridge: Cambridge University Press.

Skerrett, K. Roberts. 2005. "Political Liberalism and the Idea of Public Reason: A Response to Jeffrey Stout's *Democracy and Tradition*." *Social Theory and Practice* 31: 173–90.

Slote, Michael. 2002. *The Ethics of Care and Empathy*. London: Routledge.

Slote, Walter H. and George A. DeVos (eds.). 1998. *Confucianism and the Family*. Albany: State University of New York Press.

Smith, Rogers M. 2003. *Stories of Peoplehood: The Politics and Morals of Political Membership*. Cambridge: Cambridge University Press.

Song, Jaeyoon. 2009. "The *Zhou Li* and Constitutionalism: A Southern Song Political Theory." *Journal of Chinese Philosophy* 36: 423–38.

Spragens, Thomas A. 1999. *Civic Liberalism: Reflections on Our Democratic Ideals*. Lanham, MD: Rowman & Littlefield.

Steinberg, David I. 1997. "Civil Society and Human Rights in Korea: On Contemporary and Classical Orthodoxy and Ideology." *Korea Journal* 37: 145–65.

Stilz, Anna. 2009. *Liberal Loyalty: Freedom, Obligation, and the State*. Princeton: Princeton University Press.

Stout, Jeffrey. 2004. *Democracy & Tradition*. Princeton: Princeton University Press.

Strauss, Leo. 1952. *The Political Philosophy of Hobbes: Its Basis and Its Genesis*. Chicago: University of Chicago Press.

Sunstein, Cass. 2009. "On the Tension between Sex Equality and Religious Freedom." In *Toward a Humanist Justice: The Political Philosophy of Susan Moller Okin*, edited by Debra Satz and Rob Reich. New York: Oxford University Press, 129–39.

Talmon, J. L. 1960. *Origins of Totalitarian Democracy*. New York: Praeger.

Tamir, Yael. 1993. *Liberal Nationalism*. Princeton: Princeton University Press.

Tan, Kok-Chor. 2004. *Justice without Borders: Cosmopolitanism, Nationalism and Patriotism*. Cambridge: Cambridge University Press.

Tan, Sor-hoon. 2002. "Between Family and State: Relational Tensions in Confucian Ethics." In *Mencius: Contexts and Interpretations*, edited by Alan K. L. Chan. Honolulu: University of Hawaii Press, 169–88.

2003. "Can There Be a Confucian Civil Society?" In *The Moral Circle and the Self: Chinese and Western Approaches*, edited by Kim-chong Chong, Sor-hoon Tan, and C. L. Ten. Chicago: Open Court, 193–218.

2003. *Confucian Democracy: A Deweyan Reconstruction*. Albany: State University of New York Press.

2004. "From Cannibalism to Empowerment: An *Analects*-Inspired Attempt to Balance Community and Liberty." *Philosophy East and West* 54: 52–70.

2007. "Confucian Democracy as Pragmatic Experience: Uniting Love of Learning and Love of Antiquity." *Asian Philosophy* 17: 141–66.

2009. "Beyond Elitism: A Community Ideal for a Modern East Asia." *Philosophy East and West* 59: 537–53.

2010. "Our Country Right or Wrong: A Pragmatic Response to Anti-democratic Cultural Nationalism in China." *Contemporary Pragmatism* 7: 45–69.

Tao, Julia Tao and Andrew Brennan. 2003. "Confucian and Liberal Ethics for Public Policy: Holistic or Atomistic?" *Journal of Social Philosophy* 34: 572–89.

Taylor, Charles. 1985. "What Is Human Agency?" In *Philosophical Papers*, vol. 1. Cambridge: Cambridge University Press.

1989. "Cross-Purposes: The Liberal-Communitarian Debate." In Rosenblum, *Liberalism and the Moral Life*, 159–82.

1989. *Sources of the Self: The Making of the Modern Identity*. Cambridge, MA: Harvard University Press.

2007. *A Secular Age*. Cambridge, MA: Belknap.

Taylor, Rodney L. 1998. "The Religious Character of Confucian Tradition." *Philosophy East and West* 48: 80–107.

Thompson, Dennis F. 1980. "Moral Responsibility of Public Officials: The Problem of Many Hands." *American Political Science Review* 74: 905–16.

1987. *Political Ethics and Public Office*. Cambridge, MA: Harvard University Press.

Tismaneanu, Vladimir. 1992. *Reinventing Politics: Eastern Europe from Stalin to Havel*. New York: Free Press.

2001. "Civil Society, Pluralism, and the Future of East and Central Europe." *Social Research* 68: 977–91.

Tiwald, Justin. 2008. "A Right of Rebellion in the *Mengzi*?" *Dao* 7: 269–82.

2012. "Confucianism and Human Rights." In *Handbook of Human Rights*, edited by Thomas Cushman. London: Routledge, 244–54.

Tu, Weiming. 1968. "The Creative Tension between *Jen* and *Li*." *Philosophy East and West* 18: 29–39.

1979. *Humanity and Self-Cultivation*. Berkeley, CA: Asian Humanities Press.

1993. *Way, Learning, and Politics: Essays on the Confucian Intellectual*. Albany: State University of New York Press.

(ed.). 1996. *Confucian Traditions in East Asian Modernity: Moral Education and Economic Culture in Japan and Four Mini-Dragons*. Cambridge, MA: Harvard University Press.

1998. "Probing the 'Three Bonds' and 'Five Relationships' in Confucian Humanism." In Slote and DeVos, *Confucianism and the Family*, 121–36.

2002. "Confucianism and Liberalism." *Dao* 2: 1–20.

Van Norden, Bryan W. 2000. "Mengzi and Xunzi: Two Views of Human Agency." In *Virtue, Nature, and Moral Agency in the Xunzi*, edited by T. C. Kline III and Philip J. Ivanhoe. Indianapolis: Hackett, 103–34.

2007. *Virtue Ethics and Consequentialism in Early Chinese Philosophy*. Cambridge: Cambridge University Press.

Villa, Dana. 2001. *Socratic Citizenship*. Princeton: Princeton University Press.

2008. *Public Freedom*. Princeton: Princeton University Press.

Vincent, Andrew. 2002. *Nationalism and Particularity*. Cambridge: Cambridge University Press.

Viroli, Maurizio. 1995. *For Love of Country: An Essay on Patriotism and Nationalism*. Oxford: Clarendon.

2002. *Republicanism*, translated by Antony Shugaar. New York: Hill and Wang.

Waldron, Jeremy. 1983. *Liberal Rights*. Cambridge: Cambridge University Press.

1999. *The Dignity of Legislation*. Cambridge: Cambridge University Press.

Wall, Steven. 1998. *Liberalism, Perfectionism and Restraint*. Cambridge: Cambridge University Press.

2005. "Perfectionism, Public Reason, and Religious Accommodation." *Social Theory and Practice* 31: 281–304.

Walzer, Michael. 1981. "Philosophy and Democracy." *Political Theory* 9: 370–99.

1983. *Spheres of Justice: A Defense of Pluralism and Equality*. New York: Basic Books.

1994. *Thick and Thin: Moral Argument at Home and Abroad*. Notre Dame, IN: University of Notre Dame Press.

1996. "On Negative Politics." In Yack, *Liberalism without Illusions*, 17–24.

2007. "Deliberation and What Else?" In *Thinking Politically: Essays in Political Theory*, edited by David Miller. New Haven: Yale University Press, 134–46.

2010. "Michael Walzer Responds." *Dissent* 57: 100–101.

Wang, Xianqian. 1988. *Xunzijijie* [Collected Interpretations of the *Xunzi*]. Beijing: Zhonghua shuju.

Warren, Mark. 1992. "Democratic Theory and Self-Transformation." *American Political Science Review* 86: 8–23.

Watson, Burton (trans.). 1964. *Han Fei Tzu: Basic Writings*. New York: Columbia University Press.

Watson, Ian. 2010. "Multiculturalism in South Korea: A Critical Assessment." *Journal of Contemporary Asia* 40: 337–46.

Weber, Max. 1958. *From Max Weber: Essays in Sociology*, translated and edited by Hans H. Gerth and C. W. Mills. New York: Oxford University Press.

Williams, Bernard. 1981. *Moral Luck*. Cambridge: Cambridge University Press.

Wolin, Sheldon S. 1960. *Politics and Vision*. Boston: Little, Brown.

1989. *The Presence of the Past: Essays on the State and the Constitution*. Baltimore: Johns Hopkins University Press.

2008. *Democracy Incorporated: Managed Democracy and the Specter of Inverted Totalitarianism*. Princeton: Princeton University Press.

Wong, David B. 2002. "Reasons and Analogical Reasoning in Mengzi." In Liu and Ivanhoe, *Essays on the Moral Philosophy of Mengzi*, 187–220.

2004. "Rights and Community in Confucianism." In Shun and Wong, *Confucian Ethics*, 31–48.

Woo, Insoo. 1999. *Joseonhugi sanlimseryeok yeon'gu* [A Study on the Backwoods Literati Forces in Late Chosŏn Korea]. Seoul: Iljogak.

Yack, Bernard (ed.). 1996. *Liberalism without Illusions*. Chicago: University of Chicago Press.

Yang, Hyunah. 2002. "Unfinished Tasks for Korean Family Policy in the 1990s: Maternity Protection Policy and Abolition of the Family-Head System." *Korea Journal* 42: 68–99.

Yang, Jung-hye. 2007. "Sosuminjok ijuyeoseongui jaehyeon" [Representing Migrated Women]. *Midieo, jendeo, munhwa* 7: 47–77.

Yoon, Injin. 2008. "Han'kukdamunhwajuuiui jeon'gaewa teukseong" [The Development and Characteristics of Multiculturalism in South Korea]. *Korean Sociological Review* 42: 72–103.

Young, Iris M. 2000. *Inclusion and Democracy*. Oxford: Oxford University Press.

2007. *Global Challenges: War, Self-Determination and Responsibility for Justice*. Cambridge: Polity.

2011. *Responsibility for Justice*. Oxford: Oxford University Press.

Index